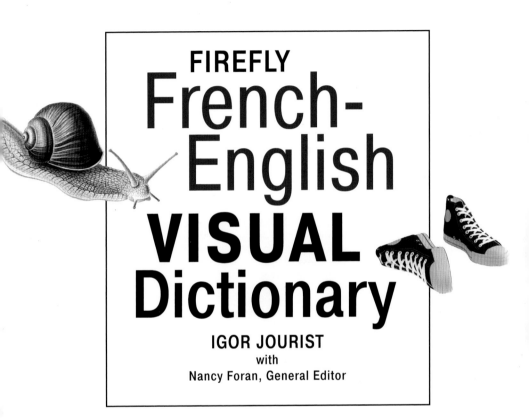

FIREFLY
French-
English
VISUAL
Dictionary

IGOR JOURIST

with

Nancy Foran, General Editor

FIREFLY BOOKS

A FIREFLY BOOK

Published by Firefly Books Ltd. 2015
Illustrations and basic text © 2015 Jourist Verlag GmbH, Hamburg
Text adaptations for this publication © 2015 Firefly Books Ltd.

First printing

Publisher Cataloging-in-Publication Data (U.S.)
Jourist, Igor.
Firefly French-English visual dictionary / Igor Jourist with Nancy Foran, general editor.
[800] pages : color illustrations ; cm.
Includes index.
Text in English and French.
Summary: A bilingual reference which presents detailed and accurate illustrations of
thousands of items, from everyday objects to highly specialized equipment.
ISBN-13: 978-1-77085-621-9
1. Picture dictionaries, French. 2. Picture dictionaries, English. 3. French
language – Dictionaries – English. 4. English language – Dictionaries –
French. I. Foran, Nancy, editor. II. Title. III. French-English visual dictionary.
443.21 dc23   PC2640.J576 2015

Library and Archives Canada Cataloguing in Publication
Jourist, Igor, author
Firefly French-English visual dictionary / Igor Jourist ; with Nancy Foran, general editor.
Includes index.
ISBN 978-1-77085-621-9 (bound)
1. Picture dictionaries, French. 2. Picture dictionaries, English.
3. French language – Dictionaries – English. 4. English language –
Dictionaries – French. I. Foran, Nancy, editor
II. Title: French-English visual dictionary.
PC2640.F57 2015   443'.21   C2015-903106-0

Published in the United States by
Firefly Books (U.S.) Inc.
P.O. Box 1338, Ellicott Station
Buffalo, New York 14205

Published in Canada by
Firefly Books Ltd.
50 Staples Avenue, Unit 1
Richmond Hill, Ontario L4B 0A7

Illustrations, terminology and production: Jourist Verlags GmbH, Hamburg

jourist

Cover design: Jacqueline Hope Raynor
Printed in China

LIST OF CHAPTERS
LISTE DE CHAPITRES

CONTENTS

LEISURE AND ENTERTAINMENT
LOISIRS ET DIVERTISSEMENT 558

OFFICE *BUREAU* 584

TRANSPORTATION
TRANSPORTS 612

HOW TO USE THE DICTIONARY
COMMENT UTILISER LE DICTIONARY

Indicator
These lines link the vocabulary with the specific part of the illustration that is being identified.
Indicateur
Ces lignes joignent le vocabulaire avec l'exacte partie de l'illustration qu'on identifie.

Subtheme | *Sous-thème*
The 14 themes are divided into more specific subjects, which group related objects together. | *Les 14 thèmes sont parfois divisés en groupes plus spécifiques, qui rassemblent des objets semblables.*

Topic
Some subthemes are divided into topics, which are more specific and more closely related groupings.
Sujet
Quelques sous-thèmes sont divisés en sujets, créant des groupes encore plus spécifiques et proches.

Subtopic
Subtopics are the smallest, most specific and most closely related groupings.
Sous-Sujet
Les sous-sujets sont les groupes les plus petits, les plus spécifiques et les plus proches.

HOUSEHOLD FURNISHINGS *ARTICLES ᴹ MÉNAGERS*
Furniture *Meubles ᴹ*

Sofas
Canapés ᴹ

sectional sofa
canapé ᴹ modulaire

backrest
dossier ᴹ

seat cushion
coussin ᴹ

leg
pied ᴹ

arm
bras ᴹ

ottoman
tabouret ᴹ

loveseat
causeuse ꜰ

chaise longe
chaise ꜰ longue

bench
banc ᴹ

208 HOUSING *HABITATION ꜰ*

Gender identification
The gender is indicated for every Spanish noun.
Identification de gendre
Le gendre est identifié pour tous les noms en français.

Object Illustration
A detailed illustration of the object being defined; for some illustrations, several parts are identified and defined.
L'illustration de l'objet
Une illustration détaillée de l'objet qu'on identifie; pour quelques illustrations, plusieurs parties sont identifiées et définies.

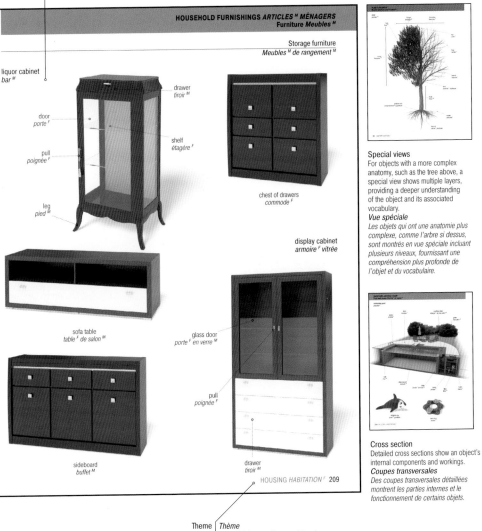

HOUSEHOLD FURNISHINGS *ARTICLES ᴹ MÉNAGERS*
Furniture *Meubles* ᴹ

Storage furniture
Meubles ᴹ *de rangement* ᴹ

liquor cabinet
bar ᴹ

drawer
tiroir ᴹ

door
porte ᶠ

shelf
étagère ᶠ

pull
poignée ᶠ

leg
pied ᴹ

chest of drawers
commode ᶠ

display cabinet
armoire ᶠ *vitrée*

sofa table
table ᶠ *de salon* ᴹ

glass door
porte ᶠ *en verre* ᴹ

pull
poignée ᶠ

sideboard
buffet ᴹ

drawer
tiroir ᴹ

HOUSING *HABITATION* ᶠ 209

Special views
For objects with a more complex anatomy, such as the tree above, a special view shows multiple layers, providing a deeper understanding of the object and its associated vocabulary.
Vue spéciale
Les objets qui ont une anatomie plus complexe, comme l'arbre si dessus, sont montrés en vue spéciale incluant plusieurs niveaux, fournissant une compréhension plus profonde de l'objet et du vocabulaire.

Cross section
Detailed cross sections show an object's internal components and workings.
Coupes transversales
Des coupes transversales détaillées montrent les parties internes et le fonctionnement de certains objets.

Theme | *Thème*
There are 14 themes, covering every important aspect of the modern world. | *Il y a 14 thèmes, qui couvrent tous les aspects importants du monde moderne.*

NATURE

NATURE

animal cell
cellule ᶠ *animale*

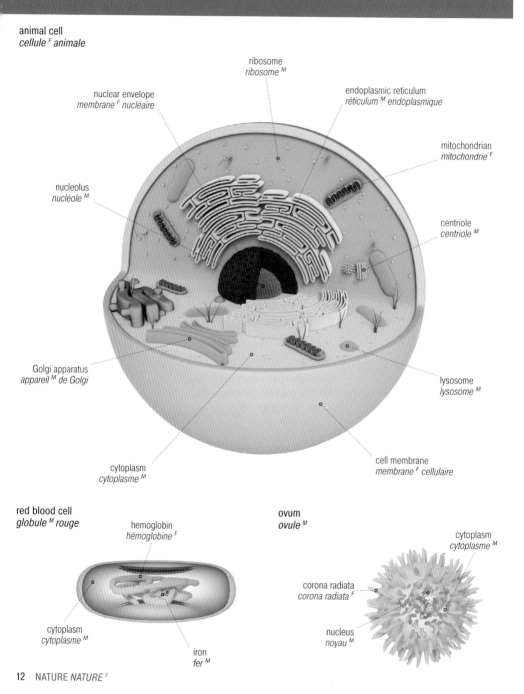

ribosome
ribosome ᴹ

nuclear envelope
membrane ᶠ *nucléaire*

endoplasmic reticulum
réticulum ᴹ *endoplasmique*

mitochondrian
mitochondrie ᶠ

nucleolus
nucléole ᴹ

centriole
centriole ᴹ

Golgi apparatus
appareil ᴹ *de Golgi*

lysosome
lysosome ᴹ

cytoplasm
cytoplasme ᴹ

cell membrane
membrane ᶠ *cellulaire*

red blood cell
globule ᴹ *rouge*

hemoglobin
hémoglobine ᶠ

ovum
ovule ᴹ

cytoplasm
cytoplasme ᴹ

corona radiata
corona radiata ᶠ

cytoplasm
cytoplasme ᴹ

iron
fer ᴹ

nucleus
noyau ᴹ

Arabian horse
cheval ^M arabe

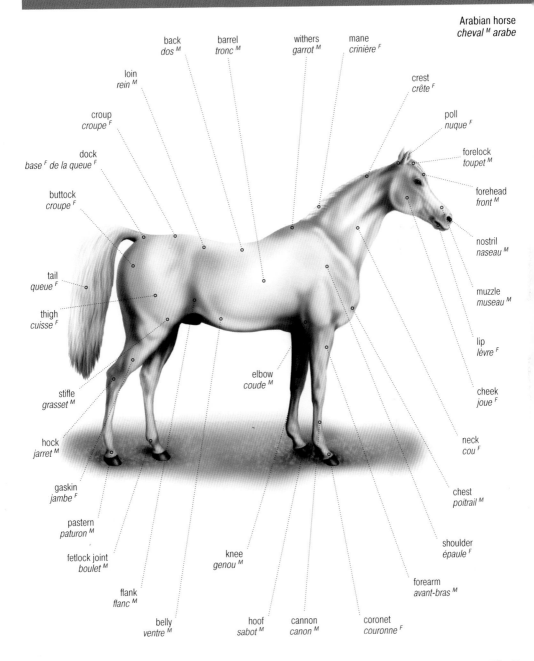

back
dos ^M

barrel
tronc ^M

withers
garrot ^M

mane
crinière ^F

loin
rein ^M

crest
crête ^F

croup
croupe ^F

poll
nuque ^F

dock
base ^F de la queue ^F

forelock
toupet ^M

buttock
croupe ^F

forehead
front ^M

nostril
naseau ^M

tail
queue ^F

muzzle
museau ^M

thigh
cuisse ^F

lip
lèvre ^F

elbow
coude ^M

cheek
joue ^F

stifle
grasset ^M

hock
jarret ^M

neck
cou ^F

gaskin
jambe ^F

chest
poitrail ^M

pastern
paturon ^M

fetlock joint
boulet ^M

knee
genou ^M

shoulder
épaule ^F

flank
flanc ^F

forearm
avant-bras ^M

belly
ventre ^M

hoof
sabot ^M

cannon
canon ^M

coronet
couronne ^F

white-tailed deer
cerf ᴹ *de Virginie*

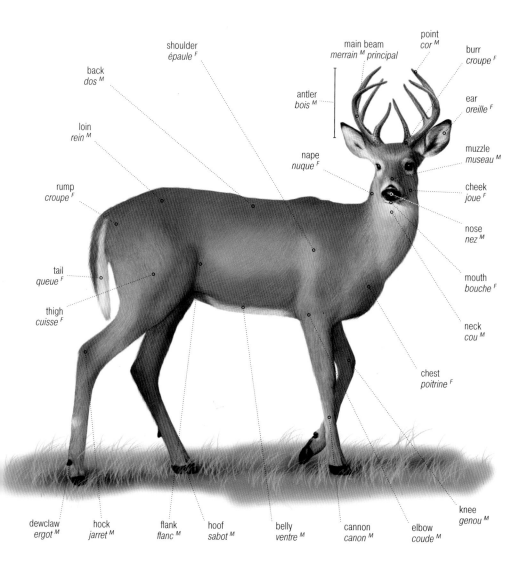

shoulder
épaule ᶠ

back
dos ᴹ

antler
bois ᴹ

loin
rein ᴹ

rump
croupe ᶠ

nape
nuque ᶠ

tail
queue ᶠ

thigh
cuisse ᶠ

main beam
merrain ᴹ *principal*

point
cor ᴹ

burr
croupe ᶠ

ear
oreille ᶠ

muzzle
museau ᴹ

cheek
joue ᶠ

nose
nez ᴹ

mouth
bouche ᶠ

neck
cou ᴹ

chest
poitrine ᶠ

knee
genou ᴹ

dewclaw
ergot ᴹ

hock
jarret ᴹ

flank
flanc ᴹ

hoof
sabot ᴹ

belly
ventre ᴹ

cannon
canon ᴹ

elbow
coude ᴹ

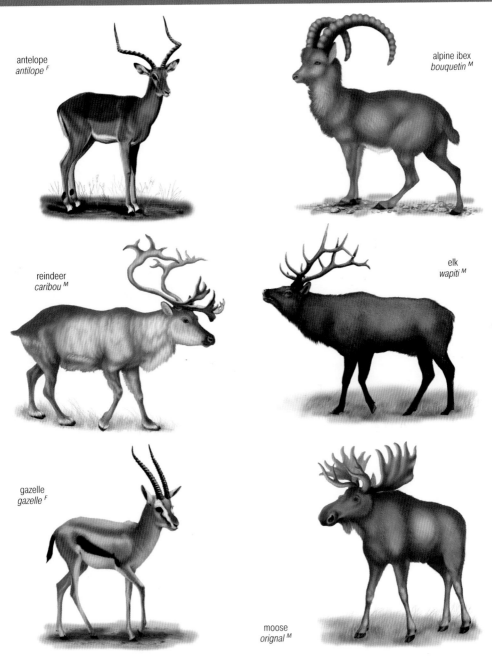

antelope
antilope ᶠ

alpine ibex
bouquetin ᴹ

reindeer
caribou ᴹ

elk
wapiti ᴹ

gazelle
gazelle ᶠ

moose
orignal ᴹ

musk ox
bœuf M *musqué*

buffalo
bison M *d'Amérique* F

bison
bison M

tapir
tapir M

goat
chèvre ᶠ

bighorn sheep
mouflon ᴹ *d'Amérique* ᶠ

cashmere goat
chèvre ᶠ *cachemire*

western roe deer
chevreuil ᴹ

mule
mulet ᴹ

rhinoceros
rhinocéros [M]

hippopotamus
hippopotame [M]

giraffe
girafe [F]

Asian elephant
éléphant [M] *d'Asie* [F]

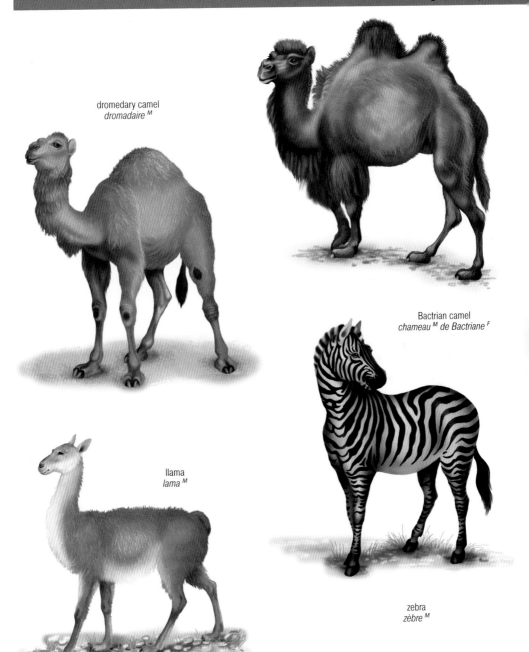

dromedary camel
dromadaire ^M

Bactrian camel
chameau ^M *de Bactriane* ^F

llama
lama ^M

zebra
zèbre ^M

cow
vache F

donkey
âne M

wild boar
sanglier M

pig
cochon M

sheep
mouton M

polar bear
ours ^M *polaire*

black bear
ours ^M *noir*

giant panda
panda ^M *géant*

grizzly bear
grizzli ^M

cougar
puma ^M

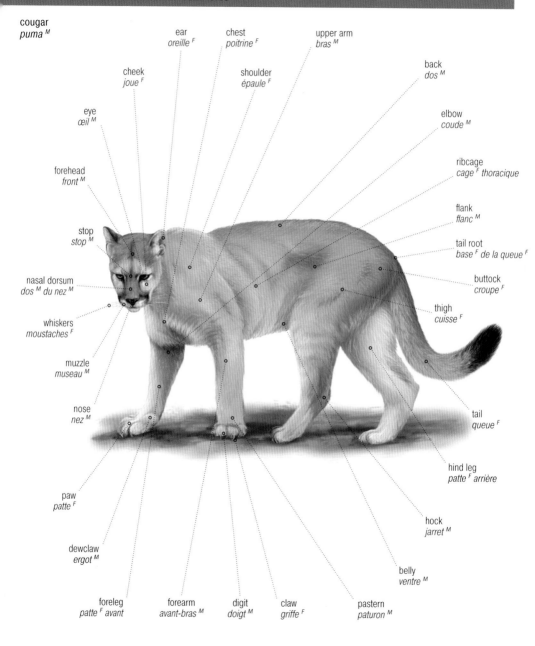

ear
oreille ^F

chest
poitrine ^F

upper arm
bras ^M

back
dos ^M

cheek
joue ^F

shoulder
épaule ^F

elbow
coude ^M

eye
œil ^M

ribcage
cage ^F *thoracique*

forehead
front ^M

flank
flanc ^M

stop
stop ^M

tail root
base ^F *de la queue* ^F

nasal dorsum
dos ^M *du nez* ^M

buttock
croupe ^F

thigh
cuisse ^F

whiskers
moustaches ^F

muzzle
museau ^M

nose
nez ^M

tail
queue ^F

hind leg
patte ^F *arrière*

paw
patte ^F

hock
jarret ^M

dewclaw
ergot ^M

belly
ventre ^M

foreleg
patte ^F *avant*

forearm
avant-bras ^M

digit
doigt ^M

claw
griffe ^F

pastern
paturon ^M

wolf
loup ^M

cheetah
guépard ^M

lion
lion ^M

jackal
chacal ^M

lynx
lynx ^M

spotted hyena
hyène ^F *tachetée*

striped hyena
hyène ^F *rayée*

snow leopard
léopard ^M *des neiges* ^F

tiger
tigre ^M

jaguar
jaguar ^M

badger
blaireau ^M

otter
loutre ^F

stoat
hermine ^F

polecat
mouffette ^F *tachetée*

skunk
mouffette ^F

racoon
raton laveur ^M

jungle cat
chaus *M*

marten
martre *F*

wolverine
carcajou *M*

wildcat
chat *M* *sauvage*

red fox
renard *M* *roux*

gray seal
phoque ^M *gris*

fur seal
otarie ^F *à fourrure* ^F

walrus
morse ^M

sea lion
otarie ^F

bulldog
bulldog ᴹ

rottweiler
rottweiler ᴹ

Siberian husky
husky ᴹ *sibérien*

collie
colley ᴹ

dachshund
teckel ᴹ

poodle
caniche ^M

German shepherd
berger ^M *allemand*

golden retriever
golden ^M *retriever*

dalmatian
dalmatien ^M

Chihuahua
chihuahua ^M

Labrador retriever
labrador M

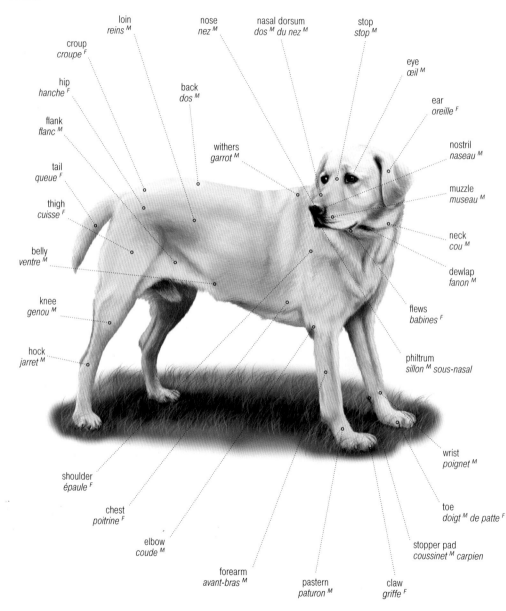

loin
reins M

nose
nez M

nasal dorsum
dos M *du nez* M

stop
stop M

croup
croupe F

eye
œil M

hip
hanche F

back
dos M

ear
oreille F

flank
flanc M

nostril
naseau M

withers
garrot M

tail
queue F

muzzle
museau M

thigh
cuisse F

neck
cou M

belly
ventre M

dewlap
fanon M

knee
genou M

flews
babines F

hock
jarret M

philtrum
sillon M *sous-nasal*

shoulder
épaule F

wrist
poignet M

chest
poitrine F

toe
doigt M *de patte* F

elbow
coude M

stopper pad
coussinet M *carpien*

forearm
avant-bras M

pastern
paturon M

claw
griffe F

British shorthair
british shorthair M

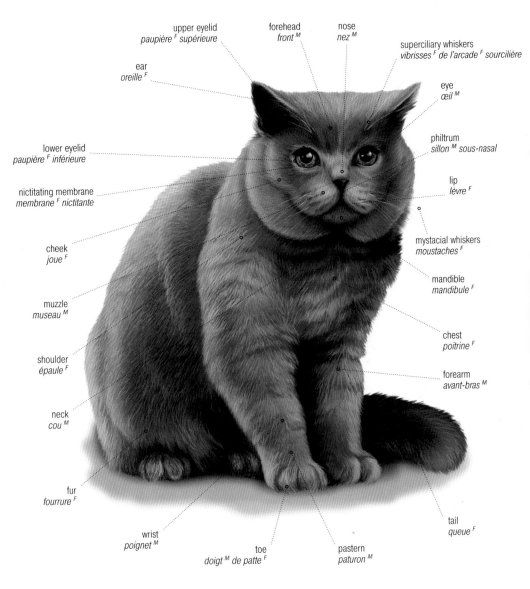

upper eyelid
paupière F *supérieure*

forehead
front M

nose
nez M

superciliary whiskers
vibrisses F *de l'arcade* F *sourcilière*

ear
oreille F

eye
œil M

philtrum
sillon M *sous-nasal*

lower eyelid
paupière F *inférieure*

lip
lèvre F

nictitating membrane
membrane F *nictitante*

mystacial whiskers
moustaches F

cheek
joue F

mandible
mandibule F

muzzle
museau M

chest
poitrine F

shoulder
épaule F

forearm
avant-bras M

neck
cou M

fur
fourrure F

tail
queue F

wrist
poignet M

toe
doigt M *de patte* F

pastern
paturon M

Norwegian forest cat
chat M norvégien

Russian blue
chat M bleu russe

Maine coon
maine coon M

Persian cat
chat M persan

Siamese cat
chat M siamois

rabbit
lapin M

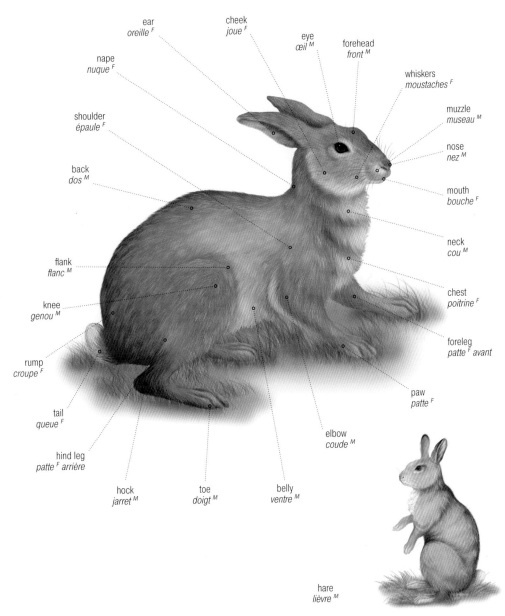

ear
oreille F

cheek
joue F

eye
œil M

forehead
front M

whiskers
moustaches F

nape
nuque F

muzzle
museau M

shoulder
épaule F

nose
nez M

back
dos M

mouth
bouche F

neck
cou M

flank
flanc M

knee
genou M

chest
poitrine F

foreleg
patte F _avant_

rump
croupe F

paw
patte F

tail
queue F

elbow
coude M

hind leg
patte F _arrière_

hock
jarret M

toe
doigt M

belly
ventre M

hare
lièvre M

koala
koala ^M

head
tête ^F

ear
oreille ^F

cheek
joue ^F

eye
œil ^M

mouth
bouche ^F

nose
nez ^M

forelimb
membre ^M *antérieur*

hind limb
membre ^M *postérieur*

chest
poitrine ^F

opposable digit
doigt ^M *opposable*

digit
doigt ^M

hind paw
patte ^F *arrière*

forepaw
patte ^F *avant*

claw
griffe ^F

opossum
opossum ^M

kangaroo
kangourou ^M

house mouse
souris [F] *commune*

tail
queue [F]

hind limb
membre [M] *postérieur*

fur
fourrure [F]

ear
oreille [M]

eye
œil [M]

hind paw
patte [F] *arrière*

digit
doigt [M]

forelimb
membre [M] *antérieur*

forepaw
patte [F] *avant*

claw
griffe [F]

whiskers
vibrisses [F]

nose
nez [M]

field vole
campagnol [M] *agreste*

brown rat
rat [M] *brun*

porcupine
porc-épic [M]

red-rumped agouti
agouti ^M doré

beaver
castor ^M

muskrat
rat ^M musqué

chinchilla
chinchilla ^M

gray squirrel
écureuil ^M gris

marmot
marmotte ^F commune

hamster
hamster ^M

guinea pig
cochon ^M *d'Inde* ^F

jerboa
gerboise ^F

chipmunk
tamia ^M *rayé*

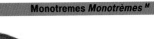

Monotremes *Monotrèmes* ^M

platypus
ornithorynque ^M

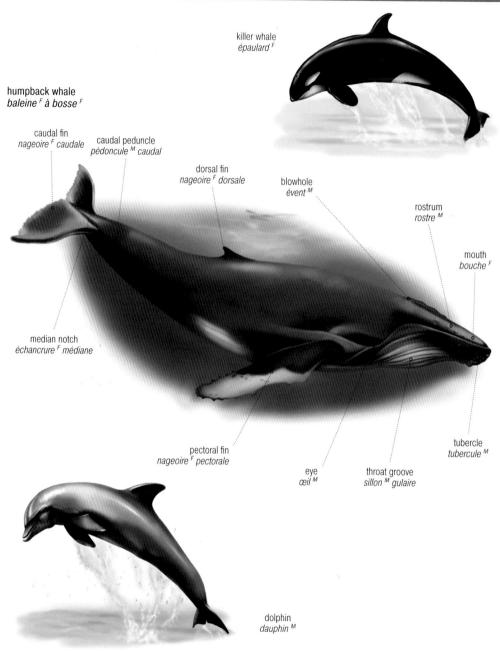

killer whale
épaulard [F]

humpback whale
baleine [F] *à bosse* [F]

caudal fin
nageoire [F] *caudale*

caudal peduncle
pédoncule [M] *caudal*

dorsal fin
nageoire [F] *dorsale*

blowhole
évent [M]

rostrum
rostre [M]

mouth
bouche [F]

median notch
échancrure [F] *médiane*

pectoral fin
nageoire [F] *pectorale*

eye
œil [M]

throat groove
sillon [M] *gulaire*

tubercle
tubercule [M]

dolphin
dauphin [M]

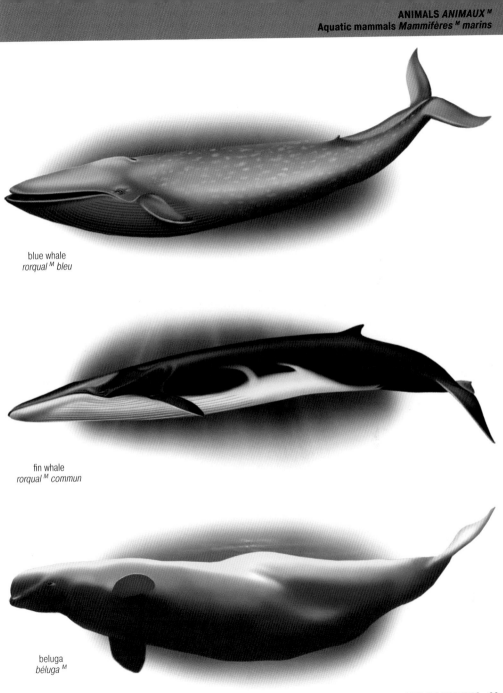

blue whale
rorqual ^M *bleu*

fin whale
rorqual ^M *commun*

beluga
béluga ^M

Galápagos tortoise
tortue [F] *géante des Galapagos* [M]

vertebral scute
plaque [F] *vertébrale*

costal scute
plaque [F] *costale*

carapace
carapace [F]

neck
cou [M]

marginal scute
plaque [F] *marginale*

eye
œil [M]

horny beak
bec corné [M]

pygal plate
plaque [F] *pygale*

mouth
bouche [F]

leg
patte [F]

scale
écaille [F]

plastron
plastron [M]

claw
griffe [F]

Blanding's turtle
tortue [F] *mouchetée*

green sea turtle
tortue [F] *verte*

chameleon
caméléon ᴹ

iguana
iguane ᴹ

monitor lizard
varan ᴹ

gecko
gecko ᴹ

common wall lizard
lézard ᴹ *des murailles*

Cuban crocodile
crocodile ᴹ *de Cuba*

caiman
caiman ᴹ

alligator
alligator ᴹ

Nile crocodile
crocodile ᴹ *du Nil* ᴹ

Snakes
Serpents [M]

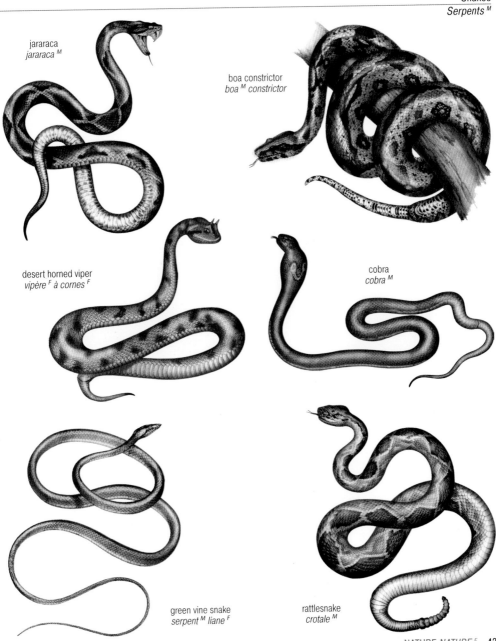

jararaca
jararaca [M]

boa constrictor
boa [M] *constrictor*

desert horned viper
vipère [F] *à cornes* [F]

cobra
cobra [M]

green vine snake
serpent [M] *liane* [F]

rattlesnake
crotale [M]

common toad
crapeau ᴹ *commun*

newt
triton ᴹ

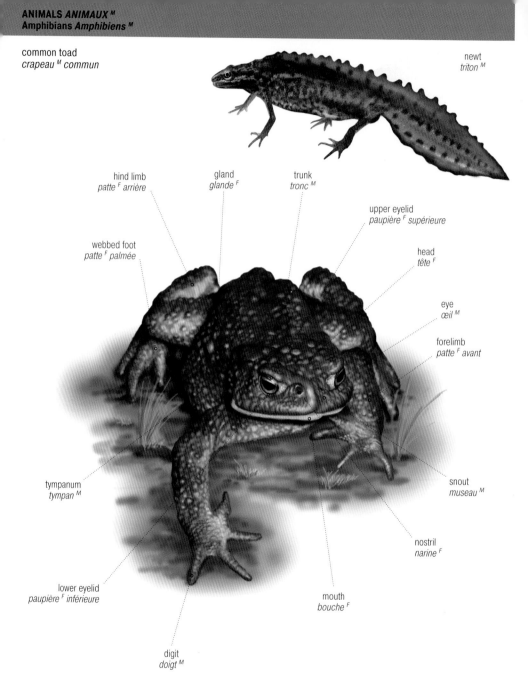

hind limb
patte ᶠ *arrière*

gland
glande ᶠ

trunk
tronc ᴹ

upper eyelid
paupière ᶠ *supérieure*

webbed foot
patte ᶠ *palmée*

head
tête ᶠ

eye
œil ᴹ

forelimb
patte ᶠ *avant*

tympanum
tympan ᴹ

snout
museau ᴹ

nostril
narine ᶠ

lower eyelid
paupière ᶠ *inférieure*

mouth
bouche ᶠ

digit
doigt ᴹ

cane toad
crapaud ^M *géant*

salamander
salamandre ^F

common frog
grenouille ^F *rousse*

tree frog
rainette ^F

edible frog
grenouille ^F *comestible*

bat
chauve-souris F

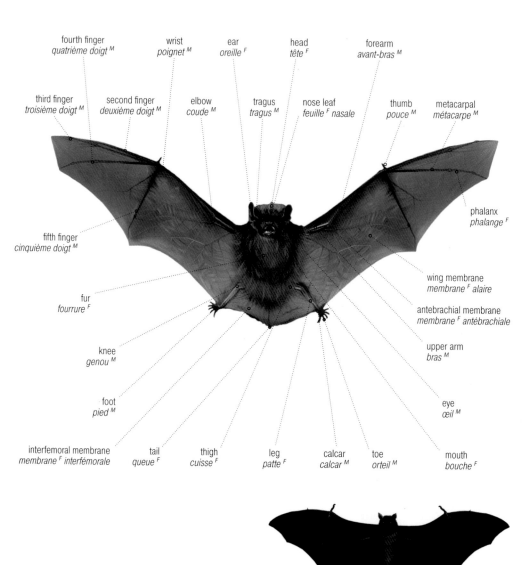

fourth finger
quatrième doigt M

wrist
poignet M

ear
oreille F

head
tête F

forearm
avant-bras M

third finger
troisième doigt M

second finger
deuxième doigt M

elbow
coude M

tragus
tragus M

nose leaf
feuille F *nasale*

thumb
pouce M

metacarpal
métacarpe M

phalanx
phalange F

fifth finger
cinquième doigt M

wing membrane
membrane F *alaire*

fur
fourrure F

antebrachial membrane
membrane F *antébrachiale*

knee
genou M

upper arm
bras M

foot
pied M

eye
œil M

interfemoral membrane
membrane F *interfémorale*

tail
queue F

thigh
cuisse F

leg
patte F

calcar
calcar M

toe
orteil M

mouth
bouche F

fruit bat
roussette F

mole
taupe ^F

head
tête ^F

eye
œil ^M

body
corps ^M

fur
fourrure ^F

snout
museau ^M

tail
queue ^F

finger
doigt ^M

claw
griffe ^F

forelimb
patte ^F *avant*

toe
doigt ^M *de patte* ^F

hind limb
patte ^F *arrière*

hedgehog
hérisson ^M

pangolin
pangolin ^M

giant anteater
tamanoir ^M

armadillo
tatou ^M

Japanese macaque
macaque M *japonais*

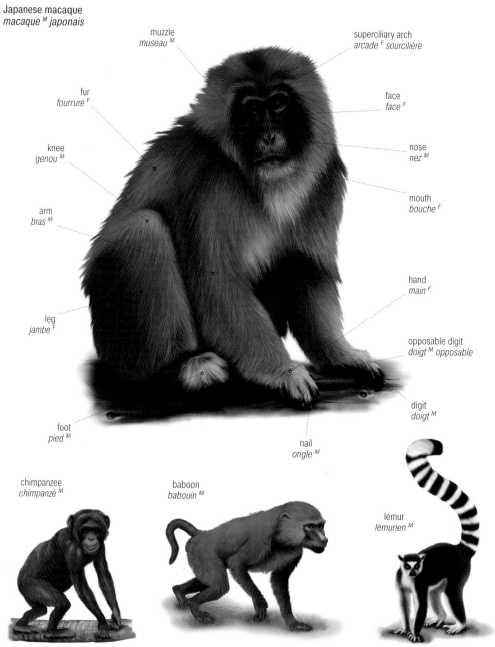

muzzle
museau M

superciliary arch
arcade F *sourcilière*

fur
fourrure F

face
face F

knee
genou M

nose
nez M

arm
bras M

mouth
bouche F

hand
main F

leg
jambe F

opposable digit
doigt M *opposable*

digit
doigt M

foot
pied M

nail
ongle M

chimpanzee
chimpanzé M

baboon
babouin M

lemur
lémurien M

lion tamarin
tamarin-lion ^M

orangutan
orang-outan ^M

red howler monkey
singe ^M *hurleur* ^M *roux*

slow loris
loris ^M

mandrill
mandrill ^M

gorilla
gorille ^M

lobster
homard M

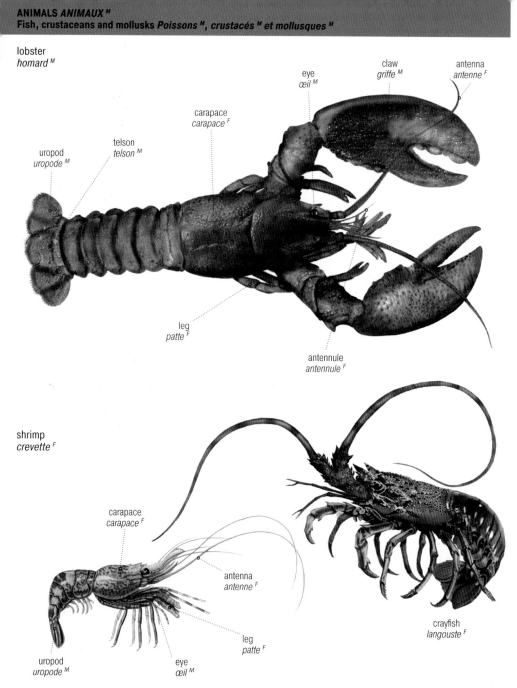

eye
œil M

claw
griffe M

antenna
antenne F

carapace
carapace F

uropod
uropode M

telson
telson M

leg
patte F

antennule
antennule F

shrimp
crevette F

carapace
carapace F

antenna
antenne F

uropod
uropode M

eye
œil M

leg
patte F

crayfish
langouste F

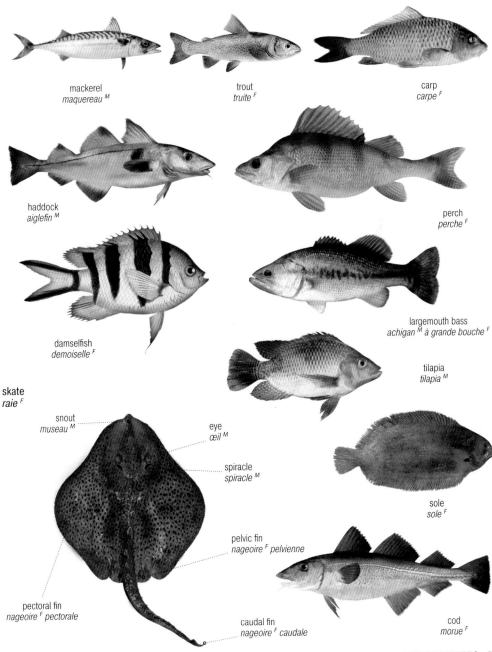

mackerel
maquereau ^M

trout
truite ^F

carp
carpe ^F

haddock
aiglefin ^M

perch
perche ^F

damselfish
demoiselle ^F

largemouth bass
achigan ^M *à grande bouche* ^F

tilapia
tilapia ^M

skate
raie ^F

snout
museau ^M

eye
œil ^M

spiracle
spiracle ^M

sole
sole ^F

pelvic fin
nageoire ^F *pelvienne*

pectoral fin
nageoire ^F *pectorale*

caudal fin
nageoire ^F *caudale*

cod
morue ^F

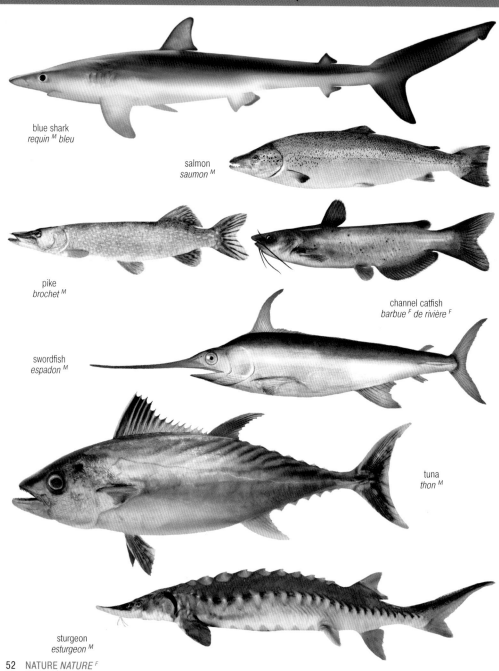

blue shark
requin M *bleu*

salmon
saumon M

pike
brochet M

channel catfish
barbue F *de rivière* F

swordfish
espadon M

tuna
thon M

sturgeon
esturgeon M

octopus
pieuvre ^F

mantle
manteau ^M

siphon
siphon ^M

eye
œil ^M

arm
bras ^M

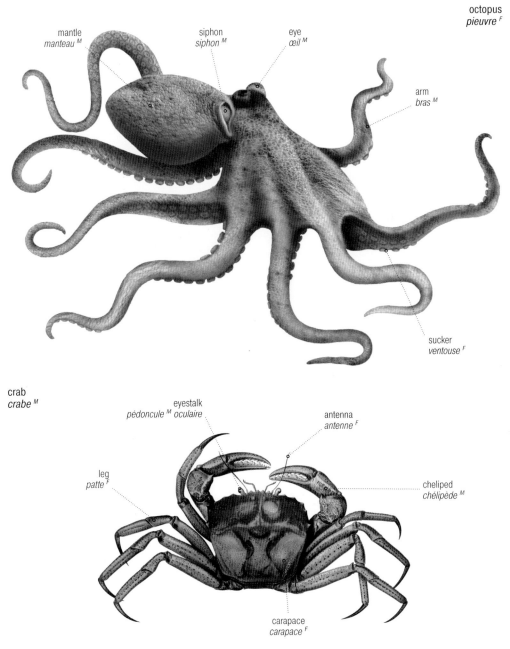

sucker
ventouse ^F

crab
crabe ^M

eyestalk
pédoncule ^M *oculaire*

antenna
antenne ^F

leg
patte ^F

cheliped
chélipède ^M

carapace
carapace ^F

Eurasian jay
geai M *des chênes* M

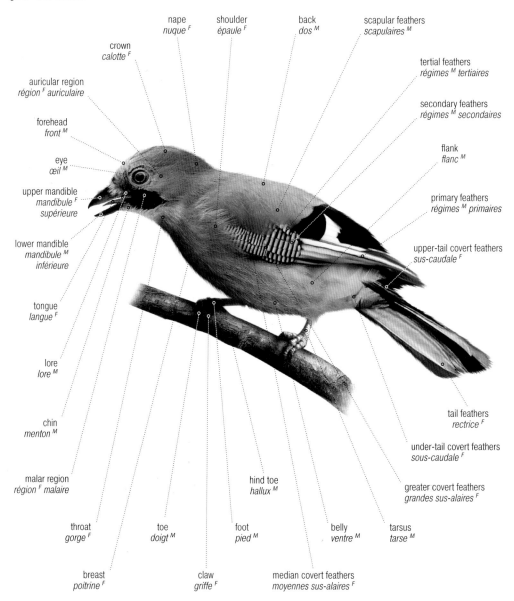

nape
nuque F

shoulder
épaule F

back
dos M

scapular feathers
scapulaires M

crown
calotte F

tertial feathers
régimes M *tertiaires*

auricular region
région F *auriculaire*

secondary feathers
régimes M *secondaires*

forehead
front M

flank
flanc M

eye
œil M

upper mandible
mandibule F
supérieure

primary feathers
régimes M *primaires*

lower mandible
mandibule M
inférieure

upper-tail covert feathers
sus-caudale F

tongue
langue F

lore
lore M

tail feathers
rectrice F

chin
menton M

under-tail covert feathers
sous-caudale F

malar region
région F *malaire*

hind toe
hallux M

greater covert feathers
grandes sus-alaires F

throat
gorge F

toe
doigt M

foot
pied M

belly
ventre M

tarsus
tarse M

breast
poitrine F

claw
griffe F

median covert feathers
moyennes sus-alaires F

Eurasian siskin
tarin ᴹ *des aulnes* ᴹ

bullfinch
bouvreuil ᴹ *pivoine*

greater titmouse
mésange ᶠ *charbonnière*

common swift
martinet ᴹ *noir*

pigeon
pigeon ᴹ

red-backed shrike
pie-grièche ᶠ *écorcheur*

blue jay
geai ᴹ *bleu*

hummingbird
colibri M

black-capped chickadee
mésange F *à tête* F *noire*

woodpecker
pic M

kingfisher
martin-pêcheur M

cockatiel
calopsitte F *élégante*

barn swallow
hirondelle F *rustique*

American goldfinch
chardonneret M *jaune*

cardinal
cardinal M

American robin
merle M *d'Amérique* F

American crow
corneille ^F *d'Amérique* ^F

thrush
grive ^F *vraie*

nightingale
rossignol ^M

sparrow
moineau ^M

starling
étourneau ^M *sansonnet*

owl
hibou ^M

stork
cigogne ^F

gyrfalcon
faucon ^M *gerfaut*

partridge
perdrix ^F

condor
condor M

ruffed grouse
gélinotte F *huppée*

bald eagle
pygargue M *à tête* F *blanche*

rooster
coq M

ostrich
autruche F

sharp-tailed grouse
tétras M *à queue* F *fine*

peacock
paon M

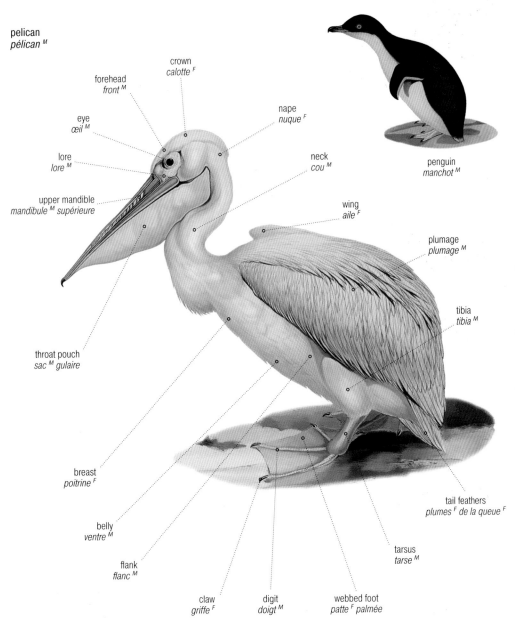

pelican
pélican M

crown
calotte F

forehead
front M

nape
nuque F

eye
œil M

lore
lore M

neck
cou M

upper mandible
mandibule M *supérieure*

wing
aile F

plumage
plumage M

penguin
manchot M

tibia
tibia M

throat pouch
sac M *gulaire*

breast
poitrine F

belly
ventre M

flank
flanc M

claw
griffe F

digit
doigt M

webbed foot
patte F *palmée*

tarsus
tarse M

tail feathers
plumes F *de la queue* F

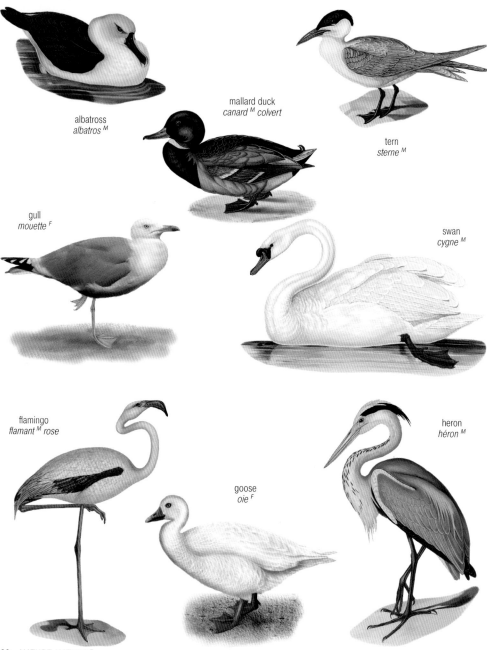

albatross
albatros M

mallard duck
canard M *colvert*

tern
sterne M

gull
mouette F

swan
cygne M

flamingo
flamant M *rose*

goose
oie F

heron
héron M

Arachnids
Arachnides [M]

scorpion
scorpion [M]

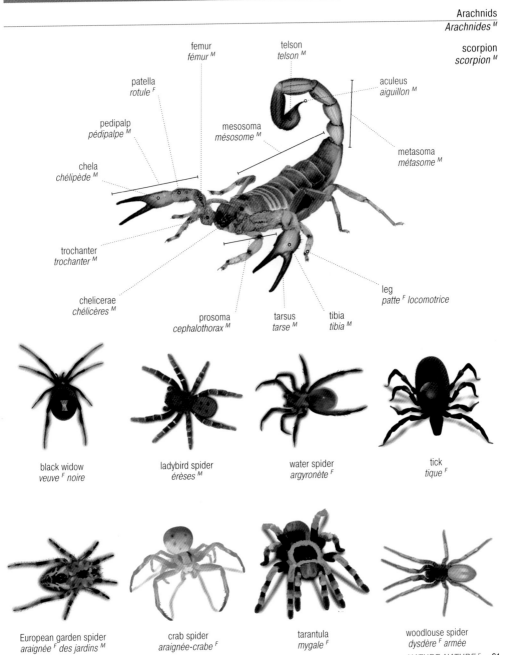

femur
fémur [M]

telson
telson [M]

aculeus
aiguillon [M]

patella
rotule [F]

mesosoma
mésosome [M]

metasoma
métasome [M]

pedipalp
pédipalpe [M]

chela
chélipède [M]

trochanter
trochanter [M]

chelicerae
chélicères [M]

prosoma
cephalothorax [M]

tarsus
tarse [M]

tibia
tibia [M]

leg
patte [F] *locomotrice*

black widow
veuve [F] *noire*

ladybird spider
érèses [M]

water spider
argyronète [F]

tick
tique [F]

European garden spider
araignée [F] *des jardins* [M]

crab spider
araignée-crabe [F]

tarantula
mygale [F]

woodlouse spider
dysdère [F] *armée*

Beetles
Coléoptères ^M

Hercules beetle
scarabée ^M *Hercule*

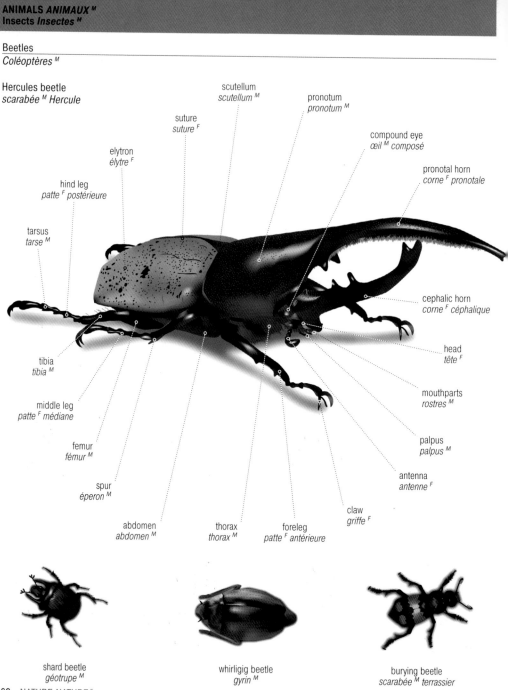

scutellum
scutellum ^M

pronotum
pronotum ^M

suture
suture ^F

compound eye
œil ^M *composé*

elytron
élytre ^F

pronotal horn
corne ^F *pronotale*

hind leg
patte ^F *postérieure*

tarsus
tarse ^M

cephalic horn
corne ^F *céphalique*

tibia
tibia ^M

head
tête ^F

middle leg
patte ^F *médiane*

mouthparts
rostres ^M

femur
fémur ^M

palpus
palpus ^M

spur
éperon ^M

antenna
antenne ^F

abdomen
abdomen ^M

thorax
thorax ^M

foreleg
patte ^F *antérieure*

claw
griffe ^F

shard beetle
géotrupe ^M

whirligig beetle
gyrin ^M

burying beetle
scarabée ^M *terrassier*

Carabus problematicus (Lat.)
carabe ^M problématique

furniture beetle
anobie ^M ponctué

Sagra buqueti (Lat.)
sagre de buquet ^M

black vine weevil
otiorhynque ^M de la vigne ^F

cockchafer
hanneton ^M commun

ladybug
coccinelle ^F

thick-legged flower beetle
œdémère ^M noble

rhinoceros beetle
scarabée-rhinocéros ^M

stag beetle
lucane ^M cerf-volant ^M

Colorado potato beetle
doryphore ^M de la pomme ^F de terre ^F

rose chafer
hanneton ^M des roses

goliath beetle
goliath ^M

larch ladybug
aphidecta obliterata ^F

dung beetle
stercoraire ^M

flower beetle
cétoine ^M

golden scarab beetle
scarabée ^M doré

Butterflies and moths
Papillons M diurnes et nocturnes

swallowtail caterpillar
chenille F de papillon M porte-queue

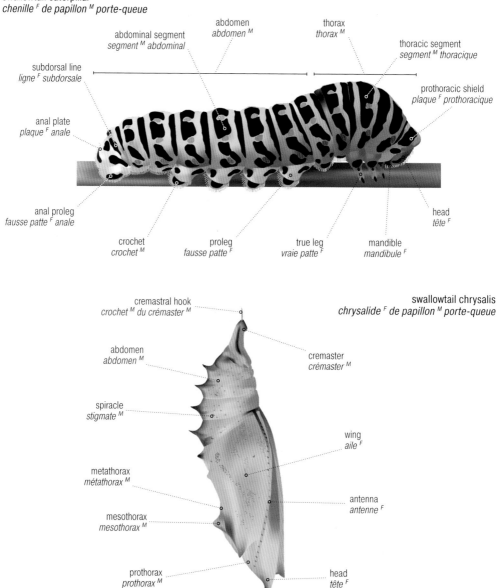

abdomen
abdomen M

thorax
thorax M

abdominal segment
segment M abdominal

thoracic segment
segment M thoracique

subdorsal line
ligne F subdorsale

prothoracic shield
plaque F prothoracique

anal plate
plaque F anale

anal proleg
fausse patte F anale

head
tête F

crochet
crochet M

proleg
fausse patte F

true leg
vraie patte F

mandible
mandibule F

cremastral hook
crochet M du crémaster M

swallowtail chrysalis
chrysalide F de papillon M porte-queue

abdomen
abdomen M

cremaster
crémaster M

spiracle
stigmate M

wing
aile F

metathorax
métathorax M

antenna
antenne F

mesothorax
mesothorax M

prothorax
prothorax M

head
tête F

tiger swallowtail
papillon M glauque du Canada M

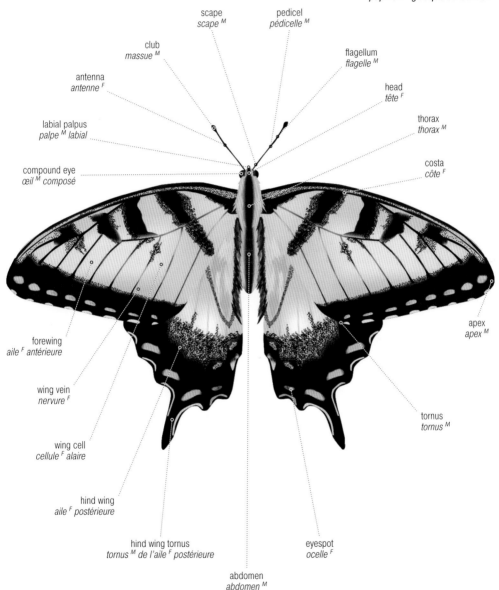

scape
scape M

pedicel
pédicelle M

club
massue M

flagellum
flagelle M

antenna
antenne F

head
tête F

labial palpus
palpe M labial

thorax
thorax M

compound eye
œil M composé

costa
côte F

forewing
aile F antérieure

apex
apex M

wing vein
nervure F

tornus
tornus M

wing cell
cellule F alaire

hind wing
aile F postérieure

hind wing tornus
tornus M de l'aile F postérieure

eyespot
ocelle F

abdomen
abdomen M

Adonis blue
azuré ^M bleu céleste

clothes moth
mite ^F

lappet moth
papillon ^M à épaulettes ^F

cabbage white
piéride ^F du chou ^M

silkmoth
bombyx ^M du mûrier ^M

monarch butterfly
monarque ^M

buff-tip
bucéphale ^F

scarce swallowtail
flambé ^M

brimstone
citron ^M

Apollo
Apollon [M]

luna moth
papillon [M] *lune*

black-veined white
piéride [F] *de l'aubépine* [F]

blue morpho
morpho [M] *bleu*

Brahmin moth
brahmaea wallichii [M]

divana diva
divana diva [F]

purple emperor
grand Mars changeant [M]

Hercules moth
coscinocera [F] *hercules*

spear-marked black moth
géomètre [M] *noir du bouleau* [M]

Wasps and wasp-like insects
Guêpes F et insectes M similaires

wasp
guêpe F

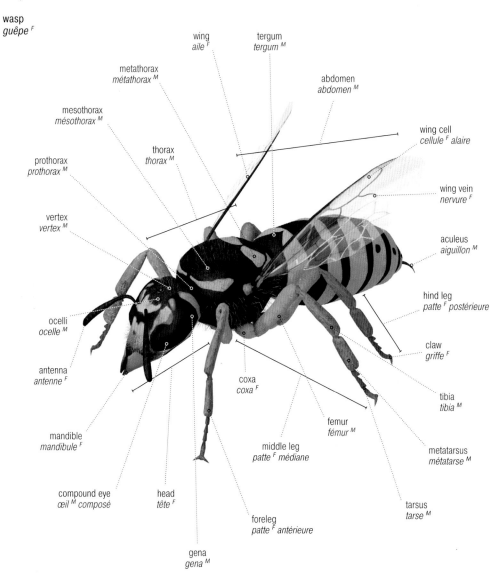

wing
aile F

tergum
tergum M

metathorax
métathorax M

abdomen
abdomen M

mesothorax
mésothorax M

wing cell
cellule F alaire

thorax
thorax M

prothorax
prothorax M

wing vein
nervure F

vertex
vertex M

aculeus
aiguillon M

hind leg
patte F postérieure

ocelli
ocelle M

claw
griffe F

antenna
antenne F

coxa
coxa F

tibia
tibia M

femur
fémur M

mandible
mandibule F

middle leg
patte F médiane

metatarsus
métatarse M

compound eye
œil M composé

head
tête F

foreleg
patte F antérieure

tarsus
tarse M

gena
gena M

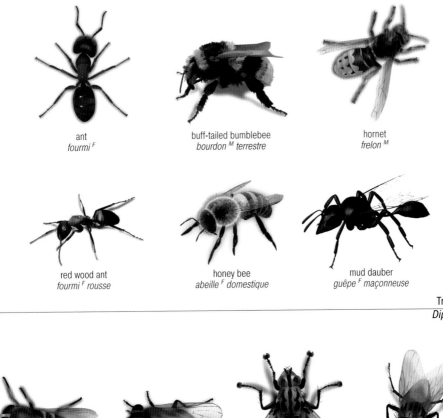

ant
fourmi ^F

buff-tailed bumblebee
bourdon ^M *terrestre*

hornet
frelon ^M

red wood ant
fourmi ^F *rousse*

honey bee
abeille ^F *domestique*

mud dauber
guêpe ^F *maçonneuse*

True flies
Diptères ^M

horsefly
taon ^M

common housefly
mouche ^F *domestique*

flesh fly
mouche ^F *à viande* ^F

little housefly
petite mouche ^F *domestique*

blackfly
simulie ^F

blowfly
calliphore ^F

mosquito
maringouin ^M

tsetse fly
mouche ^F *tsé-tsé*

Neoptera
Néoptères ᴹ

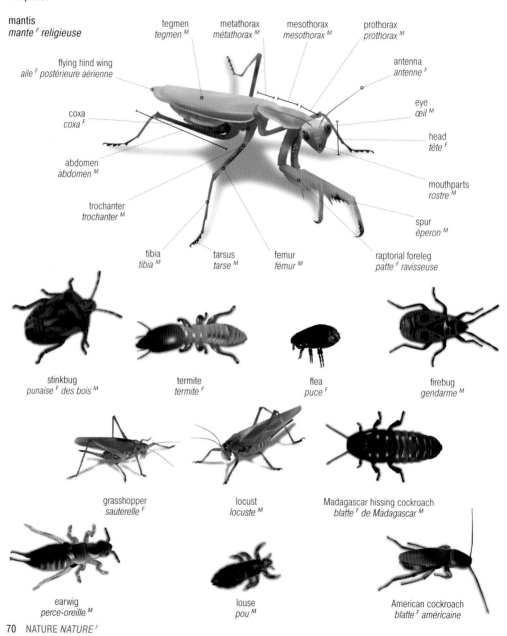

mantis
mante ᶠ *religieuse*

tegmen
tegmen ᴹ

metathorax
métathorax ᴹ

mesothorax
mesothorax ᴹ

prothorax
prothorax ᴹ

flying hind wing
aile ᶠ *postérieure aérienne*

antenna
antenne ᶠ

coxa
coxa ᶠ

eye
œil ᴹ

head
tête ᶠ

abdomen
abdomen ᴹ

mouthparts
rostre ᴹ

trochanter
trochanter ᴹ

spur
éperon ᴹ

tibia
tibia ᴹ

tarsus
tarse ᴹ

femur
fémur ᴹ

raptorial foreleg
patte ᶠ *ravisseuse*

stinkbug
punaise ᶠ *des bois* ᴹ

termite
termite ᶠ

flea
puce ᶠ

firebug
gendarme ᴹ

grasshopper
sauterelle ᶠ

locust
locuste ᴹ

Madagascar hissing cockroach
blatte ᶠ *de Madagascar* ᴹ

earwig
perce-oreille ᴹ

louse
pou ᴹ

American cockroach
blatte ᶠ *américaine*

Odonata
Odonates ^M

dragonfly
libellule ^F

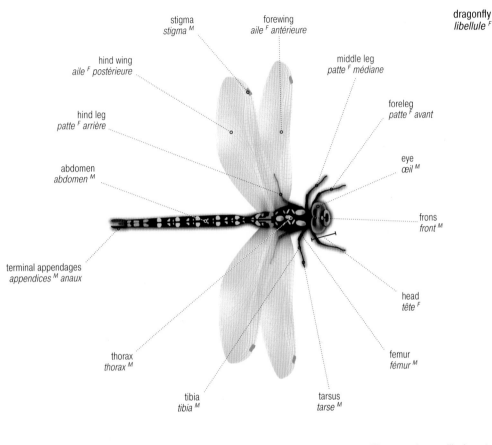

stigma
stigma ^M

forewing
aile ^F *antérieure*

middle leg
patte ^F *médiane*

hind wing
aile ^F *postérieure*

foreleg
patte ^F *avant*

hind leg
patte ^F *arrière*

eye
œil ^M

abdomen
abdomen ^M

frons
front ^M

terminal appendages
appendices ^M *anaux*

head
tête ^F

thorax
thorax ^M

femur
fémur ^M

tibia
tibia ^M

tarsus
tarse ^M

Worms and worm-like insects
Vers ^M *et insectes* ^M *similaires*

millipede
diplopode ^M

earthworm
ver de terre ^M

plant cell
*cellule *F* végétale*

chloroplast
*chloroplaste *M**

ribosome
*ribosome *M**

cell wall
*paroi *F* cellulaire*

vacuole
*vacuole *F**

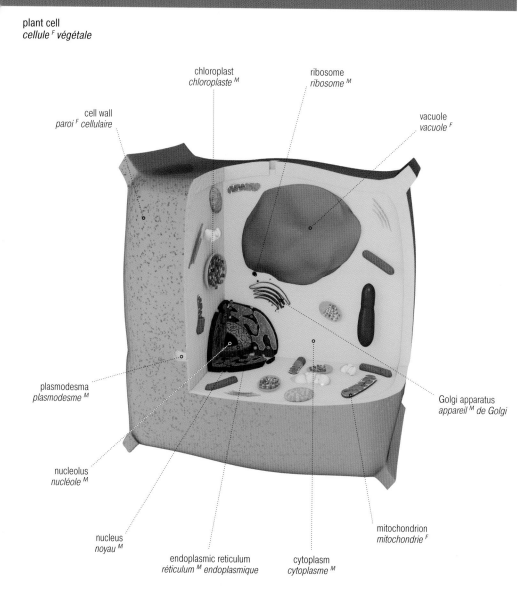

plasmodesma
*plasmodesme *M**

Golgi apparatus
*appareil *M* de Golgi*

nucleolus
*nucléole *M**

nucleus
*noyau *M**

endoplasmic reticulum
*réticulum *M* endoplasmique*

cytoplasm
*cytoplasme *M**

mitochondrion
*mitochondrie *F**

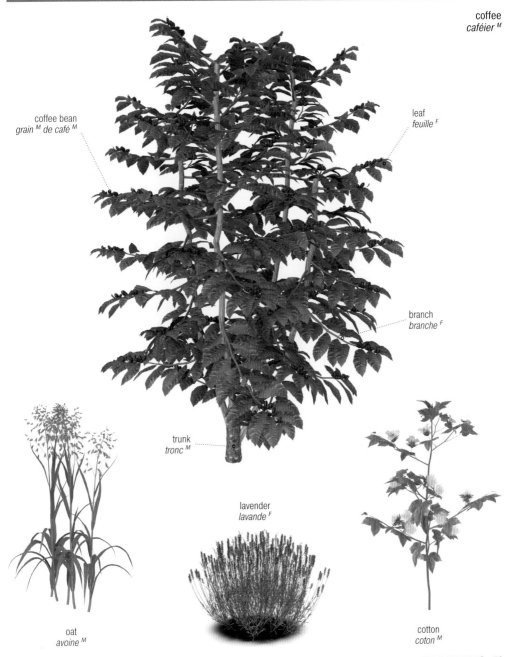

coffee
caféier ^M

coffee bean
grain ^M *de café* ^M

leaf
feuille ^F

branch
branche ^F

trunk
tronc ^M

oat
avoine ^M

lavender
lavande ^F

cotton
coton ^M

grape
raisin ^M

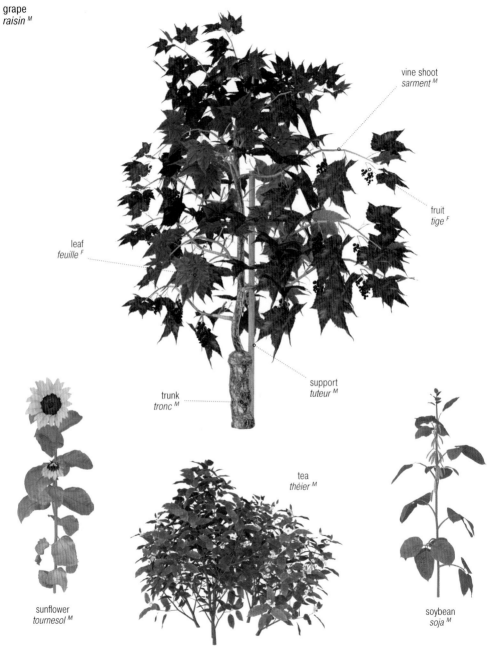

vine shoot
sarment ^M

fruit
tige ^F

leaf
feuille ^F

support
tuteur ^M

trunk
tronc ^M

tea
théier ^M

sunflower
tournesol ^M

soybean
soja ^M

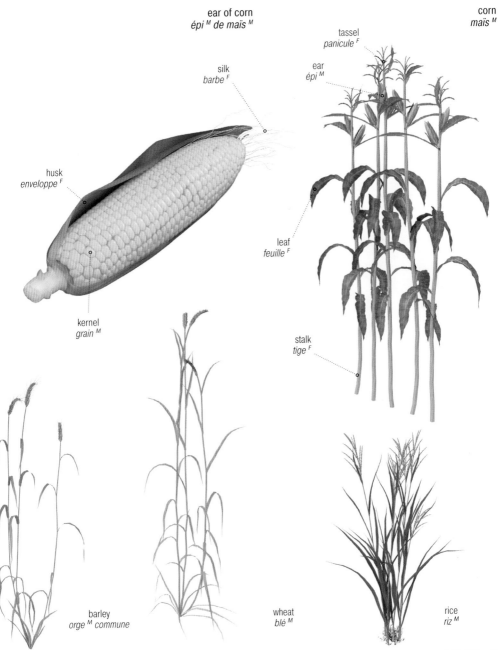

ear of corn
épi ^M *de maïs* ^M

corn
maïs ^M

tassel
panicule ^F

ear
épi ^M

silk
barbe ^F

husk
enveloppe ^F

leaf
feuille ^F

kernel
grain ^M

stalk
tige ^F

barley
orge ^M *commune*

wheat
blé ^M

rice
riz ^M

geranium
géranium ^M

flower
fleur ^F

petal
pétale ^M

flower bud
bourgeon ^M *à fleurs* ^F

stalk
tige ^F

leaf
feuille ^F

marigold
souci ^M

calla lily
arum ^M *d'Éthiopie* ^F

hydrangea
hortensia ^M

Fruits and vegetables
Fruits ^M *et légumes* ^M

strawberry
fraisier ^M

flower
fleur ^F

unripe berry
fraise ^F *non mûre*

leaf
feuille ^F

stem
tige ^F

berry
fraise ^F

broccoli
brocoli ^M

cauliflower
chou-fleur ^M

lettuce
laitue ^F

carrot
carotte F

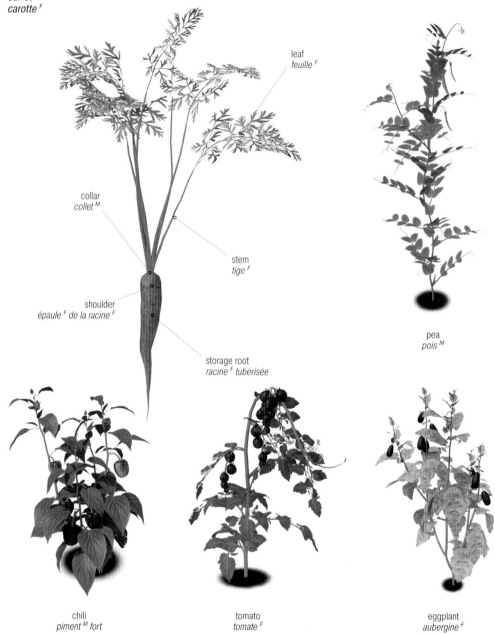

leaf
feuille F

collar
collet M

stem
tige F

shoulder
épaule F *de la racine* F

storage root
racine F *tubérisée*

pea
pois M

chili
piment M *fort*

tomato
tomate F

eggplant
aubergine F

zucchini
zucchini M

squash
courge F

watermelon
melon M *d'eau* F

cantaloupe
cantaloup M

onion
oignon M

cucumber
concombre M

pear
poirier ^M

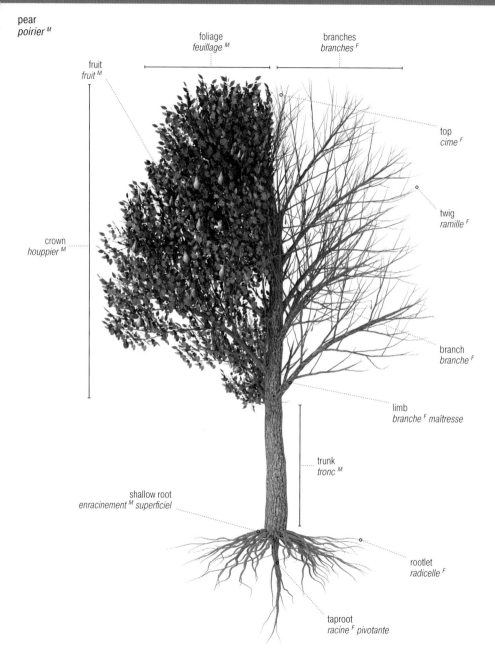

foliage
feuillage ^M

branches
branches ^F

fruit
fruit ^M

top
cime ^F

twig
ramille ^F

crown
houppier ^M

branch
branche ^F

limb
branche ^F *maîtresse*

trunk
tronc ^M

shallow root
enracinement ^M *superficiel*

rootlet
radicelle ^F

taproot
racine ^F *pivotante*

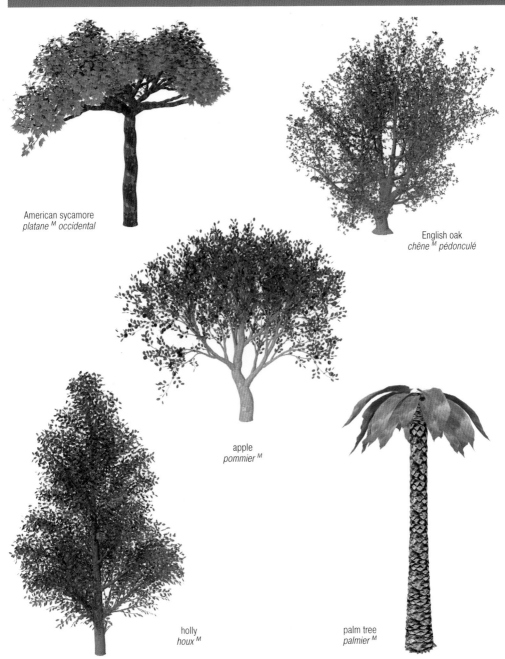

American sycamore
platane M *occidental*

English oak
chêne M *pédonculé*

apple
pommier M

holly
houx M

palm tree
palmier M

European aspen
tremble M

red oak
chêne M *rouge*

ash
frêne M

sugar maple
érable M *à sucre* M

rubber tree
hévéa M

olive
olivier M

large-leaf linden
tilleul M _à grandes feuilles_ F

black alder
aulne M _noir_

hawthorn
aubépine F

ginkgo tree
ginkgo M

American beech
hêtre ^M *à grandes feuilles* ^F

chestnut
châtaigner ^M

silver birch
bouleau ^M *blanc d'Europe* ^F

hornbeam
charme ^M

juniper
genévrier M

western red cedar
thuya M *géant*

Caucasian fir
sapin M *de Nordmann*

English yew
if M *commun*

Colorado blue spruce
épinette F *du Colorado* M

Italian cypress
cyprès M *d'Italie* F

red pine
pin M *rouge*

Norway spruce
épinette F *de Norvège* F

white pine
pin M *blanc*

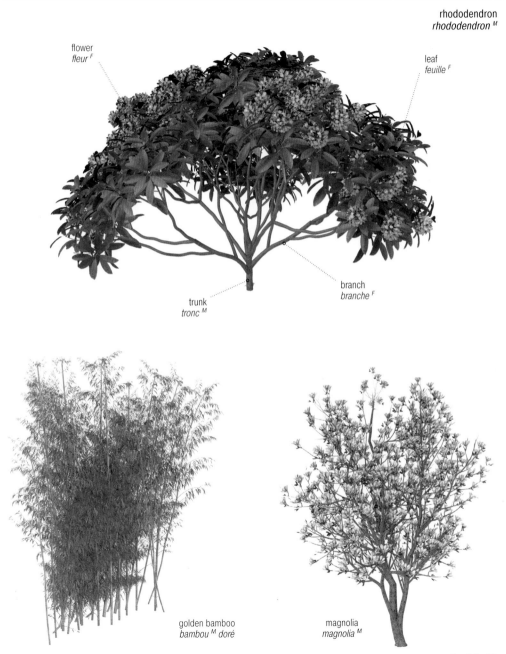

rhododendron
rhododendron M

flower
fleur F

leaf
feuille F

branch
branche F

trunk
tronc M

golden bamboo
bambou M *doré*

magnolia
magnolia M

structure of a flower
structure F *d'une fleur* F

filament
filet M

stigma
stigmate M

style
style M

petal
pétale M

anther
anthère F

receptacle
réceptacle M

ovule
ovule M

sepal
sépale M

peduncle
pédoncule M

ovary
ovaire M

rose
rose F

corolla
corolle F

petal
pétale M

amaryllis
amaryllis F

pistil
pistil M

thorn
épine F

leaf
feuille F

stamen
étamine F

stem
tige F

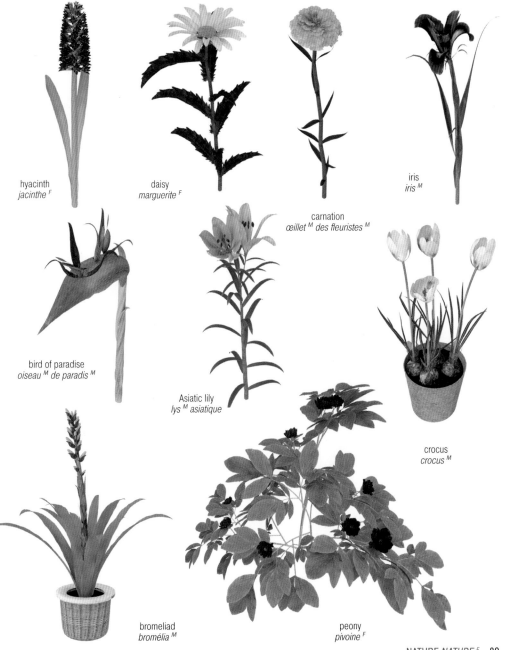

hyacinth
jacinthe [F]

daisy
marguerite [F]

carnation
œillet [M] des fleuristes [M]

iris
iris [M]

bird of paradise
oiseau [M] de paradis [M]

Asiatic lily
lys [M] asiatique

crocus
crocus [M]

bromeliad
bromélia [M]

peony
pivoine [F]

orchid
orchidée ^F

gerbera daisy
gerbera ^M *de Jameson* ^M

gladiolus
glaieul ^M

tulip
tulipe ^F

Houseplants *Plantes* ^F *d'intérieur* ^M

dragon tree
dragonnier ^M

leaf
feuille ^F

cactus
cactus ^M

trunk
tronc ^M

soil
terreau ^M

pot
pot ^M

sago palm
sagoutier ^M

weeping fig
figuier ^M pleureur

ivy
lierre ^M

croton
croton ^M

fern
fougère ^F

fan palm
talipot ^M de l'Inde ^F

Aquatic plants *Plantes* ^F *aquatiques*

lotus
lotus ^M

HUMAN BEING

ÊTRE HUMAIN

anterior view of female body
vue ^F *antérieure du corps* ^M *féminin*

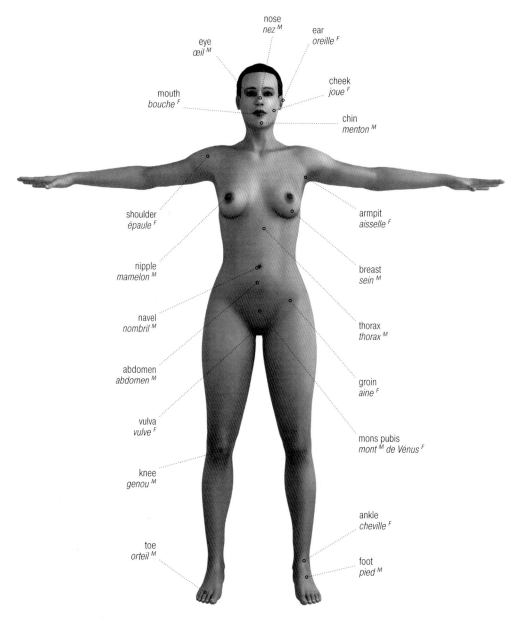

nose
nez ^M

ear
oreille ^F

eye
œil ^M

cheek
joue ^F

mouth
bouche ^F

chin
menton ^M

shoulder
épaule ^F

armpit
aisselle ^F

nipple
mamelon ^M

breast
sein ^M

navel
nombril ^M

thorax
thorax ^M

abdomen
abdomen ^M

groin
aine ^F

vulva
vulve ^F

mons pubis
mont ^M *de Vénus* ^F

knee
genou ^M

ankle
cheville ^F

toe
orteil ^M

foot
pied ^M

posterior view of female body
vue F *postérieure du corps* M *féminin*

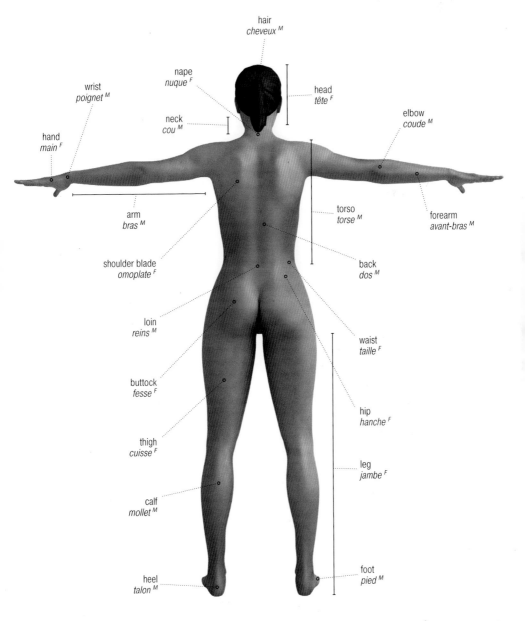

hair
cheveux M

nape
nuque F

wrist
poignet M

head
tête F

neck
cou M

elbow
coude M

hand
main F

arm
bras M

torso
torse M

forearm
avant-bras M

shoulder blade
omoplate F

back
dos M

loin
reins M

waist
taille F

buttock
fesse F

hip
hanche F

thigh
cuisse F

leg
jambe F

calf
mollet M

heel
talon M

foot
pied M

anterior view of male body
vue F *antérieure du corps* M *masculin*

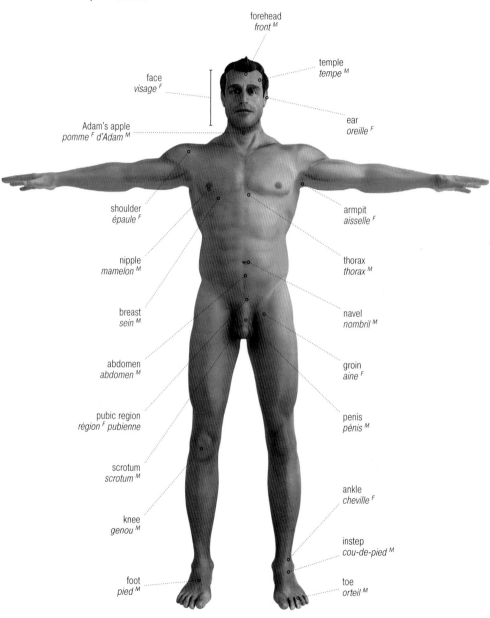

forehead
front M

temple
tempe M

face
visage F

ear
oreille F

Adam's apple
pomme F *d'Adam* M

shoulder
épaule F

armpit
aisselle F

nipple
mamelon M

thorax
thorax M

breast
sein M

navel
nombril M

abdomen
abdomen M

groin
aine F

pubic region
région F *pubienne*

penis
pénis M

scrotum
scrotum M

ankle
cheville F

knee
genou M

instep
cou-de-pied M

foot
pied M

toe
orteil M

posterior view of male body
vue F *postérieure du corps* M *masculin*

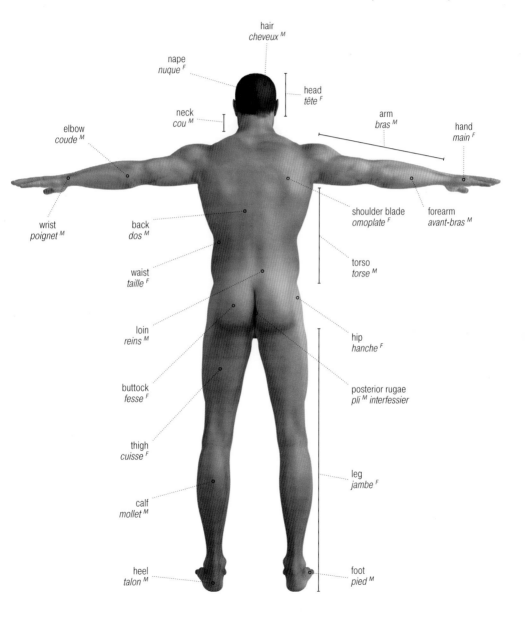

hair
cheveux M

nape
nuque F

head
tête F

neck
cou M

arm
bras M

hand
main F

elbow
coude M

shoulder blade
omoplate F

forearm
avant-bras M

wrist
poignet M

back
dos M

torso
torse M

waist
taille F

loin
reins M

hip
hanche F

buttock
fesse F

posterior rugae
pli M *interfessier*

thigh
cuisse F

leg
jambe F

calf
mollet M

heel
talon M

foot
pied M

anterior view of main muscles
vue ᶠ antérieure des muscles ᴹ principaux

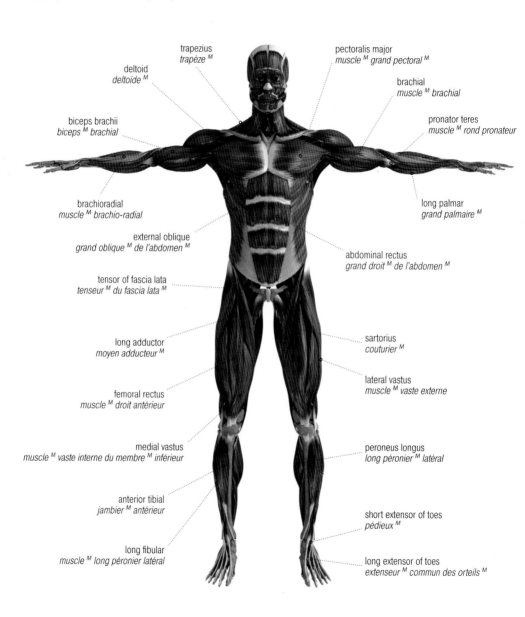

trapezius
trapèze ᴹ

pectoralis major
muscle ᴹ grand pectoral ᴹ

deltoid
deltoïde ᴹ

brachial
muscle ᴹ brachial

biceps brachii
biceps ᴹ brachial

pronator teres
muscle ᴹ rond pronateur

brachioradial
muscle ᴹ brachio-radial

long palmar
grand palmaire ᴹ

external oblique
grand oblique ᴹ de l'abdomen ᴹ

abdominal rectus
grand droit ᴹ de l'abdomen ᴹ

tensor of fascia lata
tenseur ᴹ du fascia lata ᴹ

long adductor
moyen adducteur ᴹ

sartorius
couturier ᴹ

lateral vastus
muscle ᴹ vaste externe

femoral rectus
muscle ᴹ droit antérieur

medial vastus
muscle ᴹ vaste interne du membre ᴹ inférieur

peroneus longus
long péronier ᴹ latéral

anterior tibial
jambier ᴹ antérieur

short extensor of toes
pédieux ᴹ

long fibular
muscle ᴹ long péronier latéral

long extensor of toes
extenseur ᴹ commun des orteils ᴹ

posterior view of main muscles
vue ᶠ postérieure des muscles ᴹ principaux

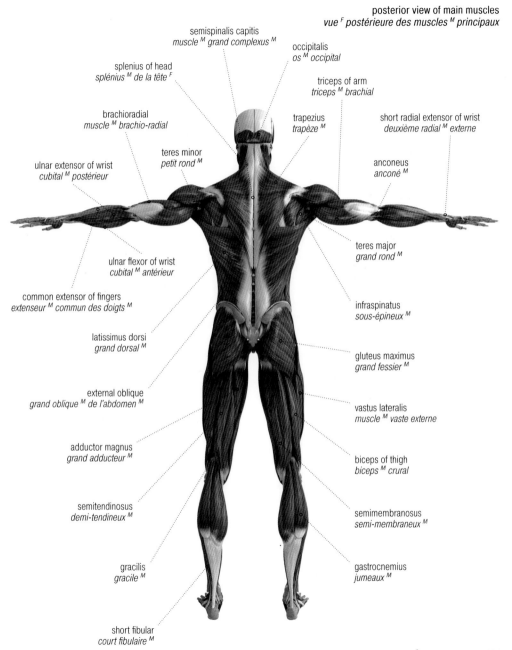

semispinalis capitis
muscle ᴹ grand complexus ᴹ

occipitalis
os ᴹ occipital

splenius of head
splénius ᴹ de la tête ᶠ

triceps of arm
triceps ᴹ brachial

brachioradial
muscle ᴹ brachio-radial

trapezius
trapèze ᴹ

short radial extensor of wrist
deuxième radial ᴹ externe

teres minor
petit rond ᴹ

anconeus
anconé ᴹ

ulnar extensor of wrist
cubital ᴹ postérieur

ulnar flexor of wrist
cubital ᴹ antérieur

teres major
grand rond ᴹ

common extensor of fingers
extenseur ᴹ commun des doigts ᴹ

infraspinatus
sous-épineux ᴹ

latissimus dorsi
grand dorsal ᴹ

gluteus maximus
grand fessier ᴹ

external oblique
grand oblique ᴹ de l'abdomen ᴹ

vastus lateralis
muscle ᴹ vaste externe

adductor magnus
grand adducteur ᴹ

biceps of thigh
biceps ᴹ crural

semitendinosus
demi-tendineux ᴹ

semimembranosus
semi-membraneux ᴹ

gracilis
gracile ᴹ

gastrocnemius
jumeaux ᴹ

short fibular
court fibulaire ᴹ

facial muscles
muscles ^M du visage ^M

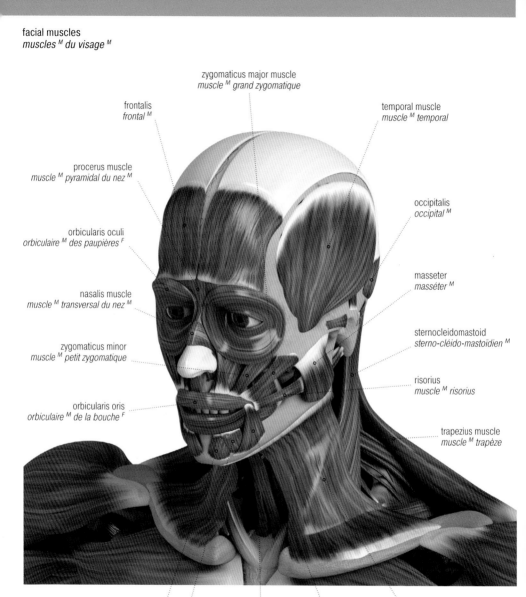

zygomaticus major muscle
muscle ^M grand zygomatique

frontalis
frontal ^M

temporal muscle
muscle ^M temporal

procerus muscle
muscle ^M pyramidal du nez ^M

occipitalis
occipital ^M

orbicularis oculi
orbiculaire ^M des paupières ^F

nasalis muscle
muscle ^M transversal du nez ^M

masseter
masséter ^M

sternocleidomastoid
sterno-cléido-mastoïdien ^M

zygomaticus minor
muscle ^M petit zygomatique

risorius
muscle ^M risorius

orbicularis oris
orbiculaire ^M de la bouche ^F

trapezius muscle
muscle ^M trapèze

mentalis
muscle ^M de la houppe ^F du menton ^M

sternothyroid muscle
muscle ^M sternothyroïdien

platysma muscle
muscle ^M peaucier du cou ^M

depressor labii inferioris muscle
muscle ^M abaisseur de la lèvre ^F inférieure

depressor anguli oris muscle
muscle ^M abaisseur de l'angle ^M de la bouche ^F

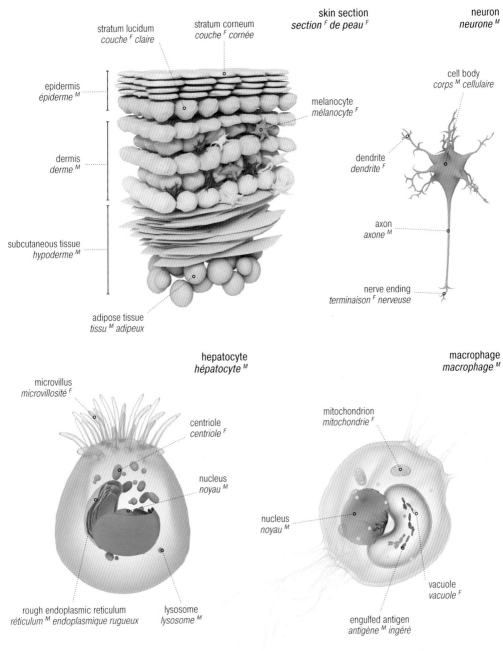

skin section
section F de peau F

neuron
neurone M

stratum lucidum
couche F claire

stratum corneum
couche F cornée

cell body
corps M cellulaire

epidermis
épiderme M

melanocyte
mélanocyte F

dermis
derme M

dendrite
dendrite F

subcutaneous tissue
hypoderme M

axon
axone M

adipose tissue
tissu M adipeux

nerve ending
terminaison F nerveuse

hepatocyte
hépatocyte M

macrophage
macrophage M

microvillus
microvillosité F

mitochondrion
mitochondrie F

centriole
centriole F

nucleus
noyau M

nucleus
noyau M

rough endoplasmic reticulum
réticulum M endoplasmique rugueux

lysosome
lysosome M

vacuole
vacuole F

engulfed antigen
antigène M ingéré

anterior view of skeleton
vue ^F *antérieure du squelette* ^M

frontal bone
os ^M *frontal*

temporal bone
os ^M *temporal*

maxilla
maxillaire ^M

zygomatic bone
os ^M *zygomatique*

mandible
mandibule ^F

clavicle
clavicule ^F

scapula
omoplate ^F

ribs
côtes ^F

sternum
sternum ^M

floating rib
côte ^F *flottante*

humerus
humérus ^M

spinal column
colonne ^F *vertébrale*

ulna
cubitus ^M

ilium
ilion ^M

radius
radius ^M

coccyx
coccyx ^M

sacrum
sacrum ^M

femur
fémur ^M

tibia
tibia ^M

patella
rotule ^F

fibula
fibula ^F

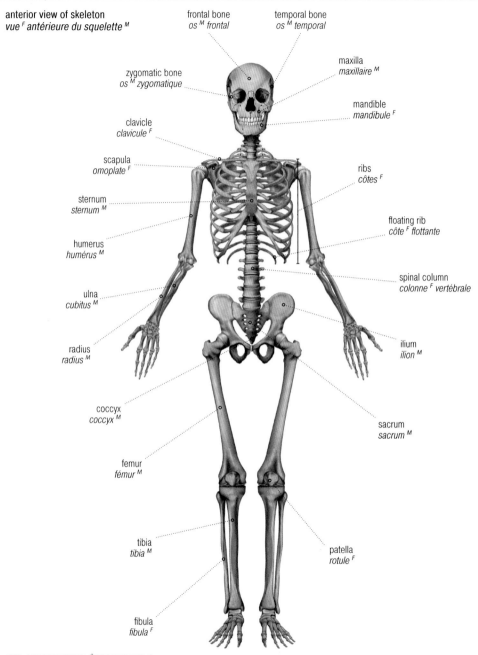

posterior view of skeleton
vue ^F postérieure du squelette ^M

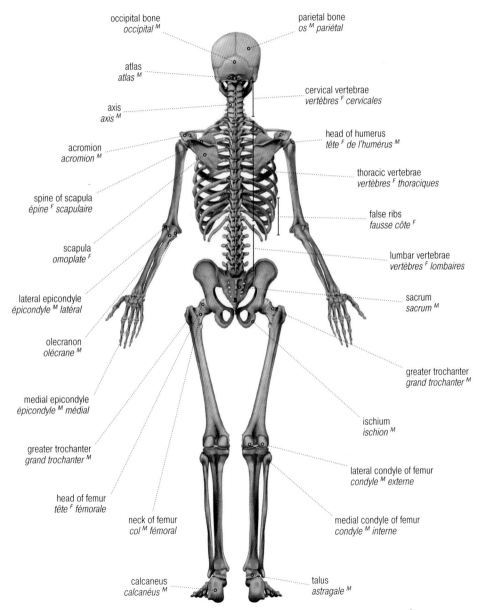

occipital bone
occipital ^M

atlas
atlas ^M

axis
axis ^M

acromion
acromion ^M

spine of scapula
épine ^F scapulaire

scapula
omoplate ^F

lateral epicondyle
épicondyle ^M latéral

olecranon
olécrane ^M

medial epicondyle
épicondyle ^M médial

greater trochanter
grand trochanter ^M

head of femur
tête ^F fémorale

neck of femur
col ^M fémoral

calcaneus
calcanéus ^M

parietal bone
os ^M pariétal

cervical vertebrae
vertèbres ^F cervicales

head of humerus
tête ^F de l'humérus ^M

thoracic vertebrae
vertèbres ^F thoraciques

false ribs
fausse côte ^F

lumbar vertebrae
vertèbres ^F lombaires

sacrum
sacrum ^M

greater trochanter
grand trochanter ^M

ischium
ischion ^M

lateral condyle of femur
condyle ^M externe

medial condyle of femur
condyle ^M interne

talus
astragale ^M

shoulder bones
os ^M de l'épaule ^F

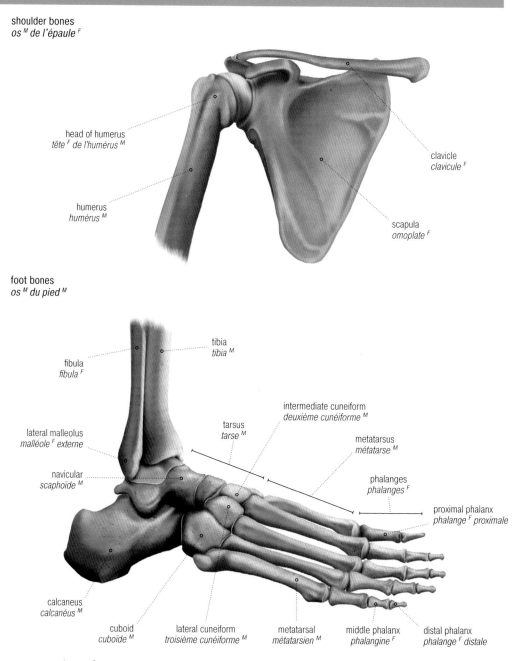

head of humerus
tête ^F de l'humérus ^M

clavicle
clavicule ^F

humerus
humérus ^M

scapula
omoplate ^F

foot bones
os ^M du pied ^M

tibia
tibia ^M

fibula
fibula ^F

intermediate cuneiform
deuxième cunéiforme ^M

tarsus
tarse ^M

metatarsus
métatarse ^M

lateral malleolus
malléole ^F externe

phalanges
phalanges ^F

navicular
scaphoïde ^M

proximal phalanx
phalange ^F proximale

calcaneus
calcanéus ^M

cuboid
cuboïde ^M

lateral cuneiform
troisième cunéiforme ^M

metatarsal
métatarsien ^M

middle phalanx
phalangine ^F

distal phalanx
phalange ^F distale

hand bones
os ᴹ de la main ᶠ

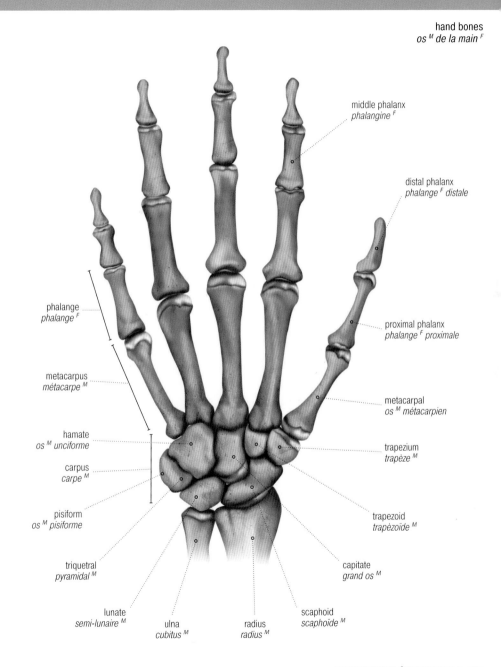

middle phalanx
phalangine ᶠ

distal phalanx
phalange ᶠ distale

phalange
phalange ᶠ

proximal phalanx
phalange ᶠ proximale

metacarpus
métacarpe ᴹ

metacarpal
os ᴹ métacarpien

hamate
os ᴹ unciforme

trapezium
trapèze ᴹ

carpus
carpe ᴹ

trapezoid
trapèzoïde ᴹ

pisiform
os ᴹ pisiforme

capitate
grand os ᴹ

triquetral
pyramidal ᴹ

lunate
semi-lunaire ᴹ

ulna
cubitus ᴹ

radius
radius ᴹ

scaphoid
scaphoïde ᴹ

knee
genou ^M

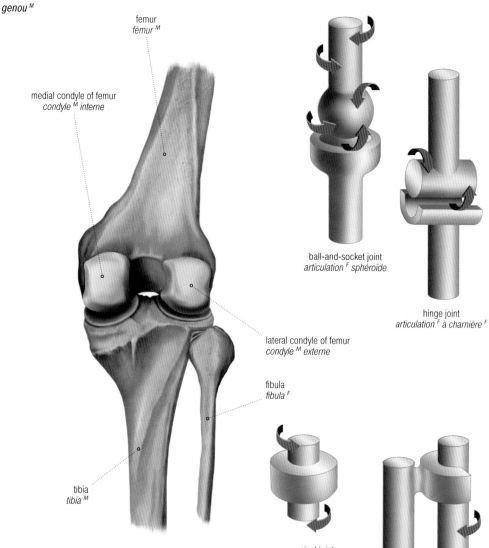

femur
fémur ^M

medial condyle of femur
condyle ^M *interne*

ball-and-socket joint
articulation ^F *sphéroïde*

hinge joint
articulation ^F *à charnière* ^F

lateral condyle of femur
condyle ^M *externe*

fibula
fibula ^F

tibia
tibia ^M

pivot joint
articulation ^F *pivot* ^M

elbow
coude ^M

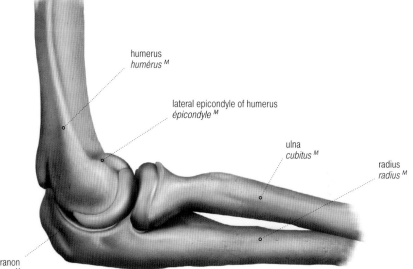

humerus
humérus ^M

lateral epicondyle of humerus
épicondyle ^M

ulna
cubitus ^M

radius
radius ^M

olecranon
olécrane ^M

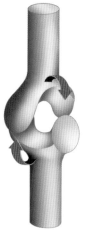

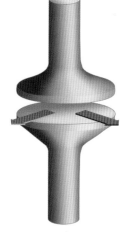

condyloid joint
articulation ^F *ellipsoïdale*

saddle joint
articulation ^F *en selle* ^F

gliding joint
articulation ^F *arthrodiale*

spinal column
colonne F *vertébrale*

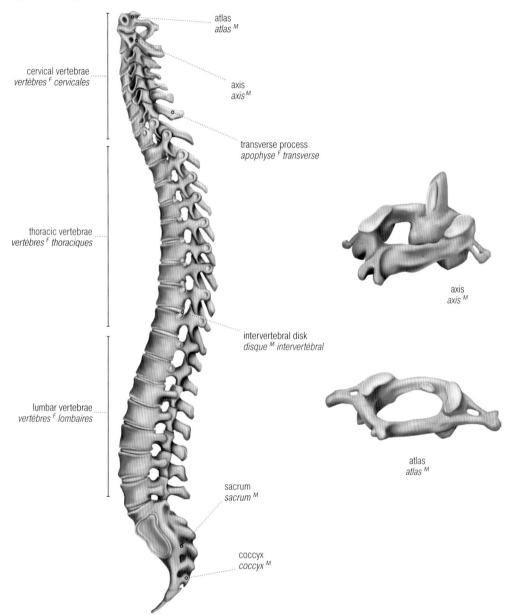

atlas
atlas M

cervical vertebrae
vertèbres F *cervicales*

axis
axis M

transverse process
apophyse F *transverse*

thoracic vertebrae
vertèbres F *thoraciques*

axis
axis M

intervertebral disk
disque M *intervertébral*

lumbar vertebrae
vertèbres F *lombaires*

atlas
atlas M

sacrum
sacrum M

coccyx
coccyx M

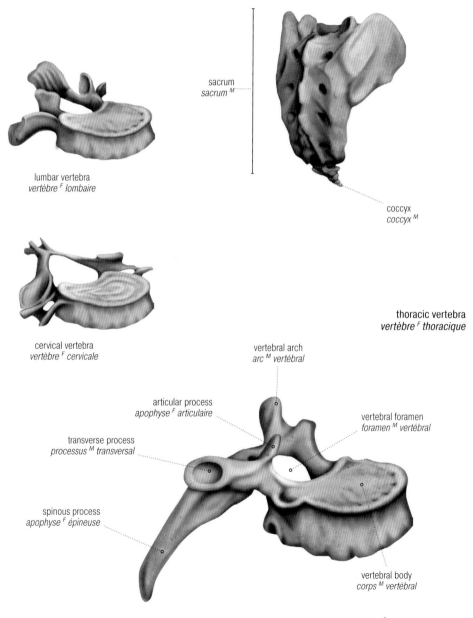

sacrum
sacrum ᴹ

sacrum
sacrum ᴹ

coccyx
coccyx ᴹ

lumbar vertebra
vertèbre ᶠ _lombaire_

thoracic vertebra
vertèbre ᶠ _thoracique_

cervical vertebra
vertèbre ᶠ _cervicale_

vertebral arch
arc ᴹ _vertébral_

articular process
apophyse ᶠ _articulaire_

vertebral foramen
foramen ᴹ _vertébral_

transverse process
processus ᴹ _transversal_

spinous process
apophyse ᶠ _épineuse_

vertebral body
corps ᴹ _vertébral_

adult's skull
crâne ᴹ d'un adulte ᴹ

squamous suture
suture ꟳ temporo-pariétale

coronal suture
suture ꟳ coronale

parietal bone
os ᴹ pariétal

frontal bone
os ᴹ frontal

sphenoid bone
sphénoïde ᴹ

nasal bone
os ᴹ nasal

zygomatic bone
os ᴹ zygomatique

lambdoid suture
suture ꟳ lambdoïde

anterior nasal spine
épine ꟳ nasale antérieure

occipital bone
occipital ᴹ

maxilla
maxillaire ᴹ

temporal bone
os ᴹ temporal

mandible
mandibule ꟳ

mastoid process
apophyse ꟳ mastoïde

external auditory canal
méat ᴹ acoustique externe

styloid process
tubercule ᴹ accessoire

child's skull
crâne ᴹ d'un enfant ᴹ

anterior fontanelle
fontanelle ꟳ antérieure

parietal bone
os ᴹ pariétal

coronal suture
suture ꟳ coronale

posterior fontanelle
fontanelle ꟳ postérieure

frontal bone
os ᴹ frontal

occipital bone
occipital ᴹ

sphenoidal fontanelle
fontanelle ꟳ sphénoïdale

mastoid fontanelle
fontanelle ꟳ mastoïdienne

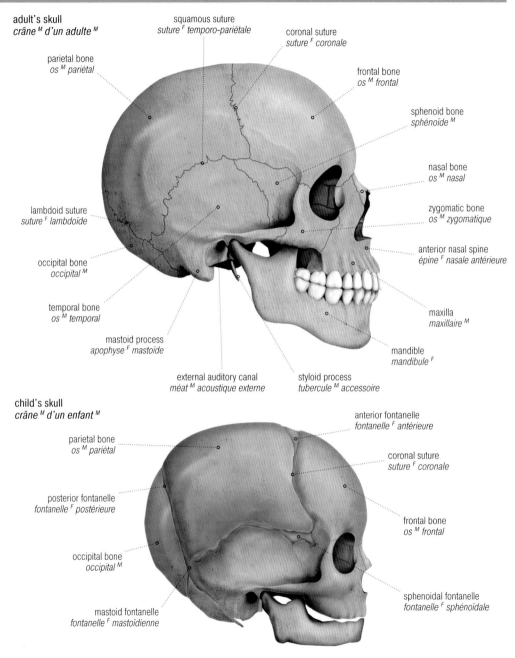

teeth and skull
dents F et crâne M

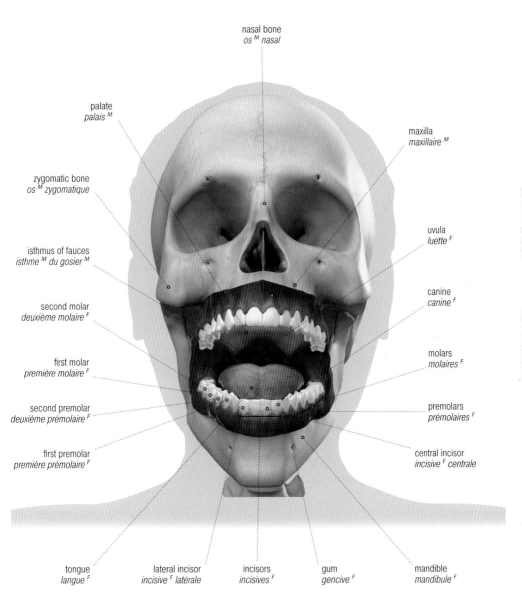

nasal bone
os M nasal

palate
palais M

maxilla
maxillaire M

zygomatic bone
os M zygomatique

uvula
luette F

isthmus of fauces
isthme M du gosier M

canine
canine F

second molar
deuxième molaire F

molars
molaires F

first molar
première molaire F

premolars
prémolaires F

second premolar
deuxième prémolaire F

central incisor
incisive F centrale

first premolar
première prémolaire F

mandible
mandibule F

tongue
langue F

lateral incisor
incisive F latérale

incisors
incisives F

gum
gencive F

cross section of molar
coupe F *transversale d'une molaire* F

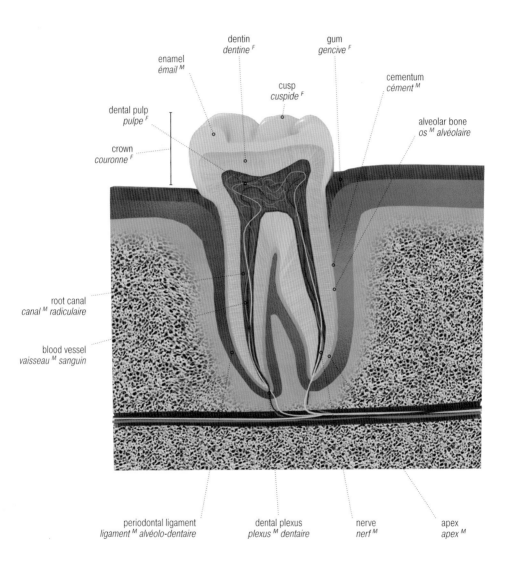

dentin
dentine F

gum
gencive F

enamel
émail M

cusp
cuspide F

cementum
cément M

dental pulp
pulpe F

alveolar bone
os M *alvéolaire*

crown
couronne F

root canal
canal M *radiculaire*

blood vessel
vaisseau M *sanguin*

periodontal ligament
ligament M *alvéolo-dentaire*

dental plexus
plexus M *dentaire*

nerve
nerf M

apex
apex M

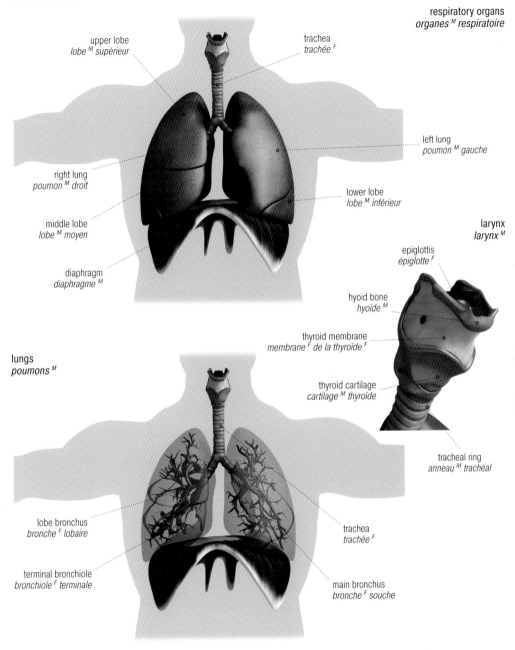

respiratory organs
organes M *respiratoire*

upper lobe
lobe M *supérieur*

trachea
trachée F

left lung
poumon M *gauche*

right lung
poumon M *droit*

lower lobe
lobe M *inférieur*

middle lobe
lobe M *moyen*

larynx
larynx M

diaphragm
diaphragme M

epiglottis
épiglotte F

hyoid bone
hyoïde M

thyroid membrane
membrane F *de la thyroïde* F

lungs
poumons M

thyroid cartilage
cartilage M *thyroïde*

tracheal ring
anneau M *trachéal*

lobe bronchus
bronche F *lobaire*

trachea
trachée F

terminal bronchiole
bronchiole F *terminale*

main bronchus
bronche F *souche*

principal arteries
artères ^F principales

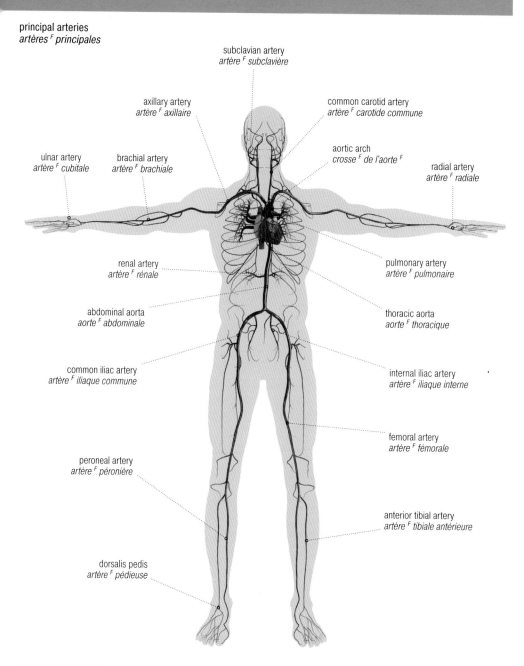

subclavian artery
artère ^F subclavière

axillary artery
artère ^F axillaire

common carotid artery
artère ^F carotide commune

ulnar artery
artère ^F cubitale

brachial artery
artère ^F brachiale

aortic arch
crosse ^F de l'aorte ^F

radial artery
artère ^F radiale

renal artery
artère ^F rénale

pulmonary artery
artère ^F pulmonaire

abdominal aorta
aorte ^F abdominale

thoracic aorta
aorte ^F thoracique

common iliac artery
artère ^F iliaque commune

internal iliac artery
artère ^F iliaque interne

femoral artery
artère ^F fémorale

peroneal artery
artère ^F péronière

anterior tibial artery
artère ^F tibiale antérieure

dorsalis pedis
artère ^F pédieuse

principal veins
veines ^F *principales*

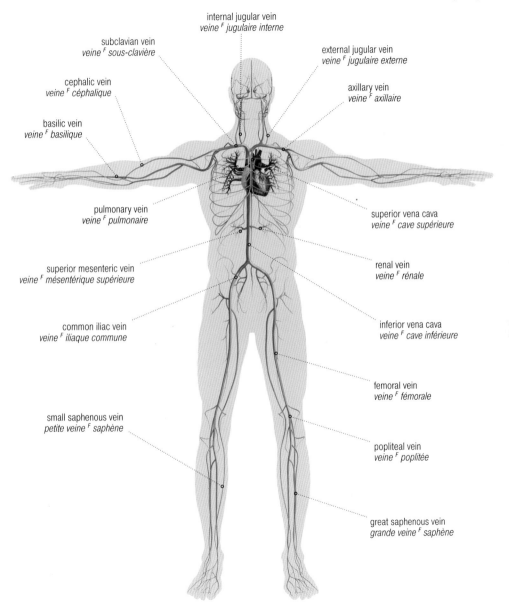

internal jugular vein
veine ^F *jugulaire interne*

subclavian vein
veine ^F *sous-clavière*

external jugular vein
veine ^F *jugulaire externe*

cephalic vein
veine ^F *céphalique*

axillary vein
veine ^F *axillaire*

basilic vein
veine ^F *basilique*

pulmonary vein
veine ^F *pulmonaire*

superior vena cava
veine ^F *cave supérieure*

superior mesenteric vein
veine ^F *mésentérique supérieure*

renal vein
veine ^F *rénale*

common iliac vein
veine ^F *iliaque commune*

inferior vena cava
veine ^F *cave inférieure*

femoral vein
veine ^F *fémorale*

small saphenous vein
petite veine ^F *saphène*

popliteal vein
veine ^F *poplitée*

great saphenous vein
grande veine ^F *saphène*

heart
cœur ^M

aortic arch
crosse ^F *de l'aorte* ^F

pulmonary trunk
tronc ^M *pulmonaire*

superior vena cava
veine ^F *cave supérieure*

left pulmonary vein
veine ^F *pulmonaire gauche*

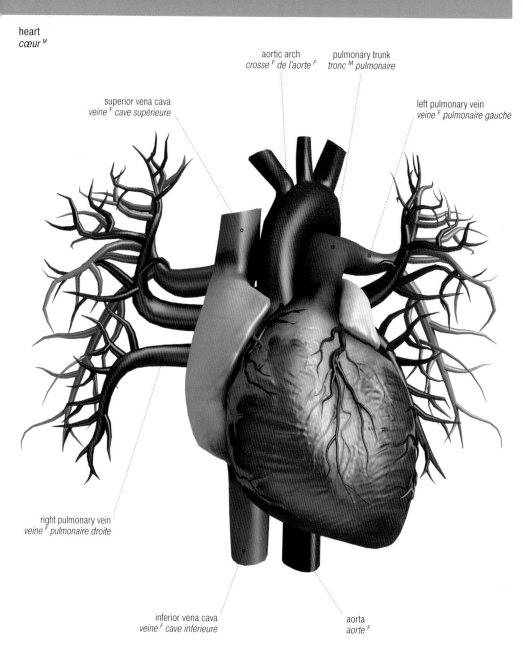

right pulmonary vein
veine ^F *pulmonaire droite*

inferior vena cava
veine ^F *cave inférieure*

aorta
aorte ^F

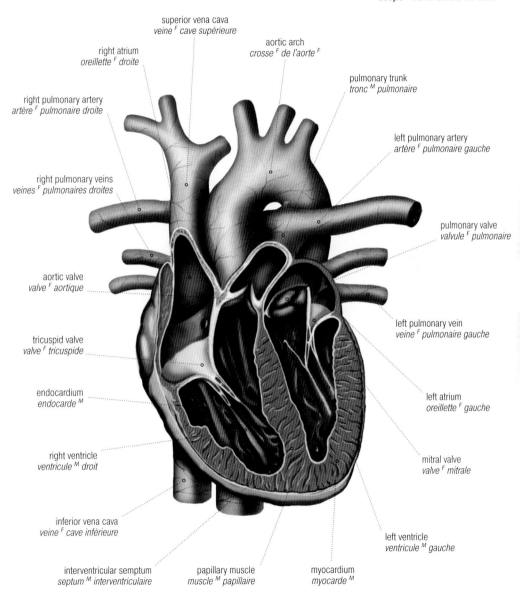

cross section of heart
coupe ᶠ *transversale du cœur* ᴹ

superior vena cava
veine ᶠ *cave supérieure*

aortic arch
crosse ᶠ *de l'aorte* ᶠ

right atrium
oreillette ᶠ *droite*

pulmonary trunk
tronc ᴹ *pulmonaire*

right pulmonary artery
artère ᶠ *pulmonaire droite*

left pulmonary artery
artère ᶠ *pulmonaire gauche*

right pulmonary veins
veines ᶠ *pulmonaires droites*

pulmonary valve
valvule ᶠ *pulmonaire*

aortic valve
valve ᶠ *aortique*

left pulmonary vein
veine ᶠ *pulmonaire gauche*

tricuspid valve
valve ᶠ *tricuspide*

endocardium
endocarde ᴹ

left atrium
oreillette ᶠ *gauche*

right ventricle
ventricule ᴹ *droit*

mitral valve
valve ᶠ *mitrale*

inferior vena cava
veine ᶠ *cave inférieure*

left ventricle
ventricule ᴹ *gauche*

interventricular semptum
septum ᴹ *interventriculaire*

papillary muscle
muscle ᴹ *papillaire*

myocardium
myocarde ᴹ

anterior view of brain
vue [F] *antérieure du cerveau* [M]

longitudinal fissure
scissure [F] *interhémisphérique*

cerebral cortex
cortex [M] *cérébral*

medulla oblongata
bulbe [M] *rachidien*

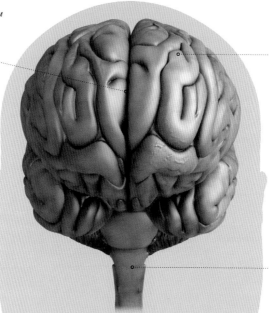

posterior view of brain
vue [F] *postérieure du cerveau* [M]

gyrus
gyrus [F]

sulcus
sillon [M]

cerebellum
cervelet [M]

brain stem
tronc [M] *cérébral*

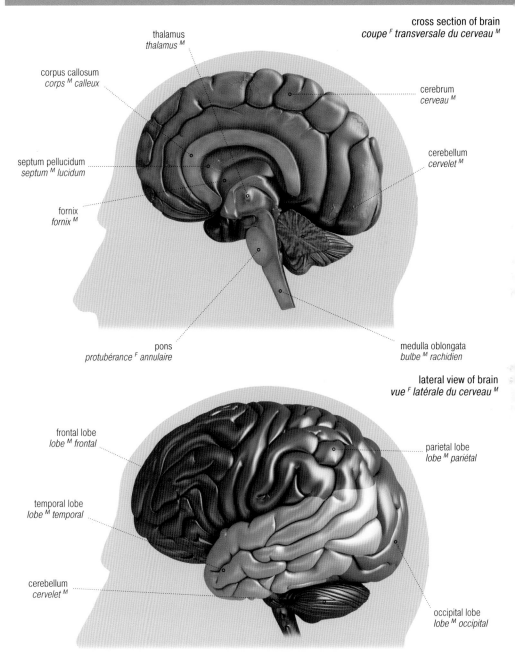

cross section of brain
coupe ꟳ transversale du cerveau ᴹ

thalamus
thalamus ᴹ

corpus callosum
corps ᴹ calleux

cerebrum
cerveau ᴹ

septum pellucidum
septum ᴹ lucidum

cerebellum
cervelet ᴹ

fornix
fornix ᴹ

pons
protubérance ꟳ annulaire

medulla oblongata
bulbe ᴹ rachidien

lateral view of brain
vue ꟳ latérale du cerveau ᴹ

frontal lobe
lobe ᴹ frontal

parietal lobe
lobe ᴹ pariétal

temporal lobe
lobe ᴹ temporal

cerebellum
cervelet ᴹ

occipital lobe
lobe ᴹ occipital

main structure of nervous system
structure ^F *principale du système* ^M *nerveux*

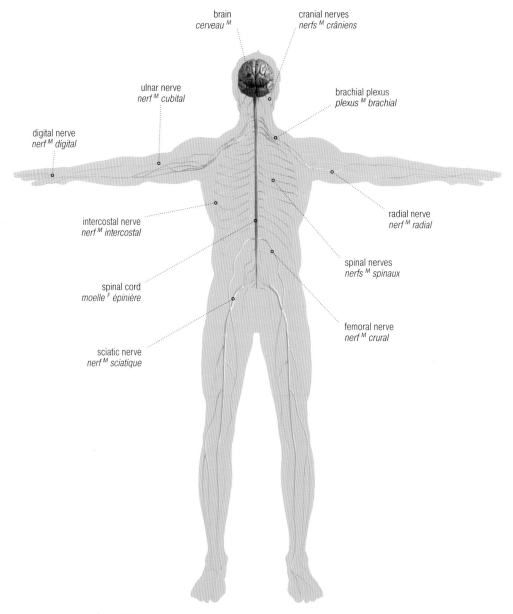

brain
cerveau ^M

cranial nerves
nerfs ^M *crâniens*

ulnar nerve
nerf ^M *cubital*

brachial plexus
plexus ^M *brachial*

digital nerve
nerf ^M *digital*

radial nerve
nerf ^M *radial*

intercostal nerve
nerf ^M *intercostal*

spinal nerves
nerfs ^M *spinaux*

spinal cord
moelle ^F *épinière*

femoral nerve
nerf ^M *crural*

sciatic nerve
nerf ^M *sciatique*

lymphatic organs
organes ᴹ lymphatiques

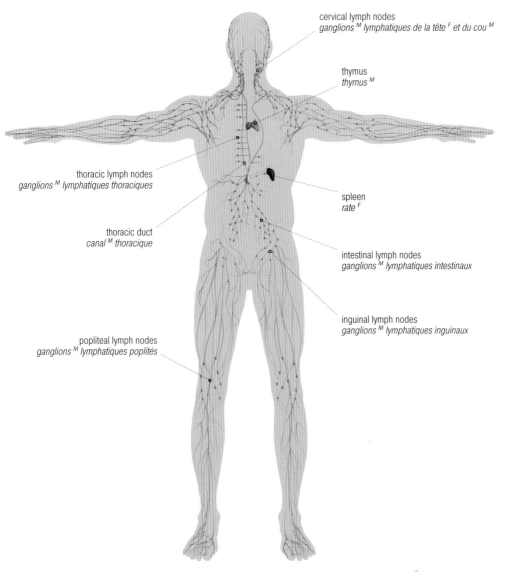

cervical lymph nodes
ganglions ᴹ lymphatiques de la tête ᶠ et du cou ᴹ

thymus
thymus ᴹ

thoracic lymph nodes
ganglions ᴹ lymphatiques thoraciques

spleen
rate ᶠ

thoracic duct
canal ᴹ thoracique

intestinal lymph nodes
ganglions ᴹ lymphatiques intestinaux

inguinal lymph nodes
ganglions ᴹ lymphatiques inguinaux

popliteal lymph nodes
ganglions ᴹ lymphatiques poplités

breast
sein [M]

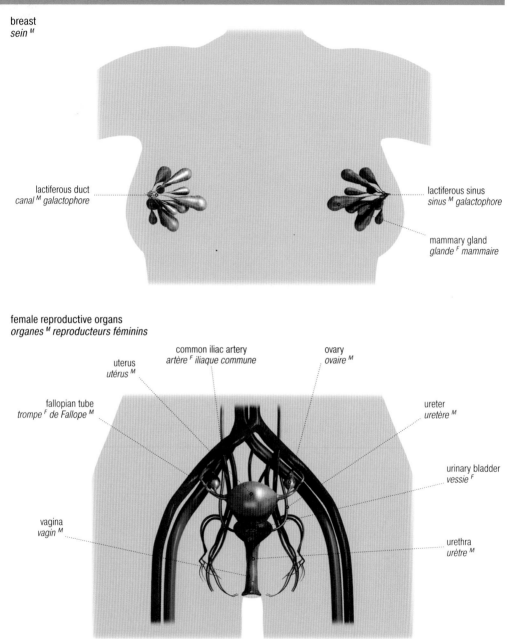

lactiferous duct
canal [M] *galactophore*

lactiferous sinus
sinus [M] *galactophore*

mammary gland
glande [F] *mammaire*

female reproductive organs
organes [M] *reproducteurs féminins*

uterus
utérus [M]

common iliac artery
artère [F] *iliaque commune*

ovary
ovaire [M]

fallopian tube
trompe [F] *de Fallope* [M]

ureter
uretère [M]

urinary bladder
vessie [F]

vagina
vagin [M]

urethra
urètre [M]

male reproductive organs
organes ᴹ reproducteurs masculins

urinary bladder
vessie ᶠ

prostate
prostate ᶠ

penis
pénis ᴹ

vas deferens
canal ᴹ déférent

testicle
testicule ᴹ

bulbocavernous muscle
muscle ᴹ bulbocaverneux

glans penis
gland ᴹ

epididymis
épididyme ᴹ

URINARY SYSTEM *APPAREIL ᴹ URINAIRE*

urinary organs
organes ᴹ urinaires

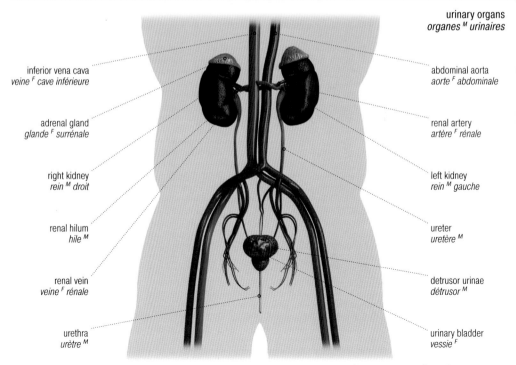

inferior vena cava
veine ᶠ cave inférieure

abdominal aorta
aorte ᶠ abdominale

adrenal gland
glande ᶠ surrénale

renal artery
artère ᶠ rénale

right kidney
rein ᴹ droit

left kidney
rein ᴹ gauche

renal hilum
hile ᴹ

ureter
uretère ᴹ

renal vein
veine ᶠ rénale

detrusor urinae
détrusor ᴹ

urethra
urètre ᴹ

urinary bladder
vessie ᶠ

anterior view of digestive system
vue F *antérieure de l'appareil* M *digestif*

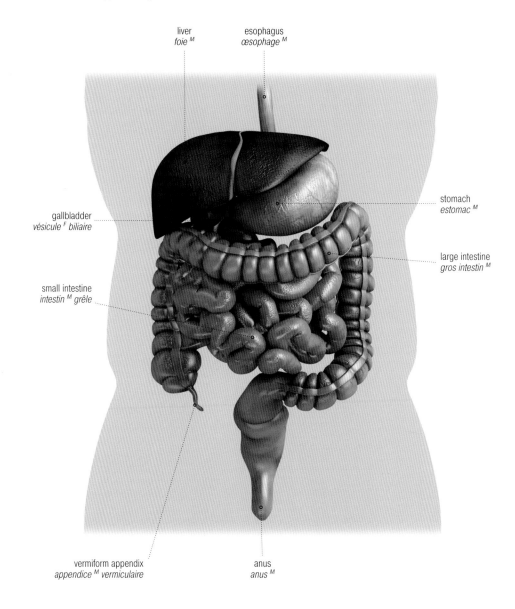

liver
foie M

esophagus
œsophage M

stomach
estomac M

gallbladder
vésicule F *biliaire*

large intestine
gros intestin M

small intestine
intestin M *grêle*

vermiform appendix
appendice M *vermiculaire*

anus
anus M

posterior view of digestive system
vue F *postérieure de l'appareil* M *digestif*

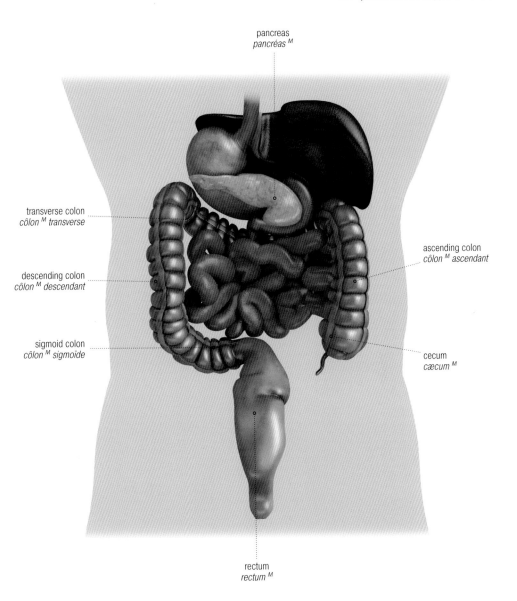

pancreas
pancréas M

transverse colon
côlon M *transverse*

descending colon
côlon M *descendant*

sigmoid colon
côlon M *sigmoïde*

ascending colon
côlon M *ascendant*

cecum
cæcum M

rectum
rectum M

female endocrine system
système ᴹ endocrinien féminin

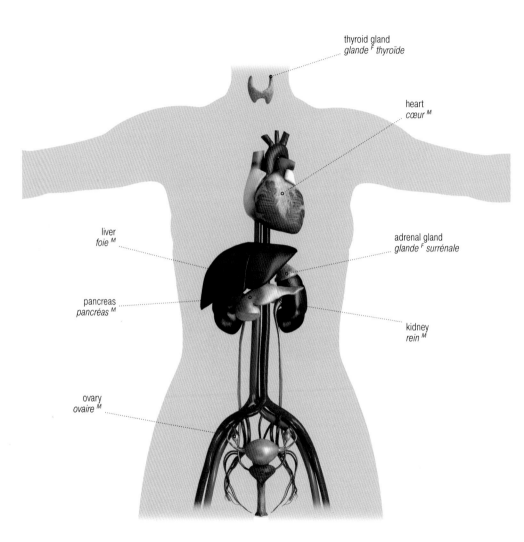

thyroid gland
glande ᶠ thyroïde

heart
cœur ᴹ

liver
foie ᴹ

adrenal gland
glande ᶠ surrénale

pancreas
pancréas ᴹ

kidney
rein ᴹ

ovary
ovaire ᴹ

hand
main F

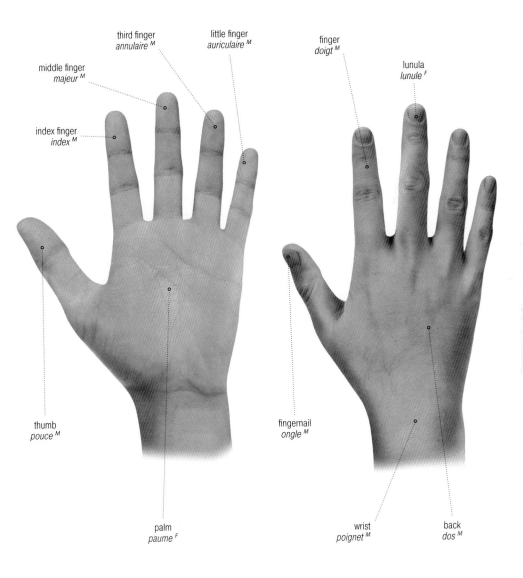

third finger
annulaire M

little finger
auriculaire M

middle finger
majeur M

index finger
index M

finger
doigt M

lunula
lunule F

thumb
pouce M

fingernail
ongle M

palm
paume F

wrist
poignet M

back
dos M

ear
oreille ᶠ

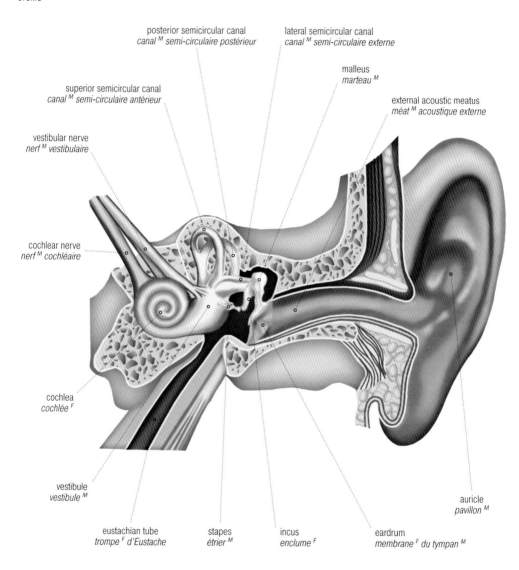

posterior semicircular canal
canal ᴹ *semi-circulaire postérieur*

lateral semicircular canal
canal ᴹ *semi-circulaire externe*

malleus
marteau ᴹ

superior semicircular canal
canal ᴹ *semi-circulaire antérieur*

external acoustic meatus
méat ᴹ *acoustique externe*

vestibular nerve
nerf ᴹ *vestibulaire*

cochlear nerve
nerf ᴹ *cochléaire*

cochlea
cochlée ᶠ

vestibule
vestibule ᴹ

auricle
pavillon ᴹ

eustachian tube
trompe ᶠ *d'Eustache*

stapes
étrier ᴹ

incus
enclume ᶠ

eardrum
membrane ᶠ *du tympan* ᴹ

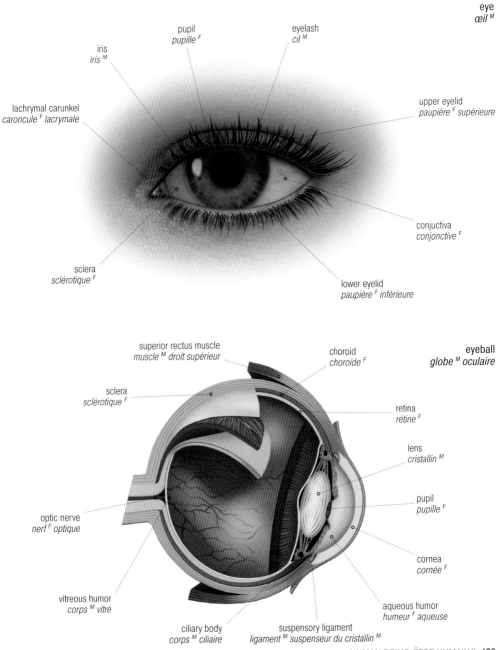

eye
œil ^M

pupil
pupille ^F

eyelash
cil ^M

iris
iris ^M

lachrymal carunkel
caroncule ^F *lacrymale*

upper eyelid
paupière ^F *supérieure*

conjuctiva
conjonctive ^F

sclera
sclérotique ^F

lower eyelid
paupière ^F *inférieure*

superior rectus muscle
muscle ^M *droit supérieur*

choroid
choroïde ^F

eyeball
globe ^M *oculaire*

sclera
sclérotique ^F

retina
rétine ^F

lens
cristallin ^M

optic nerve
nerf ^F *optique*

pupil
pupille ^F

cornea
cornée ^F

vitreous humor
corps ^M *vitré*

aqueous humor
humeur ^F *aqueuse*

ciliary body
corps ^M *ciliaire*

suspensory ligament
ligament ^M *suspenseur du cristallin* ^M

HEALTH AND MEDICINE

SANTÉ ET MÉDECINE

angiography room
salle ^F d'angiographie ^F

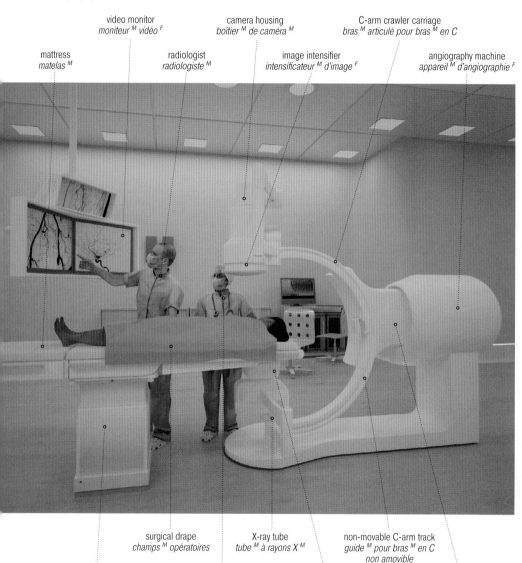

mattress
matelas ^M

video monitor
moniteur ^M vidéo ^F

radiologist
radiologiste ^M

camera housing
boîtier ^M de caméra ^M

image intensifier
intensificateur ^M d'image ^F

C-arm crawler carriage
bras ^M articulé pour bras ^M en C

angiography machine
appareil ^M d'angiographie ^F

height-adjustable pedestal
socle ^M à hauteur ^F réglable

surgical drape
champs ^M opératoires

scrub nurse
infirmière ^F en service ^M interne

X-ray tube
tube ^M à rayons X ^M

collimator housing
boîtier ^M du collimateur ^M

non-movable C-arm track
guide ^M pour bras ^M en C non amovible

support arm
bras ^M de support ^M

MRI (magnetic resonance imaging) room
salle ^F d'imagerie par résonance magnétique (IRM) ^F

file cabinet
classeur ^M

technician's room
salle ^F du technicien ^M

screened glass
écran ^M de verre ^M

display device
dispositif ^M d'affichage ^M

MRI scanner
appareil ^M d'IRM ^M

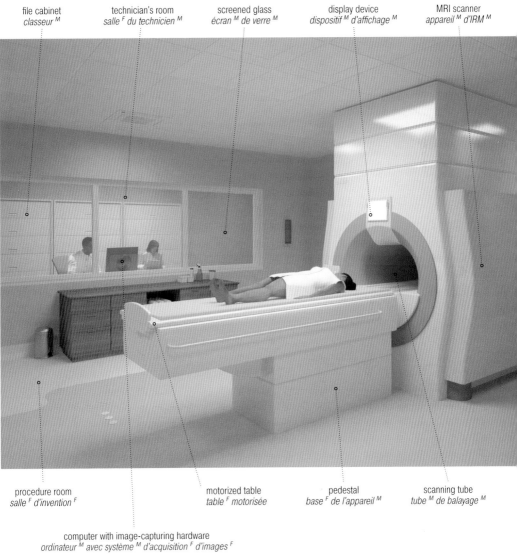

procedure room
salle ^F d'invention ^F

motorized table
table ^F motorisée

pedestal
base ^F de l'appareil ^M

scanning tube
tube ^M de balayage ^M

computer with image-capturing hardware
ordinateur ^M avec système ^M d'acquisition ^F d'images ^F

operating room
salle ^F _d'opération_ ^F

video monitor
moniteur ^M _vidéo_ ^M

surgical mask
masque ^M _chirurgical_

multi-movement pendant
suspension ^F _multimouvements_

ceiling light
plafonnier ^M

scrub nurse
infirmière ^F _en service_ ^M _interne_

anesthesiologist
anesthésiste ^M

operating light
éclairage ^M _opératoire_

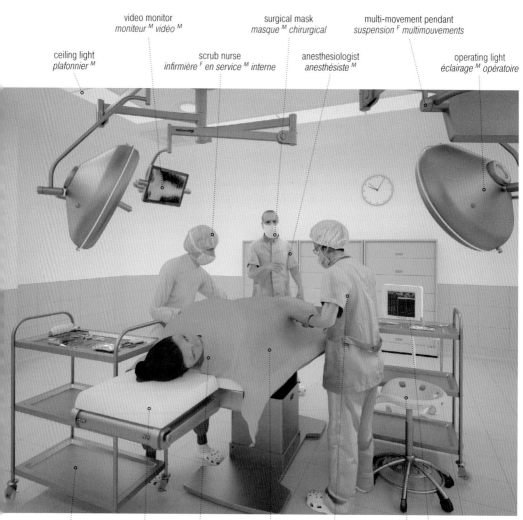

instrument cart
chariot ^M _à instruments_ ^M

patient
patient ^M

surgeon
chirurgien ^M

patient monitor
moniteur ^M _du patient_ ^M

operating table
table ^F _d'opération_ ^F

surgical drape
champs ^M _opératoires_

adjustable stool
tabouret ^M _ajustable_

hospital room
chambre F d'hôpital M

privacy screen
écran M d'intimité F

IV (intravenous) stand
tige F porte-sérum M

medical utility table
guéridon M

nurse call button
bouton M d'appel M de l'infirmière F

over-bed light
lumière F de lit M

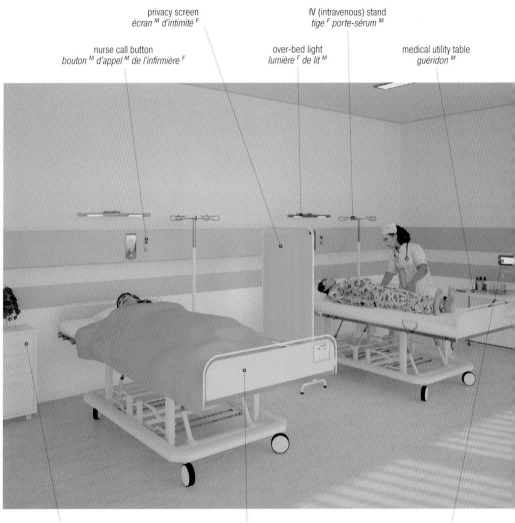

bedside table
table F de chevet M

adjustable hospital bed
lit M d'hôpital M réglable

wall light
lumière F murale

intensive care unit
unité ^F de soins ^M intensifs

patient monitor
moniteur ^M du patient ^M

patient connection panel
panneau ^M de connexion ^F au patient ^M

waveform fields
champs ^M d'ondes ^F

numeric fields
champs ^M numériques

cart
chariot ^M

bedside table
table ^F de chevet ^M

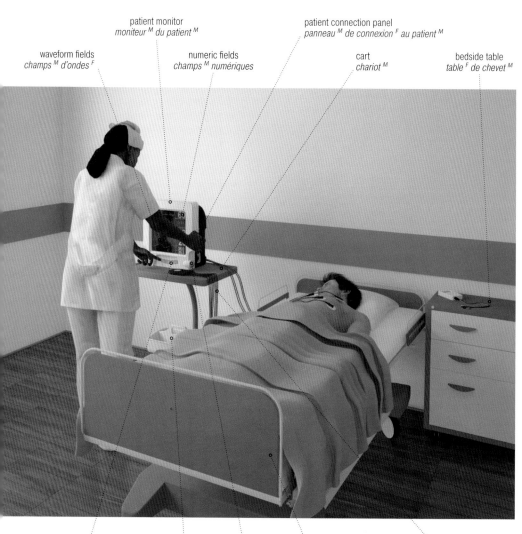

function buttons
boutons ^M de fonctions ^M

trim knob
bouton ^M de réglage ^M

adjustable hospital bed
lit ^M d'hôpital ^M réglable

cables
câbles ^M

utility basket
panier ^M tout usage ^M

physical therapy room
salle ᶠ *de physiothérapie* ᶠ

physical therapist
physiothérapeute ᴹ

treatment table
table ᶠ *de traitement* ᴹ

fitness ball
ballon ᴹ *d'exercice* ᴹ

bolster
traversin ᴹ

adjustable stool
tabouret ᴹ *ajustable*

treadmill
tapis ᴹ *roulant*

gynecological examination room
salle ᶠ d'examen ᴹ gynécologique

doctor's writing pad
bloc-notes ᴹ du médecin ᴹ

ceiling-mounted monitor
moniteur ᴹ suspendu au plafond ᴹ

examination chair
fauteuil ᴹ d'examen ᴹ

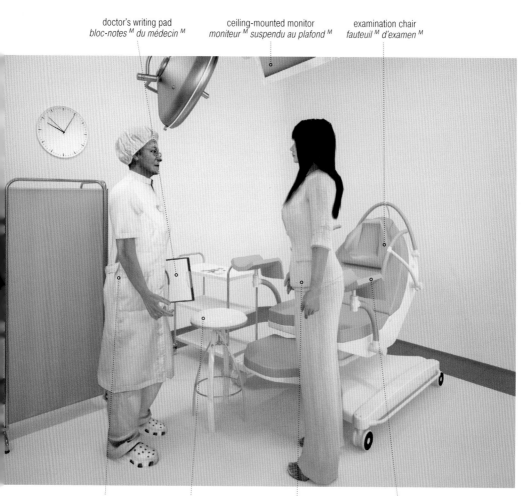

gynecologist
gynécologue ᴹ

instrument cart
chariot ᴹ d'instruments ᴹ

patient
patient ᴹ

leg support
appui-jambes ᴹ

neonatal intensive care unit
unité F *de soins* M *intensifs néonataux*

anesthesia monitor
moniteur M *d'anesthésie* F

mattress tray
socle M *pour matelas* M

incubator
incubateur M

mattress
matelas M

canopy
habitacle M

newborn
nouveau-né M

porthole
hublot M

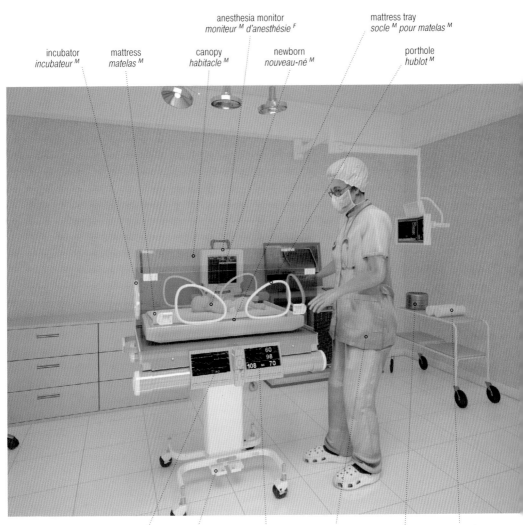

display panel
panneau M *d'affichage* F

neonatologist
néonatologiste M

underpad
protège-drap M

height-adjustment foot pedals
pédales F *pour réglage* M *de la hauteur* F

control and information panel
panneau M *de contrôle* M *et d'information* F

dressing container
récipient M *à pansements* M

dental room
cabinet ᴹ _dentaire_

emesis basin
bassin ᴹ _réniforme_

dental chair
fauteuil ᴹ _dentaire_

operating light
lampe ᶠ _d'opération_ ᶠ

delivery system
système ᴹ _d'adminstration_ ᶠ _de soins_ ᴹ

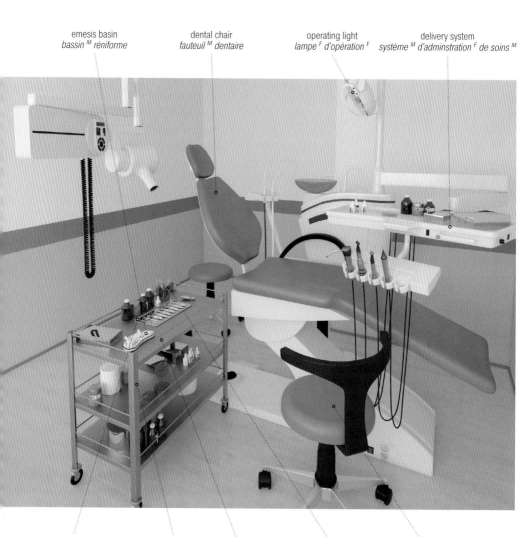

dental mirror
miroir ᴹ _buccal_

Mayo instrument stand
plateau ᴹ _à instruments_ ᴹ _Mayo_

work tray
plateau ᴹ _de travail_ ᶠ

dental tweezers
pinces ᶠ _dentaires_

adjustable stool
tabouret ᴹ _ajustable_

psychotherapy room
salle ᶠ de psychothérapie ᶠ

therapy couch
canapé ᴹ de thérapie ᶠ

therapist's chair
fauteuil ᴹ du thérapeute ᴹ

therapist's notes
notes ᶠ du thérapeute ᴹ

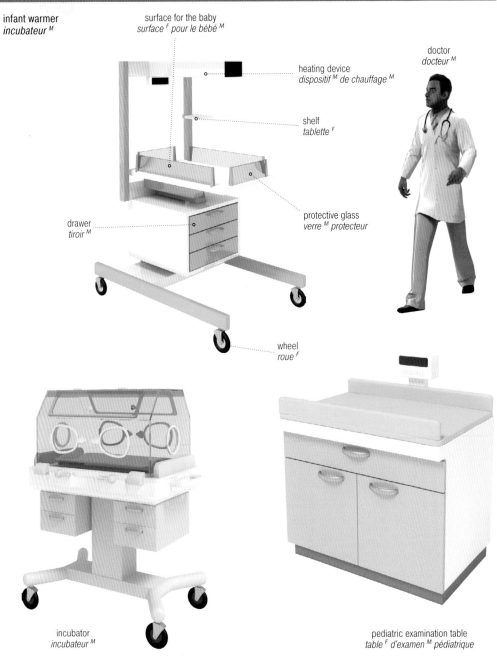

infant warmer
incubateur M

surface for the baby
surface F *pour le bébé* M

heating device
dispositif M *de chauffage* M

shelf
tablette F

doctor
docteur M

drawer
tiroir M

protective glass
verre M *protecteur*

wheel
roue F

incubator
incubateur M

pediatric examination table
table F *d'examen* M *pédiatrique*

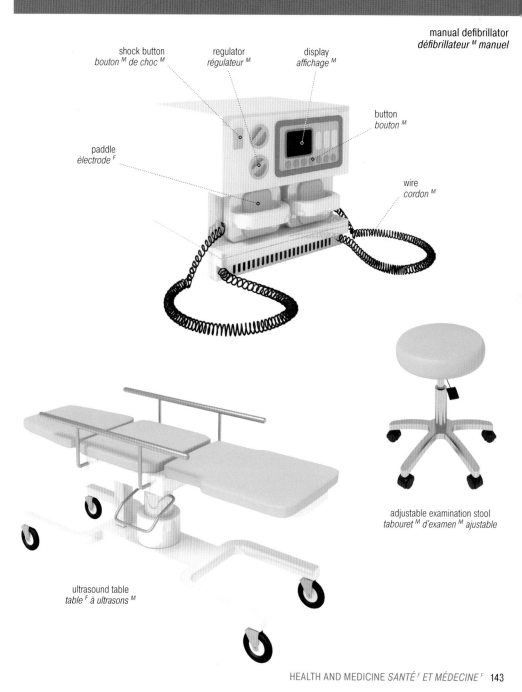

manual defibrillator
défibrillateur ᴹ *manuel*

shock button
bouton ᴹ *de choc* ᴹ

regulator
régulateur ᴹ

display
affichage ᴹ

button
bouton ᴹ

paddle
électrode ᶠ

wire
cordon ᴹ

adjustable examination stool
tabouret ᴹ *d'examen* ᴹ *ajustable*

ultrasound table
table ᶠ *à ultrasons* ᴹ

electric hospital bed
lit ᴹ d'hôpital ᴹ électrique

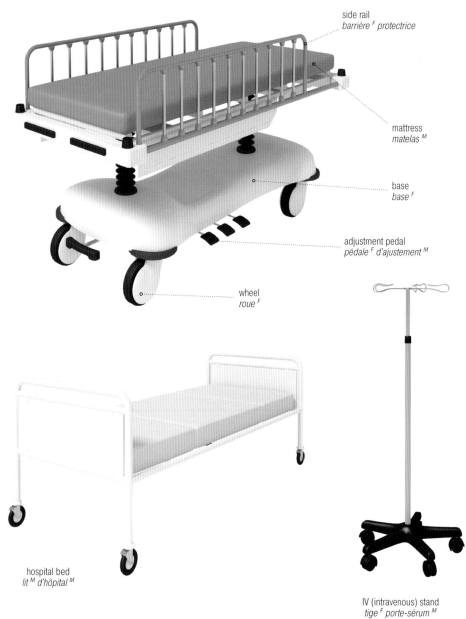

side rail
barrière ᶠ protectrice

mattress
matelas ᴹ

base
base ᶠ

adjustment pedal
pédale ᶠ d'ajustement ᴹ

wheel
roue ᶠ

hospital bed
lit ᴹ d'hôpital ᴹ

IV (intravenous) stand
tige ᶠ porte-sérum ᴹ

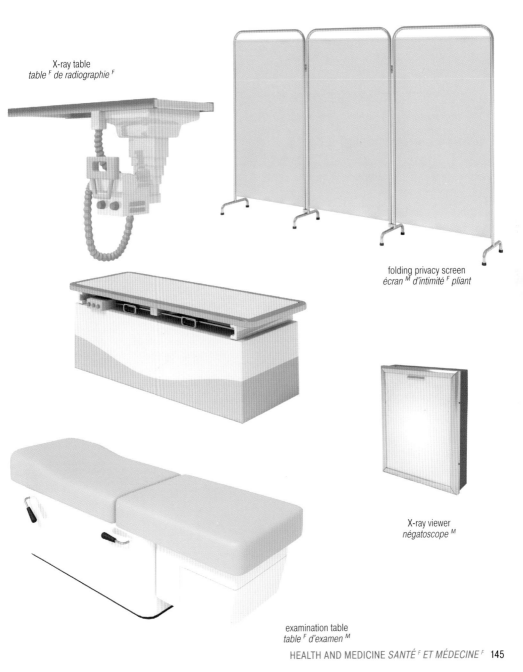

X-ray table
table ^F *de radiographie* ^F

folding privacy screen
écran ^M *d'intimité* ^F *pliant*

X-ray viewer
négatoscope ^M

examination table
table ^F *d'examen* ^M

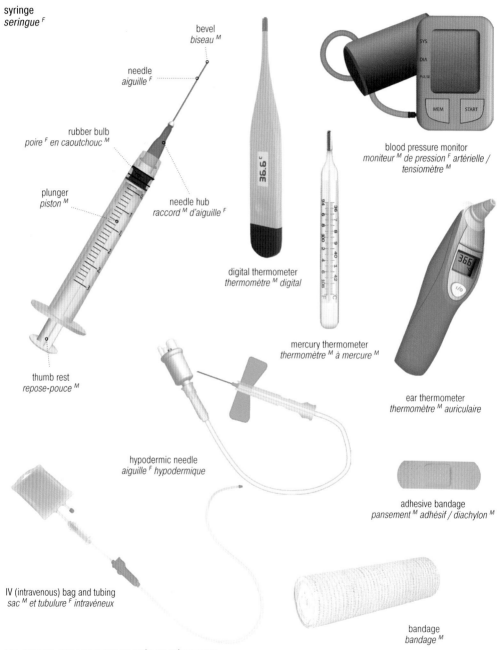

syringe
seringue ᶠ

bevel
biseau ᴹ

needle
aiguille ᶠ

rubber bulb
poire ᶠ *en caoutchouc* ᴹ

plunger
piston ᴹ

needle hub
raccord ᴹ *d'aiguille* ᶠ

thumb rest
repose-pouce ᴹ

digital thermometer
thermomètre ᴹ *digital*

mercury thermometer
thermomètre ᴹ *à mercure* ᴹ

blood pressure monitor
moniteur ᴹ *de pression* ᶠ *artérielle /
tensiomètre* ᴹ

ear thermometer
thermomètre ᴹ *auriculaire*

hypodermic needle
aiguille ᶠ *hypodermique*

adhesive bandage
pansement ᴹ *adhésif / diachylon* ᴹ

IV (intravenous) bag and tubing
sac ᴹ *et tubulure* ᶠ *intravéneux*

bandage
bandage ᴹ

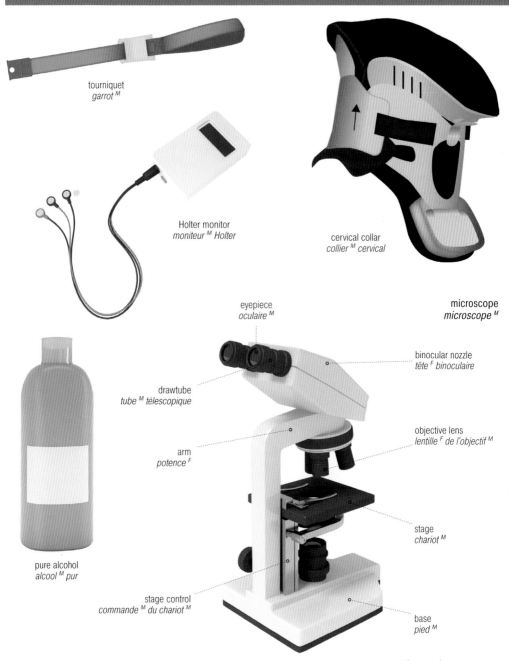

tourniquet
garrot ᴹ

Holter monitor
moniteur ᴹ Holter

cervical collar
collier ᴹ cervical

eyepiece
oculaire ᴹ

microscope
microscope ᴹ

binocular nozzle
tête ᶠ binoculaire

drawtube
tube ᴹ télescopique

objective lens
lentille ᶠ de l'objectif ᴹ

arm
potence ᶠ

stage
chariot ᴹ

pure alcohol
alcool ᴹ pur

stage control
commande ᴹ du chariot ᴹ

base
pied ᴹ

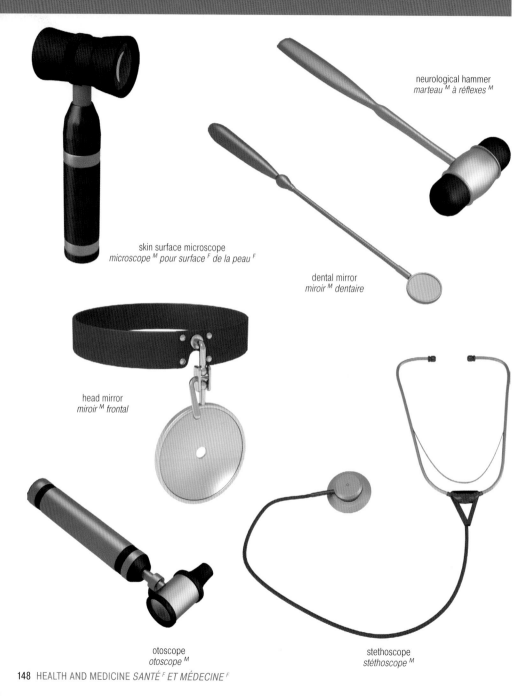

skin surface microscope
microscope ᴹ pour surface ᶠ de la peau ᶠ

neurological hammer
marteau ᴹ à réflexes ᴹ

dental mirror
miroir ᴹ dentaire

head mirror
miroir ᴹ frontal

otoscope
otoscope ᴹ

stethoscope
stéthoscope ᴹ

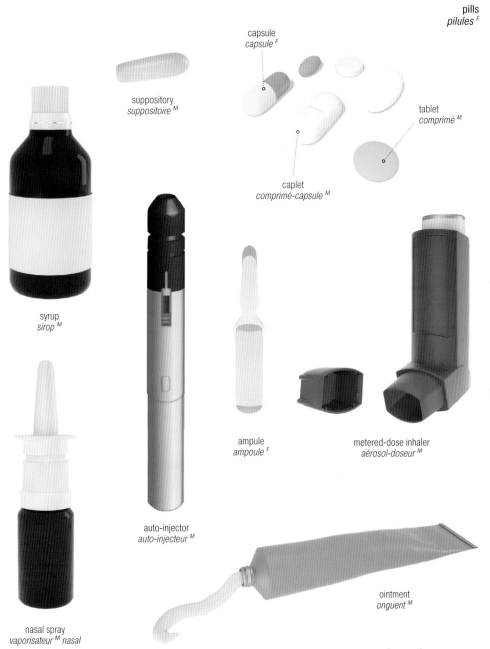

pills
pilules ^F

capsule
capsule ^F

suppository
suppositoire ^M

tablet
comprimé ^M

caplet
comprimé-capsule ^M

syrup
sirop ^M

ampule
ampoule ^F

metered-dose inhaler
aérosol-doseur ^M

auto-injector
auto-injecteur ^M

ointment
onguent ^M

nasal spray
vaporisateur ^M *nasal*

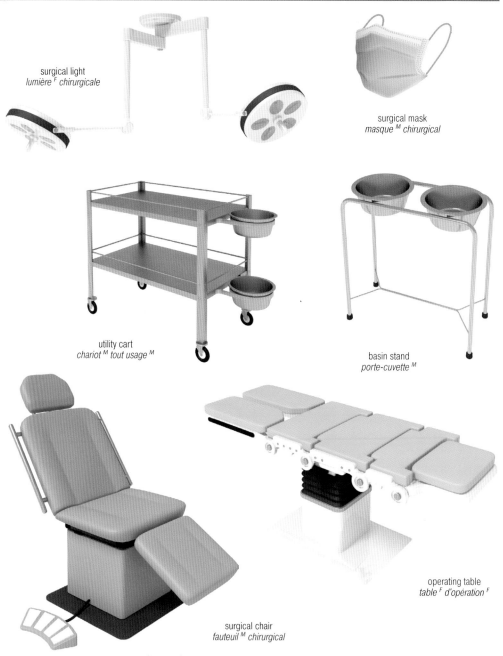

surgical light
lumière F *chirurgicale*

surgical mask
masque M *chirurgical*

utility cart
chariot M *tout usage* M

basin stand
porte-cuvette M

operating table
table F *d'opération* F

surgical chair
fauteuil M *chirurgical*

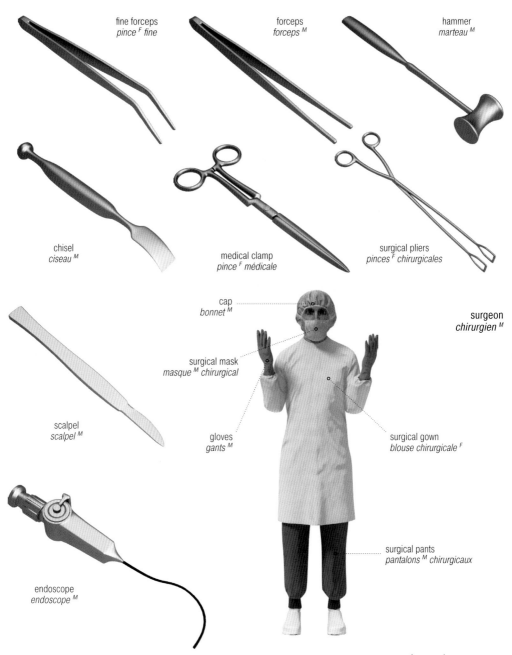

fine forceps
pince *F* *fine*

forceps
forceps *M*

hammer
marteau *M*

chisel
ciseau *M*

medical clamp
pince *F* *médicale*

surgical pliers
pinces *F* *chirurgicales*

cap
bonnet *M*

surgeon
chirurgien *M*

surgical mask
masque *M* *chirurgical*

scalpel
scalpel *M*

gloves
gants *M*

surgical gown
blouse chirurgicale *F*

endoscope
endoscope *M*

surgical pants
pantalons *M* *chirurgicaux*

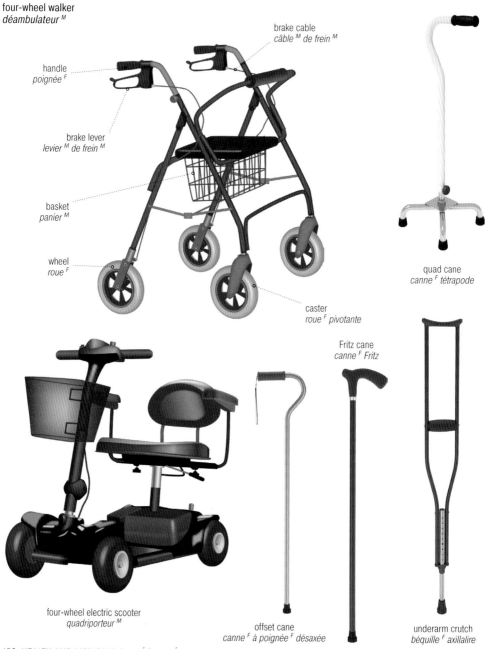

four-wheel walker
déambulateur M

brake cable
câble M de frein M

handle
poignée F

brake lever
levier M de frein M

basket
panier M

wheel
roue F

caster
roue F pivotante

quad cane
canne F tétrapode

Fritz cane
canne F Fritz

four-wheel electric scooter
quadriporteur M

offset cane
canne F à poignée F désaxée

underarm crutch
béquille F axillaire

electric wheelchair
fauteuil M *roulant électrique*

back
dossier M

control stick
levier M *de commande* M

handle
poignée M

armrest
accoudoir M

seat
siège M

electric drive
commande F *électrique*

wheel
roue F

footboard
repose-pied M

caster
roue F *pivotante*

forearm crutch
béquille F *d'avant-bras* M

back
dossier M

clothing guard
protège-vêtement M

wheelchair
fauteuil M *roulant*

handle
poignée F

arm
bras M

armrest
accoudoir M

seat
siège M

push rim
main-courante F

caster
roue F *pivotante*

hub
moyeu M

large wheel
grande roue F

footrest
repose-pied M

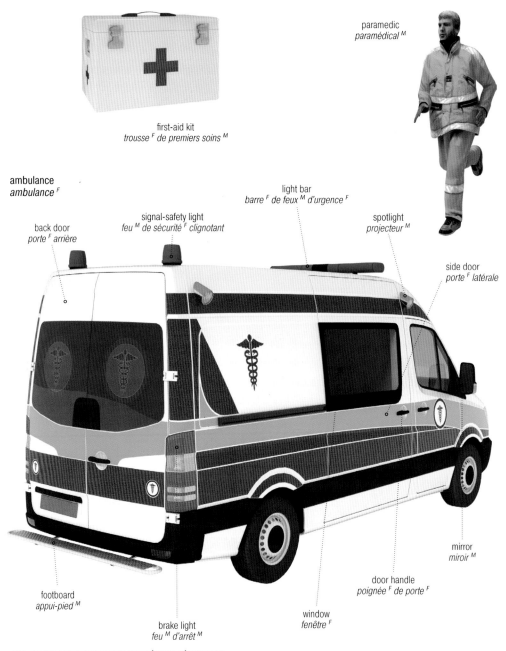

paramedic
paramédical ^M

first-aid kit
trousse ^F *de premiers soins* ^M

ambulance
ambulance ^F

light bar
barre ^F *de feux* ^M *d'urgence* ^F

signal-safety light
feu ^M *de sécurité* ^F *clignotant*

spotlight
projecteur ^M

back door
porte ^F *arrière*

side door
porte ^F *latérale*

mirror
miroir ^M

door handle
poignée ^F *de porte* ^F

footboard
appui-pied ^M

window
fenêtre ^F

brake light
feu ^M *d'arrêt* ^M

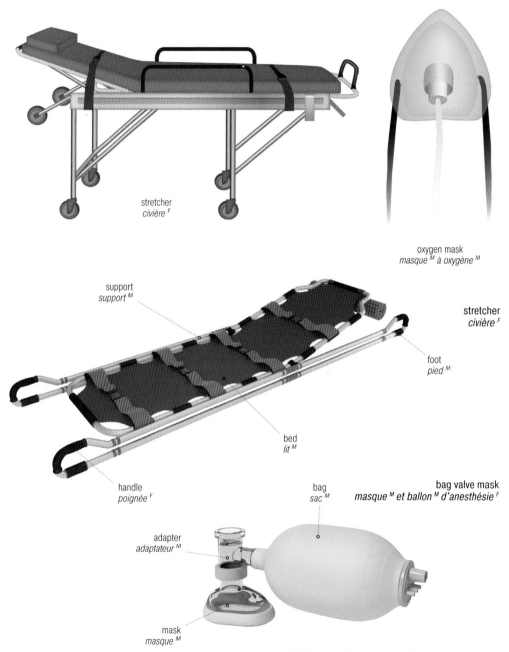

stretcher
civière ^F

oxygen mask
masque ^M *à oxygène* ^M

support
support ^M

stretcher
civière ^F

foot
pied ^M

bed
lit ^M

handle
poignée ^F

bag
sac ^M

bag valve mask
masque ^M *et ballon* ^M *d'anesthésie* ^F

adapter
adaptateur ^M

mask
masque ^M

HOUSING

HABITATION

ground floor of house
rez-de-chaussée M *de la maison* F

kitchen
cuisine F

cabinets
armoires F

powder room
salle F *de toilette* F

stairs
escalier M

refrigerator
réfrigérateur M

breakfast bar
comptoir-repas M

bar stool
tabouret M *de bar*

dining room
salle F *à manger*

mailbox
boîte F *aux lettres* F

dining table
table F *de salle* F *à manger*

picture
photographie F

dining chair
chaise F *de salle* F *à manger*

front door
porte F *d'entrée* F

front steps
marches F *à l'entrée* F

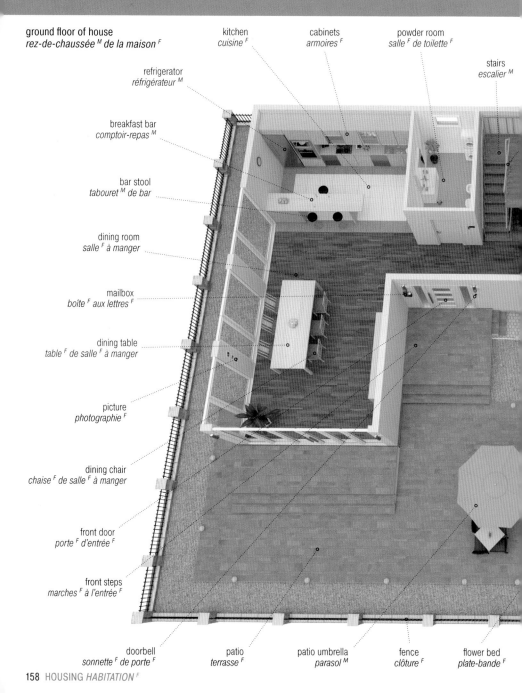

doorbell
sonnette F *de porte* F

patio
terrasse F

patio umbrella
parasol M

fence
clôture F

flower bed
plate-bande F

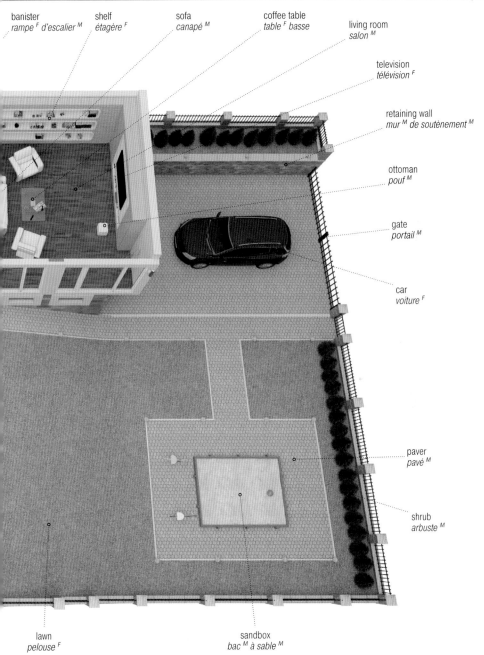

banister
rampe ᶠ *d'escalier* ᴹ

shelf
étagère ᶠ

sofa
canapé ᴹ

coffee table
table ᶠ *basse*

living room
salon ᴹ

television
télévision ᶠ

retaining wall
mur ᴹ *de soutènement* ᴹ

ottoman
pouf ᴹ

gate
portail ᴹ

car
voiture ᶠ

paver
pavé ᴹ

shrub
arbuste ᴹ

lawn
pelouse ᶠ

sandbox
bac ᴹ *à sable* ᴹ

second floor of house
premier étage ^M *de la maison* ^F

closet
placard ^M

dressing room
vestiaire ^M

bathroom
salle ^F *de bain* ^M

hall
couloir ^M

master bedroom
chambre ^F *principale*

balcony
balcon ^M

bistro set
ensemble ^M *bistro*

railing
balustrade ^F *de balcon* ^M

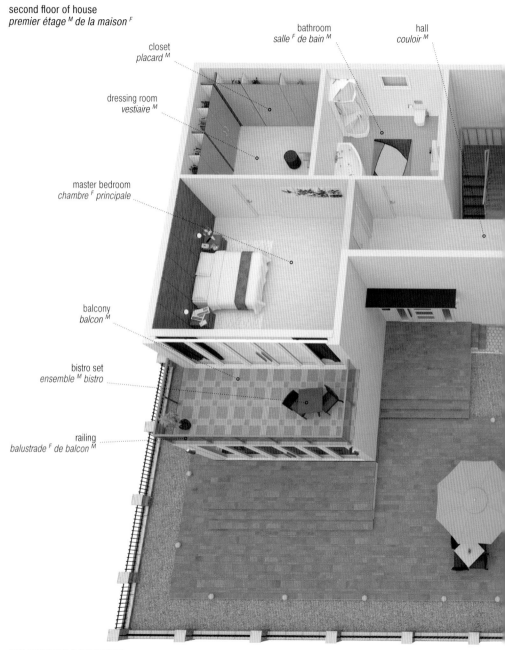

bathroom
salle ᶠ de bain ᴹ

child's bedroom
chambre ᶠ d'enfant ᴹ

nursery
chambre ᶠ de bébé ᴹ

security camera
caméra ᶠ de surveillance ᶠ

exterior of house
extérieur ᴹ de la maison ᶠ

balcony
balcon ᴹ

roof
toit ᴹ

roof hatch
trappe ᶠ de toit ᴹ

front door
porte ᶠ d'entrée ᶠ

porch
porche ᴹ

patio umbrella
parasol ᴹ

patio
terrasse ᶠ

bistro set
ensemble ᴹ bistro

flower bed
plate-bande ᶠ

lawn
pelouse ᶠ

sandbox
bac ᴹ à sable ᴹ

fence
clôture ᶠ

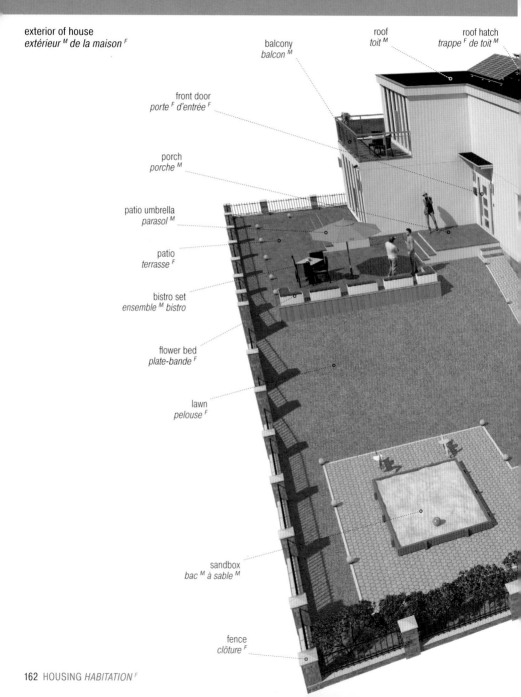

ventilation shaft
conduit ^M de ventilation ^F

solar panel
panneau ^M solaire

security camera
caméra ^F de surveillance ^F

garage door
porte ^F de garage ^M

car
voiture ^F

hedge
haie ^F

retaining wall
mur ^M de soutènement ^M

gate
portail ^M

driveway
entrée ^F de cour ^F

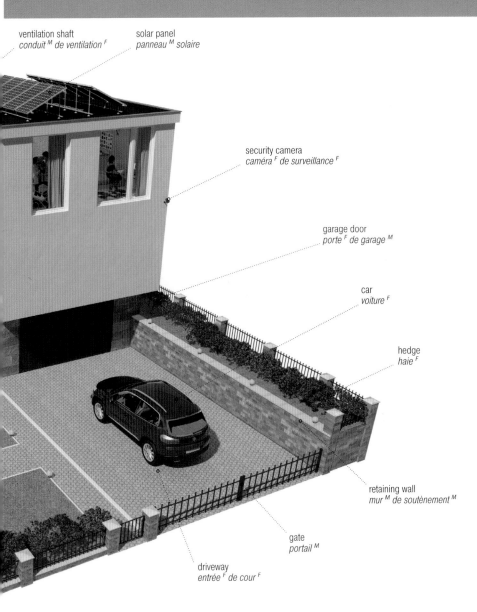

apartment building
immeuble M d'appartements M

facade
façade F

penthouse
appartement-terrasse M

balcony door
porte F de balcon M

balcony
balcon M

balcony railing
balustrade F de balcon M

resident
résident M

window
fenêtre F

intercom
interphone M

main entrance
entrée F principale

satellite dish
antenne ^F *parabolique*

antenna
antenne ^F

patio umbrella
parasol ^M

patio
terrasse ^F

living room
salon ᴹ

book
livre ᴹ

fruit bowl
bol ᴹ *à fruits* ᴹ

bookshelf
étagère ᶠ *de bibliothèque*

sofa
canapé ᴹ

magazine
magazine ᴹ

coffee table
table ᶠ *basse*

remote control
télécommande ᶠ

DVD
DVD ᴹ

DVD player
lecteur ᴹ *DVD* ᴹ

television
télévision ᶠ

shelf
étagère ᶠ

cushion
coussin ᴹ

armchair
fauteuil ᴹ

ottoman
pouf ᴹ

potted plant
plante ᶠ *en pot* ᴹ

master bedroom
chambre ᶠ principale

curtain
rideau ᴹ

light fixture
luminaire ᴹ

photograph
photographie ᶠ

nightstand
table ᶠ de nuit ᶠ

rug
tapis ᴹ

book
livre ᴹ

bed
lit ᴹ

pillow
oreiller ᴹ

light switch
interrupteur ᴹ *d'éclairage* ᴹ

closet door
porte ᶠ *de placard* ᴹ

telephone
téléphone ᴹ

electrical outlet
prise électrique ᶠ

hardwood floor
plancher ᴹ *de bois* ᴹ *franc*

bathroom
salle ᶠ de bain ᴹ

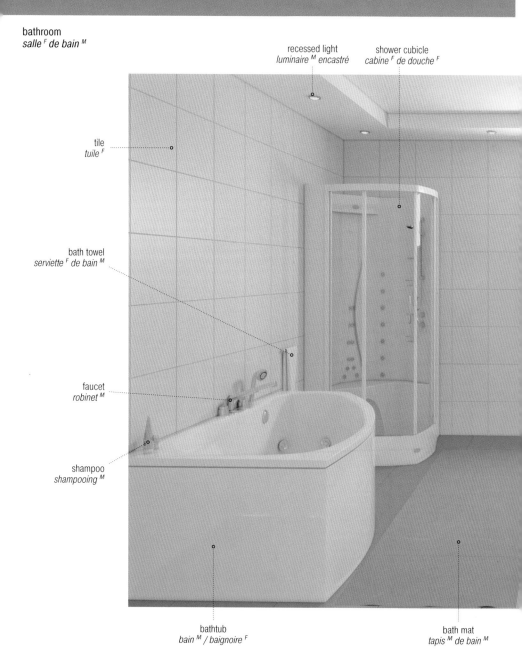

recessed light
luminaire ᴹ encastré

shower cubicle
cabine ᶠ de douche ᶠ

tile
tuile ᶠ

bath towel
serviette ᶠ de bain ᴹ

faucet
robinet ᴹ

shampoo
shampooing ᴹ

bathtub
bain ᴹ / baignoire ᶠ

bath mat
tapis ᴹ de bain ᴹ

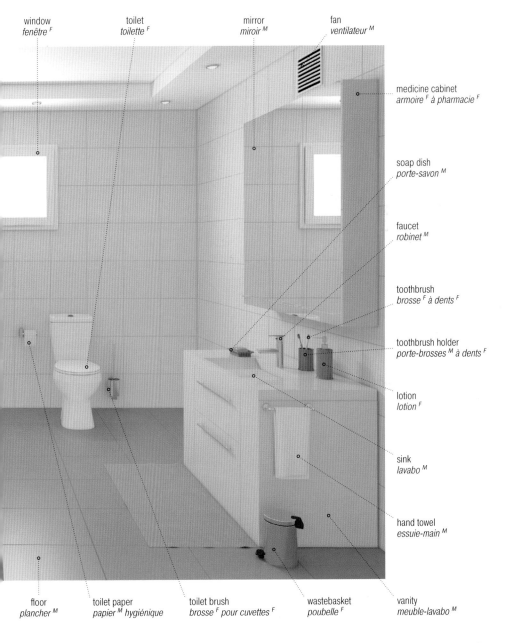

window
fenêtre ᶠ

toilet
toilette ᶠ

mirror
miroir ᴹ

fan
ventilateur ᴹ

medicine cabinet
armoire ᶠ *à pharmacie* ᶠ

soap dish
porte-savon ᴹ

faucet
robinet ᴹ

toothbrush
brosse ᶠ *à dents* ᶠ

toothbrush holder
porte-brosses ᴹ *à dents* ᶠ

lotion
lotion ᶠ

sink
lavabo ᴹ

hand towel
essuie-main ᴹ

floor
plancher ᴹ

toilet paper
papier ᴹ *hygiénique*

toilet brush
brosse ᶠ *pour cuvettes* ᶠ

wastebasket
poubelle ᶠ

vanity
meuble-lavabo ᴹ

girl's room
chambre ᶠ de fille ᶠ

wall decal
décalque ᴹ mural

clock
horloge ᶠ

photograph
photographie ᶠ

chest of drawers
commode ᶠ

pillow
oreiller ᴹ

sheets
draps ᴹ

bed
lit ᴹ

wallpaper
papier ᴹ *peint*

picture
illustration ᶠ

lamp
lampe ᶠ

toy
jouet ᴹ

nightstand
table ᶠ *de nuit* ᶠ

hardwood floor
plancher ᴹ *de bois* ᴹ *franc*

throw rug
carpette ᶠ

nursery
chambre ꟳ *de bébé* ᴹ

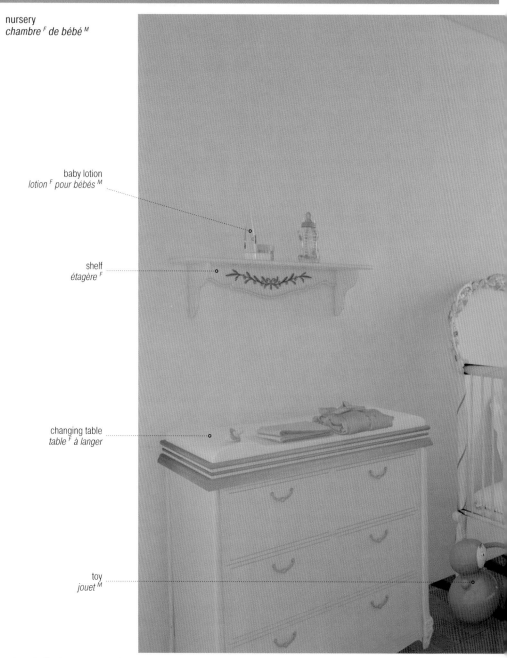

baby lotion
lotion ꟳ *pour bébés* ᴹ

shelf
étagère ꟳ

changing table
table ꟳ *à langer*

toy
jouet ᴹ

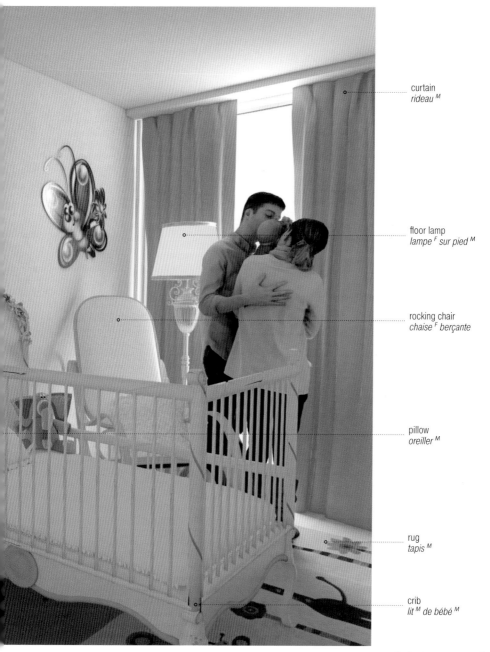

curtain
rideau M

floor lamp
lampe F *sur pied* M

rocking chair
chaise F *berçante*

pillow
oreiller M

rug
tapis M

crib
lit M *de bébé* M

Children's furniture
Meubles M *pour enfants* M

changing table
table F *à langer*

knob
bouton M

drawer
tiroir M

leg
pied M

shelf
étagère F

armoire
armoire F

high chair
chaise F *haute*

back
dossier M

desk and chair
bureau M *et chaise* F

desk
bureau M

tray
plateau M

seat
siège M

leg
pied M

footrest
repose-pied M

chair
chaise F

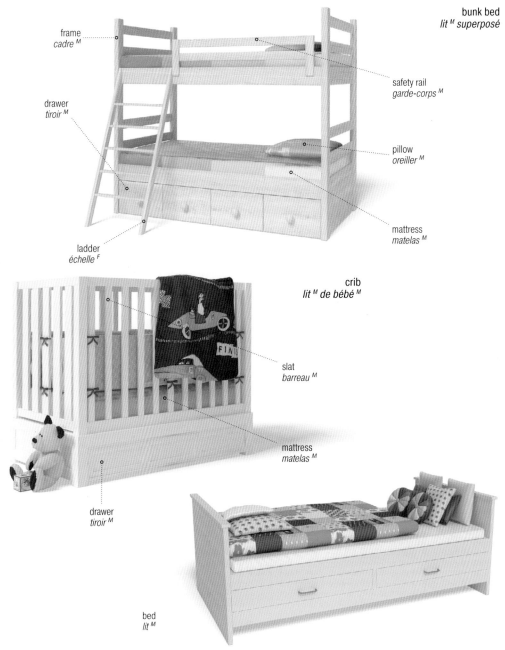

bunk bed
lit *M superposé*

frame
cadre *M*

safety rail
garde-corps *M*

drawer
tiroir *M*

pillow
oreiller *M*

mattress
matelas *M*

ladder
échelle *F*

crib
lit *M de bébé* *M*

slat
barreau *M*

mattress
matelas *M*

drawer
tiroir *M*

bed
lit *M*

kitchen
cuisine ^F

picture
photographie ^F

clock
horloge ^F

refrigerator
réfrigérateur ^M

microwave
micro-ondes ^M

breakfast bar
comptoir-repas ^M

bar stool
tabouret ^M *de bar* ^M

oven
four ^M

coffee machine
machine ^F *à espresso* ^M

wine fridge
réfrigérateur ^M *à vin* ^M

range hood
otte ᶠ *de cuisine* ᶠ

wine glass
verre ᴹ *à vin* ᴹ

canister
pot ᴹ *à ingrédient* ᴹ

cup
tasse ᶠ

faucet
robinet ᴹ

cabinet
armoire ᶠ

cooktop
plaque ᶠ *de cuisson* ᶠ

countertop
plan ᴹ *de travail* ᴹ

dishwasher
lave-vaisselle ᴹ

sink
évier ᴹ

tiled floor
carrelage ᴹ

Large appliances
Gros électroménagers ^M

refrigerator
réfrigérateur ^M

shelf
étagère ^F

egg tray
plateau ^M à œufs ^M

refrigerator compartment door
porte ^F du compartiment ^M
réfrigérateur ^M

side-by-side refrigerator and freezer
réfrigérateur-congélateur ^M côte à côte

handle
poignée ^F

microwave
micro-ondes ^M

freezer compartment
compartiment ^M congélateur ^M

crisper
bac ^M à légumes ^M

drawer
tiroir ^M

handle
poignée ^F

clock timer
horloge ^F programmatrice

freezer compartment door
porte ^F du compartiment ^M congélateur ^M

window
vitre ^F

cooktop
plaque ^F de cuisson ^F

turntable
plateau ^M tournant

door
porte ^F

control panel
panneau ^M de commande ^F

range hood
hotte[F] *de cuisine*[F]

dishwasher
lave-vaisselle[M]

ventilation duct
conduit de ventilation[M]

handle
poignée[F]

power button
bouton[M] *de mise*[F] *en marche*[F]

control knob
bouton[M] *de commande*[F]

indicator light
voyant[M] *lumineux*

door
porte[F]

filter
filtre[M]

screen
écran[M]

display
affichage[M]

gas range
cuisinière[F] *à gaz*[M]

cooktop control knob
bouton[M] *de commande*[F] *de la surface*[F]
de cuisson[F]

burner
brûleur[M]

handle
poignée[F]

oven control knob
bouton[M] *de commande*[F] *du four*[M]

electric range
cuisinière[F] *électrique*

oven
four[M]

Small appliances
Petits appareils [M]

espresso machine
machine [F] *à espresso* [M]

pressure gauge
manomètre [M]

cup-warming tray
plateau [M] *chauffant pour tasses* [F]

group head
tête [F] *supérieure*

water tank
réservoir [M] *d'eau* [F]

filter holder
porte-filtre [M]

spout
bec [M] *verseur*

handle
poignée [F]

coffee grinder
moulin [M] *à café* [M]

steam nozzle
buse [F] *à vapeur* [F]

drip tray
plateau [M] *perforé*

automatic drip coffeemaker
cafetière [F] *à filtre* [M] *électrique*

lid
couvercle [M]

water-level indicator
indicateur [M] *de niveau* [M] *d'eau* [F]

basket
panier [M]

lid-release button
bouton [M] *d'ouverture* [F] *du*
couvercle [M]

pot lid
couvercle [M]

handle
poignée [F]

pot
verseuse [F] *à café* [M]

warming plate
plaque [F] *chauffante*

water reservoir
réservoir [M] *d'eau* [F]

blender
mélangeur [M]

juicer
centrifugeuse F

pusher
poussoir M

feed tube
tube M *d'alimentation* F

filter
filtre M

lid
couvercle M

pulp container
réservoir M *à pulpe* F

safety latch
verrou M *de sécurité* F

spout
bec M *verseur*

power button
bouton M *de mise* F *en marche* F

motor housing
boîtier M *du moteur* M

immersion blender
mélangeur M *à main* F

electric kettle
bouilloire F *électrique*

electric citrus juicer
presse-agrumes M *électrique*

spout
bec M *verseur*

lid
couvercle M

lid-release button
bouton M *d'ouverture* F *du couvercle* M

reamer
cône M

strainer
passoire F

power switch
interrupteur M *d'alimentation* F

spout
bec M *verseur*

jug
cruche F

bowl
bol M

juice-level indicator
indicateur M *de niveau* M *de jus* M

motor housing
boîtier M *du moteur* M

base
socle M

indicator light
voyant M *lumineux*

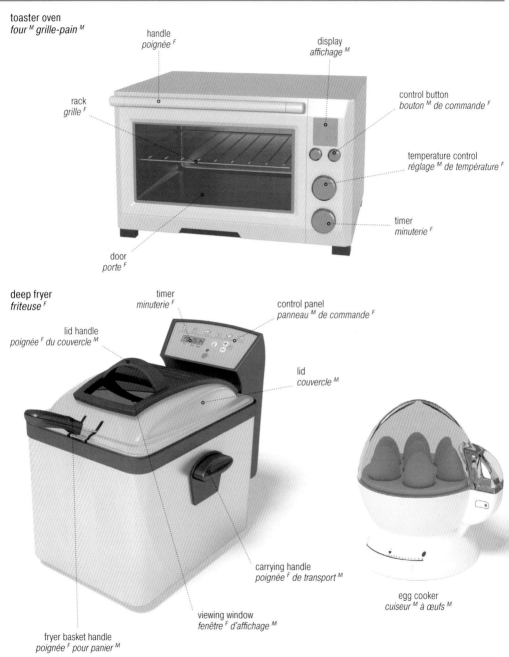

toaster oven
four M *grille-pain* M

handle
poignée F

display
affichage M

rack
grille F

control button
bouton M *de commande* F

temperature control
réglage M *de température* F

timer
minuterie F

door
porte F

deep fryer
friteuse F

timer
minuterie F

control panel
panneau M *de commande* F

lid handle
poignée F *du couvercle* M

lid
couvercle M

carrying handle
poignée F *de transport* M

viewing window
fenêtre F *d'affichage* M

fryer basket handle
poignée F *pour panier* M

egg cooker
cuiseur M *à œufs* M

slot
fente ᶠ

toaster
grille-pain ᴹ

control buttons
touches ᶠ de fonction ᶠ

lever
levier ᴹ

crumb tray
ramasse-miettes ᴹ

browning control
commande ᶠ de brunissement ᴹ

table grill
barbecue ᴹ de table ᶠ

waffle iron
gaufrier ᴹ

bread maker
machine ᶠ à pain ᴹ

window
hublot ᴹ

liquid-crystal display (LCD)
affichage ᴹ à cristaux ᴹ liquides (ACL)

lid
couvercle ᴹ

control buttons
touches ᶠ de fonction ᶠ

food processor
robot ^M *de cuisine* ^F

feed tube
entonnoir ^M

handle
poignée ^F

bowl
bol ^M

blade
lame ^F

motor housing
bloc-moteur ^M

control pad
touche ^F *de commande* ^F

control buttons
touches de fonction ^F

stand mixer
batteur ^M *sur socle* ^M

tilt-back head
tête ^F *basculante*

dehydrator
déshydrateur ^M

mixing bowl
bol ^M

beater
fouet ^M

pusher
poussoir ᴹ

electric meat grinder
hache-viande ᴹ électrique

feeder tray
plateau ᴹ d'alimentation ᶠ

feed tube
tube ᴹ d'alimentation ᶠ

grinding plate
grille ᴹ à hacher

knife housing
boîtier ᴹ du couteau ᴹ

power switch
interrupteur ᴹ d'alimentation ᶠ

motor housing
boîtier ᴹ du moteur ᴹ

slow cooker
mijoteuse ᶠ

ceramic pot
pot ᴹ céramique

lid
couvercle ᴹ

sandwich toaster
grille-sandwich ᴹ

control pad
touche ᶠ de commande ᶠ

heating base
base ᶠ chauffante

table setting
couvert M *de table* F

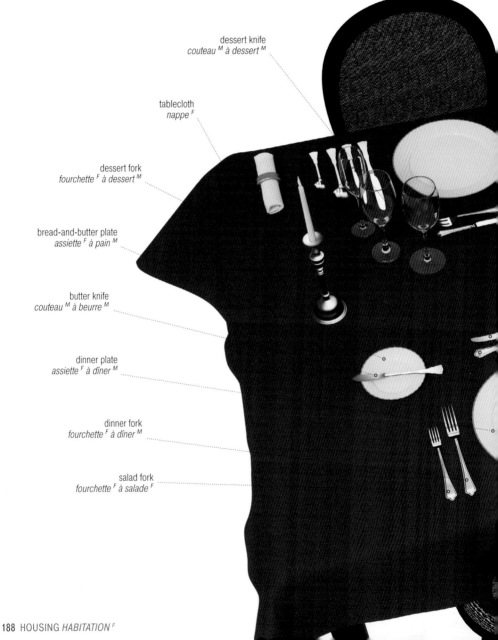

dessert knife
couteau M *à dessert* M

tablecloth
nappe F

dessert fork
fourchette F *à dessert* M

bread-and-butter plate
assiette F *à pain* M

butter knife
couteau M *à beurre* M

dinner plate
assiette F *à dîner* M

dinner fork
fourchette F *à dîner* M

salad fork
fourchette F *à salade* F

candle
bougie ^F

red wine glass
verre ^M à vin ^M rouge

candlestick
chandelier ^M

white wine glass
verre ^M à vin ^M blanc

ice bucket
seau ^M à glace ^F

champagne flute
coupe ^F de champagne ^M

napkin
serviette ^F

teaspoon
cuillère ^F à thé ^M/à café ^M

soupspoon
cuillère ^F à soupe ^F

fish knife
couteau ^M à poisson ^M

dinner knife
couteau ^M de table ^F

Cutlery
Coutellerie F

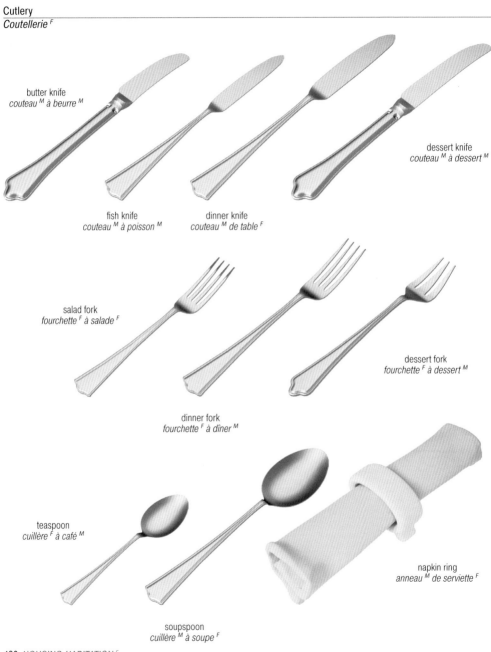

butter knife
couteau M *à beurre* M

dessert knife
couteau M *à dessert* M

fish knife
couteau M *à poisson* M

dinner knife
couteau M *de table* F

salad fork
fourchette F *à salade* F

dessert fork
fourchette F *à dessert* M

dinner fork
fourchette F *à dîner* M

teaspoon
cuillère F *à café* M

napkin ring
anneau M *de serviette* F

soupspoon
cuillère M *à soupe* F

Kitchen knives
Couteaux M de cuisine F

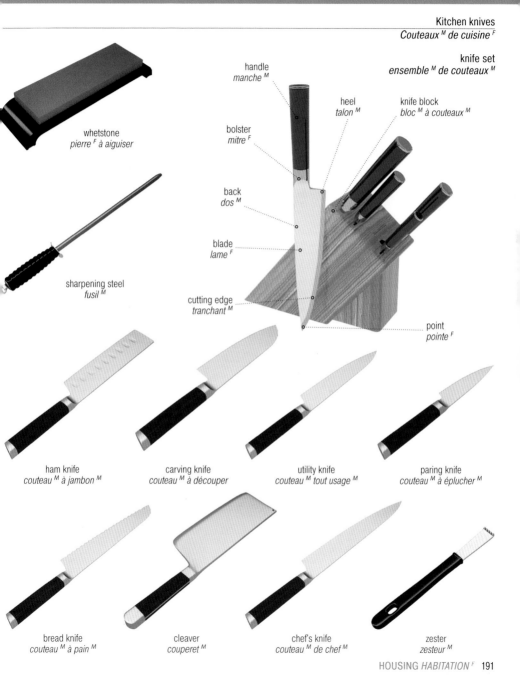

knife set
ensemble M de couteaux M

handle
manche M

heel
talon M

knife block
bloc M à couteaux M

bolster
mitre F

back
dos M

blade
lame F

cutting edge
tranchant M

point
pointe F

whetstone
pierre F à aiguiser

sharpening steel
fusil M

ham knife
couteau M à jambon M

carving knife
couteau M à découper

utility knife
couteau M tout usage M

paring knife
couteau M à éplucher M

bread knife
couteau M à pain M

cleaver
couperet M

chef's knife
couteau M de chef M

zester
zesteur M

Tableware
Vaisselle F

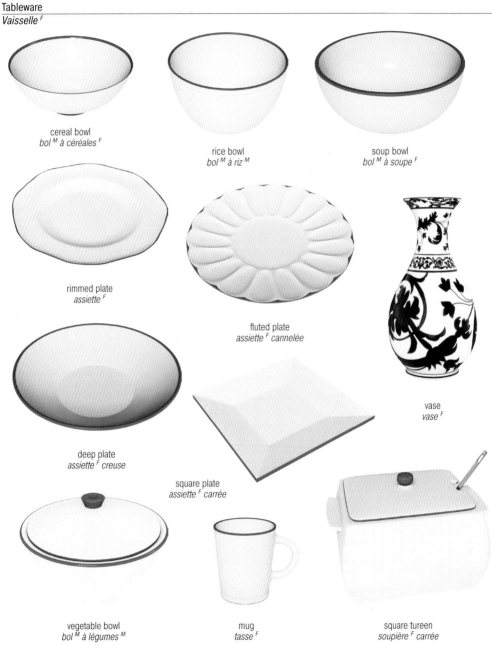

cereal bowl
bol M *à céréales* F

rice bowl
bol M *à riz* M

soup bowl
bol M *à soupe* F

rimmed plate
assiette F

fluted plate
assiette F *cannelée*

vase
vase F

deep plate
assiette F *creuse*

square plate
assiette F *carrée*

vegetable bowl
bol M *à légumes* M

mug
tasse F

square tureen
soupière F *carrée*

platter
plat ^M

dinner plate
assiette ^F à dîner ^M

dessert plate
assiette ^F à dessert ^M

spoon rest
repose-cuillère ^M

dessert bowl
coupe ^F à dessert ^M

cup and saucer
tasse ^F et soucoupe ^F

soup tureen
soupière ^F

teapot
théière ^F

creamer
pot ^M à lait

sugar bowl
sucrier ^M

Kitchen utensils
Ustensiles M de cuisine F

electronic kitchen scale
balance F de cuisine F électronique

bowl
bol M

fondue set
service M à fondue F

cube slicer
trancheur M de cubes M

fondue pot
poêlon M à fondue F

burner
réchaud M

platform
plate-forme F

stand
support M

fondue fork
fourchette F à fondue F

display
affichage M

bowl
bol M

corkscrew
tire-bouchon M

tray
plateau M

bread box
boîte F à pain M

manual coffee grinder
moulin M à café M manuel

roll-top lid
couvercle M coulissant

pastry blender
mélangeur M à pâtisserie F

citrus juicer
presse-agrumes M

pot grabber
poignée F de four M

meat thermometer
thermomètre M à viande F

mezzaluna
hachoir M berceuse F

peeler
éplucheur M

apple corer and slicer
coupe-pommes M

grater
râpe F

pastry brush
pinceau F à pâtisserie

milk frother
mousseur M à lait M

sieve
tamis M

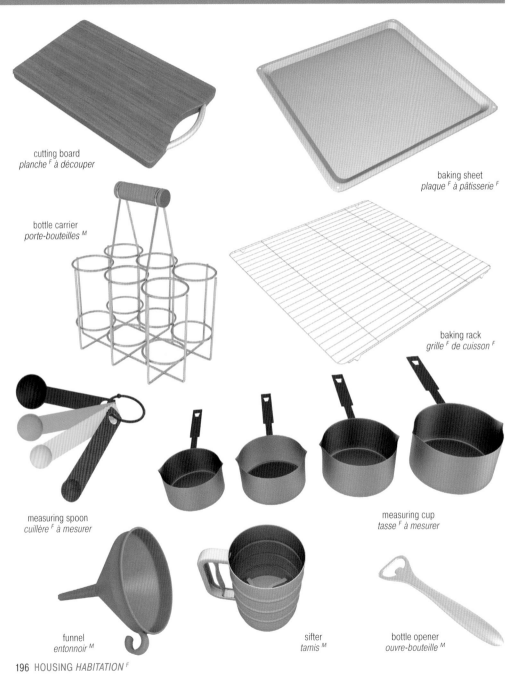

cutting board
planche F *à découper*

baking sheet
plaque F *à pâtisserie* F

bottle carrier
porte-bouteilles M

baking rack
grille F *de cuisson* F

measuring spoon
cuillère F *à mesurer*

measuring cup
tasse F *à mesurer*

funnel
entonnoir M

sifter
tamis M

bottle opener
ouvre-bouteille M

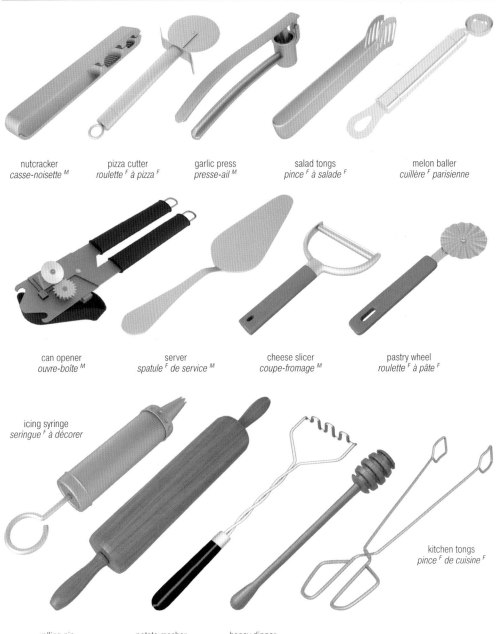

nutcracker
casse-noisette M

pizza cutter
roulette F à pizza F

garlic press
presse-ail M

salad tongs
pince F à salade F

melon baller
cuillère F parisienne

can opener
ouvre-boîte M

server
spatule F de service M

cheese slicer
coupe-fromage M

pastry wheel
roulette F à pâte F

icing syringe
seringue F à décorer

kitchen tongs
pince F de cuisine F

rolling pin
rouleau M à pâte F

potato masher
pilon M à patates F

honey dipper
cuillère F à miel M

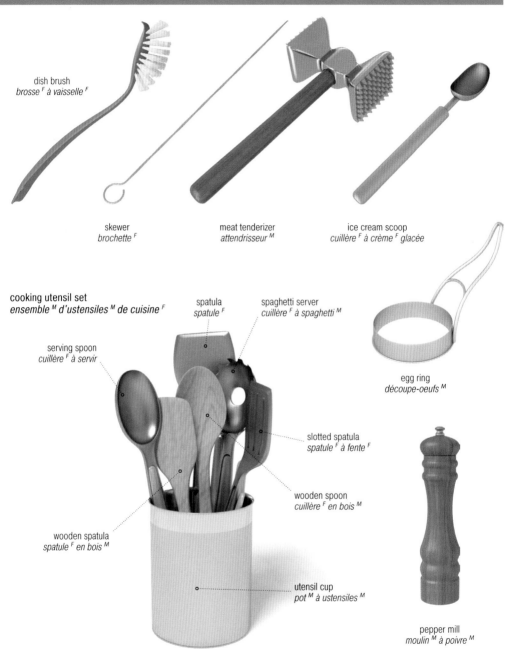

dish brush
brosse F *à vaisselle* F

skewer
brochette F

meat tenderizer
attendrisseur M

ice cream scoop
cuillère F *à crème* F *glacée*

cooking utensil set
ensemble M *d'ustensiles* M *de cuisine* F

spatula
spatule F

spaghetti server
cuillère F *à spaghetti* M

serving spoon
cuillère F *à servir*

egg ring
découpe-oeufs M

slotted spatula
spatule F *à fente* F

wooden spoon
cuillère F *en bois* M

wooden spatula
spatule F *en bois* M

utensil cup
pot M *à ustensiles* M

pepper mill
moulin M *à poivre* M

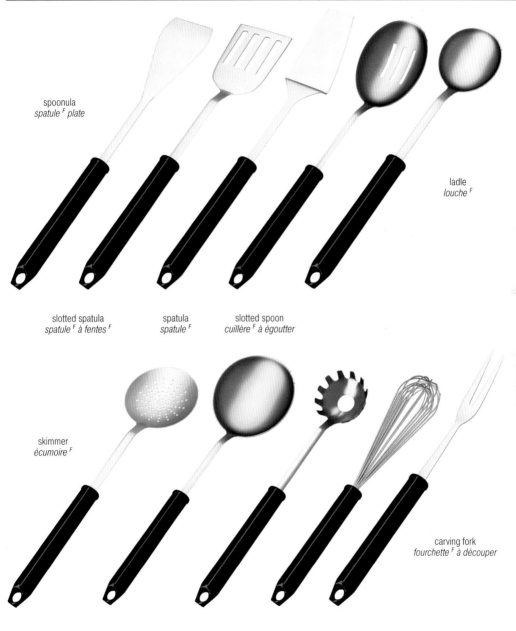

spoonula
spatule F *plate*

ladle
louche F

slotted spatula
spatule F *à fentes* F

spatula
spatule F

slotted spoon
cuillère F *à égoutter*

skimmer
écumoire F

carving fork
fourchette F *à découper*

serving spoon
cuillère F *à servir*

spaghetti server
cuillère F *à spaghetti* M

whisk
fouet M

coffee carafe
carafe F de café M

measuring cup
tasse F à mesurer

ice bucket
seau M à glace F

mold
moule M

mortar and pestle
mortier M et pilon M

plastic storage container
contenant M de plastique M

mixing bowl
bol M à mélanger

saucepan
casserole F

double boiler
bain-marie M

kettle
bouilloire F

pie dish
moule M à tarte F

wok
wok M

skillet
poêle F

frying pan
poêle M *à frire*

casserole dish
cocotte F

stock pot
marmite F

colander
passoire M

salad spinner
essoreuse F *à salade* F

loaf pan
moule M *à pain* M

roasting pan
rôtissoire F

Glassware
Verrerie F

water glass
verre M à eau F

white wine glass
verre M à vin M blanc

champagne flute
flûte F à champagne M

Alsace glass
verre M à vin M d'Alsace F

decanter
carafe F

cocktail glass
verre M à cocktail M

champagne glass
verre M à champagne M

sherry glass
verre M à sherry M

brandy snifter
verre M à cognac M

burgundy glass
verre M à bourgogne M

port glass
verre M à porto M

liqueur glass
verre M à liqueur F

red wine glass
verre M à vin M rouge

beer mug
chope F à bière F

beer glass
verre M à bière F

old-fashioned glass
verre M à whisky M

Tables
Tables ᴹ

console table
console ᶠ

nightstand
table ᶠ *de nuit* ᶠ

dining table
table ᶠ *de salle* ᶠ *à manger*

writing desk
secrétaire ᴹ

end table
table F *d'appoint* M

top
dessus M

leg
pied M

telephone table
table F *de téléphone* M

tempered glass
verre M *trempé*

patio table
table F *de jardin* M

base
base F

vanity
coiffeuse F

coffee table
table F *basse*

Chairs
Chaises ^F

bergère
bergère ^F

leather armchair
fauteuil ^M *en cuir* ^M

back
dossier ^M

arm
bras ^M

seat
siège ^M

leg
pied ^M

armchair
fauteuil ^M

stool
tabouret ^M

Voltaire chair
Voltaire ^M

easy chair
fauteuil ^M

cushioned armchair
fauteuil ^M *rembourré* ^M

kitchen chair
chaise ^F *de cuisine* ^F

folding chair
chaise ^F *pliante*

stacking chair
chaise ^F *empilable*

bar stool
tabouret ^M *de bar* ^M

rocking chair
chaise ^F *berçante*

director's chair
fauteuil ^M *de metteur* ^M *en scène* ^F

dining chair
chaise ^F *de salle* ^F *à manger*

back
dossier ^M

seat
siège ^M

upholstery
rembourrage ^M

back leg
pied ^M *arrière*

front leg
pied ^M *avant*

Sofas
Canapés ᴹ

sectional sofa
canapé ᴹ *modulaire*

backrest
dossier ᴹ

seat cushion
coussin ᴹ

leg
pied ᴹ

arm
bras ᴹ

ottoman
tabouret ᴹ

loveseat
causeuse ᶠ

chaise longe
chaise ᶠ *longue*

bench
banc ᴹ

Storage furniture
Meubles M *de rangement* M

liquor cabinet
bar M

door
porte F

pull
poignée F

leg
pied M

drawer
tiroir M

shelf
étagère F

chest of drawers
commode F

display cabinet
armoire F *vitrée*

sofa table
table F *de salon* M

glass door
porte F *en verre* M

pull
poignée F

sideboard
buffet M

drawer
tiroir M

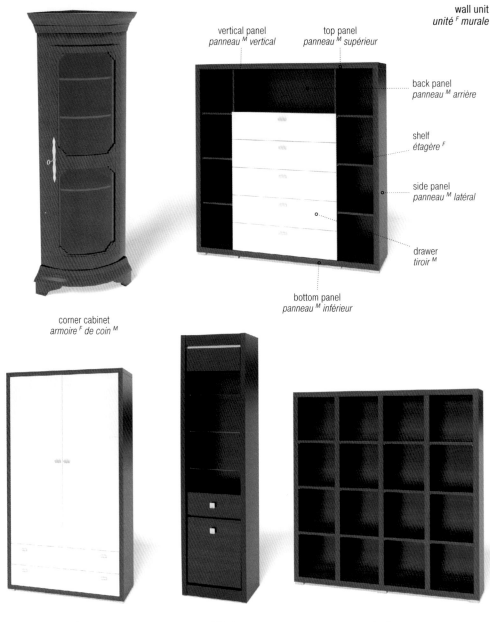

wall unit
unité F *murale*

vertical panel
panneau M *vertical*

top panel
panneau M *supérieur*

back panel
panneau M *arrière*

shelf
étagère F

side panel
panneau M *latéral*

drawer
tiroir M

bottom panel
panneau M *inférieur*

corner cabinet
armoire F *de coin* M

armoire
armoire F

chiffonier
chiffonnier M

bookcase
bibliothèque F

Domestic appliances
Appareils électroménagers ^M

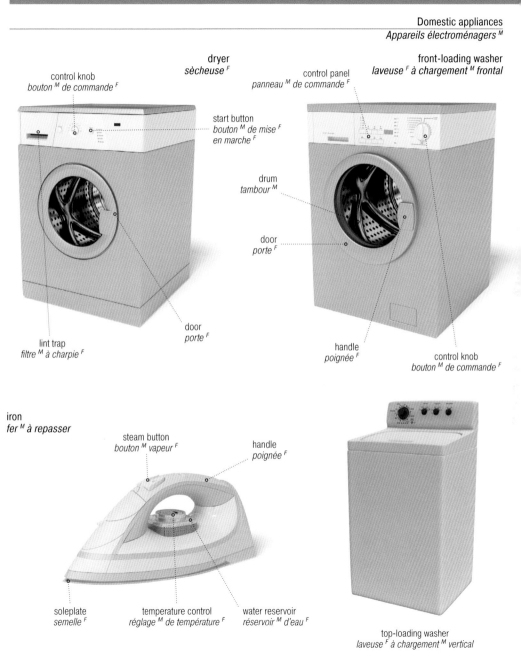

dryer
sècheuse ^F

front-loading washer
laveuse ^F *à chargement* ^M *frontal*

control knob
bouton ^M *de commande* ^F

control panel
panneau ^M *de commande* ^F

start button
bouton ^M *de mise* ^F
en marche ^F

drum
tambour ^M

door
porte ^F

door
porte ^F

lint trap
filtre ^M *à charpie* ^F

handle
poignée ^F

control knob
bouton ^M *de commande* ^F

iron
fer ^M *à repasser*

steam button
bouton ^M *vapeur* ^F

handle
poignée ^F

soleplate
semelle ^F

temperature control
réglage ^M *de température* ^F

water reservoir
réservoir ^M *d'eau* ^F

top-loading washer
laveuse ^F *à chargement* ^M *vertical*

ceiling fan
ventilateur M *de plafond* M

pedestal fan
ventilateur M *sur pied* M

oscillation control
commande F *d'oscillation* F

blade
lame F

ceiling mount
support M *de plafond* M

safety guard
grille F *de protection* F

motor housing
boîtier M *du moteur* M

rod
tige F

motor housing
boîtier M *du moteur* M

speed control
commande F *de vitesse* F

height adjustment
réglage M *de la hauteur* F

blade
pale F

stand
pied M

ductless air conditioner
climatiseur M *sans conduites* F

base
base F

canister vacuum cleaner
aspirateur-traîneau M

power switch
interrupteur d'alimentation M

pipe
tube M

handheld vacuum cleaner
aspirateur M *portatif*

hose
tuyau M

storage compartment release button
bouton M *déclencheur* M *du compartiment* M
de rangement M

wheel
roue F

ventilation grille
grille F *de ventilation* F

rug and floor brush
brosse F *à tapis* M
et planchers M

robotic vacuum cleaner
aspirateur M *robot* M

upright vacuum cleaner
aspirateur M *vertical/*
balai

Audiovisual equipment
Matériel ^M *audiovisuel*

television
télévision ^F

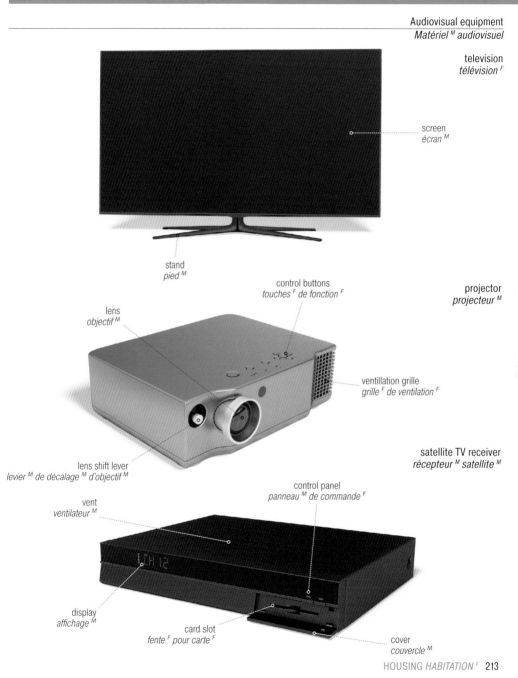

screen
écran ^M

stand
pied ^M

control buttons
touches ^F *de fonction* ^F

projector
projecteur ^M

lens
objectif ^M

ventillation grille
grille ^F *de ventilation* ^F

lens shift lever
levier ^M *de décalage* ^M *d'objectif* ^M

satellite TV receiver
récepteur ^M *satellite* ^M

vent
ventilateur ^M

control panel
panneau ^M *de commande* ^F

display
affichage ^M

card slot
fente ^F *pour carte* ^F

cover
couvercle ^M

sound system
chaîne ᶠ audio

main speaker
haut-parleur ᴹ principal

subwoofer
haut-parleur ᴹ d'extrêmes graves ᴹ

surround speaker
haut-parleur ᴹ ambiophonique

stand
support ᴹ

base
base ᶠ

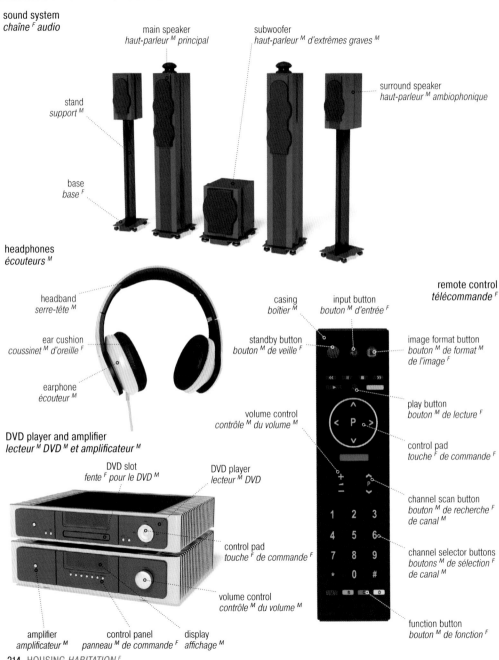

headphones
écouteurs ᴹ

remote control
télécommande ᶠ

headband
serre-tête ᴹ

casing
boîtier ᴹ

input button
bouton ᴹ d'entrée ᶠ

image format button
*bouton ᴹ de format ᴹ
de l'image ᶠ*

ear cushion
coussinet ᴹ d'oreille ᶠ

standby button
bouton ᴹ de veille ᶠ

earphone
écouteur ᴹ

play button
bouton ᴹ de lecture ᶠ

volume control
contrôle ᴹ du volume ᴹ

control pad
touche ᶠ de commande ᶠ

DVD player and amplifier
lecteur ᴹ DVD ᴹ et amplificateur ᴹ

DVD slot
fente ᶠ pour le DVD ᴹ

DVD player
lecteur ᴹ DVD

channel scan button
*bouton ᴹ de recherche ᶠ
de canal ᴹ*

control pad
touche ᶠ de commande ᶠ

channel selector buttons
*boutons ᴹ de sélection ᶠ
de canal ᴹ*

volume control
contrôle ᴹ du volume ᴹ

amplifier
amplificateur ᴹ

control panel
panneau ᴹ de commande ᶠ

display
affichage ᴹ

function button
bouton ᴹ de fonction ᶠ

Lightbulbs
Ampoules ^F

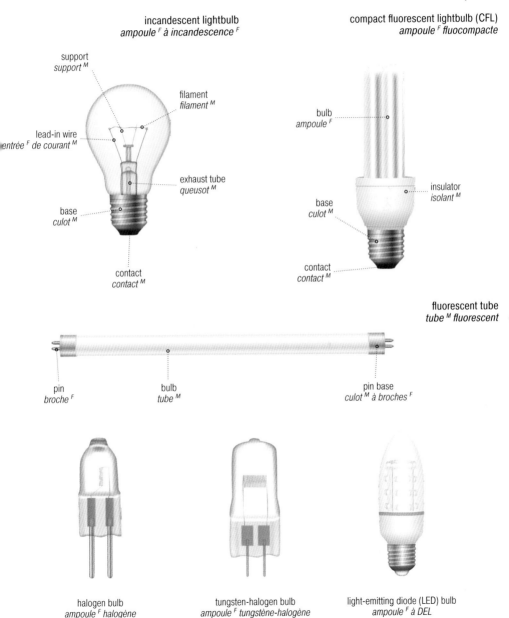

incandescent lightbulb
ampoule ^F *à incandescence* ^F

compact fluorescent lightbulb (CFL)
ampoule ^F *fluocompacte*

support
support ^M

filament
filament ^M

lead-in wire
entrée ^F *de courant* ^M

bulb
ampoule ^F

exhaust tube
queusot ^M

insulator
isolant ^M

base
culot ^M

base
culot ^M

contact
contact ^M

contact
contact ^M

fluorescent tube
tube ^M *fluorescent*

pin
broche ^F

bulb
tube ^M

pin base
culot ^M *à broches* ^F

halogen bulb
ampoule ^F *halogène*

tungsten-halogen bulb
ampoule ^F *tungstène-halogène*

light-emitting diode (LED) bulb
ampoule ^F *à DEL*

Light fixtures and lamps
Luminaires M *et lampes* F

chandelier
lustre M

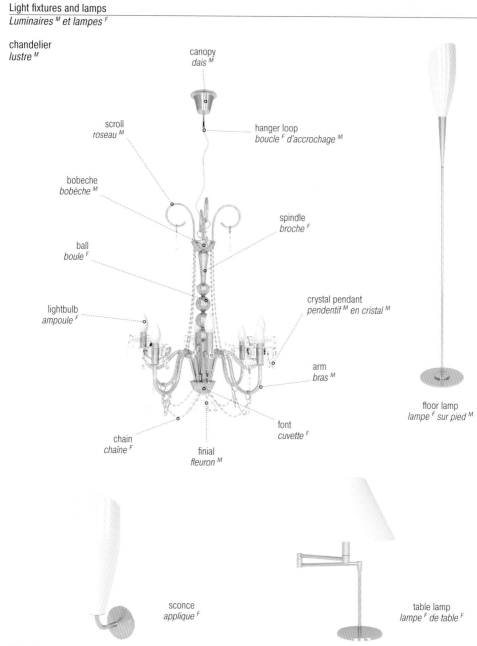

canopy
dais M

scroll
roseau M

hanger loop
boucle F *d'accrochage* M

bobeche
bobèche M

spindle
broche F

ball
boule F

crystal pendant
pendentif M *en cristal* M

lightbulb
ampoule F

arm
bras M

chain
chaîne F

font
cuvette F

finial
fleuron M

floor lamp
lampe F *sur pied* M

sconce
applique F

table lamp
lampe F *de table* F

floor lamp
lampe ^F *sur pied* ^M

hanging pendant
luminaire ^M *suspendu*

lampshade
abat-jour ^M

ceiling mount
support ^M *de plafond* ^M

wire
fil ^M

swivel arm
bras ^M *pivotant*

shade
abat-jour ^M

stand
pied ^M

base
base ^F

hanging track lighting
éclairage ^M *sur rail* ^M *suspendu*

ceiling mount
support ^M *de plafond* ^M

suspension wire
fils de suspension ^M

ceiling fixture
plafonnier ^M

track
rail ^M

lightbulb
ampoule ^F

Electrical fittings
Raccords ᴹ électriques

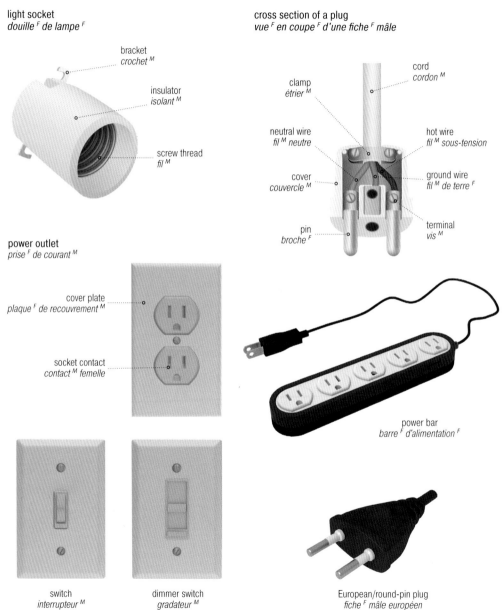

light socket
douille ᶠ de lampe ᶠ

bracket
crochet ᴹ

insulator
isolant ᴹ

screw thread
fil ᴹ

cross section of a plug
vue ᶠ en coupe ᶠ d'une fiche ᶠ mâle

cord
cordon ᴹ

clamp
étrier ᴹ

neutral wire
fil ᴹ neutre

hot wire
fil ᴹ sous-tension

cover
couvercle ᴹ

ground wire
fil ᴹ de terre ᶠ

pin
broche ᶠ

terminal
vis ᴹ

power outlet
prise ᶠ de courant ᴹ

cover plate
plaque ᶠ de recouvrement ᴹ

socket contact
contact ᴹ femelle

power bar
barre ᶠ d'alimentation ᶠ

switch
interrupteur ᴹ

dimmer switch
gradateur ᴹ

European/round-pin plug
fiche ᶠ mâle européen

flat mop
balai ^M à laver plat

mop
vadrouille ^F

handle
manche ^F

broom
balai ^M

mop head
tête ^F de vadrouille ^F

bucket
seau ^M

scrub brush
brosse ^F à récurage ^M

dustpan
porte-poussière ^M

wastebasket
poubelle ^F

aquarium
aquarium M

lighting hood
hotte F *de lumière* F

decorative rock
roche F *décorative*

fish
poisson F

gravel
gravier M

plant
plante F

tank
réservoir M

air pump
pompe F *à air* M

terrarium
terrarium M

ventilation screen
écran M *de ventilation* F

heating light
lampe F *chauffante*

plant
plante F

decorative background
fond M *décoratif*

tank
réservoir M

chameleon
caméléon M

latch
loquet M

driftwood
bois flotté M

swinging door
porte F *battante*

ventilation
ventilation F

water bowl
bol M *d'eau* F

base
base F

sand
sable M

birdcage
cage ^F *à oiseaux* ^M

hanging ring
anneau ^M *de suspension* ^F

wire bar
fil ^M *de fer* ^M

leash
laisse ^F

access door
porte d'accès ^F

parrot
perroquet ^M

food and water bowls
bols ^M *pour eau* ^F *et nourriture* ^F

feeding dish
mangeoire ^F

perch
perchoir ^M

collar
collier ^M

muzzle
muselière ^F

covered litter box
bac ^M *à litière* ^F *couvert*

pet carrier
cage ^F *de transport* ^M

small animal cage
petite cage ^F *pour animaux* ^M

Curtain rods
Tringles ^F *à rideaux* ^M

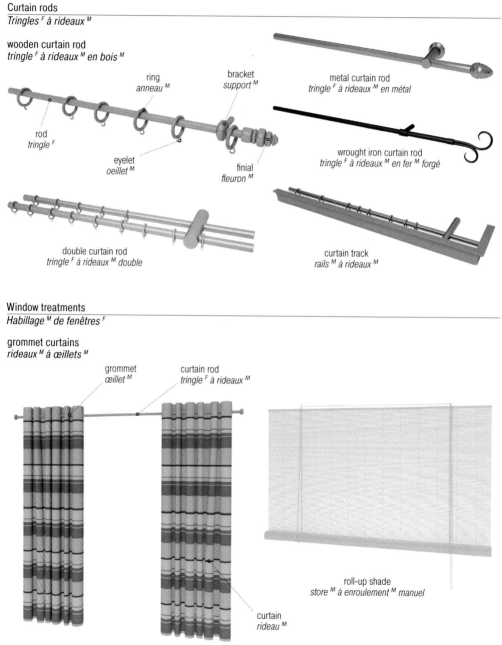

wooden curtain rod
tringle ^F *à rideaux* ^M *en bois* ^M

ring
anneau ^M

bracket
support ^M

metal curtain rod
tringle ^F *à rideaux* ^M *en métal*

rod
tringle ^F

eyelet
oeillet ^M

finial
fleuron ^M

wrought iron curtain rod
tringle ^F *à rideaux* ^M *en fer* ^M *forgé*

double curtain rod
tringle ^F *à rideaux* ^M *double*

curtain track
rails ^M *à rideaux* ^M

Window treatments
Habillage ^M *de fenêtres* ^F

grommet curtains
rideaux ^M *à œillets* ^M

grommet
œillet ^M

curtain rod
tringle ^F *à rideaux* ^M

roll-up shade
store ^M *à enroulement* ^M *manuel*

curtain
rideau ^M

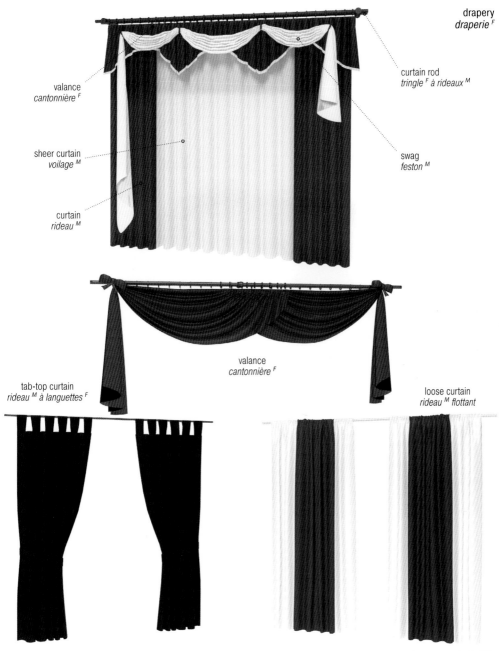

drapery
draperie ᶠ

valance
cantonnière ᶠ

curtain rod
tringle ᶠ à rideaux ᴹ

sheer curtain
voilage ᴹ

swag
feston ᴹ

curtain
rideau ᴹ

valance
cantonnière ᶠ

tab-top curtain
rideau ᴹ à languettes ᶠ

loose curtain
rideau ᴹ flottant

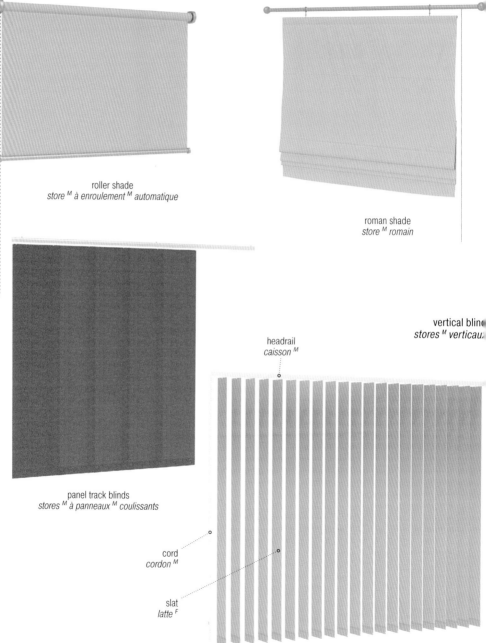

roller shade
store [M] *à enroulement* [M] *automatique*

roman shade
store [M] *romain*

vertical blind
stores [M] *verticaux*

headrail
caisson [M]

panel track blinds
stores [M] *à panneaux* [M] *coulissants*

cord
cordon [M]

slat
latte [F]

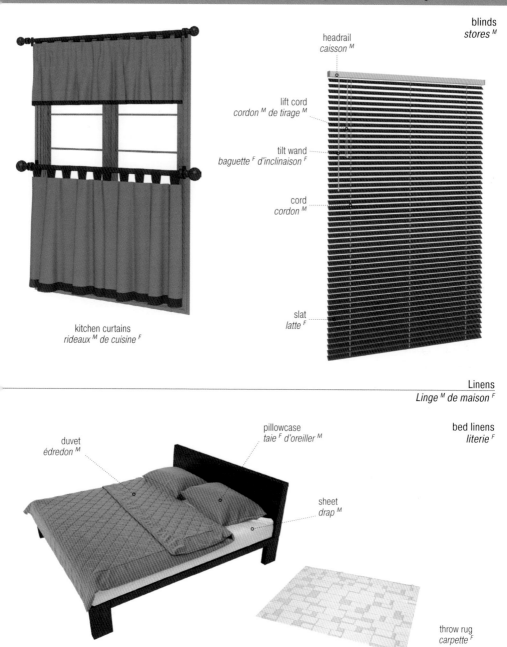

blinds
stores ᴹ

headrail
caisson ᴹ

lift cord
cordon ᴹ *de tirage* ᶠ

tilt wand
baguette ᶠ *d'inclinaison* ᶠ

cord
cordon ᴹ

slat
latte ᶠ

kitchen curtains
rideaux ᴹ *de cuisine* ᶠ

Linens
Linge ᴹ *de maison* ᶠ

duvet
édredon ᴹ

pillowcase
taie ᶠ *d'oreiller* ᴹ

bed linens
literie ᶠ

sheet
drap ᴹ

throw rug
carpette ᶠ

brick house
maison ᶠ de brique ᶠ

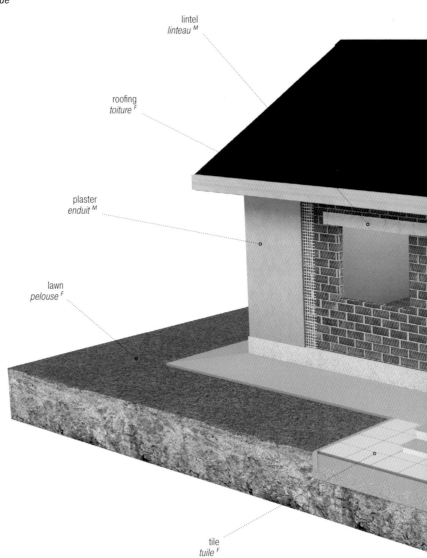

lintel
linteau ᴹ

roofing
toiture ᶠ

plaster
enduit ᴹ

lawn
pelouse ᶠ

tile
tuile ᶠ

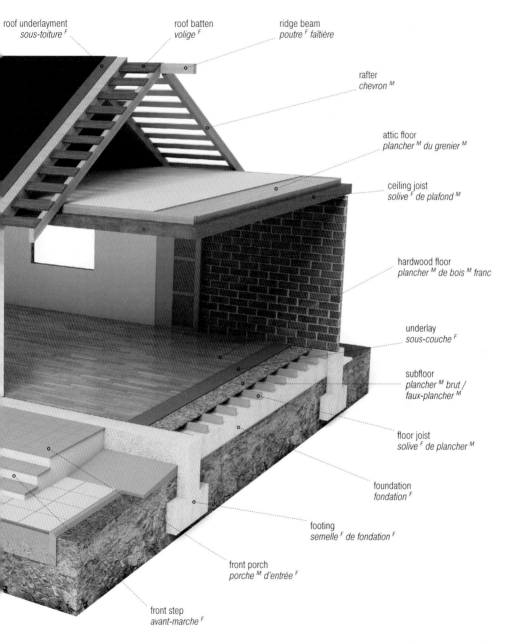

roof underlayment
sous-toiture ᶠ

roof batten
volige ᶠ

ridge beam
poutre ᶠ faîtière

rafter
chevron ᴹ

attic floor
plancher ᴹ du grenier ᴹ

ceiling joist
solive ᶠ de plafond ᴹ

hardwood floor
plancher ᴹ de bois ᴹ franc

underlay
sous-couche ᶠ

subfloor
*plancher ᴹ brut /
faux-plancher ᴹ*

floor joist
solive ᶠ de plancher ᴹ

foundation
fondation ᶠ

footing
semelle ᶠ de fondation ᶠ

front porch
porche ᴹ d'entrée ᶠ

front step
avant-marche ᶠ

reinforced concrete house
maison ᶠ en béton ᴹ armé

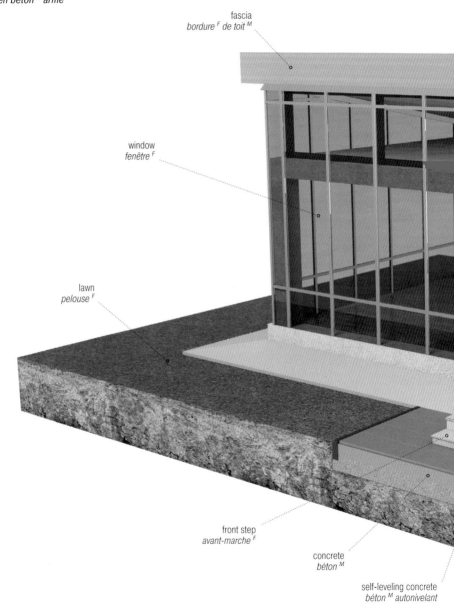

fascia
bordure ᶠ de toit ᴹ

window
fenêtre ᶠ

lawn
pelouse ᶠ

front step
avant-marche ᶠ

concrete
béton ᴹ

self-leveling concrete
béton ᴹ autonivelant

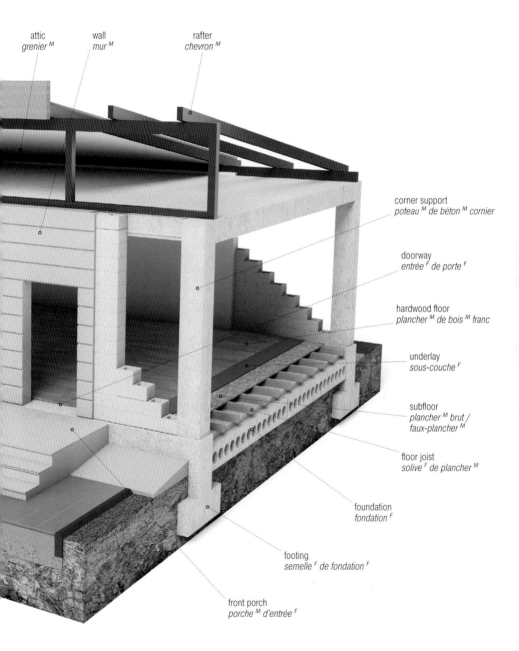

attic
grenier ^M

wall
mur ^M

rafter
chevron ^M

corner support
poteau ^M *de béton* ^M *cornier*

doorway
entrée ^F *de porte* ^F

hardwood floor
plancher ^M *de bois* ^M *franc*

underlay
sous-couche ^F

subfloor
plancher ^M *brut /*
faux-plancher ^M

floor joist
solive ^F *de plancher* ^M

foundation
fondation ^F

footing
semelle ^F *de fondation* ^F

front porch
porche ^M *d'entrée* ^F

wooden-frame house
maison ^F *à ossature* ^F *en bois* ^M

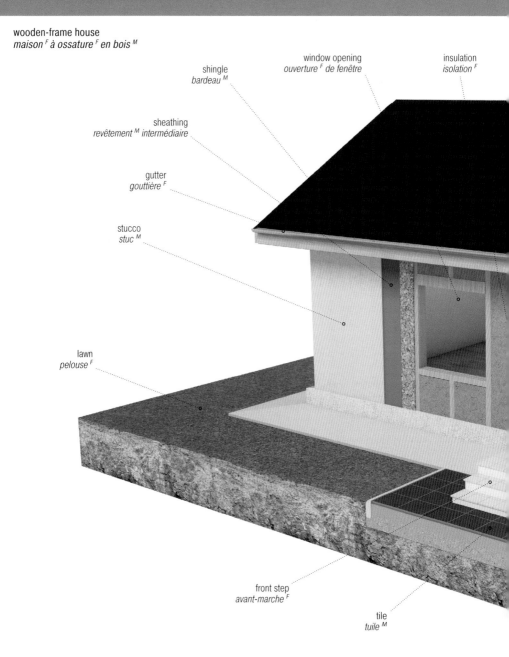

shingle
bardeau ^M

window opening
ouverture ^F *de fenêtre*

insulation
isolation ^F

sheathing
revêtement ^M *intermédiaire*

gutter
gouttière ^F

stucco
stuc ^M

lawn
pelouse ^F

front step
avant-marche ^F

tile
tuile ^M

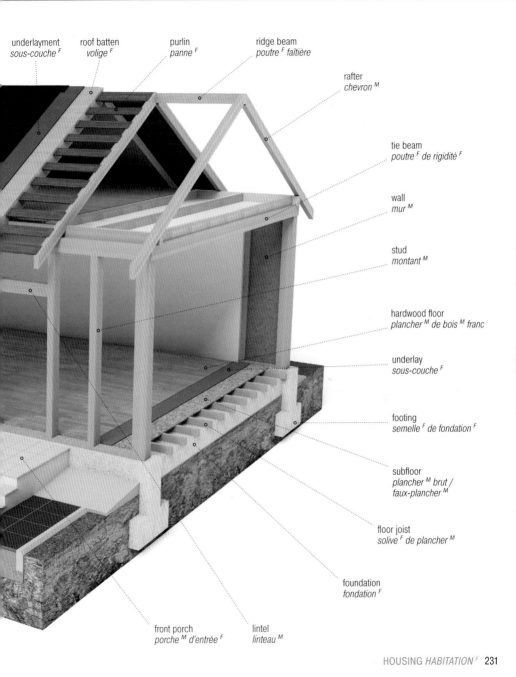

underlayment
sous-couche F

roof batten
volige F

purlin
panne F

ridge beam
poutre F *faîtière*

rafter
chevron M

tie beam
poutre F *de rigidité* F

wall
mur M

stud
montant M

hardwood floor
plancher M *de bois* M *franc*

underlay
sous-couche F

footing
semelle F *de fondation* F

subfloor
plancher M *brut /*
faux-plancher M

floor joist
solive F *de plancher* M

foundation
fondation F

front porch
porche M *d'entrée* F

lintel
linteau M

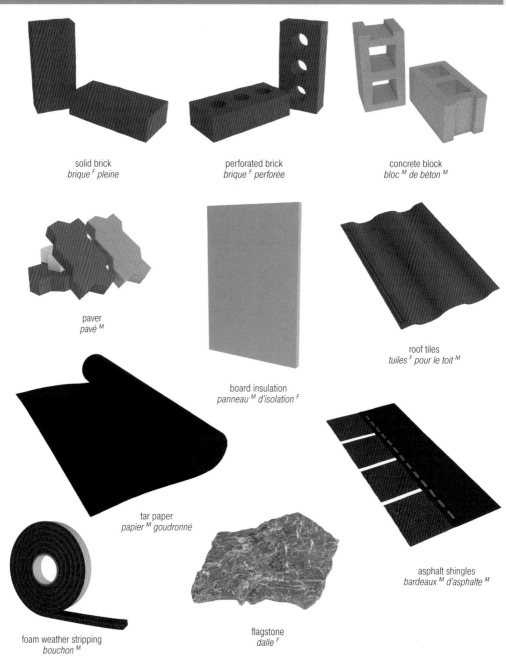

solid brick
brique ᶠ pleine

perforated brick
brique ᶠ perforée

concrete block
bloc ᴹ de béton ᴹ

paver
pavé ᴹ

board insulation
panneau ᴹ d'isolation ᶠ

roof tiles
tuiles ᶠ pour le toit ᴹ

tar paper
papier ᴹ goudronné

asphalt shingles
bardeaux ᴹ d'asphalte ᴹ

foam weather stripping
bouchon ᴹ

flagstone
dalle ᶠ

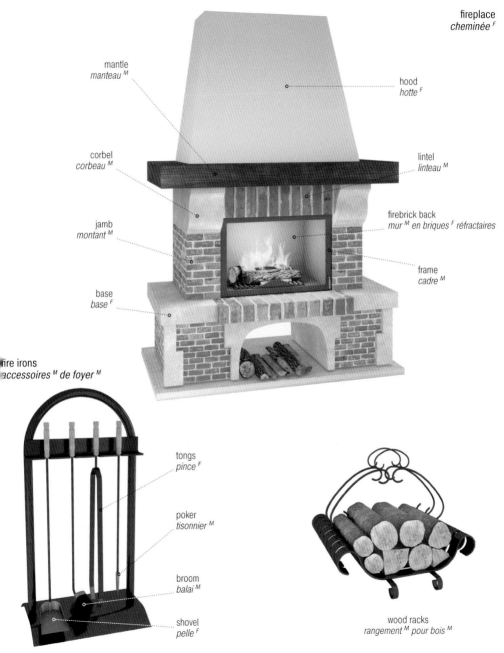

fireplace
cheminée ^F

mantle
manteau ^M

hood
hotte ^F

corbel
corbeau ^M

lintel
linteau ^M

firebrick back
mur ^M *en briques* ^F *réfractaires*

jamb
montant ^M

frame
cadre ^M

base
base ^F

fire irons
accessoires ^M *de foyer* ^M

tongs
pince ^F

poker
tisonnier ^M

broom
balai ^M

shovel
pelle ^F

wood racks
rangement ^M *pour bois* ^M

forced-air heating and air-conditioning system
système ᴹ de chauffage ᴹ et de climatisation ᶠ à air ᴹ forcé

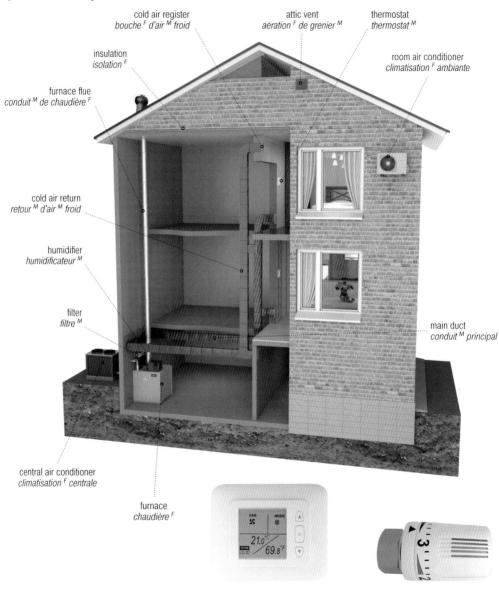

cold air register
bouche ᶠ d'air ᴹ froid

attic vent
aération ᶠ de grenier ᴹ

thermostat
thermostat ᴹ

insulation
isolation ᶠ

room air conditioner
climatisation ᶠ ambiante

furnace flue
conduit ᴹ de chaudière ᶠ

cold air return
retour ᴹ d'air ᴹ froid

humidifier
humidificateur ᴹ

filter
filtre ᴹ

main duct
conduit ᴹ principal

central air conditioner
climatisation ᶠ centrale

furnace
chaudière ᶠ

room thermostat
thermostat ᴹ ambiant

radiator thermostat
thermostat ᴹ de radiateur ᴹ

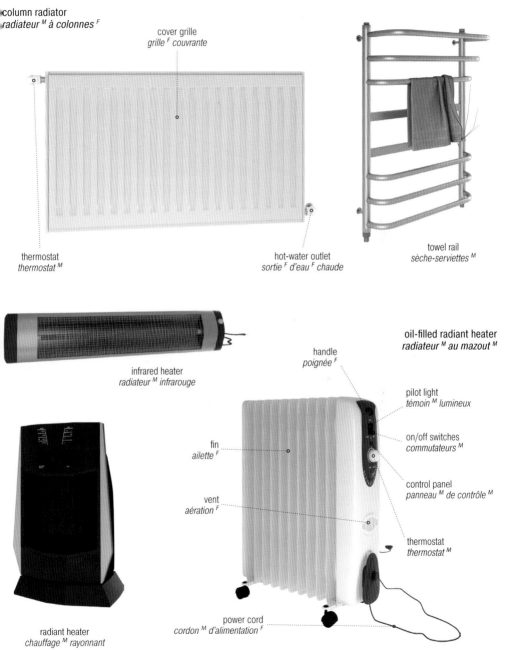

column radiator
radiateur M *à colonnes* F

cover grille
grille F *couvrante*

thermostat
thermostat M

hot-water outlet
sortie F *d'eau* F *chaude*

towel rail
sèche-serviettes M

infrared heater
radiateur M *infrarouge*

oil-filled radiant heater
radiateur M *au mazout* M

handle
poignée F

pilot light
témoin M *lumineux*

on/off switches
commutateurs M

fin
ailette F

control panel
panneau M *de contrôle* M

vent
aération F

thermostat
thermostat M

radiant heater
chauffage M *rayonnant*

power cord
cordon M *d'alimentation* F

plumbing system
tuyauterie ᶠ

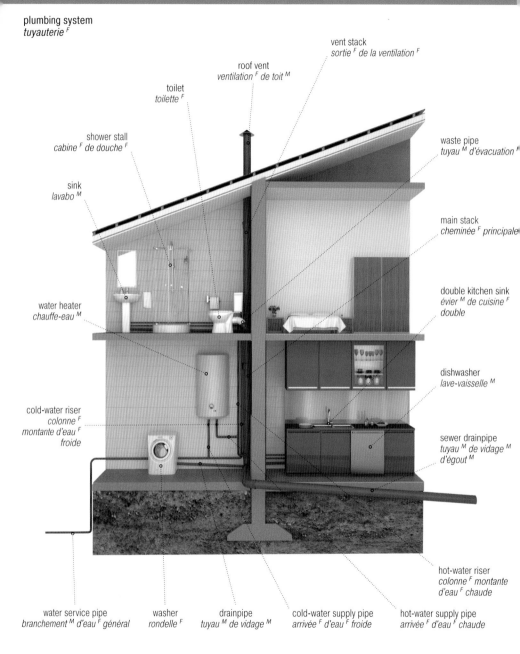

vent stack
sortie ᶠ *de la ventilation* ᶠ

roof vent
ventilation ᶠ *de toit* ᴹ

toilet
toilette ᶠ

shower stall
cabine ᶠ *de douche* ᶠ

waste pipe
tuyau ᴹ *d'évacuation* ᴹ

sink
lavabo ᴹ

main stack
cheminée ᶠ *principale*

double kitchen sink
évier ᴹ *de cuisine* ᶠ
double

water heater
chauffe-eau ᴹ

dishwasher
lave-vaisselle ᴹ

cold-water riser
colonne ᶠ
montante d'eau ᶠ
froide

sewer drainpipe
tuyau ᴹ *de vidage* ᴹ
d'égout ᴹ

hot-water riser
colonne ᶠ *montante*
d'eau ᶠ *chaude*

water service pipe
branchement ᴹ *d'eau* ᶠ *général*

washer
rondelle ᶠ

drainpipe
tuyau ᴹ *de vidage* ᴹ

cold-water supply pipe
arrivée ᶠ *d'eau* ᶠ *froide*

hot-water supply pipe
arrivée ᶠ *d'eau* ᶠ *chaude*

cartridge faucet
robinet ᴹ à cartouche ᶠ

handle
poignée ᶠ

nut
tige ᶠ

spline
cannelure ᶠ

ceramic disc
disque ᴹ en céramique ᶠ

thread
filetage ᴹ

tap valve
valve ᶠ de robinet ᴹ

spout
bec ᴹ

retaining ring
bague ᶠ de serrage ᴹ

O-ring
joint ᴹ torique

disc faucet
robinet ᴹ à disque ᴹ

setscrew
vis ᶠ de pression ᶠ

handle
poignée ᶠ

aerator body
corps ᴹ de l'aérateur ᴹ

aerator insert
insert ᴹ pour aérateur ᴹ

mounting screw
vis ᶠ de montage ᴹ

bonnet
enjoliveur ᴹ

cylinder
cylindre ᴹ

post
support ᴹ

aerator insert
insert ᴹ pour aérateur ᴹ

seal
joint ᴹ

aerator body
aérateur ᴹ

spout
bec ᴹ

spout sleeve
manchon ᴹ

water inlet
arrivée ᶠ d'eau ᶠ

spot shank
tige ᶠ de fixation ᶠ

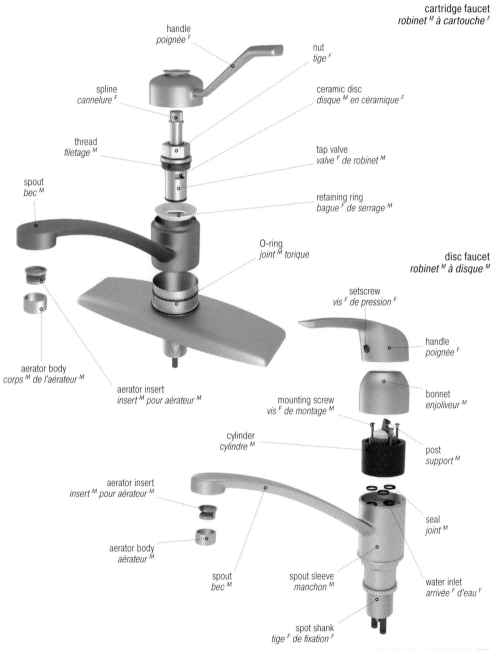

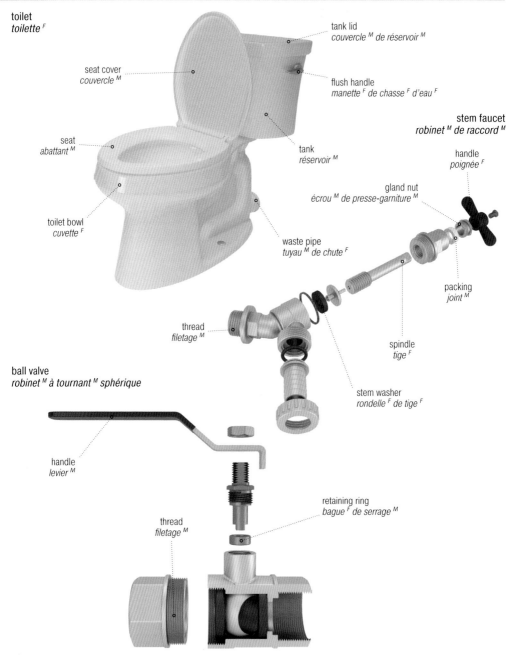

toilet
toilette F

tank lid
couvercle M *de réservoir* M

seat cover
couvercle M

flush handle
manette F *de chasse* F *d'eau* F

stem faucet
robinet M *de raccord* M

seat
abattant M

handle
poignée F

tank
réservoir M

gland nut
écrou M *de presse-garniture* M

toilet bowl
cuvette F

waste pipe
tuyau M *de chute* F

packing
joint M

thread
filetage M

spindle
tige F

ball valve
robinet M *à tournant* M *sphérique*

stem washer
rondelle F *de tige* F

handle
levier M

retaining ring
bague F *de serrage* M

thread
filetage M

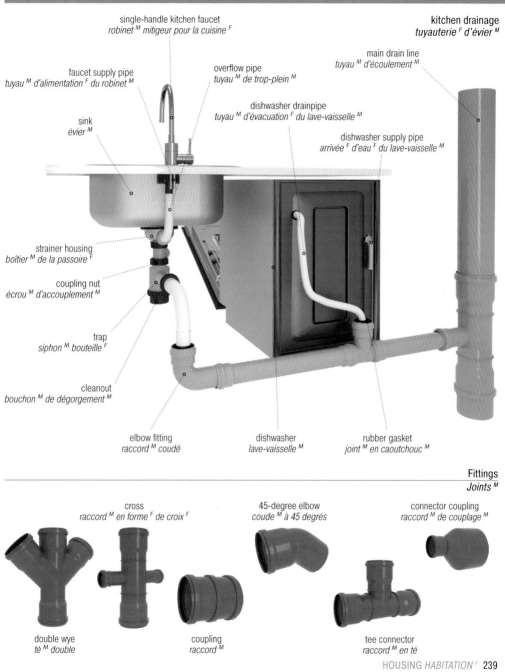

single-handle kitchen faucet
robinet ᴹ *mitigeur pour la cuisine* ᶠ

kitchen drainage
tuyauterie ᶠ *d'évier* ᴹ

main drain line
tuyau ᴹ *d'écoulement* ᴹ

faucet supply pipe
tuyau ᴹ *d'alimentation* ᶠ *du robinet* ᴹ

overflow pipe
tuyau ᴹ *de trop-plein* ᴹ

dishwasher drainpipe
tuyau ᴹ *d'évacuation* ᶠ *du lave-vaisselle* ᴹ

sink
évier ᴹ

dishwasher supply pipe
arrivée ᶠ *d'eau* ᶠ *du lave-vaisselle* ᴹ

strainer housing
boîtier ᴹ *de la passoire* ᶠ

coupling nut
écrou ᴹ *d'accouplement* ᴹ

trap
siphon ᴹ *bouteille* ᶠ

cleanout
bouchon ᴹ *de dégorgement* ᴹ

elbow fitting
raccord ᴹ *coudé*

dishwasher
lave-vaisselle ᴹ

rubber gasket
joint ᴹ *en caoutchouc* ᴹ

Fittings
Joints ᴹ

cross
raccord ᴹ *en forme* ᶠ *de croix* ᶠ

45-degree elbow
coude ᴹ *à 45 degrés*

connector coupling
raccord ᴹ *de couplage* ᴹ

double wye
té ᴹ *double*

coupling
raccord ᴹ

tee connector
raccord ᴹ *en té*

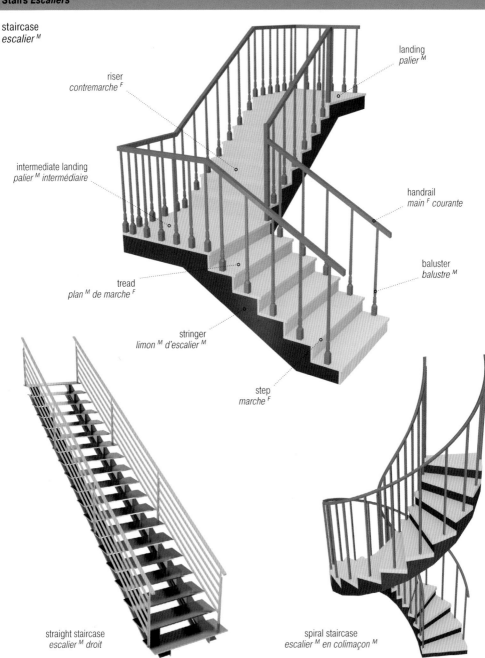

staircase
escalier [M]

riser
contremarche [F]

landing
palier [M]

intermediate landing
palier [M] *intermédiaire*

handrail
main [F] *courante*

baluster
balustre [M]

tread
plan [M] *de marche* [F]

stringer
limon [M] *d'escalier* [M]

step
marche [F]

straight staircase
escalier [M] *droit*

spiral staircase
escalier [M] *en colimaçon* [M]

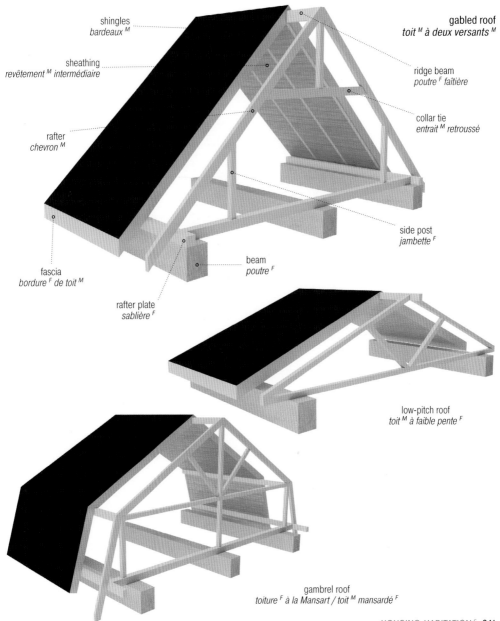

shingles
bardeaux [M]

sheathing
revêtement [M] *intermédiaire*

rafter
chevron [M]

fascia
bordure [F] *de toit* [M]

rafter plate
sablière [F]

beam
poutre [F]

gabled roof
toit [M] *à deux versants* [M]

ridge beam
poutre [F] *faîtière*

collar tie
entrait [M] *retroussé*

side post
jambette [F]

low-pitch roof
toit [M] *à faible pente* [F]

gambrel roof
toiture [F] *à la Mansart / toit* [M] *mansardé* [F]

roof construction
construction ^M *de la toiture* ^F

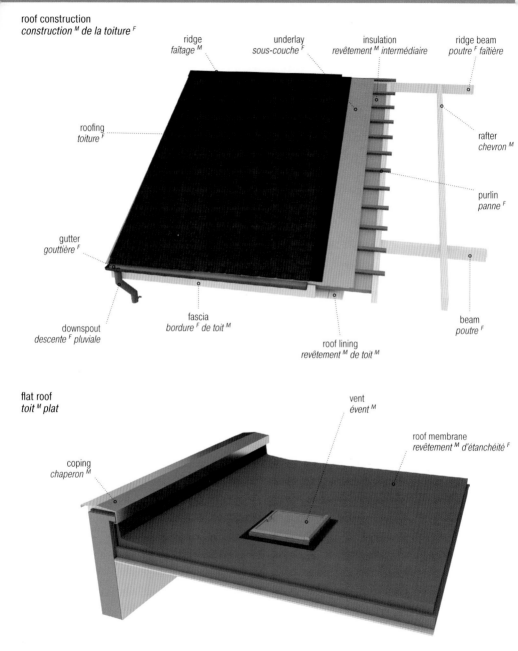

ridge
faîtage ^M

underlay
sous-couche ^F

insulation
revêtement ^M *intermédiaire*

ridge beam
poutre ^F *faîtière*

roofing
toiture ^F

rafter
chevron ^M

purlin
panne ^F

gutter
gouttière ^F

downspout
descente ^F *pluviale*

fascia
bordure ^F *de toit* ^M

beam
poutre ^F

roof lining
revêtement ^M *de toit* ^M

flat roof
toit ^M *plat*

vent
évent ^M

roof membrane
revêtement ^M *d'étanchéité* ^F

coping
chaperon ^M

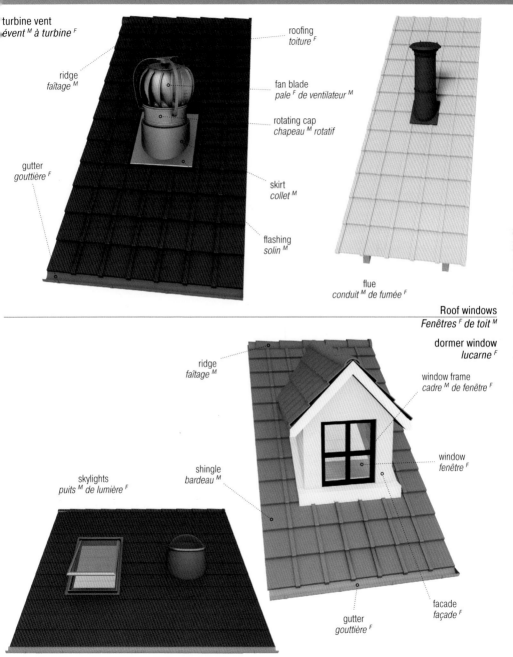

turbine vent
évent ^M *à turbine* ^F

ridge
faîtage ^M

gutter
gouttière ^F

roofing
toiture ^F

fan blade
pale ^F *de ventilateur* ^M

rotating cap
chapeau ^M *rotatif*

skirt
collet ^M

flashing
solin ^M

flue
conduit ^M *de fumée* ^F

Roof windows
Fenêtres ^F *de toit* ^M

dormer window
lucarne ^F

ridge
faîtage ^M

window frame
cadre ^M *de fenêtre* ^F

window
fenêtre ^F

skylights
puits ^M *de lumière* ^F

shingle
bardeau ^M

facade
façade ^F

gutter
gouttière ^F

swimming pool
piscine F

ladder
échelle F

deck
terrasse F

overflow drain
vidange F de trop-plein M

gutter
trop-plein M

wall
mur M

diving board
tremplin M

drain
bonde F de fond M

pump
pompe F

filter
filtre M

hatch
trappe F

inflatable toy
jouet M gonflable

swim ring
bouée F

sauna
sauna M

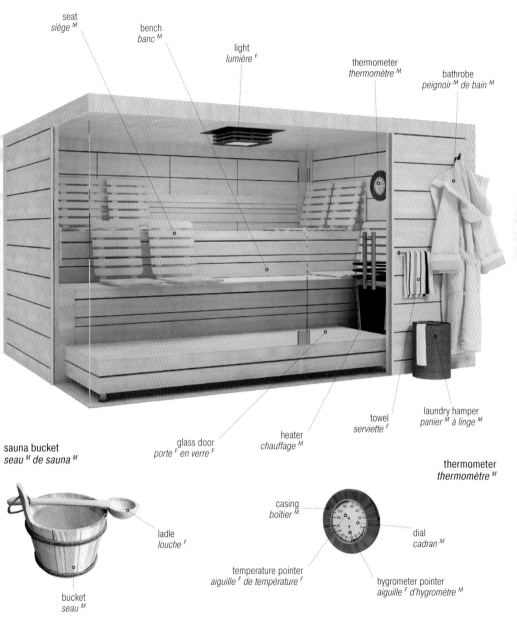

seat
siège M

bench
banc M

light
lumière F

thermometer
thermomètre M

bathrobe
peignoir M *de bain* M

sauna bucket
seau M *de sauna* M

glass door
porte F *en verre* F

heater
chauffage M

towel
serviette F

laundry hamper
panier M *à linge* M

thermometer
thermomètre M

ladle
louche F

casing
boîtier M

dial
cadran M

temperature pointer
aiguille F *de température* F

hygrometer pointer
aiguille F *d'hygromètre* M

bucket
seau M

gazebo
belvédère ^M

roof
toit ^M

table
table ^F

bench
banc ^M

deck chair
transatlantique ^M

support beam
poutre ^F *de soutien* ^M

floor
plancher ^M

bistro set
ensemble ^M *bistro*

table
table ^F

chair
chaise ^F

bench
banc ^M

lounger
chaise F *longue*

sofa
canapé M

folding table
table F *pliante*

folding bench
banc M *pliant*

porch swing
balancelle F

bridge
pont M

patio umbrella
parasol ^M

fountain
fontaine ^F

fence
clôture ^F

patio heater
radiateur ^M *d'extérieur* ^M

reflector
réflecteur ^M

shade
abat-jour ^M

burner
brûleur ^M

sconce
applique ^F

ventilation hole
trou ^M *de ventilation* ^F

propane tank housing
boîtier ^M *de la bonbonne* ^F
de propane ^M

base
base ^F

decorative light
lumière ^F *décorative*

lamppost
lampadaire ^M

stake light
lampe ^F *sur piquet* ^M

barbecue
barbecue ^M

lid
couvercle ^M

control pad
touche ^F *de commande* ^F

grill rack
grille ^F *de barbecue* ^M

meat
viande ^F

gas cylinder
bouteille ^F *de gaz* ^M

wheel
roue ^F

storage rack
étagère ^F *de rangement* ^M

outdoor fireplace
foyer ^M *extérieur*

hibachi
gril ^M

grill
grille ^F

lid
couvercle ^M

bowl
cuve ^F

electric grill
gril ^M *électrique*

barbecue utensils
ustensiles M *de barbecue* M

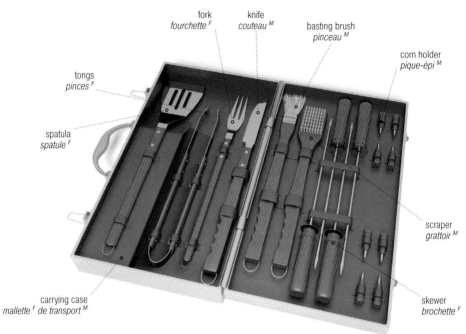

fork
fourchette F

knife
couteau M

basting brush
pinceau M

corn holder
pique-épi M

tongs
pinces F

spatula
spatule F

scraper
grattoir M

carrying case
mallette F *de transport* M

skewer
brochette F

TOOLS *OUTILS* M
Gardening tools *Outils* M *de jardinage* M

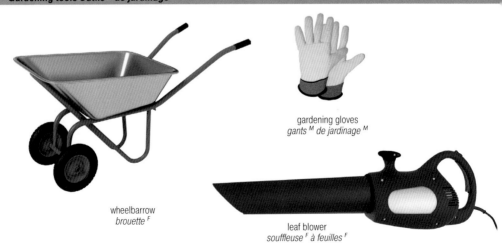

gardening gloves
gants M *de jardinage* M

wheelbarrow
brouette F

leaf blower
souffleuse F *à feuilles* F

snow scoop
pousse-neige ^M

plastic snow shovel
pelle ^F *à neige* ^F *en plastique* ^M

metal snow shovel
pelle ^F *à neige* ^F *en métal* ^M

leaf rake
râteau ^M *à feuilles* ^F

level rake
râteau ^M *à niveler*

garden fork
fourche ^F *à bêcher*

hoe
houe ^F

weeder
truelle ^F

hand rake
râteau ^M *à main* ^F

hand cultivator
cultivateur ^M *à main* ^F

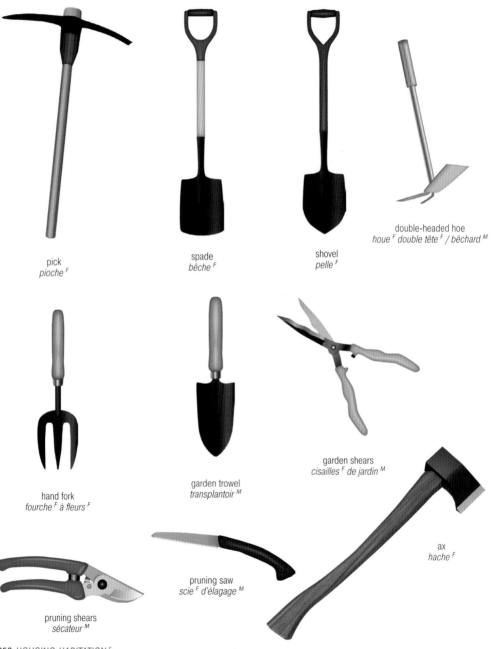

pick
pioche ^F

spade
bêche ^F

shovel
pelle ^F

double-headed hoe
houe ^F *double tête* ^F / *bêchard* ^M

hand fork
fourche ^F *à fleurs* ^F

garden trowel
transplantoir ^M

garden shears
cisailles ^F *de jardin* ^M

pruning shears
sécateur ^M

pruning saw
scie ^F *d'élagage* ^M

ax
hache ^F

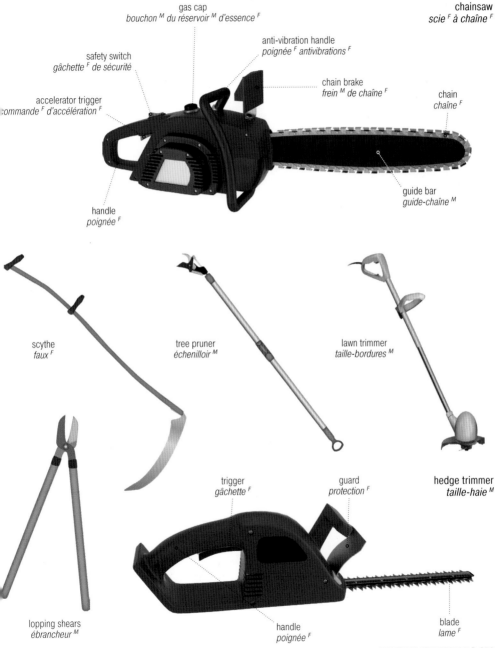

gas cap
bouchon [M] *du réservoir* [M] *d'essence* [F]

chainsaw
scie [F] *à chaîne* [F]

anti-vibration handle
poignée [F] *antivibrations* [F]

safety switch
gâchette [F] *de sécurité*

chain brake
frein [M] *de chaîne* [F]

accelerator trigger
commande [F] *d'accélération* [F]

chain
chaîne [F]

handle
poignée [F]

guide bar
guide-chaîne [M]

scythe
faux [F]

tree pruner
échenilloir [M]

lawn trimmer
taille-bordures [M]

trigger
gâchette [F]

guard
protection [F]

hedge trimmer
taille-haie [M]

lopping shears
ébrancheur [M]

handle
poignée [F]

blade
lame [F]

lawn mower
tondeuse ^F *à gazon* ^M

control lever
levier ^M *de commande* ^F

handle
poignée ^F

safety handle
poignée ^F *de sécurité* ^F

gas tank
réservoir ^M *de carburant* ^M

string trimmer
tondeuse ^F *à fouet* ^M

grass catcher
collecteur ^M *d'herbe* ^M

air filter
filtre ^M *à air* ^M

wheel
roue ^F

impulse sprinkler
arroseur ^M *canon* ^M

oscillating sprinkler
arroseur ^M *oscillant*

watering wand
lance ^F *d'arrosage* ^M

pistol nozzle
pistolet ^M *d'arrosage* ^M

watering can
arrosoir ^M

garden hose
tuyau ^M *d'arrosage* ^M

hose reel
enrouleur ^M

flaring tool
outil ^M _à évaser_

wing nut
écrou ^M _à oreilles_ ^F

clamp
pince ^F

tube slot
fente ^F _du tuyau_ ^M

mount
montage ^M

pipe wrench
clé ^F _à tuyau_ ^M

pipe cutter
coupe-tuyau ^M

plumber's snake
furet ^M

plunger
ventouse ^F

tongue-and-groove pliers
pince ^F _multiprise_

pipe threader
fileteuse ^F _de tuyaux_ ^M

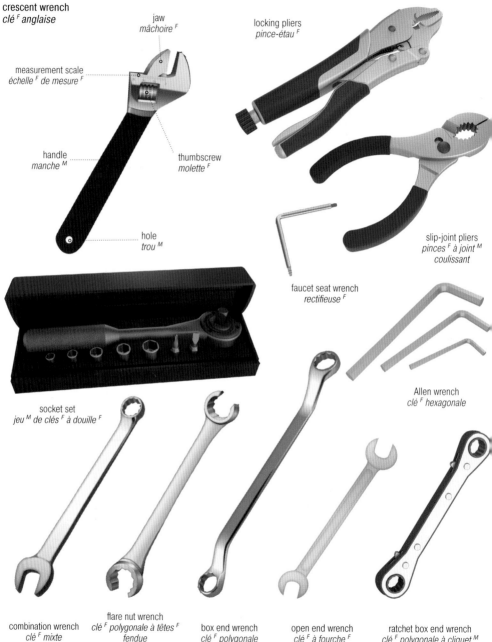

crescent wrench
clé ^F anglaise

jaw
mâchoire ^F

measurement scale
échelle ^F de mesure ^F

handle
manche ^M

thumbscrew
molette ^F

hole
trou ^M

locking pliers
pince-étau ^F

slip-joint pliers
*pinces ^F à joint ^M
coulissant*

faucet seat wrench
rectifieuse ^F

Allen wrench
clé ^F hexagonale

socket set
jeu ^M de clés ^F à douille ^F

combination wrench
clé ^F mixte

flare nut wrench
*clé ^F polygonale à têtes ^F
fendue*

box end wrench
clé ^F polygonale

open end wrench
clé ^F à fourche ^F

ratchet box end wrench
clé ^F polygonale à cliquet ^M

circular saw
scie ^F *circulaire*

motor housing
boîtier ^M *du moteur* ^M

jigsaw
scie ^F *sauteuse*

handle
poignée ^F

handle
poignée ^F

blade guard
protège-lame ^M

blade
lame ^F

power cord
cordon ^M *d'alimentation* ^F

blade
lame ^F

vent
coffre ^M *d'aspiration* ^F

motor housing
boîtier ^M *du moteur* ^M

handle
poignée ^F

blade
lame ^F

hacksaw
scie ^F *à métaux* ^M

frame
monture ^F

bolt
boulon ^M

nut
écrou ^M

wing nut
écrou ^M *à oreilles* ^F

table saw
scie ^F *circulaire à table* ^F

hand saw
scie ^M *égoïne*

backsaw
scie ^F *à dos* ^M

compass saw
scie ^F *à guichet* ^M

Sanding and polishing tools *Outils* ^M *de ponçage* ^M *et de polissage* ^M

orbital sander
ponceuse ^F *orbitale*

power cord
cordon ^M *d'alimentation* ^F

motor housing
boîtier ^M *du moteur* ^M

electric grinder
meuleuse ^F *électrique*

dust collection bag
sac ^M *à poussière* ^F

belt sander
ponceuse ^F *à ruban*

motor housing
boîtier ^M *du moteur* ^M

fastening
fixation ^F

sanding pad
plateau ^M *de ponçage* ^M

power cord
cordon ^M *d'alimentation* ^F

sanding belt
bande de ponçage ^F

dust collection bag
sac ^M *à poussière* ^F

pulley
poulie ^F

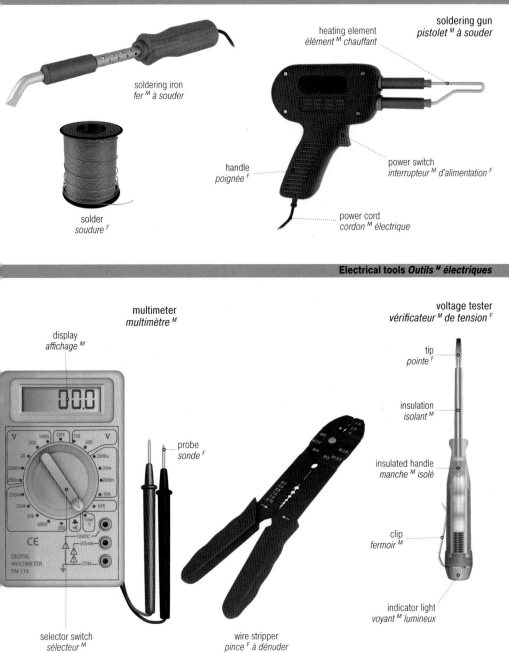

soldering gun
pistolet ^M *à souder*

heating element
élément ^M *chauffant*

soldering iron
fer ^M *à souder*

handle
poignée ^F

power switch
interrupteur ^M *d'alimentation* ^F

solder
soudure ^F

power cord
cordon ^M *électrique*

Electrical tools *Outils* ^M *électriques*

multimeter
multimètre ^M

voltage tester
vérificateur ^M *de tension* ^F

display
affichage ^M

tip
pointe ^F

probe
sonde ^F

insulation
isolant ^M

insulated handle
manche ^M *isolé*

clip
fermoir ^M

selector switch
sélecteur ^M

wire stripper
pince ^F *à dénuder*

indicator light
voyant ^M *lumineux*

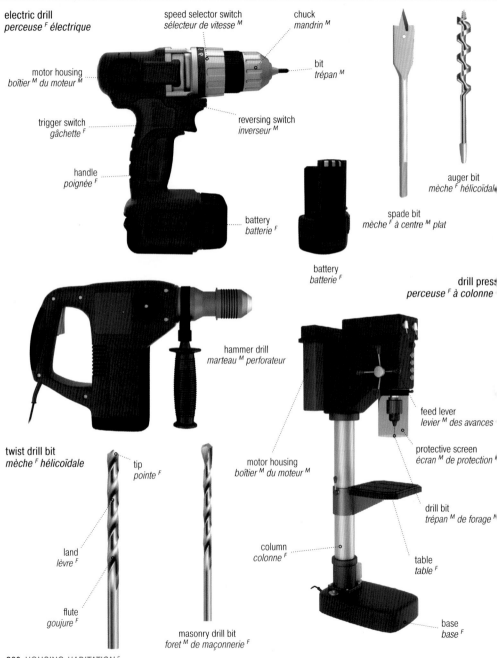

electric drill
perceuse F *électrique*

speed selector switch
sélecteur de vitesse M

chuck
mandrin M

bit
trépan M

motor housing
boîtier M *du moteur* M

trigger switch
gâchette F

reversing switch
inverseur M

handle
poignée F

battery
batterie F

auger bit
mèche F *hélicoïdale*

spade bit
mèche F *à centre* M *plat*

battery
batterie F

drill press
perceuse F *à colonne*

hammer drill
marteau M *perforateur*

feed lever
levier M *des avances*

protective screen
écran M *de protection*

twist drill bit
mèche F *hélicoïdale*

tip
pointe F

motor housing
boîtier M *du moteur* M

drill bit
trépan M *de forage*

land
lèvre F

column
colonne F

table
table F

flute
goujure F

masonry drill bit
foret M *de maçonnerie* F

base
base F

aw hammer
arteau M de charpentier M

claw
panne F

face
frappe F

shaft
manche M

handle
manche M

crowbar
pied-de-biche M

masonry hammer
marteau M à maçonnerie F

mallet
maillet M

nail gun
cloueuse F

nail set
chasse-clou M

electric stapler
agrafeuse F électrique

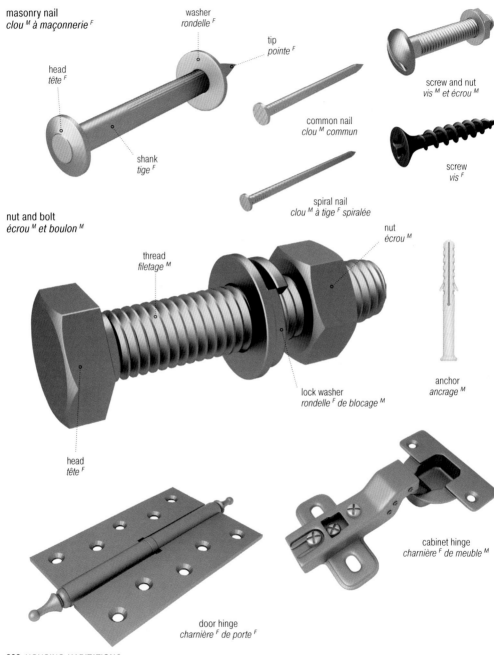

masonry nail
clou [M] *à maçonnerie* [F]

washer
rondelle [F]

tip
pointe [F]

head
tête [F]

shank
tige [F]

common nail
clou [M] *commun*

spiral nail
clou [M] *à tige* [F] *spiralée*

screw and nut
vis [M] *et écrou* [M]

screw
vis [F]

nut and bolt
écrou [M] *et boulon* [M]

nut
écrou [M]

thread
filetage [M]

lock washer
rondelle [F] *de blocage* [M]

anchor
ancrage [M]

head
tête [F]

cabinet hinge
charnière [F] *de meuble* [M]

door hinge
charnière [F] *de porte* [F]

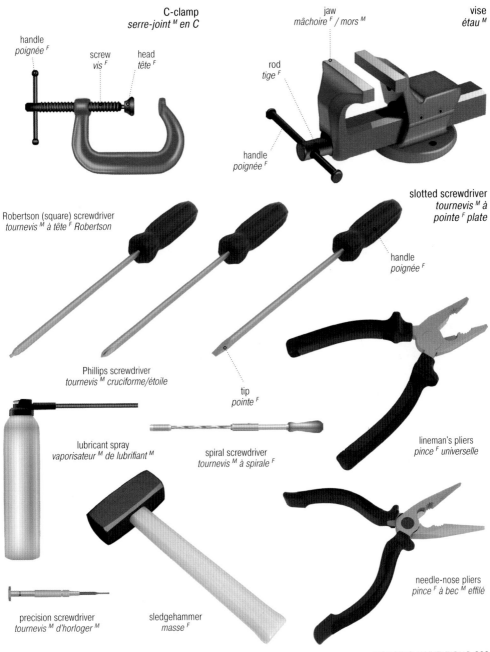

C-clamp
serre-joint ^M *en C*

handle
poignée ^F

screw
vis ^F

head
tête ^F

jaw
mâchoire ^F / *mors* ^M

vise
étau ^M

rod
tige ^F

handle
poignée ^F

slotted screwdriver
tournevis ^M *à pointe* ^F *plate*

Robertson (square) screwdriver
tournevis ^M *à tête* ^F *Robertson*

handle
poignée ^F

Phillips screwdriver
tournevis ^M *cruciforme/étoile*

tip
pointe ^F

lubricant spray
vaporisateur ^M *de lubrifiant* ^M

spiral screwdriver
tournevis ^M *à spirale* ^F

lineman's pliers
pince ^F *universelle*

precision screwdriver
tournevis ^M *d'horloger* ^M

sledgehammer
masse ^F

needle-nose pliers
pince ^F *à bec* ^M *effilé*

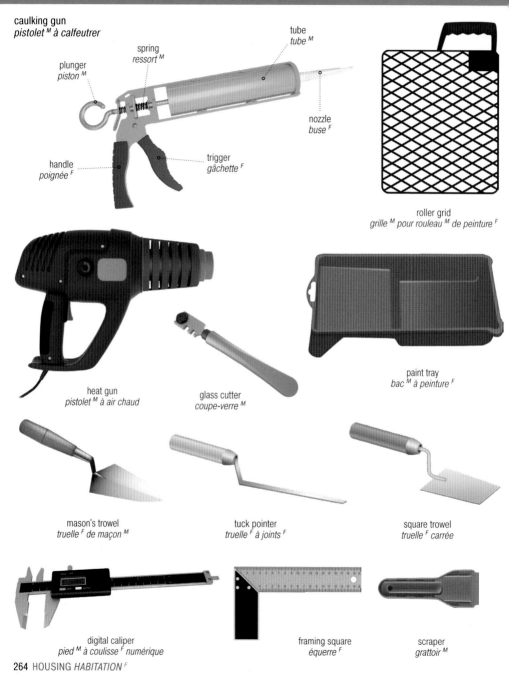

caulking gun
pistolet ᴹ *à calfeutrer*

plunger
piston ᴹ

spring
ressort ᴹ

tube
tube ᴹ

nozzle
buse ᶠ

handle
poignée ᶠ

trigger
gâchette ᶠ

roller grid
grille ᴹ *pour rouleau* ᴹ *de peinture* ᶠ

heat gun
pistolet ᴹ *à air chaud*

glass cutter
coupe-verre ᴹ

paint tray
bac ᴹ *à peinture* ᶠ

mason's trowel
truelle ᶠ *de maçon* ᴹ

tuck pointer
truelle ᶠ *à joints* ᶠ

square trowel
truelle ᶠ *carrée*

digital caliper
pied ᴹ *à coulisse* ᶠ *numérique*

framing square
équerre ᶠ

scraper
grattoir ᴹ

cement mixer
bétonnière ^F

platform stepladder
escabeau ^M

shelf
tablette ^F

leg
montant ^M

leg tip
embout ^M *du montant* ^M

extension ladder
échelle ^F *à coulisse* ^F

step
marche ^F

tape measure
ruban ^M *à mesurer*

spirit level
niveau ^M *à bulle* ^F

paint sprayer
pistolet ^M *à peindre*

paint reservoir
réservoir ^M *de peinture* ^F

bricklayer's hammer
marteau ^M *de briqueteur* ^M

paintbrush
pinceau ^M

paint roller
rouleau ^M *à peindre*

trigger
gâchette ^F

handle
poignée ^F

fluid adjustment screw
vis ^F *de réglage* ^M *du fluide* ^M

roller
rouleau ^M

nozzle
buse ^F

handle
poignée ^F

FOOD

NOURRITURE

bacon
bacon ^M

bologna
bologne ^M

cooked sausage
saucisse ^F *cuite*

foie gras
foie ^M *gras*

breakfast sausage
saucisse ^F

sausage meat
chair ^F *à saucisse* ^F

kielbasa sausage
saucisse ^F *kielbasa*

prosciutto
prosciutto ^M

bratwurst sausage
saucisse ^F *bratwurst*

salami
salami ^M

pâté
pâté ^M

weiner
saucisse ^F *fumée*

Variety meats *Abats* ^M

beef liver
foie ^M *de bœuf* ^M

chicken liver
foie ^M *de poulet* ^M

heart
cœur ^M

kidney
rein ^M

tongue
langue ^F

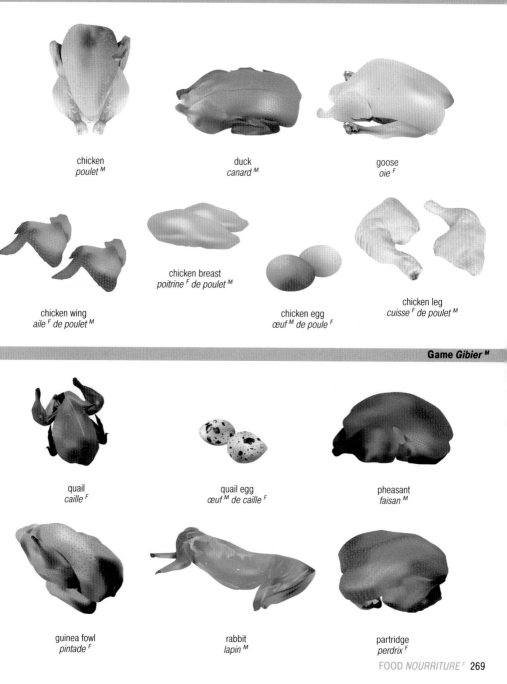

chicken
poulet M

duck
canard M

goose
oie F

chicken breast
poitrine F *de poulet* M

chicken wing
aile F *de poulet* M

chicken egg
œuf M *de poule* F

chicken leg
cuisse F *de poulet* M

Game *Gibier* M

quail
caille F

quail egg
œuf M *de caille* F

pheasant
faisan M

guinea fowl
pintade F

rabbit
lapin M

partridge
perdrix F

Lamb
Agneau ^M

cuts of lamb
coupes ^F *d'agneau* ^M

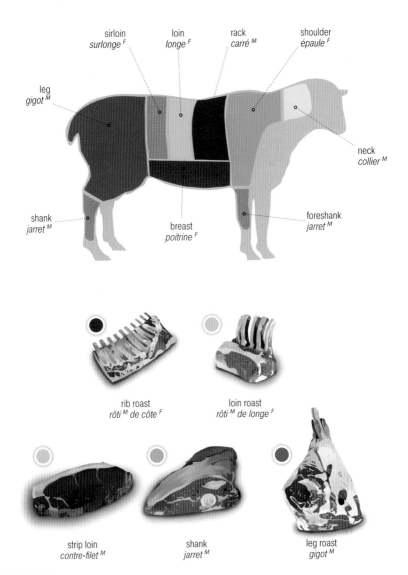

sirloin
surlonge ^F

loin
longe ^F

rack
carré ^M

shoulder
épaule ^F

leg
gigot ^M

neck
collier ^M

shank
jarret ^M

breast
poitrine ^F

foreshank
jarret ^M

rib roast
rôti ^M *de côte* ^F

loin roast
rôti ^M *de longe* ^F

strip loin
contre-filet ^M

shank
jarret ^M

leg roast
gigot ^M

Pork
Porc M

cuts of pork
coupes F *de porc* M

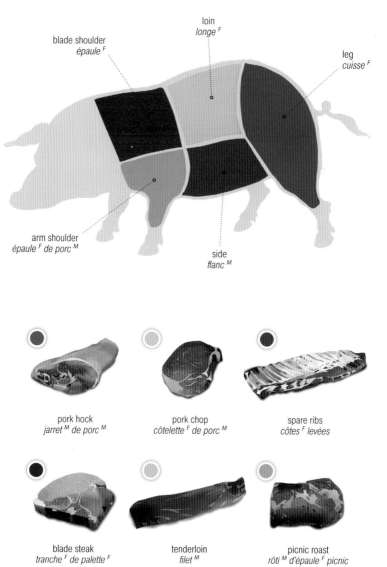

blade shoulder
épaule F

loin
longe F

leg
cuisse F

arm shoulder
épaule F *de porc* M

side
flanc M

pork hock
jarret M *de porc* M

pork chop
côtelette F *de porc* M

spare ribs
côtes F *levées*

blade steak
tranche F *de palette* F

tenderloin
filet M

picnic roast
rôti M *d'épaule* F *picnic*

Beef
Bœuf M

cuts of beef
coupes F de bœuf M

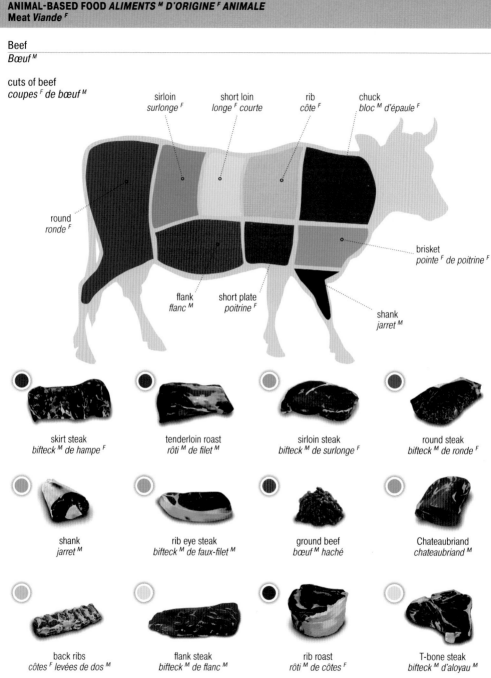

sirloin
surlonge F

short loin
longe F courte

rib
côte F

chuck
bloc M d'épaule F

round
ronde F

brisket
pointe F de poitrine F

flank
flanc M

short plate
poitrine F

shank
jarret M

skirt steak
bifteck M de hampe F

tenderloin roast
rôti M de filet M

sirloin steak
bifteck M de surlonge F

round steak
bifteck M de ronde F

shank
jarret M

rib eye steak
bifteck M de faux-filet M

ground beef
bœuf M haché

Chateaubriand
chateaubriand M

back ribs
côtes F levées de dos M

flank steak
bifteck M de flanc M

rib roast
rôti M de côtes F

T-bone steak
bifteck M d'aloyau M

Veal
Veau ᴹ

cuts of veal
coupes ᶠ *de veau* ᴹ

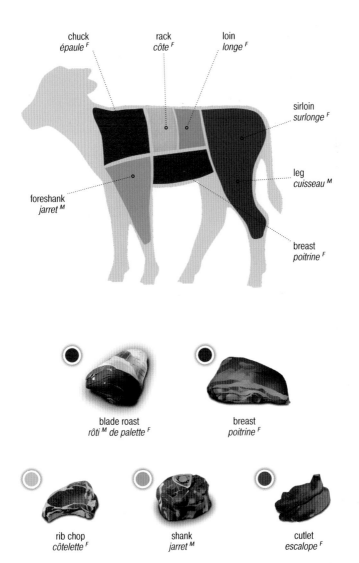

chuck
épaule ᶠ

rack
côte ᶠ

loin
longe ᶠ

sirloin
surlonge ᶠ

leg
cuisseau ᴹ

foreshank
jarret ᴹ

breast
poitrine ᶠ

blade roast
rôti ᴹ *de palette* ᶠ

breast
poitrine ᶠ

rib chop
côtelette ᶠ

shank
jarret ᴹ

cutlet
escalope ᶠ

Milk and cream
Lait **M** *et crème* **F**

kefir
kéfir **M**

cow's milk
lait **M** *de vache* **F**

goat's milk
lait **M** *de chèvre* **F**

lactose-free milk
lait **M** *sans lactose* **M**

evaporated milk
lait **M** *condensé*

sour cream
crème **F** *sure*

whipped cream
crème **F** *fouettée*

yogurt
yogourt **M**

cream cheese
fromage **M** *à la crème* **F**

butter
beurre **M**

buttermilk
babeurre **M**

Cheeses
Fromages **M**

mozzarella
mozzarella **F**

cottage cheese
fromage **M** *cottage*

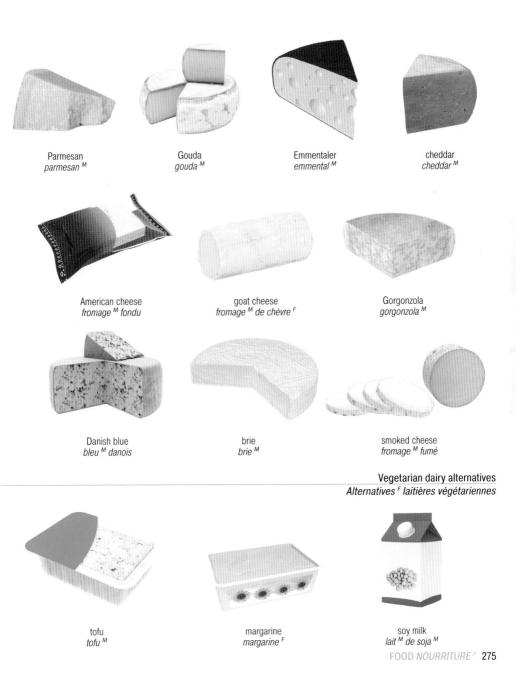

Parmesan
parmesan ^M

Gouda
gouda ^M

Emmentaler
emmental ^M

cheddar
cheddar ^M

American cheese
fromage ^M fondu

goat cheese
fromage ^M de chèvre ^F

Gorgonzola
gorgonzola ^M

Danish blue
bleu ^M danois

brie
brie ^M

smoked cheese
fromage ^M fumé

Vegetarian dairy alternatives
Alternatives ^F laitières végétariennes

tofu
tofu ^M

margarine
margarine ^F

soy milk
lait ^M de soja ^M

salmon roe
œufs ^M *de saumon* ^M

caviar
caviar ^M

mussel
moule ^F

scallop
pétoncle ^M

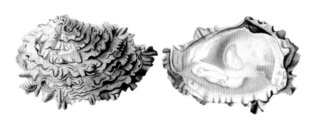

clam
palourde ^F

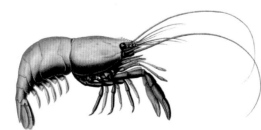

shrimp
crevette ^F

snail
escargot ^M

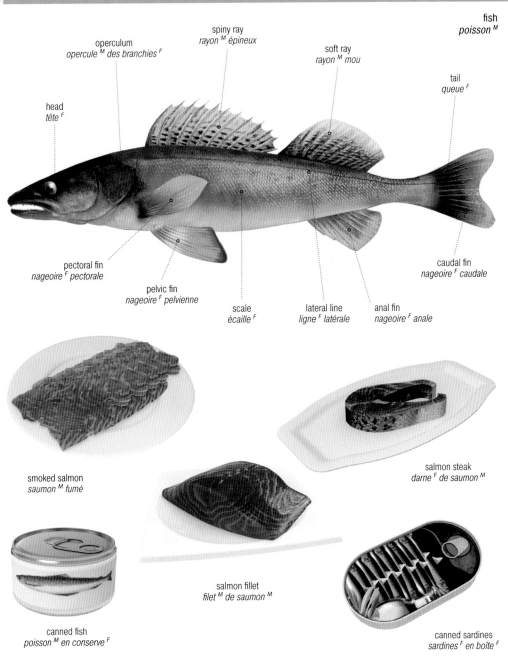

fish
poisson ^M

spiny ray
rayon ^M *épineux*

soft ray
rayon ^M *mou*

operculum
opercule ^M *des branchies* ^F

tail
queue ^F

head
tête ^F

pectoral fin
nageoire ^F *pectorale*

pelvic fin
nageoire ^F *pelvienne*

scale
écaille ^F

lateral line
ligne ^F *latérale*

anal fin
nageoire ^F *anale*

caudal fin
nageoire ^F *caudale*

smoked salmon
saumon ^M *fumé*

salmon steak
darne ^F *de saumon* ^M

canned fish
poisson ^M *en conserve* ^F

salmon fillet
filet ^M *de saumon* ^M

canned sardines
sardines ^F *en boîte* ^F

Leaf vegetables
Légumes ^M *à feuilles* ^F

red cabbage
chou ^M *rouge*

Brussels sprout
chou ^M *de Bruxelles*

white cabbage
chou ^M *blanc*

Belgian endive
endive ^F

corn salad
mâche ^F

curly kale
chou ^M *frisé*

garden sorrel
oseille ^F

Boston lettuce
laitue ^F *Boston*

iceberg lettuce
laitue ^F *iceberg*

Chinese cabbage
chou ^M *chinois*

radicchio
radicchio ^M

arugula
roquette ^F

romaine lettuce
laitue ^F *romaine*

green cabbage
chou ^M *pommé vert*

spinach
épinards ^M

bok choy
bok choy ^M

Bulb vegetables
Légumes ᴹ *à bulbes* ᴹ

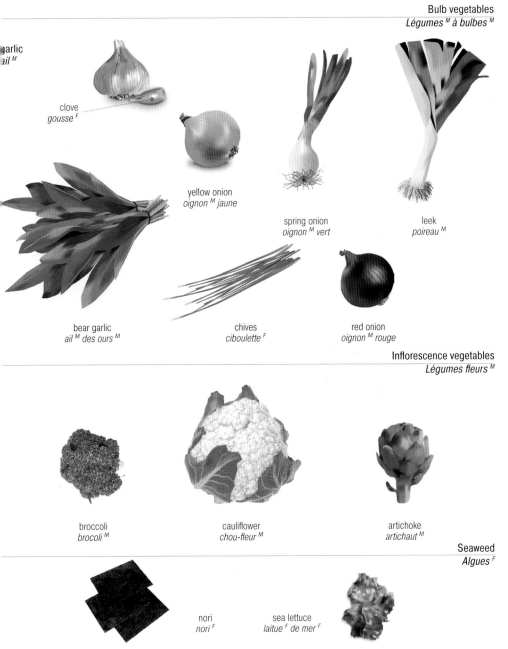

garlic
ail ᴹ

clove
gousse ᶠ

yellow onion
oignon ᴹ jaune

spring onion
oignon ᴹ vert

leek
poireau ᴹ

bear garlic
ail ᴹ des ours ᴹ

chives
ciboulette ᶠ

red onion
oignon ᴹ rouge

Inflorescence vegetables
Légumes fleurs ᴹ

broccoli
brocoli ᴹ

cauliflower
chou-fleur ᴹ

artichoke
artichaut ᴹ

Seaweed
Algues ᶠ

nori
nori ᶠ

sea lettuce
laitue ᶠ de mer ᶠ

Fruit vegetables
Légumes-fruits ^M

olives
olives ^F

black olive
olives ^F *noires*

green olive
olives ^F *vertes*

avocado
avocat ^M

tomatoes on the vine
tomate ^M *en grappe* ^F

vine
vigne ^F

zucchini
zucchini ^M

pattypan squash
pâtisson ^M

okra
gombo ^M

green chili pepper
piment ^M *vert*

tomato
tomate ^F

red chili pepper
piment ^M *de Cayenne*

buttercup squash
courge ^F *Buttercup*

pumpkin
citrouille ^F

yellow pepper
poivron ^M *jaune*

sweet pepper
poivron ^M

acorn squash
courge ^M *poivrée*

red pepper
poivron ^M *rouge*

green pepper
poivron ^M *vert*

eggplant
aubergine ^F

cucumber
concombre ^M

Root vegetables
Légumes-racines ᴹ

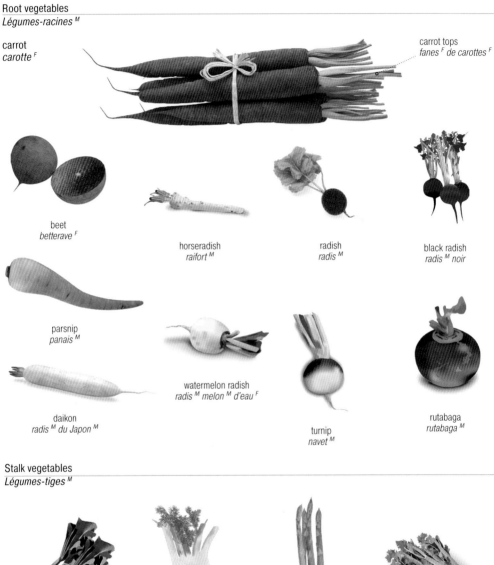

carrot
carotte ᶠ

carrot tops
fanes ᶠ *de carottes* ᶠ

beet
betterave ᶠ

horseradish
raifort ᴹ

radish
radis ᴹ

black radish
radis ᴹ *noir*

parsnip
panais ᴹ

watermelon radish
radis ᴹ *melon* ᴹ *d'eau* ᶠ

turnip
navet ᴹ

rutabaga
rutabaga ᴹ

daikon
radis ᴹ *du Japon* ᴹ

Stalk vegetables
Légumes-tiges ᴹ

rhubarb
rhubarbe ᶠ

fennel
fenouil ᴹ

asparagus
asperge ᶠ

celery
céleri ᴹ

Tuber vegetables
Légumes-tubercules ^M

Jerusalem artichoke
topinambour ^M

kohlrabi
chou-rave ^M

potato
pomme ^F *de terre* ^F

sweet potato
patate ^F *douce*

Legumes
Légumineuses ^F

white kidney bean
haricot ^M *blanc*

black-eyed pea
haricot ^M *à oeil* ^M *noir*

chickpea
pois ^M *chiche*

lentil
lentille ^F

adzuki bean
haricot ^M *adzuki*

red kidney bean
haricot ^M *rouge*

pinto bean
haricot ^M *pinto*

peanut
arachide ^F

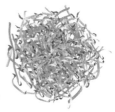

mung bean
haricot ^M *mungo*

green bean
haricot ^M *vert*

pea
pois ^M

bean sprouts
germes ^M *de haricot* ^M

porcini mushroom
cèpes ᴹ

stem
tige ᶠ

cap
chapeau ᴹ

oyster mushroom
pleurote ᴹ en forme ᶠ d'huître ᶠ

enoki mushroom
collybie ᶠ à pied ᴹ velouté

cremini
champignon ᴹ de Paris

button mushroom
champignon ᴹ en bouton ᴹ

chanterelle
chanterelle ᶠ

honey mushroom
armillaire ᶠ couleur ᶠ de miel ᴹ

morel
morille ᶠ

wood ear
oreille-de-Judas ᴹ

truffle
truffe ᶠ

russula
russule ᶠ

saffron milk cap
lactaire ᴹ délicieux

shiitake
shiitake ᴹ

slippery jack
bolet ᴹ jaune

bay bolete
bolet ᴹ *bai*

red aspen bolete
bolet ᴹ *orangé*

birch bolete
bolet ᴹ *rude*

suede bolete
bolet ᴹ *subtomenteux*

Nuts *Noix* ᶠ

walnut
noix ᶠ

shell
coquille ᶠ

almond
amande ᶠ

hazelnut
noisette ᶠ

coconut
noix ᶠ *de coco* ᴹ

pine nut
pignon ᴹ *de pin* ᴹ

Brazil nut
noix ᶠ *du Brésil* ᶠ

cashew
noix ᶠ *de cajou* ᴹ

macadamia nut
noix ᶠ *de macadam* ᴹ

chestnut
châtaigne ᶠ

pistachio
pistache ᶠ

pecan
pacane ᶠ

black mustard
moutarde ^F *noire*

black pepper
poivre ^M *noir*

caraway
carvi ^M

cardamom
cardamome ^F

white pepper
poivre ^M *blanc*

cinnamon
cannelle ^F

bird's eye chili pepper
piment ^M *oiseau* ^M

dried chili
piment ^F *séché*

ginger
gingembre ^M

ground pepper
poivre ^M *moulu*

jalapeño
jalapeño ^M

juniper berry
baie ^F *de genévrier* ^M

nutmeg
noix ^F *de muscade* ^F

paprika
paprika ^M

pink peppercorn
poivre ^M *rose*

poppy seed
graines ^F *de pavot* ^M

clove
clou ^M *de girofle* ^F

saffron
safran ^M

white mustard
moutarde ^F *blanche*

cayenne pepper
piment ^M *de Cayenne* ^F

table salt
sel ^M *de table* ^F

turmeric
curcuma ^M

sea salt
sel ^M *de mer* ^F

curry powder
poudre ^F *de curry* ^M

anise
anis ᴹ

basil
basilic ᴹ

bay leaf
feuille ᶠ de laurier ᴹ

caper
câpres ᶠ

cilantro
coriandre ᴹ

dill
aneth ᴹ

rosemary
romarin ᴹ

fennel
fenouil ᴹ

garden cress
cresson ᴹ alénois

parsley
persil ᴹ

lemongrass
citronnelle ᶠ

mint
menthe ᶠ

mugwort
armoise ᶠ

sage
sauge ᶠ

thyme
thym ᴹ

tarragon
estragon ᴹ

PLANT-BASED FOOD *ALIMENTS ᴹ D'ORIGINE ᶠ VÉGÉTALE*
Herbs *Fines herbes* ᶠ

oregano
origan ᴹ

purple basil
basilic ᴹ *pourpre*

lemon balm
mélisse ᶠ

Tea and coffee *Thé* ᴹ *et café* ᴹ

black tea
thé ᴹ *noir*

herbal tea
tisane ᶠ

green coffee bean
grain ᴹ *de café* ᴹ *vert*

ground coffee
café ᴹ *moulu*

instant coffee
café ᴹ *instantané*

oolong tea
thé ᴹ *oolong*

green tea
thé ᴹ *vert*

white tea
thé ᴹ *blanc*

roasted coffee bean
grains ᴹ *de café* ᴹ *torréfiés*

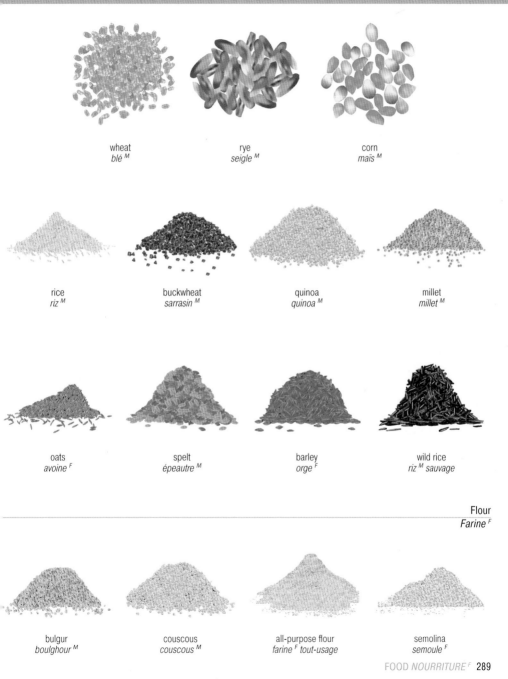

wheat
blé M

rye
seigle M

corn
maïs M

rice
riz M

buckwheat
sarrasin M

quinoa
quinoa M

millet
millet M

oats
avoine F

spelt
épeautre M

barley
orge F

wild rice
riz M *sauvage*

Flour
Farine F

bulgur
boulghour M

couscous
couscous M

all-purpose flour
farine F *tout-usage*

semolina
semoule F

Tropical fruits
Fruits [M] *tropicaux*

banana
banane [F]

flesh
chair [F]

papaya
papaye [F]

flesh
chair [F]

skin
peau [F]

seeds
graines [F]

lychee
litchi [M]

carambola
carambole [F]

cherimoya
chérimole [F]

durian
durian [M]

fig
figue [F]

guava
goyave [F]

Asian pear
pomme-poire [F]

horned melon
melon [M] *à cornes* [F]

pomegranate
grenade F

skin
peau F

membrane
membrane F

aril
graine F

pineapple
ananas M

feijoa
feijoa M

kiwifruit
kiwi M

mango
mangue F

mangosteen
mangoustan M

dragon fruit
pitaya M

persimmon
kaki M

passion fruit
fruit M *de la passion* F

rambutan
ramboutan M

tamarillo
tamarillo M

Citrus fruits
Agrumes ^M

clementine
clémentine ^F

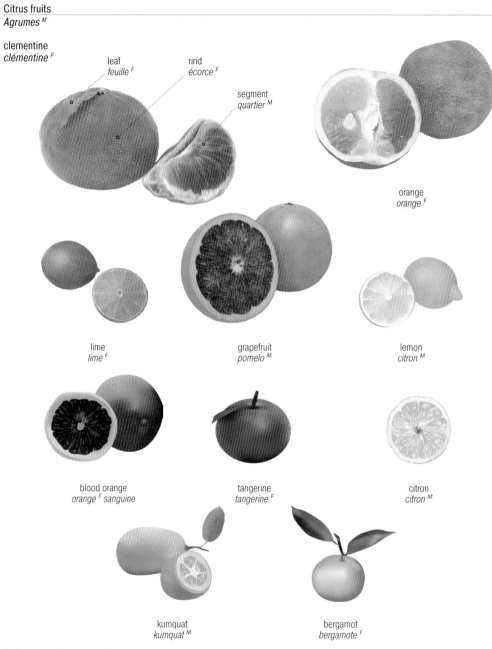

leaf
feuille ^F

rind
écorce ^F

segment
quartier ^M

orange
orange ^F

lime
lime ^F

grapefruit
pomelo ^M

lemon
citron ^M

blood orange
orange ^F *sanguine*

tangerine
tangerine ^F

citron
citron ^M

kumquat
kumquat ^M

bergamot
bergamote ^F

Berries
Baies ^F

cranberry
canneberge ^F

red grape
raisin ^M *rouge*

white grape
raisin ^M *blanc*

red currant
groseille ^F *rouge*

cloudberry
chicouté ^F

strawberry
fraise ^F

gooseberry
groseille ^F *à maquereau* ^M

raspberry
framboise ^F

blackberry
mûre ^F

black currant
cassis ^M

blueberry
bleuet ^M

cape gooseberry
groseille ^F *du Cap* ^M

elderberry
sureau ^M

lingonberry
airelles ^F *rouges*

Melons
Melons ^M

cantaloupe
cantaloup ^M

watermelon
melon ^M *d'eau* ^F

yellow watermelon
melon ^M *à chair* ^F *jaune*

honeydew melon
melon ^M *miel*

canary melon
melon ^M *brésilien*

Pome fruits
Fruits ^M *à pépins* ^M

pear
poire ^F

leaf
feuille ^F

stalk
tige ^F

red apple
pomme ^F *rouge*

seed
pépin ^M

flesh
chair ^F

skin
peau ^F

stamen
étamine ^F

loquat
nèfle ^F *du Japon* ^M

green apple
pomme ^F *verte*

ya pear
poire ^F *Yali*

Stone fruits
Fruits ^M *à noyau* ^M

plum
prune ^F

peach
pêche ^F

nectarine
nectarine ^F

apricot
abricot ^M

black cherry
cerise ^F *noire*

Saturn peach
pêche ^F *plate*

seed
noyau ^M

acerola
cerise ^F *des Antilles* ^F

greengage
reine-claude ^F

cherry
cerise ^F

sour cherry
cerise ^F *acide*

date
datte ^F

aioli
aïoli ^M

barbecue sauce
sauce ^F *barbecue*

salsa
salsa ^F

mustard
moutarde ^F

Italian dressing
vinaigrette ^F *italienne*

ketchup
ketchup ^M

mayonnaise
mayonnaise ^F

French dressing
vinaigrette ^F *française*

harissa
harissa ^F

pesto
pesto ^M

rémoulade
rémoulade ^F

sambal oelek
sambal oelek ^M

tomato paste
purée ^F *de tomates* ^F

tamarind paste
pâte ^F *de tamarin* ^M

wasabi
wasabi ^M

tomato puree
coulis ^M *de tomates* ^F

balsamic vinegar
vinaigre ^M *balsamique*

cider vinegar
vinaigre ^M *de cidre* ^M

chili oil
sauce ^F *piquante*

white wine vinegar
vinaigre ^M *de vin* ^M *blanc*

soy sauce
sauce ^F *de soja* ^M

white vinegar
vinaigre blanc

Oils *Huiles* ^F

sunflower oil
huile ^F *de tournesol* ^M

walnut oil
huile ^F *de noix* ^F

soybean oil
huile ^F *de soja* ^M

sesame oil
huile ^F *de sésame* ^M

corn oil
huile ^F *de maïs* ^M

olive oil
huile ^F *d'olive* ^F

peanut oil
huile ^F *d'arachide* ^F

pumpkin seed oil
huile ^F *de pépins* ^M *de citrouille* ^F

spaghetti
spaghetti M

lasagna
lasagne F

udon
udon M

cannelloni
cannelloni M

ramen
ramen M

tagliatelle
tagliatelle F

rice noodles
nouilles F de riz M

fusilli
fusilli M

penne
penne F

conchiglie
coquille F

rigatoni
rigatoni M

gnocchi
gnocchi M

ravioli
ravioli M

tortellini
tortellini M

farfalle
farfalle F

multi-grain bread
pain ^M *multicéréales*

baguette
baguette ^F

crust
croûte ^F

slice
tranche ^F

sunflower seed
graine ^F *de tournesol* ^M

crumb
mie ^M

white bread
pain ^M *blanc*

toast
rôtie ^F

challah
hallah ^F

bagel
bagel ^M

pretzel
bretzel ^M

stuffed pastry
pâtisserie ^F *farcie*

whole wheat roll
petit pain ^M *de blé* ^M *entier*

coarse rye bread
pain ^M *de seigle* ^M

sourdough bread
pain ^M *au levain* ^M

jelly doughnut
beigne ᴹ *à la gelée* ᶠ

powdered sugar
sucre ᴹ *à glacer*

doughnut
beigne ᴹ

sugar cookie
biscuit ᴹ *au sucre* ᴹ

chocolate cookie
biscuit ᴹ *au chocolat* ᴹ

kifli
kifli ᴹ

Spritzkuchen
Spritzkuchen ᴹ

butter cookie
biscuit ᴹ *au beurre* ᴹ

layer cake
gâteau ᴹ *étagé*

jelly roll
roulé ᴹ *à la gelée* ᶠ

bread roll
petit pain ᴹ

oatmeal cookie
biscuit ᴹ *à l'avoine* ᶠ

vatrushka
vatrouchka ᶠ

croissant
croissant ᴹ

waffle
gaufre ᶠ

rusk
biscotte ᶠ

cheesecake
gâteau ^M *au fromage* ^M

fruit sauce
sauce ^F *aux fruits* ^M

Bundt cake
gâteau ^M *Bundt*

cupcake
petit gâteau ^M

fruit tartlet
tartelette ^F *aux fruits* ^M

cherry tart
clafoutis ^M *aux cerises*

blueberry pie
tarte ^F *aux bleuets* ^M

banana bread
pain ^M *aux bananes* ^F

cake
gâteau ^M

chocolate torte
torte ^F *au chocolat* ^M

ice cream cone
cornet M *de crème* F *glacée*

sundae
coupe F *glacée*

wafer
gaufrette F

chocolate sauce
sauce F *au chocolat* M

ice cream
crème F *glacée*

cone
cornet M

crushed nut
noix F *concassée*

scoop of ice cream
boule F *de crème* F *glacée*

dessert
dessert M

fruit coulis
coulis M *de fruits* M

panna cotta
panna cotta F

sundae glass
coupe F *à crème* F *glacée*

jam
confiture F

jar
pot M

lid
couvercle M

whipped cream
crème F *fouettée*

honey
miel M

jar
pot M

rubber seal
joint M *en caoutchouc* M

candy-coated chocolates
chocolats M *enrobés de bonbons* M

sugar cubes
carrés M *de sucre* M

chocolate truffle
truffe M *au chocolat* M

hard candy
bonbons M *durs*

sugar crystals
cristaux M *de sucre* M

chocolate candy
confiserie F *au chocolat* M

chocolate coating
enrobage M *de chocolat* M

wrapper
emballage M

gummy candy
bonbons M *gommeux*

filling
garniture F

Chocolate
Chocolat M

cocoa
cacao M

aerated chocolate
chocolat M *aéré*

dark chocolate
chocolat M *noir*

milk chocolate
chocolat M *au lait* M

white chocolate
chocolat M *blanc*

hot dog
hot-dog ᴹ

mustard
moutarde ᶠ

hot dog bun
petit pain ᴹ

weiner
saucisse ᶠ

Greek salad
salade ᶠ grecque

chips
croustilles ᶠ

french fries
frites ᶠ

pizza
pizza ᶠ

toppings
garnitures ᶠ

crust
croûte ᶠ

slice of pizza
pointe ᶠ de pizza ᶠ

pizza peel
pelle ᶠ à pizza ᶠ

cola
cola ᴹ

chips and dip
croustilles F et trempette F

salsa
salsa F

sandwich
sandwich M

wrap
roulé M

coffee
café M

popcorn
maïs M soufflé

hamburger
hamburger M

doner kebab / shawarma / gyro
doner kébab M / chawarma M / gyros M

breakfast cereal
céréales ᶠ *pour petit déjeuner* ᴹ

milk
lait ᴹ

rolled oats
flocons ᴹ *d'avoine* ᶠ

blueberry
bleuet ᴹ

soft-boiled egg
œuf ᴹ *à la coque* ᶠ

cream of vegetable soup
crème ᶠ *de légumes* ᴹ

fried egg
œuf ᴹ *poêlé*

appetizer
hors-d'oeuvre ᴹ

olive oil
huile ᶠ *d'olive* ᶠ

bread
pain ᴹ

dipping bowl
pot ᴹ *à tremper*

green olive
olive ᶠ *verte*

black olive
olive ᶠ *noire*

serving board
plateau ᴹ *de service* ᴹ

roast turkey
dinde *F* *rôtie*

breast
poitrine *F*

leg
cuisse *F*

stuffing
farce *F*

tomato soup
soupe *F* *de tomate* *F*

wing
aile *F*

spaghetti and sauce
spaghetti *M* *et sauce* *F*

spaghetti
spagettis *M*

hors d'oeuvre
hors-d'oeuvre *M*

skewer
cure-dents *M*

bocconcini
bocconcini *M*

grated cheese
fromage *M* *râpé*

tomato sauce
sauce *F* *tomate* *F*

whipped cream
crème *F* *fouettée*

pancakes
crêpes *F*

crouton
croûton *M*

basil
basilic *M*

cherry tomato
tomate *F* *cerise* *F*

pancake
crêpes *F*

green tea
thé M *vert*

sushi
sushi M

teapot
théière F

avocado
avocat M

rice
riz M

tea
thé M

tea bowl
bol M *à thé* M

nori
nori M

tobiko (flying fish roe)
tobiko (œufs M *de poisson* M *volant)*

chopsticks
baguettes F *chinoises*

chopstick
baguette F

gari (pickled ginger)
gari M *(gingembre* M *mariné)*

soy sauce
sauce F *soya*

chopstick rest
porte-baguettes M

chopstick
baguette F *chinoise*

chow mein
chow mein M

miso soup
soupe F *de tofu* M

fortune cookie
biscuit M *chinois*

cappuccino
cappuccino M

espresso
espresso M

black tea
thé M *noir*

hot chocolate
chocolat M *chaud*

creamer
crémier M

coffee
café M

milkshake
lait M *frappé*

straw
paille F

fruit
fruit M

beverage with ice and lime
boisson F *avec glace* F *et lime* M

lemonade
limonade *F*

pineapple juice
jus *M* *d'ananas* *M*

orange juice
jus *M* *d'orange* *F*

peach juice
jus *M* *de pêche* *F*

pomegranate juice
jus *M* *de grenade* *F*

apple juice
jus *M* *de pomme* *F*

grape juice
jus *M* *de raisin* *M*

tomato juice
jus *M* *de tomate* *F*

bottled water
eau *F* *embouteillée*

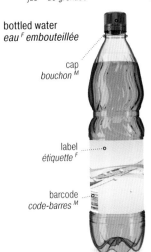

cap
bouchon *M*

label
étiquette *F*

barcode
code-barres *M*

sparkling water
eau *F* *gazeuse*

still mineral water
eau *F* *minérale*

canned pop
canette *F* *de boisson* *F*
gazeuse

wine stopper
bouchon ᴹ *à vin* ᴹ

red wine
vin ᴹ *rouge*

white wine
vin ᴹ *blanc*

champagne
champagne ᴹ

vodka
vodka ᶠ

cognac
cognac ᴹ

whiskey
whisky ᴹ

garnish
garniture ᶠ

cocktail
cocktail ᴹ

beer
bière ᶠ

cocktail glass
verre ᴹ *à cocktail* ᴹ

CLOTHING AND ACCESSORIES

VÊTEMENTS ET ACCESSOIRES

fashion show
défilé ᴹ de mode ᶠ

truss
structure ᶠ

spotlight
projecteur ᴹ

designer
styliste ᴹ

cameraman
caméraman ᴹ

video camera
caméra ᶠ

audience
spectateur ᴹ

sign
panneau ^M

model
mannequin ^M

photographer
photographe ^M

uplight
éclairage ^M *vers le haut* ^M

runway
passerelle ^F

wardrobe
garde-robe ^F

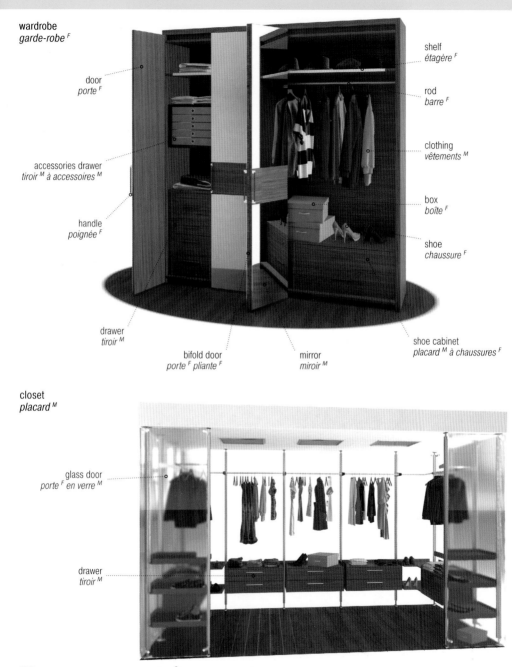

shelf
étagère ^F

door
porte ^F

rod
barre ^F

accessories drawer
tiroir ^M à accessoires ^M

clothing
vêtements ^M

box
boîte ^F

handle
poignée ^F

shoe
chaussure ^F

drawer
tiroir ^M

shoe cabinet
placard ^M à chaussures ^F

bifold door
porte ^F pliante ^F

mirror
miroir ^M

closet
placard ^M

glass door
porte ^F en verre ^M

drawer
tiroir ^M

coat
manteau ^M

collar
col ^M

sleeve
manche ^F

pocket
poche ^F

button
bouton ^M

jacket
veste ^F

trench coat
trench-coat ^M

fleece jacket
veste ^F polaire

sweat suit
survêtement ^M

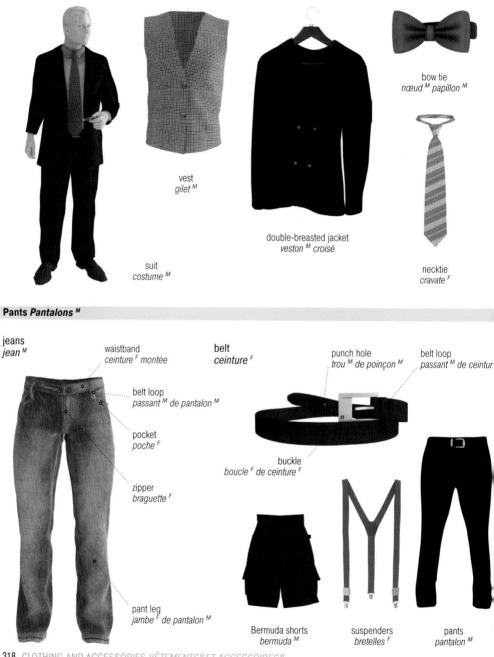

bow tie
nœud M papillon M

vest
gilet M

double-breasted jacket
veston M croisé

suit
costume M

necktie
cravate F

Pants *Pantalons M*

jeans
jean M

waistband
ceinture F montée

belt loop
passant M de pantalon M

pocket
poche F

zipper
braguette F

pant leg
jambe F de pantalon M

belt
ceinture F

punch hole
trou M de poinçon M

belt loop
passant M de ceintur

buckle
boucle F de ceinture F

Bermuda shorts
bermuda M

suspenders
bretelles F

pants
pantalon M

hoodie
chandail ^M *à capuchon* ^M

sweatshirt
chandail ^M *en molleton* ^M

three-button sweater
chandail ^M *à trois boutons* ^M

zip-front cardigan
veste ^F *à fermeture* ^F *éclair frontale*

sweater
chandail ^M

zip hoodie
veste ^F *zippée à capuche* ^F

cardigan
cardigan ^M

dress shirt
chemise ᶠ habillée

collar
col ᴹ

sleeve
manche ᶠ

button
bouton ᴹ

cuff
manchette ᶠ

plaid shirt
chemise ᶠ à carreaux ᴹ

polo shirt
polo ᶠ

V-neck
col ᴹ *en V*

T-shirt
t-shirt ᴹ

short sleeve
manches ᶠ courtes

double-pocket shirt
chemise ᶠ à doubles poches ᶠ

short-sleeved shirt
chemise ᶠ à manches ᶠ courtes

swim briefs
slip *M* *de bain* *M*

square-cut trunks
maillot *M* *boxer*

trunks
maillot *M* *de bain* *M*

boxer shorts
caleçon *M* *boxeur*

briefs
caleçon *M* *pour homme* *M*

ocks
haussettes *F*

ribbed top
bord-côte *F*

leg
jambe *F*

heel
talon *M*

foot
pied *M*

toe
pointe *F*

sole
semelle *F*

long underwear
sous-vêtements *M* *longs*

undershirt
maillot *M* *de corps* *M*

trench coat
trench-coat ^F

collar
col ^M

button
bouton ^M

belt
ceinture ^F

sleeve
manche ^F

parka
parka ^M

biker jacket
veste ^F *de motard* ^M

peacoat
caban ^M

poncho
poncho ^M

fur coat
manteau ^M *de fourrure* ^F

denim jacket
veste F *en denim* M

wool coat
manteau M *en laine* F

double-breasted overcoat
pardessus M *croisé*

sheepskin jacket
veste F *en peau* F *de mouton* M

overcoat
pardessus M

down coat
manteau M *de duvet* M

maternity pants
pantalon ^M *de grossesse*

belt loop
passant ^M *de ceinture* ^F

waistband
ceinture ^F *montée*

pocket
poche ^F

seam
couture ^F

slim-fit pants
pantalon ^M *à coupe* ^F *étroite*

wide-leg pants
pantalon ^M *coupe* ^F *ample*

jeggings
collant-jean ^M

pant leg
jambe ^F *de pantalon* ^M

bell-bottomed jeans
jean ^M *à pattes* ^F *d'éléphant* ^M

slim-fit jeans
jean ^M *à coupe* ^F *étroite*

straight-leg jeans
jean ^M *droit* ^M

shorts
short ^M

aghetti strap dress
be ^F à bretelles ^F fines

sheath dress
robe ^F fourreau ^M

strap
bretelle ^F

draped neckline
décolleté ^M drapé

belt
ceinture ^F

skirt
jupe ^F

halter dress
robe ^F à dos ^M nu

drop-waist dress
robe ^F à taille ^F basse

shirtdress
robe-chemisier ^F

A-line dress
robe F *silhouette* F *trapèze*

sleeve
manche F

jersey dress
robe F *de cocktail* M

strapless gown
robe-bustier F

maxi skirt
jupe F *longue*

jumpsuit
combinaison F

sundress
robe F *d'été* M

cap-sleeve dress
robe F *à manches* F *capes*

V-neck
encolure F *en V*

bodice
corsage M

skirt
jupe F

wedding dress
robe F *de mariée* F

pencil skirt
jupe F *droite*

maxi dress
robe F *longue*

minidress
minirobe F

short-sleeved shirt
chandail M *à manches* F *courtes*

sleeve
manche F

button
bouton M

bolero
boléro M

tunic sweater
chandail tunique M

tank top
débardeur M

ruffled top
chemisier M *à volants* M

spencer
spencer M

peasant blouse
blouse F *paysanne*

blouse
blouse F

blazer
blazer M

batwing-sleeve top
chandail M *à manches* F *chauve-souris* F

pocket
poche F

long cardigan
cardigan M *long*

T-shirt
t-shirt M

polo shirt
polo M

three-quarter sleeve top
haut M *à manches* F *trois-quarts*

short cardigan
cardigan M *court*

sweater vest
gilet M *en tricot* M

elastic-waist top
haut M *avec taille* F *élastique*

cover-up
cache-maillot M

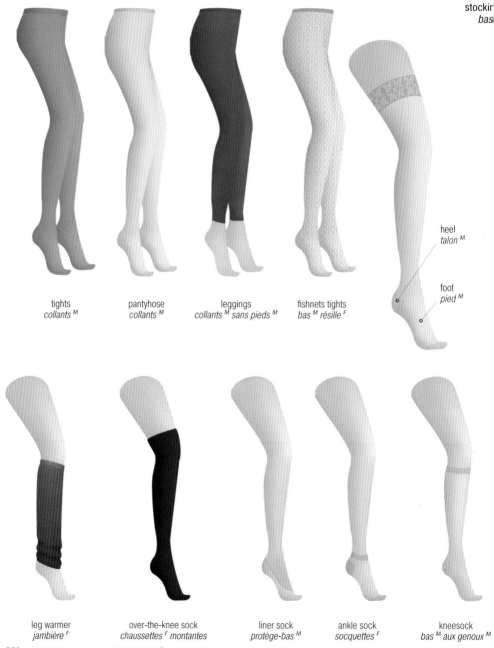

stockir
bas

heel
talon ᴹ

foot
pied ᴹ

tights
collants ᴹ

pantyhose
collants ᴹ

leggings
collants ᴹ *sans pieds* ᴹ

fishnets tights
bas ᴹ *résille* ᶠ

leg warmer
jambière ᶠ

over-the-knee sock
chaussettes ᶠ *montantes*

liner sock
protège-bas ᴹ

ankle sock
socquettes ᶠ

kneesock
bas ᴹ *aux genoux* ᴹ

rselet
mbiné ^M

shoulder strap
bretelle ^F

cup
bonnet ^M

zipper
fermeture ^F *éclair*

dressing gown
robe ^F *de chambre* ^F

camisole and briefs
camisole ^F *et culotte* ^F

baby-doll
nuisette ^F

corset
corset ^M

body shaper
combiné ^M *galbant de correction* ^F

slip
combinaison ^F

push-up bra and panties
soutien-gorge M *pigeonnant et culotte* F

shoulder strap
bretelle F

bra
soutien-gorge M

cup
bonnet M

waistband
ceinture F

panties
culotte F

sweat suit
survêtement M

sports bra
soutien-gorge M *de sport* M

nightgown
chemise F *de nuit* F

teddy
combinaison-culotte F

pajamas
pyjama M

garter belt
porte-jarretelles M

garter
jarretelle F

camisole
camisole F

bra and thong set
ensemble M *de soutien-gorge* M *et string* M

nursing bra
soutien-gorge M *d'allaitement* M

bathrobe
peignoir M *de bain* M

Swimwear *Maillot* M *de bain* M

tankini
tankini M

one-piece swimsuit
maillot M *de bain* M *une pièce* F

sarong
sarong M

bikini
bikini M

diaper bag
sac ᴹ à couches ᶠ

baby sling
écharpe ᶠ porte-bébé ᴹ

cloth baby carrier
porte-bébé ᴹ en toile ᶠ

bib
bavoir ᴹ

nursing pillow
coussin ᴹ d'allaitement ᴹ

hooded towel
serviette ᶠ à capuchon ᴹ

pacifier
sucette ᶠ

pacifier clip
attache-sucette ᶠ

teething ring
anneau ᴹ de dentition ᶠ

baby monitor
moniteur ᴹ pour bébé ᴹ

baby bouncer
exerciseur ᴹ pour bébé ᴹ

harness
harnais ᴹ

backpack baby carrier
sac à dos ᴹ porte-bébé ᴹ

stroller
landau ᴹ / pousette ᶠ

hood
capote ᴹ

handle
poignée ᶠ

wheel
roue ᶠ

lightweight stroller
poussette ᶠ / poussette ᶠ pliante

basket
panier ᴹ

brake
frein ᴹ

play mat
tapis ᴹ de jeu ᴹ

toy
jouet ᴹ

mat
tapis ᴹ

baby bathtub
baignoire ᶠ pour bébés ᴹ

tub
cuve ᶠ

onesie
onesie ᴹ

potty chair
pot ᴹ

toilet seat reducer
siège ᴹ de toilette ᶠ réducteur

disposable diaper
couche ᶠ

fastener
attache ᶠ

tongue
languette F

backstay
contrefort M

dress shoes
chaussures F habillées

quarter
quartier M

sole
semelle F

lace
lacet M

heel
talon M

toe cap
bout M

sneaker
espadrilles F

cross-trainer
chaussures F multisports M

basketball shoe
chaussures F de basketball M

high-top sneaker
espadrilles F hautes

oxford
richelieu M

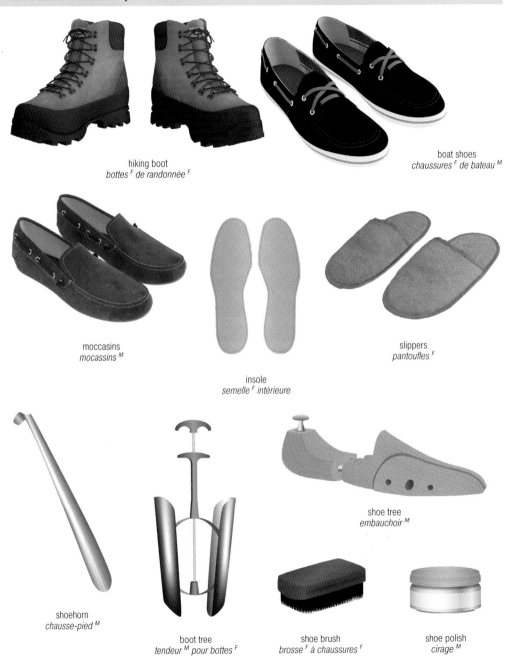

hiking boot
bottes ^F *de randonnée* ^F

boat shoes
chaussures ^F *de bateau* ^M

moccasins
mocassins ^M

insole
semelle ^F *intérieure*

slippers
pantoufles ^F

shoe tree
embauchoir ^M

shoehorn
chausse-pied ^M

boot tree
tendeur ^M *pour bottes* ^F

shoe brush
brosse ^F *à chaussures* ^F

shoe polish
cirage ^M

ankle-strap sandals
sandales [F] *à bride* [F] *de cheville* [F]

platform pumps
escarpins [M] *à semelle* [F] *plate-forme* [F]

heel
talon [M]

platform
semelle [F] *plate-forme*

strap
bride [F]

toe
bout [M]

sole
semelle [F]

ballet flats
chaussons [M] *de ballet* [M]

high-heeled boot
bottes [F] *à talons* [M] *hauts*

high-heeled sandal
sandales [F] *à talons* [M] *hauts*

sandal
sandales [F]

slippers
pantoufles ^F

peep-toe flat
chaussures ^F *plates à bout* ^M *ouvert*

peep-toe ankle boot
bottines ^F *à bout* ^M *ouvert*

biker boots
bottes ^F *de motard* ^M

ankle boots
bottines ^F

wedge boot
bottes ^F *au genou* ^M

peep-toe pump
escarpins ^M *à bout* ^M *ouvert*

pump
escarpins ^M

wedge sandal
sandales ^F *à talon* ^M *compensé*

pom-pom
pompon^M

stocking cap
tuque^F

sun hat
chapeau^M de soleil^M

hatband
ruban^M de chapeau^M

crown
calotte^F

brim
bord^M

straw hat
chapeau^M de paille^F

fedora
chapeau^M mou

cloche
chapeau^M cloche^F

cap
casquette^F

flatcap
casquette^F plate

earflap cap
casquette^F avec cache-oreilles^M

baseball cap
casquette^F de baseball^M

scarf
écharpe^F

gloves
gants^M

fingerless gloves
gants^M sans doigt^M

umbrella
parapluie ^M

ring
coulant ^F

canopy
toile ^M

shank
tige ^F

spreader
rayon ^M

rib
baleine ^F

handle
poignée ^F

garment bag
housse ^F *à vêtements* ^M

backpack
sac ^M *à dos* ^M

telescopic umbrella
parapluie ^M *télescopique*

briefcase
serviette ^F

retractable handle
poignée ^F *rétractable*

suitcase
valise ^F

carry-on bag
sac ^M *de vol* ^M

handle
poignée ^F

pocket
pochette ^F

zipper
fermeture ^F *éclair* ^M

strap
sangle ^F

pocket
pochette ^F

document case
porte-document M

cell-phone case
étui F *pour téléphone* M *cellulaire*

checkbook holder
porte-chéquier M

card case
porte-cartes M

key case
étui M *porte-clés* M

coin purse
porte-monnaie M

underarm portfolio
porte-documents M *plat*

wallet
portefeuille M

clutch
pochette F

writing case
écritoire M

evening bag
sac M *de soirée* F

passport holder
étui M *pour passeport* M

backpack purse
sac M *à dos* M *sac* M *à main* M

shoulder bag
sac M *à bandoulière* F

men's bag
sac M *pour hommes* M

carrier bag
sac M à provisions F

schoolbag
cartable M

sea bag
sac M marin

handbag
polochon M

vanity bag
mallette F de toilette F

drawstring bag
sac M à cordonnet M

laptop bag
sac M pour ordinateur M portatif

tote purse
sac M fourre-tout

attaché case
attaché-case M

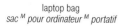

pocket watch
montre ^F *de poche* ^F

analogue watch
montre ^F *à affichage* ^M *analogique*

watchband
bracelet ^M *de montre* ^F

case
boîtier ^M

crown
couronne ^F

hour hand
aiguille ^F *des heures* ^F

face
cadran ^M

ring
anneau ^M

minute hand
grande aiguille ^F

second hand
trotteuse ^F

chain
chaîne ^F

women's watch
montre ^F *pour femme*

digital watch
montre ^F *digitale*

sunglasses
lunettes ^F *de soleil* ^M

nose pad
plaquette ^F

bridge
arête ^F *nasale*

temple
branche ^F

frame
cercle ^M

lens
verre ^M

eyeglasses
lunettes ^F

half-rimmed glasses
lunettes ^F *à demi-monture* ^F

clip-on sunglasses
clip solaire ^M

bifocal lens
lentille ^F *à double foyer* ^M

opera glasses
jumelles ^F *de théâtre* ^M

monocle
monocle ^M

soft contact lenses
lentilles F *de contact* M *souples*

hard contact lenses
lentilles F *de contact* M *dures*

disposable contact lenses
lentilles F *de contact* M *jetables*

lens case
étui M *pour lentilles* F *de contact* M

antique lens case
étui M *antique pour lentilles* F *de contact* M

multipurpose solution
solution F *multiusage*

lubricant eye drops
gouttes F *lubrifiantes pour les yeux* M

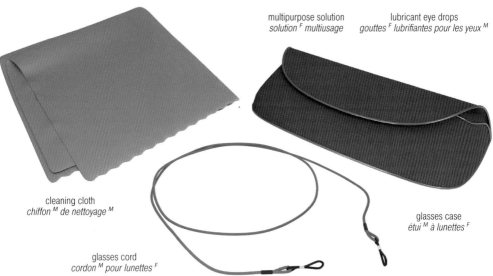

cleaning cloth
chiffon M *de nettoyage* M

glasses case
étui M *à lunettes* F

glasses cord
cordon M *pour lunettes* F

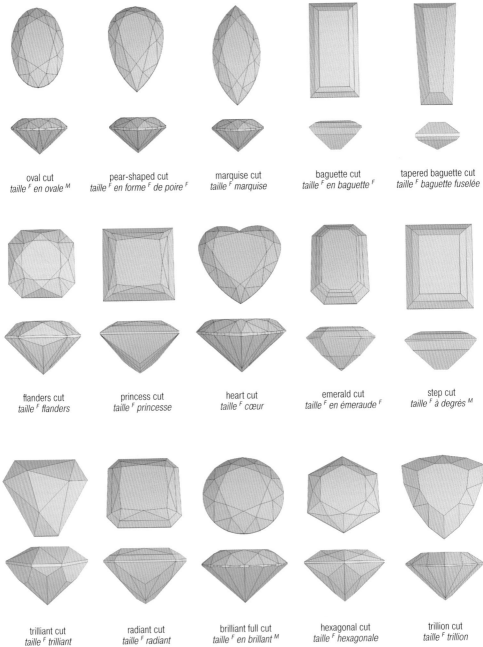

oval cut
taille F *en ovale* M

pear-shaped cut
taille F *en forme* F *de poire* F

marquise cut
taille F *marquise*

baguette cut
taille F *en baguette* F

tapered baguette cut
taille F *baguette fuselée*

flanders cut
taille F *flanders*

princess cut
taille F *princesse*

heart cut
taille F *cœur*

emerald cut
taille F *en émeraude* F

step cut
taille F *à degrés* M

trilliant cut
taille F *trilliant*

radiant cut
taille F *radiant*

brilliant full cut
taille F *en brillant* M

hexagonal cut
taille F *hexagonale*

trillion cut
taille F *trillion*

diamond
diamant ^M

amethyst
améthyste ^F

aquamarine
aigue-marine ^F

tourmaline
tourmaline ^F

blue topaz
topaze ^F bleue

ruby
rubis ^M

emerald
émeraude ^F

garnet
grenat ^M

sapphire
saphir ^M

quartz crystal
cristal ^M de quartz ^M

malachite
malachite ^F

moonstone
pierre ^F de lune ^F

jade
jade ^M

onyx
onyx ^M

opal
opale ^F

ivory
ivoire ^M

lapis lazuli
lapis-lazuli ^M

turquoise
turquoise ^F

tigereye
œil-de-tigre ^M

agate
agate ^F

tiara
tiare [F]

charm bracelet
bracelet [M] *à breloques* [F]

cuff
bracelet-manchette [M]

leather bangle
bracelet [M] *en cuir* [M]

locket
médaillon [M]

rhinestone
pierre [F] *du Rhin* [M]

cameo
camée [M]

choker
ras-du-cou [M]

pearl necklace
collier [M] *de perles* [F]

brooch
broche [F]

filigree pendant
pendentif [M] *filigrane*

pendant
pendentif [M]

navel ring stud
boucle [F] *de nombril* [M]

silver pendant
pendentif [M] *en argent* [M]

jewelry box
boîte [F] *à bijoux* [M]

screw earring
boucle ^F *d'oreille* ^F *à vis* ^F

drop earring
pendant ^M *d'oreilles* ^F

stud
bouton ^M *d'oreilles* ^F

hoop earring
créole ^F

Men's jewelry *Bijoux* ^M *pour hommes* ^M

tie bar
épingle ^F *de cravate* ^F

cuff link
bouton ^M *de manchette* ^F

tiepin
épingle ^F *de cravate* ^F

Rings *Bagues* ^F

band
jonc ^M

class ring
bague ^F *d'étudiant* ^M

engagement ring
bague ^F *de fiançailles* ^F

platinum ring
anneau ^M *en platine* ^M

solitaire ring
solitaire ^M

wedding ring
anneau ^M *de mariage* ^M

signet ring
chevalière ^F

powder blush
fard ^M *à joues* ^F

mirror
miroir ^M

blush
fard ^M *à joues* ^F

makeup brush
pinceau ^M

compact
boîtier ^M

eye shadow
fard ^M *à paupières* ^F

powder puff
houppette ^F

washcloth
débarbouillette ^F

loose eye shadow
fard ^M *à paupières* ^F *en poudre* ^F *libre*

makeup remover pad
tampons ^M *démaquillants*

pressed face powder
poudre ^F *compacte*

face cream
crème ^F *pour le visage* ^M

loose face powder
poudre ^F *libre*

makeup remover
démaquillant ^M

cotton swab
coton-tiges M

eyelash curler
courbe-cils M

brow brush and lash comb
brosse F *pour sourcils* M *et peigne-cils* M

tweezers
pinces F *à épiler*

lip gloss
brillant M *à lèvres* F

eye cream
crème F *pour les yeux* M

concealer
cache-cernes M

lipstick
rouge M *à lèvres* F

lip balm
baume M *pour les lèvres* F

loose powder brush
pinceau M *pour poudre* F *libre*

liquid eye shadow
fard M *à paupières* F *liquide*

liquid eyeliner
eyeliner M *liquide*

mascara
mascara M

lip brush
pinceau M *pour les lèvres* F

eyebrow pencil
crayon M *à sourcils* M

fan brush
pinceau M *en éventail* M

lip liner
crayon M *contour* M *des lèvres* F

liquid foundation
fond M *de teint* M *liquide*

Manicure and pedicure *Manucure* **F** *et pédicure* **F**

nail polish
vernis M *à ongles* M

nail polish remover
dissolvant M *à vernis* M *à ongles* M

cuticle nippers
pince F *pour cuticules* F

nail clippers
coupe-ongles M

safety scissors
ciseaux M *de sureté* F

toenail scissors
ciseaux M *pour ongles* M *des pieds* M

nail scissors
ciseaux M *à ongles* M

cuticle scissors
ciseaux M *pour cuticules* F

manicure set
trousse ^F *à manucure* ^F

nail scissors
ciseaux ^M *pour ongles* ^M

nail file
lime ^F *à ongles* ^M

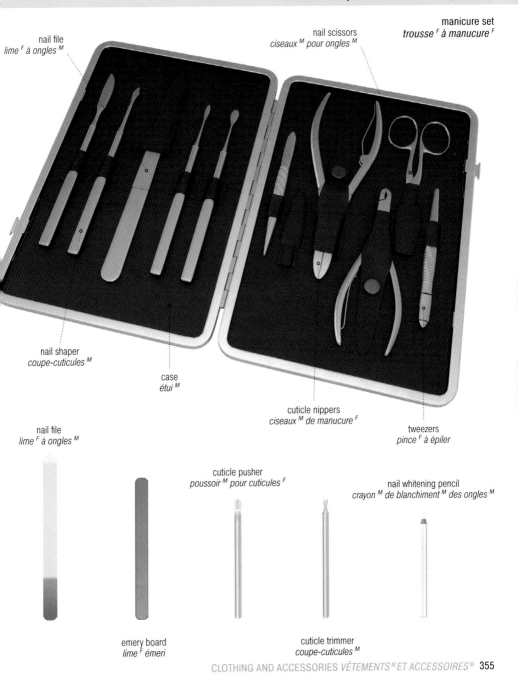

nail shaper
coupe-cuticules ^M

case
étui ^M

cuticle nippers
ciseaux ^M *de manucure* ^F

tweezers
pince ^F *à épiler*

nail file
lime ^F *à ongles* ^M

cuticle pusher
poussoir ^M *pour cuticules* ^F

nail whitening pencil
crayon ^M *de blanchiment* ^M *des ongles* ^M

emery board
lime ^F *émeri*

cuticle trimmer
coupe-cuticules ^M

electric shaver
rasoir *M* *électrique*

head
tête *F*

housing
boîtier *M*

power button
bouton *M* *d'alimentation* *F*

flexible power cord
cordon *M* *d'alimention* *F* *flexible*

shaving cream
crème *F* *à raser*

disposible razor blade
lame *F* *de rasoir* *M* *jetable*

aftershave
lotion *F* *après-rasage* *M*

cleaning brush
brosse *F* *de nettoyage* *M*

disposable razor
rasoir *M* *jetable*

men's razor
rasoir *M* *pour hommes* *M*

hair clippers
tondeuse *F*

head
tête *F*

blade
lame *F*

lubricating strip
bande *F* *hydratante*

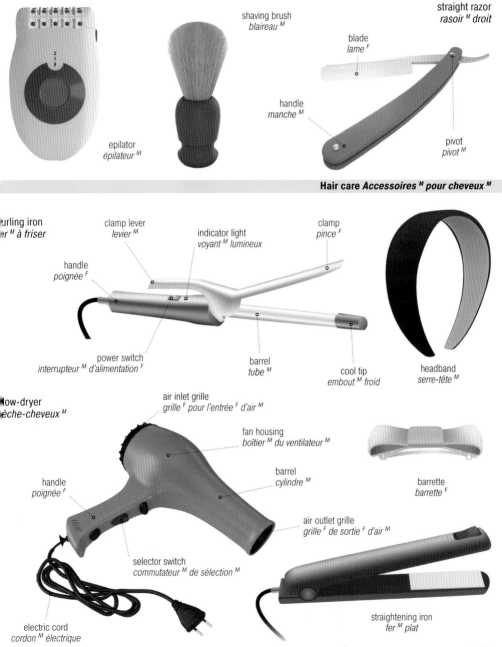

shaving brush
blaireau ^M

straight razor
rasoir ^M *droit*

blade
lame ^F

handle
manche ^M

pivot
pivot ^M

epilator
épilateur ^M

Hair care *Accessoires* ^M *pour cheveux* ^M

curling iron
fer ^M *à friser*

clamp lever
levier ^M

indicator light
voyant ^M *lumineux*

clamp
pince ^F

handle
poignée ^F

power switch
interrupteur ^M *d'alimentation* ^F

barrel
tube ^M

cool tip
embout ^M *froid*

headband
serre-tête ^M

blow-dryer
sèche-cheveux ^M

air inlet grille
grille ^F *pour l'entrée* ^F *d'air* ^M

fan housing
boîtier ^M *du ventilateur* ^M

barrel
cylindre ^M

handle
poignée ^F

selector switch
commutateur ^M *de sélection* ^M

air outlet grille
grille ^F *de sortie* ^F *d'air* ^M

barrette
barrette ^F

straightening iron
fer ^M *plat*

electric cord
cordon ^M *électrique*

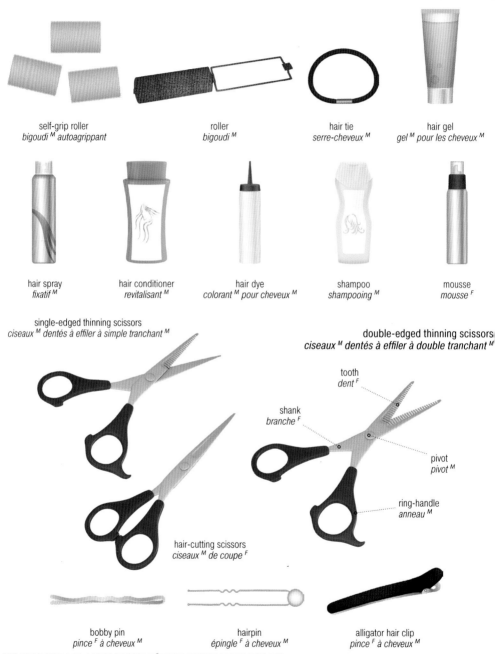

self-grip roller
bigoudi M *autoagrippant*

roller
bigoudi M

hair tie
serre-cheveux M

hair gel
gel M *pour les cheveux* M

hair spray
fixatif M

hair conditioner
revitalisant M

hair dye
colorant M *pour cheveux* M

shampoo
shampooing M

mousse
mousse F

single-edged thinning scissors
ciseaux M *dentés à effiler à simple tranchant* M

double-edged thinning scissors
ciseaux M *dentés à effiler à double tranchant* M

tooth
dent F

shank
branche F

pivot
pivot M

ring-handle
anneau M

hair-cutting scissors
ciseaux M *de coupe* F

bobby pin
pince F *à cheveux* M

hairpin
épingle F *à cheveux* M

alligator hair clip
pince F *à cheveux* M

rake comb
peigne ^M *râteau* ^M

quill brush
brosse ^F *anglaise*

vent brush
brosse-arraignée ^F

round brush
brosse ^F *ronde*

tint brush
pinceau ^M *pour coloration* ^F

wave clip
pince ^F *pour cheveux* ^M

hair pick
peigne ^M *fourchette* ^F

paddle brush
brosse ^F *plate*

tail comb
peigne ^M *à queue* ^F

pitchfork comb
peigne ^M *fourche*

barber comb
peigne ^M *de barbier* ^M

teaser comb
peigne ^M *à crêper*

battery-operated toothbrush
brosse F *à dents* F *électrique*

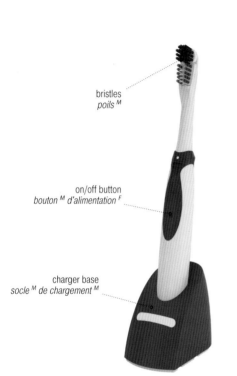

bristles
poils M

on/off button
bouton M *d'alimentation* F

charger base
socle M *de chargement* M

toothbrush
brosse F *à dents* F

gum stimulator
stimulateur M *de gencives* F

dental floss
soie F *dentaire* F

toothpaste
dentifrice M

mouthwash
rince-bouche M

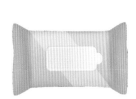

sanitary pad
serviette ᶠ *hygiénique*

tampon
tampon ᴹ

pantyliner
protège-dessous ᴹ

wipe
lingette ᶠ

natural sponge
éponge ᶠ *naturelle*

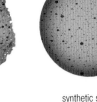

synthetic sponge
éponge ᶠ *synthétique*

toilet paper
papier ᴹ *de toilette* ᶠ

wax strip
bande ᶠ *de cire* ᶠ

soap dish
porte-savon ᴹ

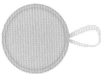

soap
savon ᴹ

loofah
luffa ᴹ

condom
préservatif ᴹ

depilatory cream
crème ᶠ *dépilatoire*

sunscreen
écran ᴹ *solaire*

bronzer
lotion ᶠ *de bronzage* ᴹ

liquid soap
savon ᴹ *liquide*

eau de parfum
eau ^F *de parfum* ^M

bubble bath
bain ^M *moussant*

shower gel
gel ^M *douche*

spray-on deodorant
désodorisant ^M *en aérosol* ^M

eau de toilette
eau ^F *de toilette* ^F

nail brush
brosse ^F *à ongles* ^M

moisturizer
hydratant ^M

solid deodorant
désodorisant ^M

bath bomb
bombe ^F *pour le bain* ^M

toiletry bag
trousse ^F *de toilette* ^F

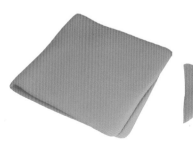

bath sheet
drap ^M *de bain* ^M

exfoliating glove
gant ^M *exfoliant*

bath towel
serviette ^F *de bain* ^M

washing symbols
lavage M

do not wash
ne pas laver

wash in warm water
laver à l'eau F *tiède*

hand wash
laver à la main F

drying symbols
séchage M

tumble dry at any heat
sécher par culbutage M *à toute température* F

tumble dry at low heat
sécher par culbutage M *à basse température* F

tumble dry at medium heat
sécher par culbutage M *à moyenne température* F

do not tumble dry
ne pas sécher par culbutage M

ironing symbols
repassage M

iron at low setting
repasser à basse température F

iron at medium setting
repasser à moyenne température F

iron at high setting
repasser à haute température F

do not iron
ne pas repasser

bleaching symbols
blanchiment M

use any bleach
utiliser tout agent M *de blanchiment* M

use non-chlorine bleach only
utiliser un agent M *de blanchiment* M *non chloré seulement*

do not bleach
ne pas utiliser d'agent M *de blanchiment* M

dry cleaning
nettoyage M *à sec*

dry clean
faire nettoyer à sec

do not dry clean
ne pas faire nettoyer à sec

SOCIETY

SOCIÉTÉ

parents and children
parents ^M et enfants ^M

grandparents and grandchildren
grands-parents ^M et petits-enfants ^M

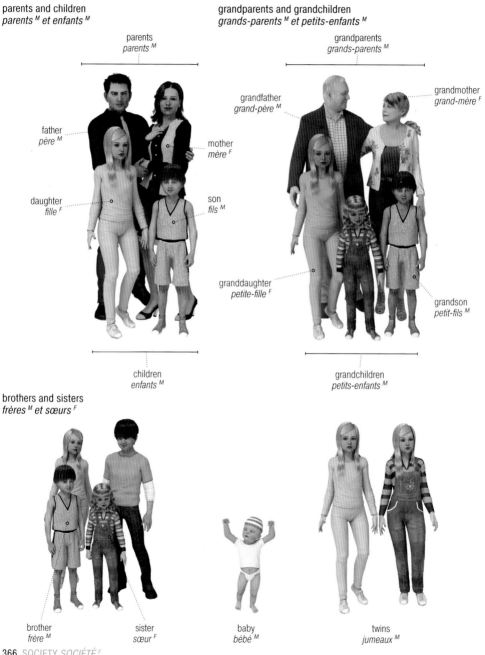

parents
parents ^M

grandparents
grands-parents ^M

father
père ^M

mother
mère ^F

grandfather
grand-père ^M

grandmother
grand-mère ^F

daughter
fille ^F

son
fils ^M

granddaughter
petite-fille ^F

grandson
petit-fils ^M

children
enfants ^M

grandchildren
petits-enfants ^M

brothers and sisters
frères ^M et sœurs ^F

brother
frère ^M

sister
sœur ^F

baby
bébé ^M

twins
jumeaux ^M

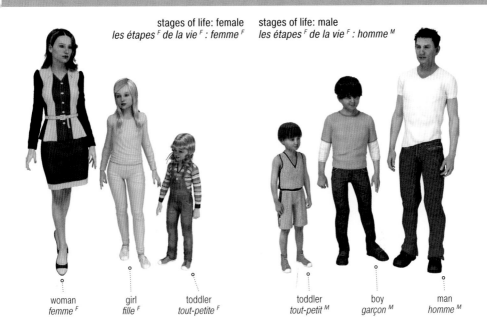

stages of life: female
les étapes F de la vie F : femme F

stages of life: male
les étapes F de la vie F : homme M

woman
femme F

girl
fille F

toddler
tout-petite F

toddler
tout-petit M

boy
garçon M

man
homme M

Body types
Types M de morphologies F

overweight
corpulent

average
moyen

slim
maigre

athletic
athlétique

classroom
salle ^F *de classe* ^F

teacher
professeur ^M

blackboard
tableau ^M *noir*

globe
globe ^M *terrestre*

chair
chaise ^F

teacher's desk
bureau ^M *du professeur* ^M

student
élève ^M

chalk
craie ^F

bulletin board
panneau [M] d'affichage [M]

bookcase
bibliothèque [F]

desk
bureau [M]

lecture hall
amphithéâtre M

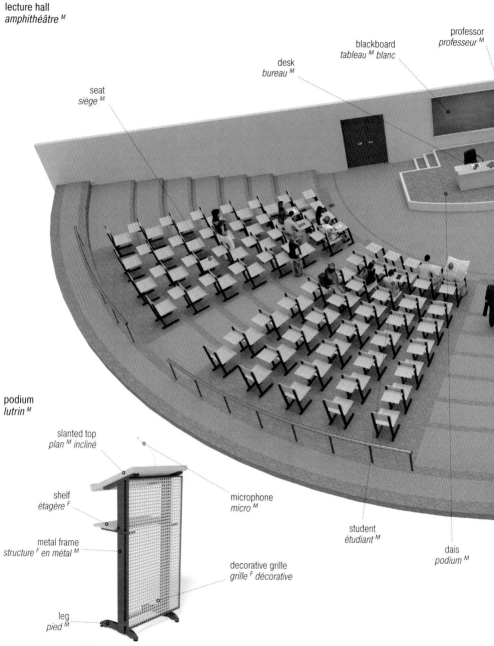

professor
professeur M

blackboard
tableau M *blanc*

desk
bureau M

seat
siège M

podium
lutrin M

slanted top
plan M *incliné*

shelf
étagère F

microphone
micro M

metal frame
structure F *en métal* M

decorative grille
grille F *décorative*

student
étudiant M

dais
podium M

leg
pied M

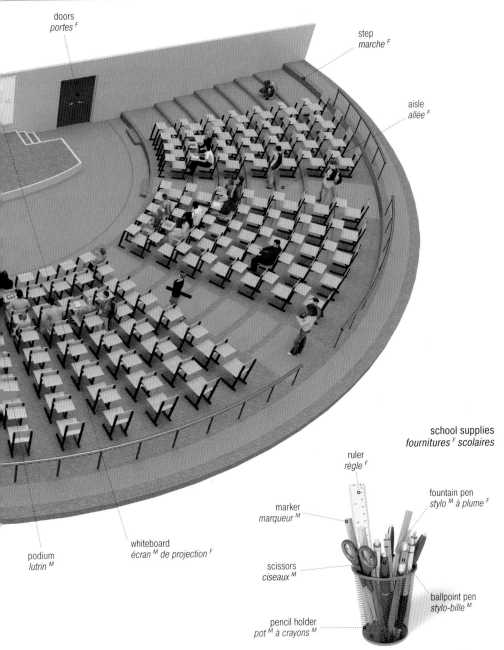

doors
portes F

step
marche F

aisle
allée F

school supplies
fournitures F *scolaires*

ruler
règle F

marker
marqueur M

fountain pen
stylo M *à plume* F

scissors
ciseaux M

ballpoint pen
stylo-bille M

whiteboard
écran M *de projection* F

podium
lutrin M

pencil holder
pot M *à crayons* M

residential neighborhood
quartier ^M résidentiel

high-rise apartment building
tour ^F d'habitation ^F

intersection
intersection ^F

parking lot
parc ^M de stationnement ^M

townhouse
maison ^M de ville ^F

front yard
jardin ^M

low-rise apartment building
*immeuble ^M de faible
hauteur ^F*

house
maison ^F

coffee shop
café ^M

swimming pool
piscine ^F

hotel
hôtel ^M

road
route ^F

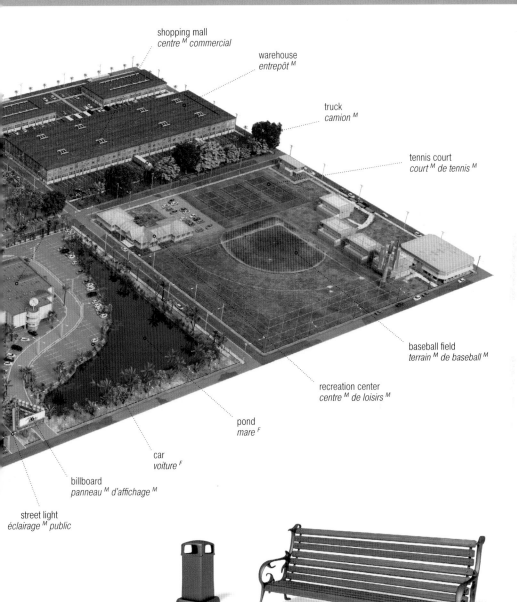

shopping mall
centre M commercial

warehouse
entrepôt M

truck
camion M

tennis court
court M de tennis M

baseball field
terrain M de baseball M

recreation center
centre M de loisirs M

pond
mare F

car
voiture F

billboard
panneau M d'affichage M

street light
éclairage M public

trash can
poubelle F

bench
banc M

downtown
centre-ville M

helipad
héliport M

helicopter
hélicoptère M

crane
grue F

skyscraper
gratte-ciel M

construction site
chantier M *de constuction* F

restaurant
restaurant M

museum
musée M

building
bâtiment M

container
conteneur M

truck
camion M

cement truck
camion M *malaxeur*

satellite dish
antenne F *parabolique*

solar panel
panneau M *solaire*

car
voiture F

road
route F

hospital
hôpital M

supermarket
supermarché M

antenna
antenne F

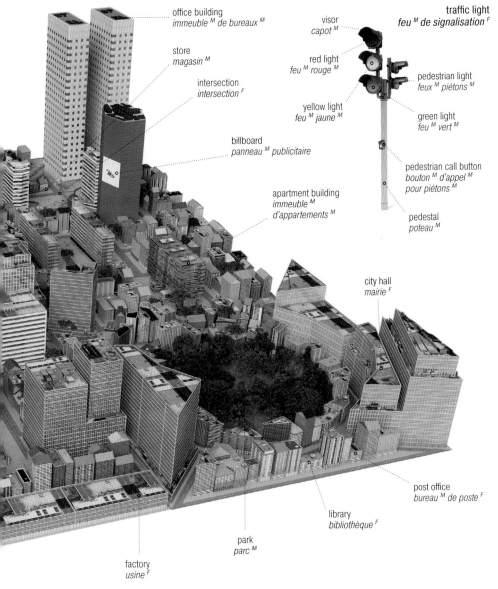

office building
immeuble ^M *de bureaux* ^M

store
magasin ^M

intersection
intersection ^F

billboard
panneau ^M *publicitaire*

apartment building
immeuble ^M
d'appartements ^M

visor
capot ^M

red light
feu ^M *rouge* ^M

yellow light
feu ^M *jaune* ^M

traffic light
feu ^M *de signalisation* ^F

pedestrian light
feux ^M *piétons* ^M

green light
feu ^M *vert* ^M

pedestrian call button
bouton ^M *d'appel* ^M
pour piétons ^M

pedestal
poteau ^M

city hall
mairie ^F

post office
bureau ^M *de poste* ^F

library
bibliothèque ^F

park
parc ^M

factory
usine ^F

penthouse
penthouse ^M

shopping mall
centre ^M *commercial*

sporting goods store
magasin ^M *d'articles* ^M *de sport* ^M

travel agency
agence ^F *de voyage* ^M

cosmetics store
boutique ^F *de produits* ^M *de beauté* ^F

maintenance worker
préposé ^M *à l'entretien* ^M

jewelry store
bijouterie ^F

skylight
lucarne ^F

railing
garde-corps ^M

potted plant
plante ^F *en pot*

bridge
passerelle ^F

clothing store
magasin ^M *de vêtements* ^M

housewares store
magasin ^M *d'articles* ^M
ménagers

vending machine
distributrice ^F *automatique*

security guard
agent ^M *de sécurité* ^F

bench
banc ^M

menswear store
magasin ^M *de vêtements* ^M *pour homme* ^M

department store
grand magasin ^M

trash can
poubelle ^F

customer
cliente ^F

information stand
kiosque ^M *d'information*

electronics store
magasin ^M *d'électronique* ^F

information display
kiosque ^M *d'information* ^F

newsstand
kiosque ^M *à journaux* ^M

toy store
magasin ^M *de jouets* ^M

lighting store
magasin ^M *de luminaires* ^M

coffee shop
café ^M

automated teller machine (ATM)
guichet ^M *automatique bancaire*

bakery
boulangerie ^F

table and chairs
table ^F *et chaises* ^F

baby-changing room
table ^F *à langer*

restroom
toilettes ^F

janitor
concierge ^M

supermarket
supermarché [M]

prepared foo
plats [M] *prépar*

display freezer
rayon [M] *surgelés* [M]

drinks fridge
boissons [F] *réfrigérées*

baked goods
rayon [M] *boulangerie* [F]

frozen foods
produits [M] *congelés*

locker
consigne [F] *automatique*

drinks
boissons [F]

security guard
agent [M] *de sécurité* [M]

conveyor belt
tapis [M] *roulant*

cashier
caissière [F]

chair
chaise [F]

counter
comptoir [M]

basket
panier [M]

customer
cliente [F]

railing
rampe [F]

store entrance/exit
entrée [F]/*sortie* [F]
du magasin [M]

anti-theft sensor
portique [M] *anti-vol*

fruits and vegetables
fruits [M] *et légumes* [M]

shopping cart
chariot [M]

magazine stand
porte-revues [M]

newspaper and magazine rack
présentoir à revues [M] *et à journaux*

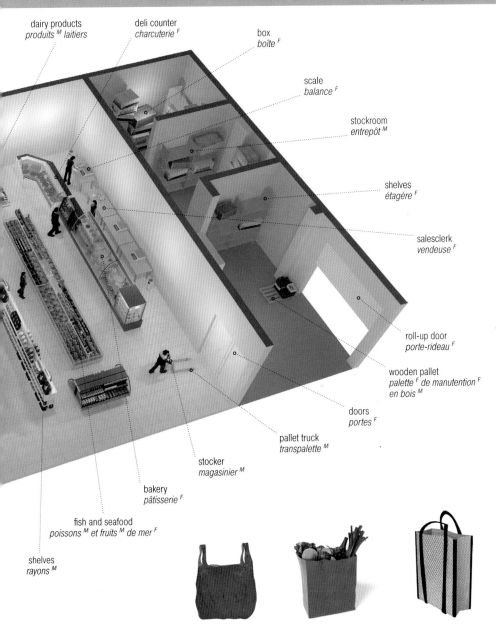

dairy products
produits M laitiers

deli counter
charcuterie F

box
boîte F

scale
balance F

stockroom
entrepôt M

shelves
étagère F

salesclerk
vendeuse F

roll-up door
porte-rideau F

wooden pallet
palette F de manutention F
en bois M

doors
portes F

pallet truck
transpalette M

stocker
magasinier M

bakery
pâtisserie F

fish and seafood
poissons M et fruits M de mer F

shelves
rayons M

plastic bag
sac M plastique

paper grocery bag
sac M de papier M

reusable grocery bag
sac M d'épicerie F réutilisable

coffee house
café M

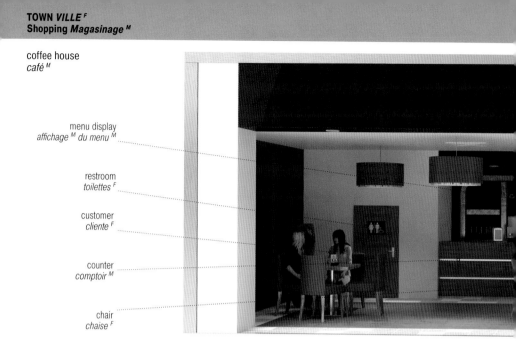

menu display
affichage M *du menu* M

restroom
toilettes F

customer
cliente F

counter
comptoir M

chair
chaise F

bakery
boulangerie F

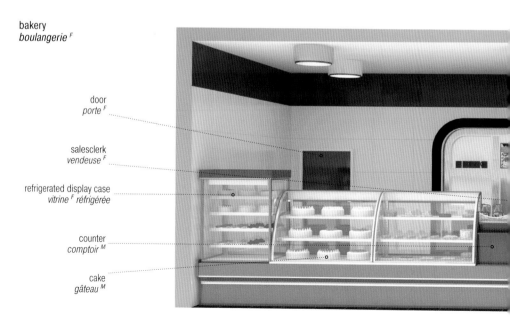

door
porte F

salesclerk
vendeuse F

refrigerated display case
vitrine F *réfrigérée*

counter
comptoir M

cake
gâteau M

storefront sign
enseigne ^F *de vitrine* ^F

exhaust fan
aération ^F

pendant light
suspension ^F

barista
barista ^M

waitress
serveuse ^F

table
table ^F

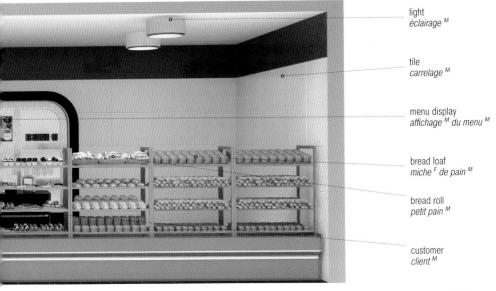

light
éclairage ^M

tile
carrelage ^M

menu display
affichage ^M *du menu* ^M

bread loaf
miche ^F *de pain* ^M

bread roll
petit pain ^M

customer
client ^M

cosmetics store
boutique F *de produits* M
de beauté F

mirror
miroir M

display
étalage M

store manager
directrice F *de magasin* M

computer
ordinateur M

counter
comptoir M

electronics store
magasin M *d'électronique* F

tablet
tablette F

monitor
laveur M *de vitres* F

cellular phone
cellulaire M

counter
comptoir M

light
lumière F

shampoo
shampooing M

sales assistant
assistante F aux ventes F

customer
cliente F

perfume
parfum M

lipstick
rouge M à lèvres F

light
lumière F

display
présentoir M

sales assistant
assistant M aux ventes M

customer
client M

laptop
ordinateur M portatif

clothing store
magasin ^M *de vêtements* ^M

hooks
crochets ^M

curtain
rideau ^M

hangers
cintres ^M

fitting room
cabine ^F *d'essayage* ^M

bench
banc ^M

full-length mirror
miroir ^M *de plain-pied* ^M

display table
table ^F *de présentation* ^F

clothes rod
tringle F à vêtements M

mannequin
mannequin M

shelves
étagères F

checkout computer
caisse F

sales and merchandise area
zone F de vente F et d'exposition F

counter
comptoir M

bar
bar [M]

draft beer taps
robinets [M] *de bière* [F] *pression* [F]

patron
cliente [F]

waitress
serveuse [F]

bar counter
comptoir [M] *du bar* [M]

bar stool
tabouret [M] *de bar* [M]

liquor bottle
bouteille F *d'alcool* M

coffee machine
machine F *à café* M

point-of-sale computer
ordinateur M *de point* M *de vente* F

wine rack
casier M *à vin* M

bartender
barman M

rack of glasses
égouttoir M *pour verres* M

napkin dispenser
distributeur M *de serviettes* F

refrigerator
réfrigérateur M

restaurant
restaurant [M]

prep table
table [F] *de préparation*

chef
chef [M]

kitchen
cuisine [F]

bus cart
desserte [F]

storage room
chambre [F] *d'entreposage* [M]

walk-in cooler
chambre [F] *froide*

grand piano
piano [M] *à queue* [F]

bartender
barman [M]

bar counter
comptoir [M] *du bar* [M]

piano bar
piano-bar [M]

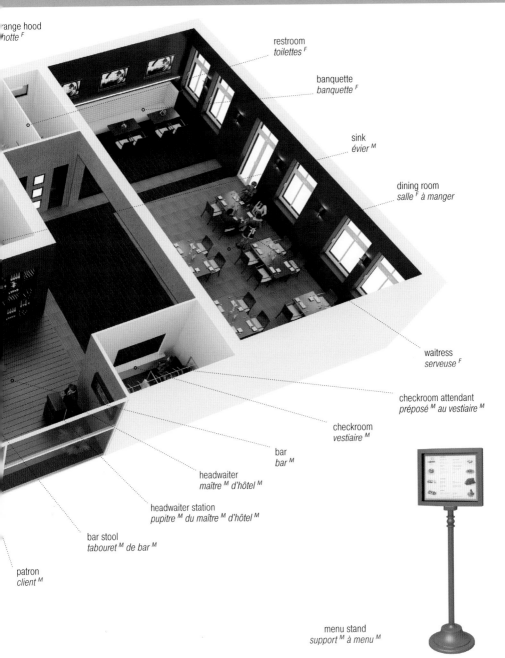

range hood
hotte F

restroom
toilettes F

banquette
banquette F

sink
évier M

dining room
salle F *à manger*

waitress
serveuse F

checkroom attendant
préposé M *au vestiaire* M

checkroom
vestiaire M

bar
bar M

headwaiter
maître M *d'hôtel* M

headwaiter station
pupitre M *du maître* M *d'hôtel* M

bar stool
tabouret M *de bar* M

patron
client M

menu stand
support M *à menu* M

fast-food restaurant
restaurant M *rapide*

cash register
caisse M *enregistreuse*

beverage dispenser
distributrice F *de boissons* F

menu board
panneau M *d'affichage* M *du menu* M

salt and pepper shakers
salière F *et poivrière* F

counter
comptoir M

napkin dispenser
distributeur M *de serviettes*

waitress
serveuse F

glasses
verres M

light
luminaire ^M

table
table ^F

patron
client ^M

window
fenêtre ^F

chair
chaise ^F

squeeze bottle
flacon ^M *pressable*

napkin holder
support ^M *pour serviettes* ^F

banquette
banquette ^F

reception
réception F

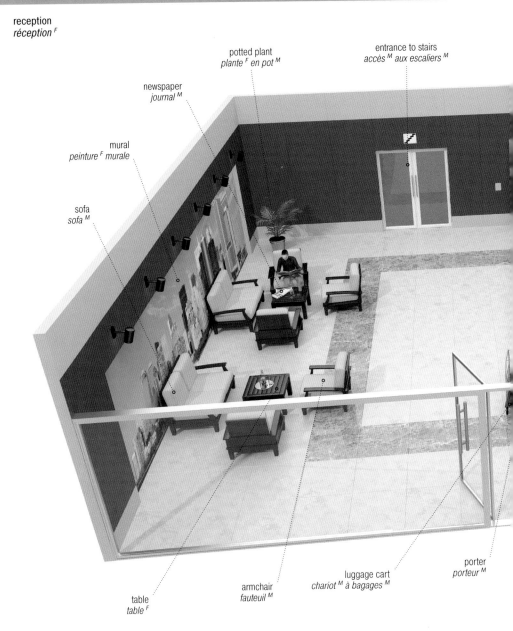

potted plant
plante F *en pot* M

entrance to stairs
accès M *aux escaliers* M

newspaper
journal M

mural
peinture F *murale*

sofa
sofa M

porter
porteur M

luggage cart
chariot M *à bagages* M

armchair
fauteuil M

table
table F

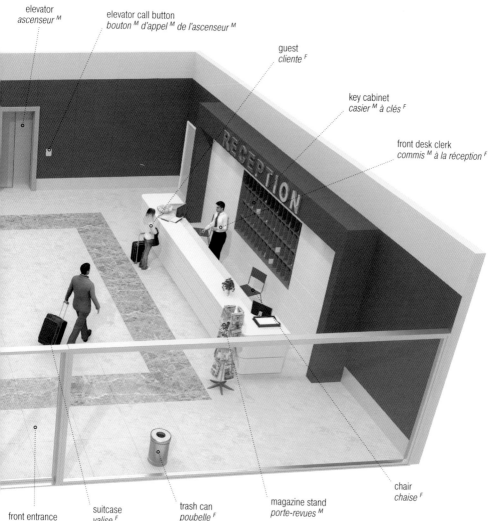

elevator
ascenseur M

elevator call button
bouton M *d'appel* M *de l'ascenseur* M

guest
cliente F

key cabinet
casier M *à clés* F

front desk clerk
commis M *à la réception* F

RECEPTION

chair
chaise F

front entrance
entrée F *principale*

suitcase
valise F

trash can
poubelle F

magazine stand
porte-revues M

hotel room
chambre F d'hôtel M

ventilation fan
aération F

toilet paper
papier M toilette F

toilet
toilette F

flush buttons
bouton M de chasse F

toilet brush
brosse F de toilettes F

bathtub
baignoire F

trash can
poubelle F

towel
serviette F

mirror
miroir M

sink
évier M

bath mat
tapis M de bain M

front door
porte F d'entrée F

tiled floor
carrelage M

coat hook
patère F

shelf
étagère F

shower enclosure
cabine F de douche F

closet
placard M

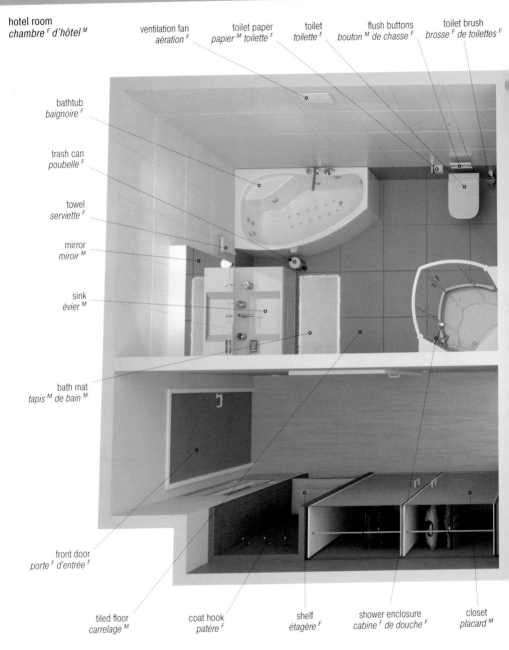

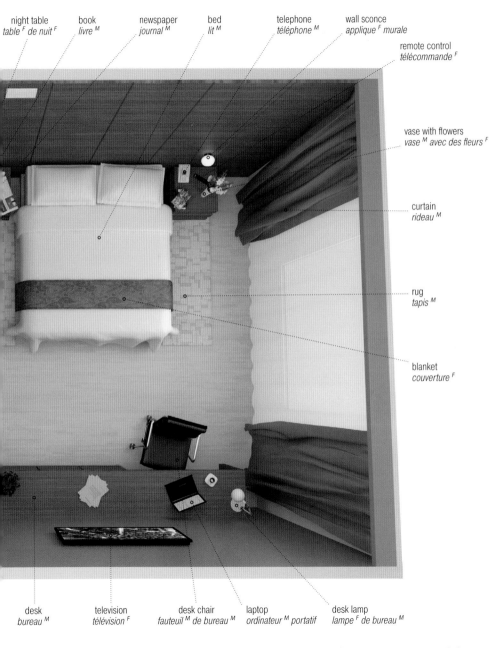

night table
table F *de nuit* F

book
livre M

newspaper
journal M

bed
lit M

telephone
téléphone M

wall sconce
applique F *murale*

remote control
télécommande F

vase with flowers
vase M *avec des fleurs* F

curtain
rideau M

rug
tapis M

blanket
couverture F

desk
bureau M

television
télévision F

desk chair
fauteuil M *de bureau* M

laptop
ordinateur M *portatif*

desk lamp
lampe F *de bureau* M

auditorium
auditorium ^M

projector screen
écran ^M *de projection* ^F

head table
table ^F *d'honneur* ^M

podium
lutrin ^M

microphone
micro ^M

gooseneck
micro ^M *directionnel*

grille
grille ^F

dais
estrade ^F

indicator light
lampe ^F *témoin*

power switch
commutateur ^M

control button
bouton ^M *de commande* ^F

base
base ^F

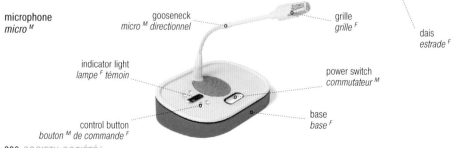

microphone
micro M

video camera
caméra F *vidéo* F

simultaneous interpretation booth
cabine F *de traduction* F *simultanée*

soundproof window
fenêtre F *insonorisée*

conference table
table F *de conférence* F

desk chair
chaise F *de bureau* M

door
porte F

floor
sol M

Police department
Service ^M _de police_ ^F

police officer
agent ^M _de police_ ^F

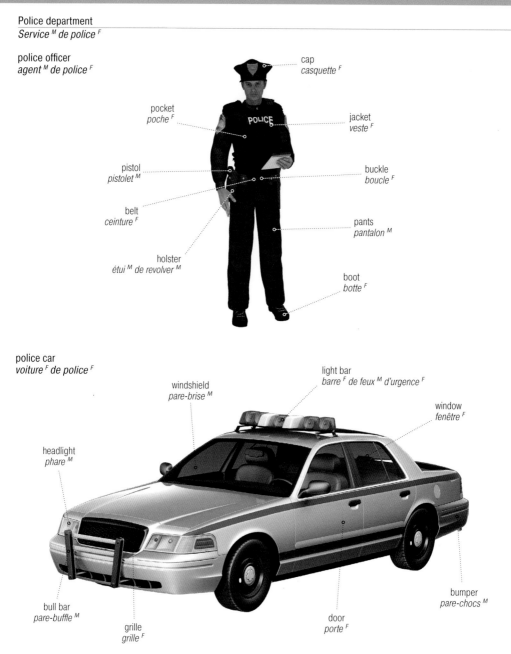

cap
casquette ^F

pocket
poche ^F

jacket
veste ^F

pistol
pistolet ^M

buckle
boucle ^F

belt
ceinture ^F

pants
pantalon ^M

holster
étui ^M _de revolver_ ^M

boot
botte ^F

police car
voiture ^F _de police_ ^F

light bar
barre ^F _de feux_ ^M _d'urgence_ ^F

windshield
pare-brise ^M

window
fenêtre ^F

headlight
phare ^M

bull bar
pare-buffle ^M

grille
grille ^F

door
porte ^F

bumper
pare-chocs ^M

rotor hub
moyeu [M] de rotor [M]

police helicopter
hélicoptère [M] de police [F]

rotor blade
pale [F] de rotor [M]

anti-torque tail rotor
rotor [M] anticouple

fuselage
fuselage [M]

horizontal stabilizer
stabilisateur [M] horizontal

searchlight
projecteur [M]

door
porte [F]

tail boom
poutre [M] de queue [F]

skid
patin [M]

police motorcycle
moto [F] de police [F]

mirror
miroir [M]

windshield
pare-brise [M]

beacon
gyrophare [M]

handlebars
guidon [M]

seat
siège [M]

fender
garde-boue [M]

crash bar
arceau [M] de sécurité [F]

footrest
repose-pied [M]

tire
pneu [M]

Fire department
Service[M] *d'incendie*[M]

firefighter
pompier[M]

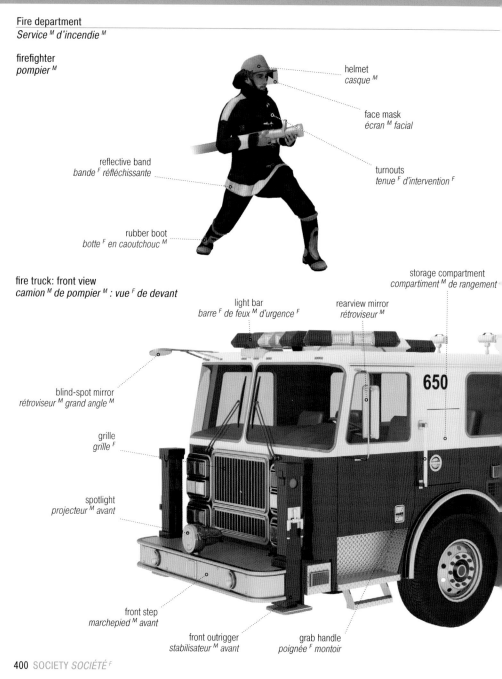

helmet
casque[M]

face mask
écran[M] *facial*

reflective band
bande[F] *réfléchissante*

turnouts
tenue[F] *d'intervention*[F]

rubber boot
botte[F] *en caoutchouc*[M]

storage compartment
compartiment[M] *de rangement*

fire truck: front view
camion[M] *de pompier*[M] : *vue*[F] *de devant*

light bar
barre[F] *de feux*[M] *d'urgence*[F]

rearview mirror
rétroviseur[M]

blind-spot mirror
rétroviseur[M] *grand angle*[M]

650

grille
grille[F]

spotlight
projecteur[M] *avant*

front step
marchepied[M] *avant*

front outrigger
stabilisateur[M] *avant*

grab handle
poignée[F] *montoir*

fire truck: back view
camion ^M *de pompier* ^M : *vue* ^F *de derrière*

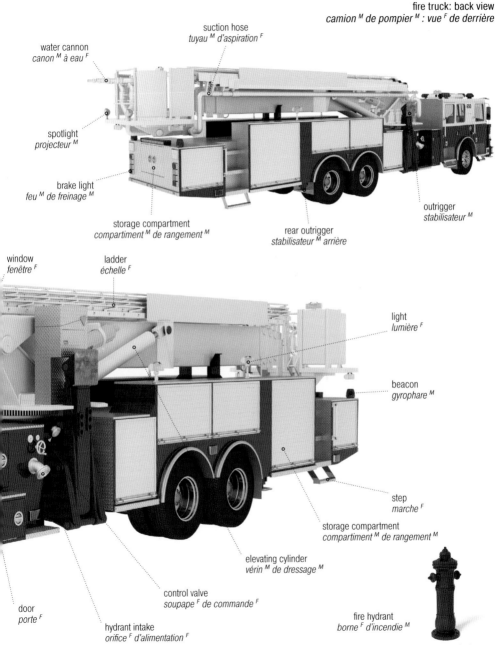

water cannon
canon ^M *à eau* ^F

suction hose
tuyau ^M *d'aspiration* ^F

spotlight
projecteur ^M

brake light
feu ^M *de freinage* ^M

storage compartment
compartiment ^M *de rangement* ^M

rear outrigger
stabilisateur ^M *arrière*

outrigger
stabilisateur ^M

window
fenêtre ^F

ladder
échelle ^F

light
lumière ^F

beacon
gyrophare ^M

step
marche ^F

storage compartment
compartiment ^M *de rangement* ^M

elevating cylinder
vérin ^M *de dressage* ^M

control valve
soupape ^F *de commande* ^F

door
porte ^F

hydrant intake
orifice ^F *d'alimentation* ^F

fire hydrant
borne ^F *d'incendie* ^M

Information signs
Panneaux ᴹ d'information ᶠ

telephone
téléphone ᴹ

post office
bureau ᴹ de poste ᴹ

currency exchange
bureau ᴹ de change ᴹ

first aid
premiers soins ᴹ

lost and found
objets ᴹ trouvés

checkroom
vestiaire ᴹ

baggage lockers
consigne ᶠ à bagages ᴹ

down escalator
escalier ᴹ mécanique descendant

up escalator
escalier ᴹ mécanique ascendant

stairs
escaliers ᴹ

elevator
ascenseur ᴹ

men's restroom
toilettes ᶠ pour hommes ᴹ

women's restroom
toilettes ᶠ pour femmes ᶠ

restroom
toilettes ᶠ

baby changing area
table ᶠ à langer

waiting room
salle ᶠ d'attente ᶠ

information
information [F]

lodging
hôtel [M]

airport
aéroport [M]

litter barrel
poubelle [F]

taxi stand
station [F] *de taxi* [M]

bus stop
arrêt [M] *d'autobus* [M]

ground transportation
transport [M] *terrestre*

train station
gare [F] *ferroviaire*

ferry terminal
gare [F] *maritime*

car rental
location [F] *de voiture* [F]

restaurant
restaurant [M]

coffee shop
café [M]

bar
bar [M]

baggage claim
bagages [M]

parking
stationnement [M]

smoking area
zone [F] *fumeur* [M]

wheelchair access
*accès ^M pour fauteuils ^M
roulants*

tent camping
camping ^M sous la tente ^F

trailer camping
campement ^M de remorques ^F

hospital
hôpital ^M

picnic area
aire ^F de pique-nique ^M

fire extinguisher
extincteur ^M

service station
station-service ^F

Wi-Fi zone
zone ^F Wi-Fi ^M

campfire area
zone ^F de feux ^M de camp ^M

automatic teller machine (ATM)
guichet ^M automatique bancaire

dog-walking area
aire ^F d'exercice ^M pour chiens ^M

swimming area
baignade ^F

drinking water
eau ^F potable

video surveillance
vidéosurveillance ^F

hiking trail
sentier ^M de randonnée ^F pédestre

auto mechanic
mécanicien ^M

Hazard signs
Panneaux [M] *indicateurs de danger* [M]

corrosive to skin and metals
corrosif pour la peau [F]
et les métaux [M]

gases under pressure
gaz [M] *sous pression* [F]

flammable materials, self-reactives,
organic peroxides
matières [F] *inflammables, matières* [F]
autoréactives, peroxydes [M] *organiques*

explosives, self-reactives
explosifs, [M] *autoréactifs* [M]

aquatic toxicity
toxicité [F] *aquatique*

oxidizers
agents [M] *oxydants*

health hazard
danger [M] *pour la santé* [F]

acute toxicity
toxicité [F] *aiguë*

Workplace safety signs
Panneaux [M] *de sécurité* [F] *au travail* [M]

eye protection
protection [F] *des yeux* [M]

respiratory system protection
protection [F] *respiratoire*

foot protection
protection [F] *des pieds* [M]

hand protection
protection [F] *des mains* [F]

head protection
protection [F] *de la tête* [F]

protective clothing
vêtements [M] *de protection* [F]

face shield
écran [M] *facial*

ear protection
protection [F] *auditive*

Warning signs
Panneaux ᴹ d'avertissement ᴹ

poison
poison

radioactive
radioactif

irritant
irritant

flammable
inflammable

magnetic field
champ ᴹ magnétique

high voltage
haute tension ᶠ

slippery
glissant

corrosive to skin and metals
*corrosif pour la peau ᶠ
et les métaux ᴹ*

Prohibition signs
Panneaux ᴹ d'interdiction ᶠ

not drinking water
eau ᶠ non potable

cell phone use prohibited
cellulaire ᴹ interdit

no open flame
flamme ᶠ nue interdite

photography prohibited
*interdiction ᶠ de
prendre des photos ᶠ*

no smoking
interdiction ᶠ de fumer

pets prohibited
animaux ᴹ interdits

no access
accès ᴹ interdit

stop
arrêt ᴹ

Emergency signs
Panneaux ᴹ d'urgence

first aid
premiers soins ᴹ

emergency telephone
téléphone ᴹ d'urgence

assembly point
point ᴹ de rassemblement ᴹ

automated external defibrillator
(AED)
défibrillateur ᴹ externe automatique

eye wash station
bassin ᴹ oculaire

doctor
médecin ᴹ

in case of emergency break glass
briser la vitre ᶠ en cas ᴹ d'urgence ᶠ

emergency exit
sortie ᶠ de secours ᴹ

Fire safety signs
Panneaux ᴹ de sécurité ᶠ incendie ᴹ

fire hose
tuyau ᴹ d'incendie ᴹ

ladder
échelle ᶠ

fire extinguisher
extincteur ᴹ

fire alarm
alarme ᶠ incendie ᴹ

fire-fighting equipment
matériel ᴹ d'incendie ᴹ

emergency phone
téléphone ᴹ d'urgence

directional arrow
flèche ᶠ de direction ᶠ

Asia
Asie *F*

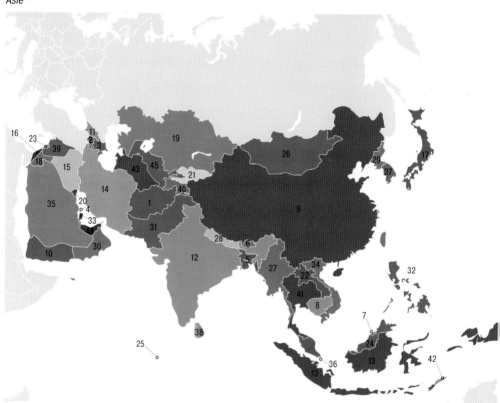

1
Afghanistan
Afghanistan *M*

2
Armenia
Arménie *F*

3
Azerbaijan
Azerbaïdjan *M*

4
Bahrain
Bahrein *M*

5
Bangladesh
Bangladesh *M*

6
Bhutan
Bhoutan *M*

7
Brunei
Brunei *M*

8
Cambodia
Cambodge *M*

9
Republic of China
République *F* *populaire* *F* *de Chine* *F*

10
Yemen
Yémen *M*

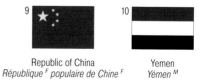

11
Georgia
Géorgie ^F

12
India
Inde ^F

13
Indonesia
Indonésie ^F

14
Iran
Iran ^M

15
Iraq
Irak ^M

16
Israel
Israël ^M

17
Japan
Japon ^M

18
Jordan
Jordanie ^F

19
Kazakhstan
Kazakhstan ^M

20
Kuwait
Koweït ^M

21
Kyrgyzstan
Kirghizistan ^M

22
Laos
Laos ^M

23
Lebanon
Liban ^M

24
Federation of Malaysia
Fédération ^F *de Malaisie* ^F

25
Maldives
Maldives ^F

26
Mongolia
Mongolie ^F

27
Myanmar
Myanmar ^M

28
Nepal
Népal ^M

29
North Korea
Corée ^F *du Nord* ^M

30
Oman
Oman ^M

31
Pakistan
Pakistan ^M

32
Philippines
Philippines ^F

33
Qatar
Qatar ^M

34
Vietnam
Vietnam ^M

35
Saudi Arabia
Arabie Saoudite ^F

36
Singapore
Singapour ^M

37
South Korea
Corée ^F *du Sud* ^M

38
Sri Lanka
Sri Lanka ^M

39
Syria
Syrie ^F

40
Tajikistan
Tadjikistan ^M

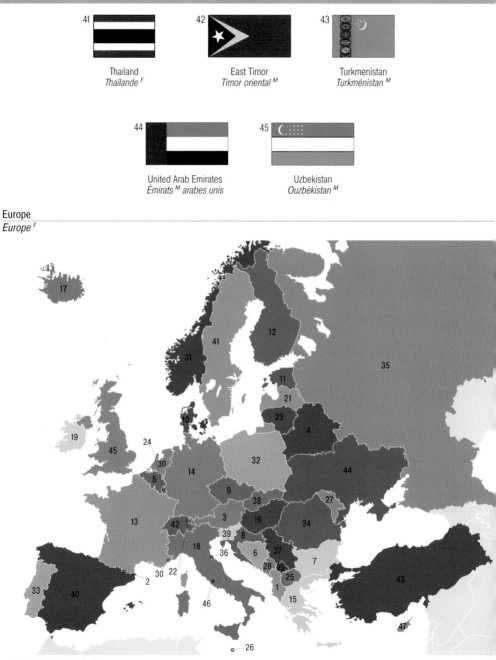

41

Thailand
Thaïlande^F

42

East Timor
Timor oriental^M

43

Turkmenistan
Turkménistan^M

44

United Arab Emirates
Émirats^M *arabes unis*

45

Uzbekistan
Ouzbékistan^M

Europe
Europe^F

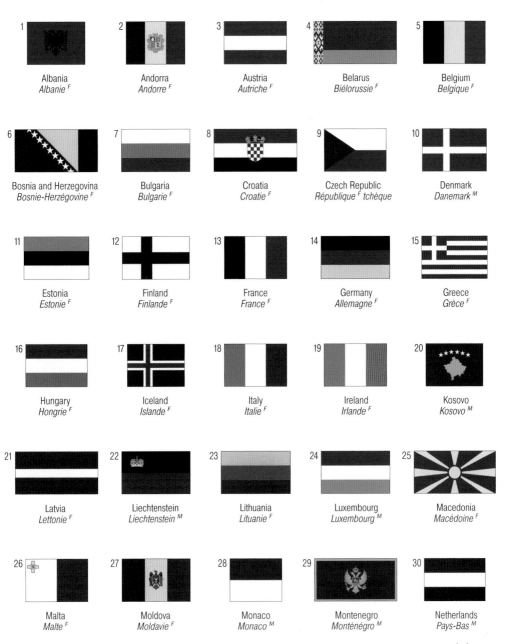

1 Albania
Albanie [F]

2 Andorra
Andorre [F]

3 Austria
Autriche [F]

4 Belarus
Biélorussie [F]

5 Belgium
Belgique [F]

6 Bosnia and Herzegovina
Bosnie-Herzégovine [F]

7 Bulgaria
Bulgarie [F]

8 Croatia
Croatie [F]

9 Czech Republic
République [F] tchèque

10 Denmark
Danemark [M]

11 Estonia
Estonie [F]

12 Finland
Finlande [F]

13 France
France [F]

14 Germany
Allemagne [F]

15 Greece
Grèce [F]

16 Hungary
Hongrie [F]

17 Iceland
Islande [F]

18 Italy
Italie [F]

19 Ireland
Irlande [F]

20 Kosovo
Kosovo [M]

21 Latvia
Lettonie [F]

22 Liechtenstein
Liechtenstein [M]

23 Lithuania
Lituanie [F]

24 Luxembourg
Luxembourg [M]

25 Macedonia
Macédoine [F]

26 Malta
Malte [F]

27 Moldova
Moldavie [F]

28 Monaco
Monaco [M]

29 Montenegro
Monténégro [M]

30 Netherlands
Pays-Bas [M]

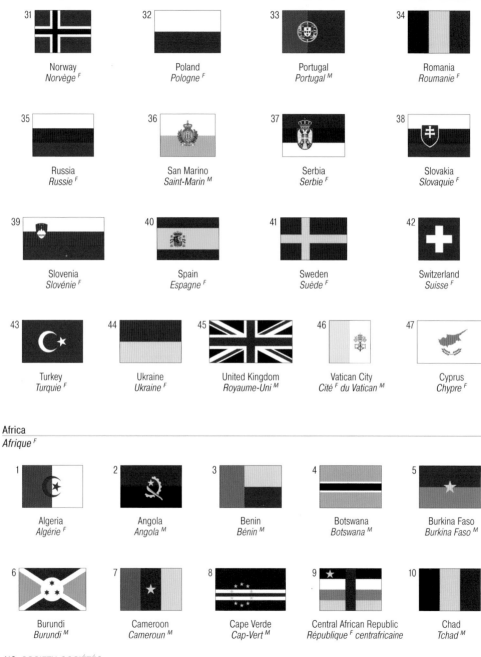

31 Norway
Norvège [F]

32 Poland
Pologne [F]

33 Portugal
Portugal [M]

34 Romania
Roumanie [F]

35 Russia
Russie [F]

36 San Marino
Saint-Marin [M]

37 Serbia
Serbie [F]

38 Slovakia
Slovaquie [F]

39 Slovenia
Slovénie [F]

40 Spain
Espagne [F]

41 Sweden
Suède [F]

42 Switzerland
Suisse [F]

43 Turkey
Turquie [F]

44 Ukraine
Ukraine [F]

45 United Kingdom
Royaume-Uni [M]

46 Vatican City
Cité [F] *du Vatican* [M]

47 Cyprus
Chypre [F]

Africa
Afrique [F]

1 Algeria
Algérie [F]

2 Angola
Angola [M]

3 Benin
Bénin [M]

4 Botswana
Botswana [M]

5 Burkina Faso
Burkina Faso [M]

6 Burundi
Burundi [M]

7 Cameroon
Cameroun [M]

8 Cape Verde
Cap-Vert [M]

9 Central African Republic
République [F] *centrafricaine*

10 Chad
Tchad [M]

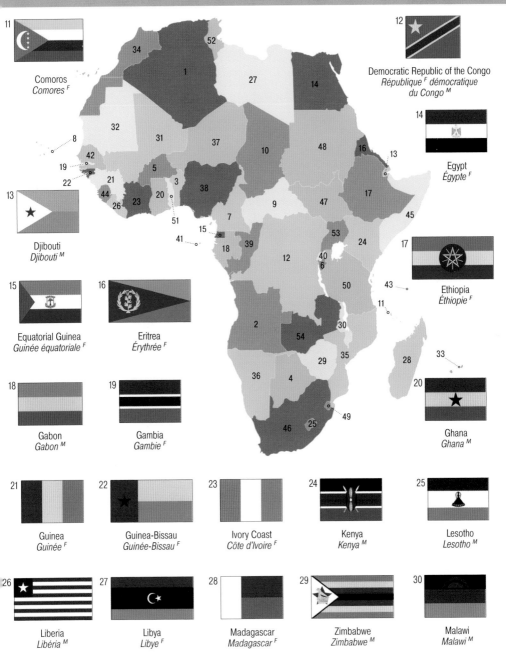

11 Comoros
Comores F

12 Democratic Republic of the Congo
République F démocratique
du Congo M

13 Djibouti
Djibouti M

14 Egypt
Égypte F

15 Equatorial Guinea
Guinée équatoriale F

16 Eritrea
Érythrée F

17 Ethiopia
Éthiopie F

18 Gabon
Gabon M

19 Gambia
Gambie F

20 Ghana
Ghana M

21 Guinea
Guinée F

22 Guinea-Bissau
Guinée-Bissau F

23 Ivory Coast
Côte d'Ivoire F

24 Kenya
Kenya M

25 Lesotho
Lesotho M

26 Liberia
Libéria M

27 Libya
Libye F

28 Madagascar
Madagascar F

29 Zimbabwe
Zimbabwe M

30 Malawi
Malawi M

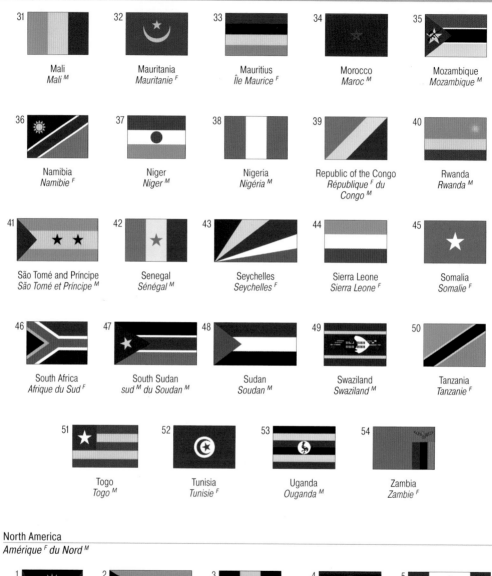

31 Mali
Mali ^M

32 Mauritania
Mauritanie ^F

33 Mauritius
Île Maurice ^F

34 Morocco
Maroc ^M

35 Mozambique
Mozambique ^M

36 Namibia
Namibie ^F

37 Niger
Niger ^M

38 Nigeria
Nigéria ^M

39 Republic of the Congo
République ^F *du Congo* ^M

40 Rwanda
Rwanda ^M

41 São Tomé and Príncipe
São Tomé et Príncipe ^M

42 Senegal
Sénégal ^M

43 Seychelles
Seychelles ^F

44 Sierra Leone
Sierra Leone ^F

45 Somalia
Somalie ^F

46 South Africa
Afrique du Sud ^F

47 South Sudan
sud ^M *du Soudan* ^M

48 Sudan
Soudan ^M

49 Swaziland
Swaziland ^M

50 Tanzania
Tanzanie ^F

51 Togo
Togo ^M

52 Tunisia
Tunisie ^F

53 Uganda
Ouganda ^M

54 Zambia
Zambie ^F

North America
Amérique ^F *du Nord* ^M

1 Antigua & Barbuda
Antigua-et-Barbuda ^F

2 Bahamas
Bahamas ^F

3 Barbados
Barbade ^F

4 Belize
Bélize ^M

5 Canada
Canada ^M

6
Costa Rica
Costa Rica [M]

7
Cuba
Cuba [F]

8
Dominica
Dominique [F]

9
Dominican Republic
République [F] *dominicaine*

10
El Salvador
Salvador [M]

11
Grenada
Grenade [F]

12
Guatemala
Guatemala [M]

13
Haiti
Haïti [M]

14
Honduras
Honduras [M]

15
Jamaica
Jamaïque [F]

16
Mexico
Mexique [M]

17
Nicaragua
Nicaragua [M]

18
Panama
Panama [M]

19
Saint Kitts-Nevis
Saint-Kitts-et-Nevis [F]

20
Saint Lucia
Sainte-Lucie [F]

21
Saint Vincent and
the Grenadines
Saint-Vincent-et-les-Grenadines [F]

22
United States of America
États-Unis [M] *d'Amérique* [F]

South America
Amérique ^F *du Sud* ^M

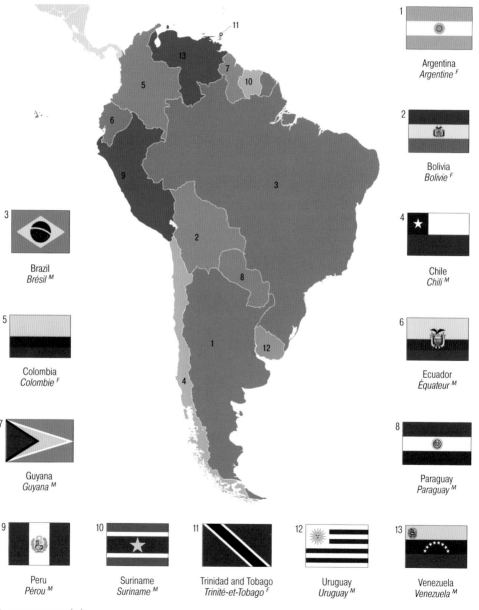

1 Argentina
Argentine ^F

2 Bolivia
Bolivie ^F

3 Brazil
Brésil ^M

4 Chile
Chili ^M

5 Colombia
Colombie ^F

6 Ecuador
Équateur ^M

7 Guyana
Guyana ^M

8 Paraguay
Paraguay ^M

9 Peru
Pérou ^M

10 Suriname
Suriname ^M

11 Trinidad and Tobago
Trinité-et-Tobago ^F

12 Uruguay
Uruguay ^M

13 Venezuela
Venezuela ^M

Australia and Oceania
Australie _F_ et _Océanie_ _F_

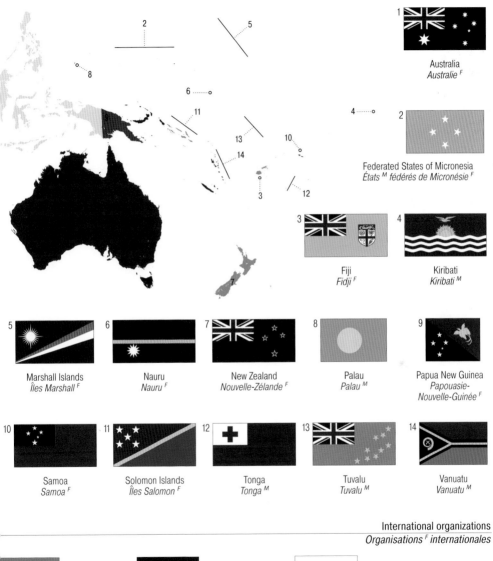

1

Australia
Australie _F_

2

Federated States of Micronesia
États _M_ _fédérés de Micronésie_ _F_

3
Fiji
Fidji _F_

4
Kiribati
Kiribati _M_

5
Marshall Islands
Îles Marshall _F_

6
Nauru
Nauru _F_

7
New Zealand
Nouvelle-Zélande _F_

8
Palau
Palau _M_

9
Papua New Guinea
_Papouasie-
Nouvelle-Guinée_ _F_

10
Samoa
Samoa _F_

11
Solomon Islands
Îles Salomon _F_

12
Tonga
Tonga _M_

13
Tuvalu
Tuvalu _M_

14
Vanuatu
Vanuatu _M_

International organizations
Organisations _F_ _internationales_

United Nations
Nations _F_ _unies_

European Union
Union _F_ _européenne_ _F_

International Olympic Committee
Comité _M_ _international olympique_

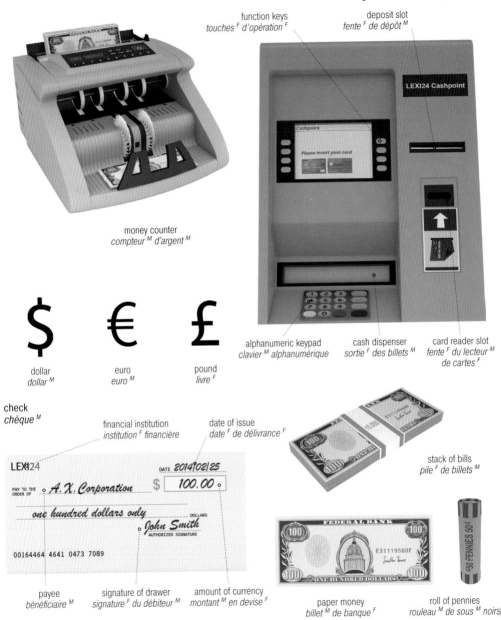

automatic teller machine (ATM)
guichet ^M automatique bancaire

function keys
touches ^F d'opération ^F

deposit slot
fente ^F de dépôt ^M

LEXI24 Cashpoint

Cashpoint

Please insert your card

money counter
compteur ^M d'argent ^M

$

€

£

dollar
dollar ^M

euro
euro ^M

pound
livre ^F

alphanumeric keypad
clavier ^M alphanumérique

cash dispenser
sortie ^F des billets ^M

card reader slot
*fente ^F du lecteur ^M
de cartes ^F*

check
chèque ^M

financial institution
institution ^F financière

date of issue
date ^F de délivrance ^F

LEXI24   DATE 2014|02|25

PAY TO THE
ORDER OF   *A. X. Corporation* $ 100.00

one hundred dollars only   DOLLARS
John Smith
AUTHORIZED SIGNATURE

00164464: 4641 0473 7089

stack of bills
pile ^F de billets ^M

E31119560F

FEDERAL BANK
E31119560F
ONE HUNDRED DOLLARS

50 PENNIES 50¢

payee
bénéficiaire ^M

signature of drawer
signature ^F du débiteur ^M

amount of currency
montant ^M en devise ^F

paper money
billet ^M de banque ^F

roll of pennies
rouleau ^M de sous ^M noirs

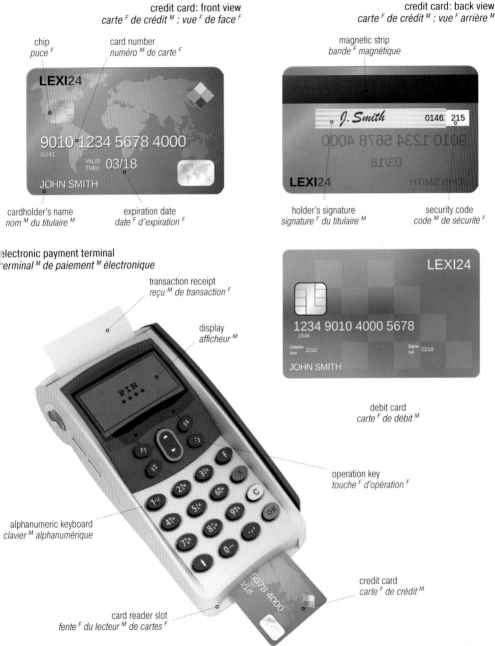

credit card: front view
carte F de crédit M : vue F de face F

credit card: back view
carte F de crédit M : vue F arrière M

chip
puce F

card number
numéro M de carte F

magnetic strip
bande F magnétique

LEXI24

9010 1234 5678 4000
5041
VALID THRU 03/18
JOHN SMITH

J. Smith   0146   215

LEXI24

cardholder's name
nom M du titulaire M

expiration date
date F d'expiration F

holder's signature
signature F du titulaire M

security code
code M de sécurité F

electronic payment terminal
terminal M de paiement M électronique

transaction receipt
reçu M de transaction F

display
afficheur M

LEXI24

1234 9010 4000 5678
1546
Customer since 2010   Expires End 02/19
JOHN SMITH

PIN
****

debit card
carte F de débit M

operation key
touche F d'opération F

alphanumeric keyboard
clavier M alphanumérique

credit card
carte F de crédit M

card reader slot
fente F du lecteur M de cartes F

pistol
pistolet [M]

front sight
guidon [M]

barrel
baril [M]

takedown lever
levier [M] *de démontage* [M]

rear sight
hausse [F]

hammer
chien [M]

muzzle
canon [M]

safety catch
cran [M] *d'arrêt* [M]

trigger
détente [F]

slide
cadre [M]

magazine
chargeur [M]

trigger guard
pontet [M]

magazine catch
arrêtoir [M] *de chargeur* [M]

butt
manche [M]

grip panel
plaquette [F]

cartridge case
douille [F]

magazine
chargeur [M]

bullet
balle [F]

front sight
guidon [M]

barrel
barillet [M]

cylinder
cylindre [M]

revolver
revolver [M]

hammer
chien [M]

muzzle
canon [M]

butt
manche [M]

trigger guard
pontet [M]

trigger
détente [F]

main battle tank (MBT)
char [M] *de combat* [M] *principal*

turret
tourelle [F]

periscope
périscope [M]

cannon
canon [M]

armor
blindage [M]

headlight
phare [M]

hatch
trappe [F]

wheel
roue [F]

track
chenille [F]

infantry fighting vehicle (IFV)
véhicule [M] *de combat* [M] *d'infanterie* [F]

heavy tank
char [M] *lourd*

high mobility multipurpose wheeled vehicle (humvee)
véhicule [M] *sur roues* [F] *polyvalent à grande mobilité* [F]

shield
écran [M]

machine gun
mitrailleuse [F]

air intake
tube [M] *d'arrivée* [F] *d'air* [M]

hood
capot [M]

reflector
réflecteur [M]

turn signal
clignolant [M]

grille
grille [F]

headlight
phare [M]

tow hook
crochet [M] *de remorquage* [M]

front bumper
pare-chocs [M] *avant*

tire
roue [F]

armor
armure [F]

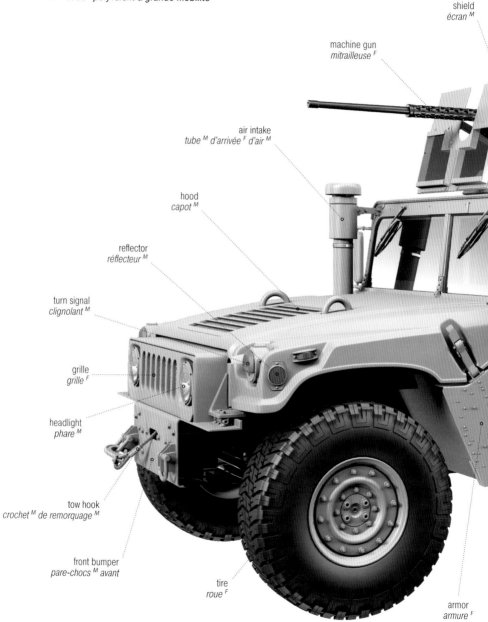

machine gun magazine
chargeur ^M *de la mitrailleuse* ^F

machine gunner
mitrailleur ^M

antenna
antenne ^F

exhaust stack
cheminée ^F *d'échappement* ^M

turret
tourelle ^F

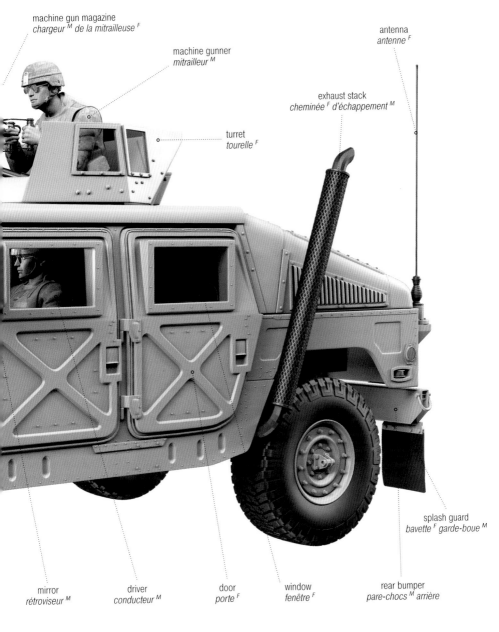

splash guard
bavette ^F *garde-boue* ^M

mirror
rétroviseur ^M

driver
conducteur ^M

door
porte ^F

window
fenêtre ^F

rear bumper
pare-chocs ^M *arrière*

humvee: bottom view
véhicule ^M militaire tous terrains : vue ^F de dessous ^M

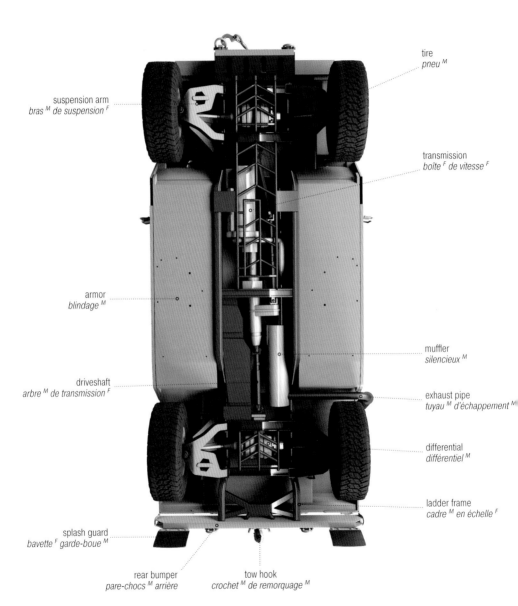

tire
pneu ^M

suspension arm
bras ^M de suspension ^F

transmission
boîte ^F de vitesse ^F

armor
blindage ^M

muffler
silencieux ^M

driveshaft
arbre ^M de transmission ^F

exhaust pipe
tuyau ^M d'échappement ^M

differential
différentiel ^M

ladder frame
cadre ^M en échelle ^F

splash guard
bavette ^F garde-boue ^M

rear bumper
pare-chocs ^M arrière

tow hook
crochet ^M de remorquage ^M

truck
camion ^M

Czech hedgehog
hérisson ^M *tchèque*

dish antenna
antenne ^F *parabolique*

transreceiving dish
antenne ^F *émettrice et réceptrice*

satellite
satellite ^M

load-bearing frame
cadre ^M *porteur*

parabolic reflector
réflecteur ^M *parabolique*

feed horn
cornet ^M *d'alimentation* ^F

solar panel
panneau ^M *solaire*

elevation adjustment
ajustement ^M *d'élévation* ^F

azimuth adjustment
ajustement ^M *azimut*

transmission dish
antenne ^F *d'émission* ^F

railing
garde-corps ^M

stairs
escalier ^M

Airplanes
Avions [M]

interceptor
intercepteur [M]

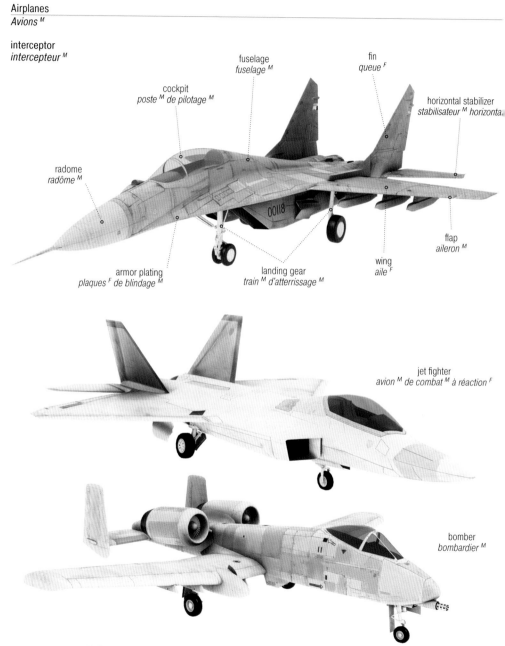

fuselage
fuselage [M]

fin
queue [F]

cockpit
poste [M] *de pilotage* [M]

horizontal stabilizer
stabilisateur [M] *horizontal*

radome
radôme [M]

flap
aileron [M]

armor plating
plaques [F] *de blindage* [M]

landing gear
train [M] *d'atterrissage* [M]

wing
aile [F]

jet fighter
avion [M] *de combat* [M] *à réaction* [F]

bomber
bombardier [M]

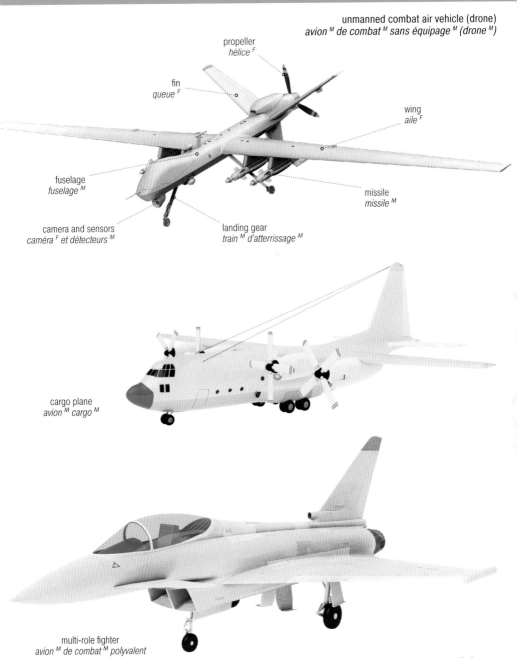

unmanned combat air vehicle (drone)
avion [M] *de combat* [M] *sans équipage* [M] *(drone* [M]*)*

propeller
hélice [F]

fin
queue [F]

wing
aile [F]

fuselage
fuselage [M]

missile
missile [M]

camera and sensors
caméra [F] *et détecteurs* [M]

landing gear
train [M] *d'atterrissage* [M]

cargo plane
avion [M] *cargo* [M]

multi-role fighter
avion [M] *de combat* [M] *polyvalent*

Helicopter
Hélicoptère [M]

utility helicopter: side view
hélicoptère [M] *polyvalent : vue* [F] *de côté*

rotor hub
moyeu [M] *de rotor* [M]

engine
moteur [M]

window
hublot [M]

rotor blade
pale [F] *de rotor* [M]

fuselage
fuselage [M]

cockpit
poste [M] *de pilotage* [M]

cockpit door
porte du poste [M] *de pilotage* [M]

landing window
hublot [M] *d'atterrissage* [M]

landing gear
train [M] *d'atterrissage* [M]

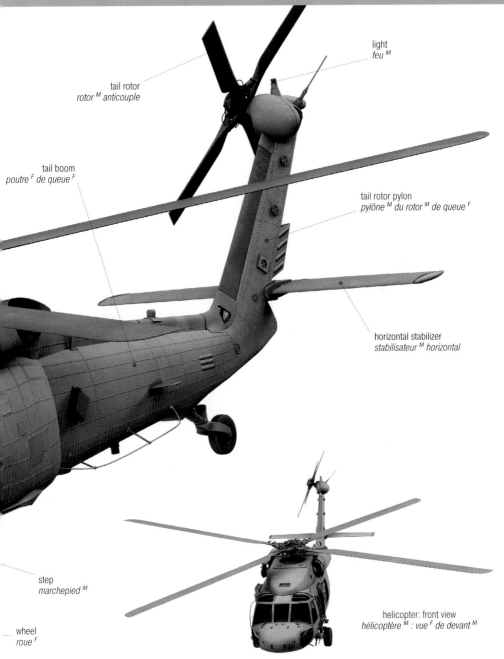

light
feu ^M

tail rotor
rotor ^M *anticouple*

tail boom
poutre ^F *de queue* ^F

tail rotor pylon
pylône ^M *du rotor* ^M *de queue* ^F

horizontal stabilizer
stabilisateur ^M *horizontal*

step
marchepied ^M

wheel
roue ^F

helicopter: front view
hélicoptère ^M : *vue* ^F *de devant* ^M

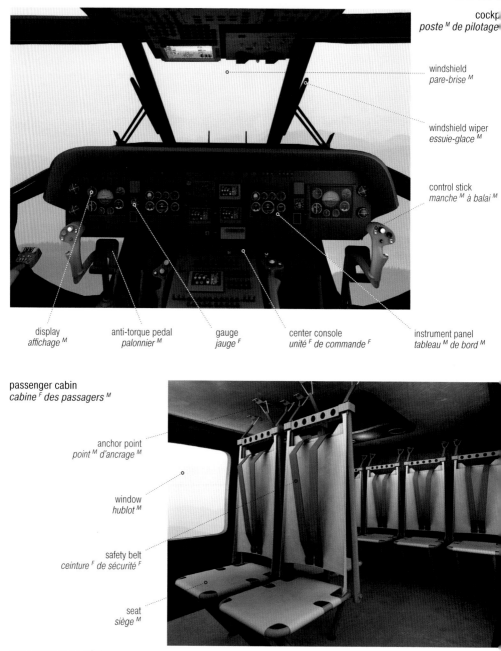

cockpit
poste [M] *de pilotage*

windshield
pare-brise [M]

windshield wiper
essuie-glace [M]

control stick
manche [M] *à balai* [M]

display
affichage [M]

anti-torque pedal
palonnier [M]

gauge
jauge [F]

center console
unité [F] *de commande* [F]

instrument panel
tableau [M] *de bord* [M]

passenger cabin
cabine [F] *des passagers* [M]

anchor point
point [M] *d'ancrage* [M]

window
hublot [M]

safety belt
ceinture [F] *de sécurité* [F]

seat
siège [M]

search and rescue (SAR) helicopter
hélicoptère ^M de recherche ^F et de sauvetage ^M

transport helicopter
hélicoptère ^M pour le transport ^M

attack helicopter
hélicoptère ^M d'attaque ^F

patrol coastal ship
navire [M] *de patrouille* [F] *côtière*

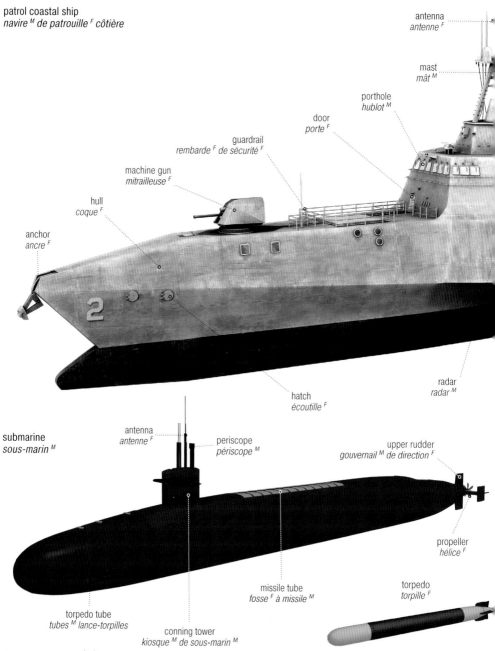

antenna
antenne [F]

mast
mât [M]

porthole
hublot [M]

door
porte [F]

guardrail
rembarde [F] *de sécurité* [F]

machine gun
mitrailleuse [F]

hull
coque [F]

anchor
ancre [F]

radar
radar [M]

hatch
écoutille [F]

submarine
sous-marin [M]

antenna
antenne [F]

periscope
périscope [M]

upper rudder
gouvernail [M] *de direction* [F]

propeller
hélice [F]

missile tube
fosse [F] *à missile* [M]

torpedo
torpille [F]

torpedo tube
tubes [M] *lance-torpilles*

conning tower
kiosque [M] *de sous-marin* [M]

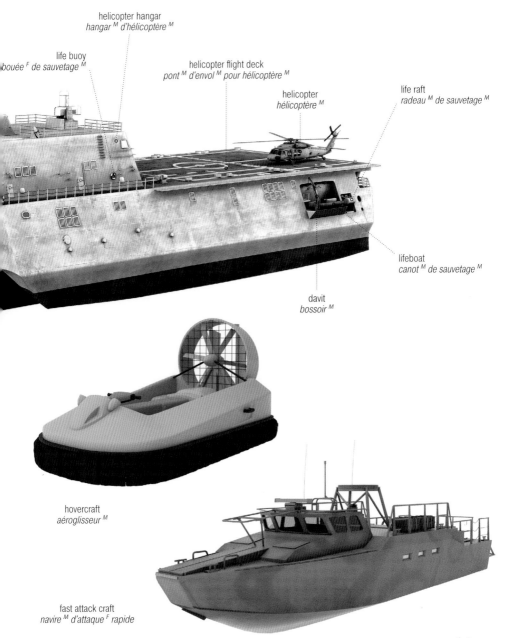

helicopter hangar
hangar [M] *d'hélicoptère* [M]

life buoy
bouée [F] *de sauvetage* [M]

helicopter flight deck
pont [M] *d'envol* [M] *pour hélicoptère* [M]

helicopter
hélicoptère [M]

life raft
radeau [M] *de sauvetage* [M]

lifeboat
canot [M] *de sauvetage* [M]

davit
bossoir [M]

hovercraft
aéroglisseur [M]

fast attack craft
navire [M] *d'attaque* [F] *rapide*

propeller
hélice ^F

blade
pale ^F

shaft
tige ^F

hub
moyeu ^M

main deck
pont ^M *principal*

radar
radar ^M

aircraft carrier
porte-avion ^M

hull
coque ^F

helicopter
hélicoptère ^M

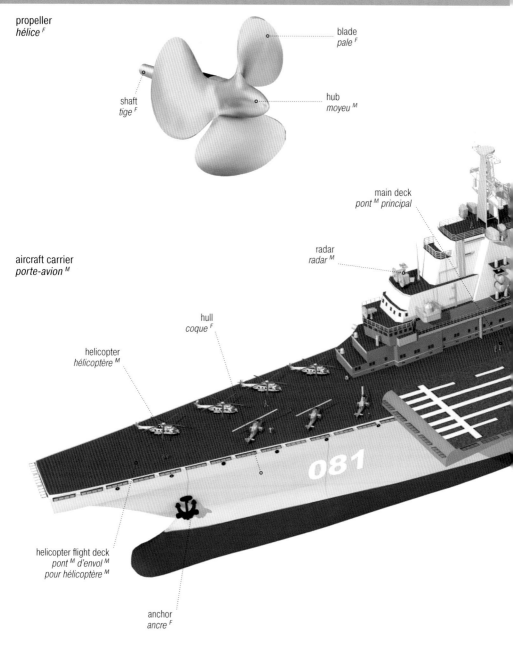

081

helicopter flight deck
pont ^M *d'envol* ^M
pour hélicoptère ^M

anchor
ancre ^F

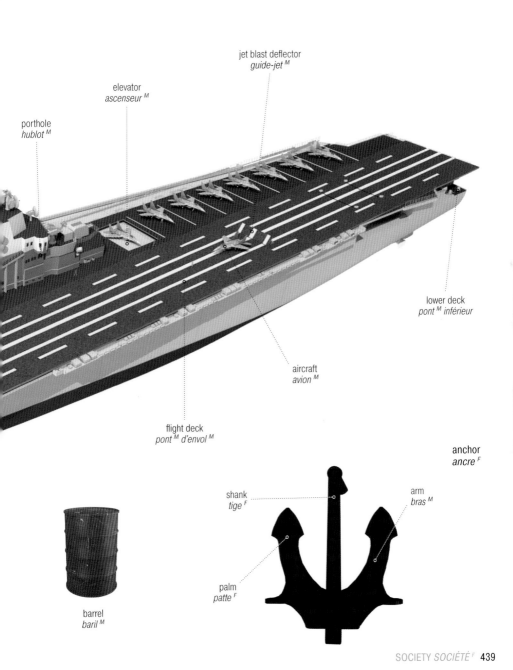

jet blast deflector
guide-jet ^M

elevator
ascenseur ^M

porthole
hublot ^M

lower deck
pont ^M *inférieur*

aircraft
avion ^M

flight deck
pont ^M *d'envol* ^M

anchor
ancre ^F

shank
tige ^F

arm
bras ^M

palm
patte ^F

barrel
baril ^M

ARTS AND ARCHITECTURE

ARTS ET ARCHITECTURE

band
groupe ^M *de musique* ^F

block of lights
bloc ^M *de projecteurs* ^M

parabolic aluminized reflector light
lampe ^F *à réflecteur* ^M *parabolique aluminé*

guitarist
guitariste ^M

electric guitar
guitare ^F

loudspeaker
haut-parleur ^M

cable
câble ^M

monitor
haut-parleur ^M *de contrôle* ^M

synthesizer
synthétiseur ^M

keyboardist
claviériste ^M

audio engineer
ingénieur ^M *du son* ^M

singer
chanteuse ᶠ

drummer
batteur ᴹ

drum kit
batterie ᶠ

bassist
bassiste ᴹ

trussing
structure ᶠ

console
console ᶠ

chair
chaise ᶠ

laptop computer
ordinateur ᴹ portatif

table
table ᶠ

bass guitar
basse ᶠ

stage
scène ᶠ

movie theater
cinéma [F]

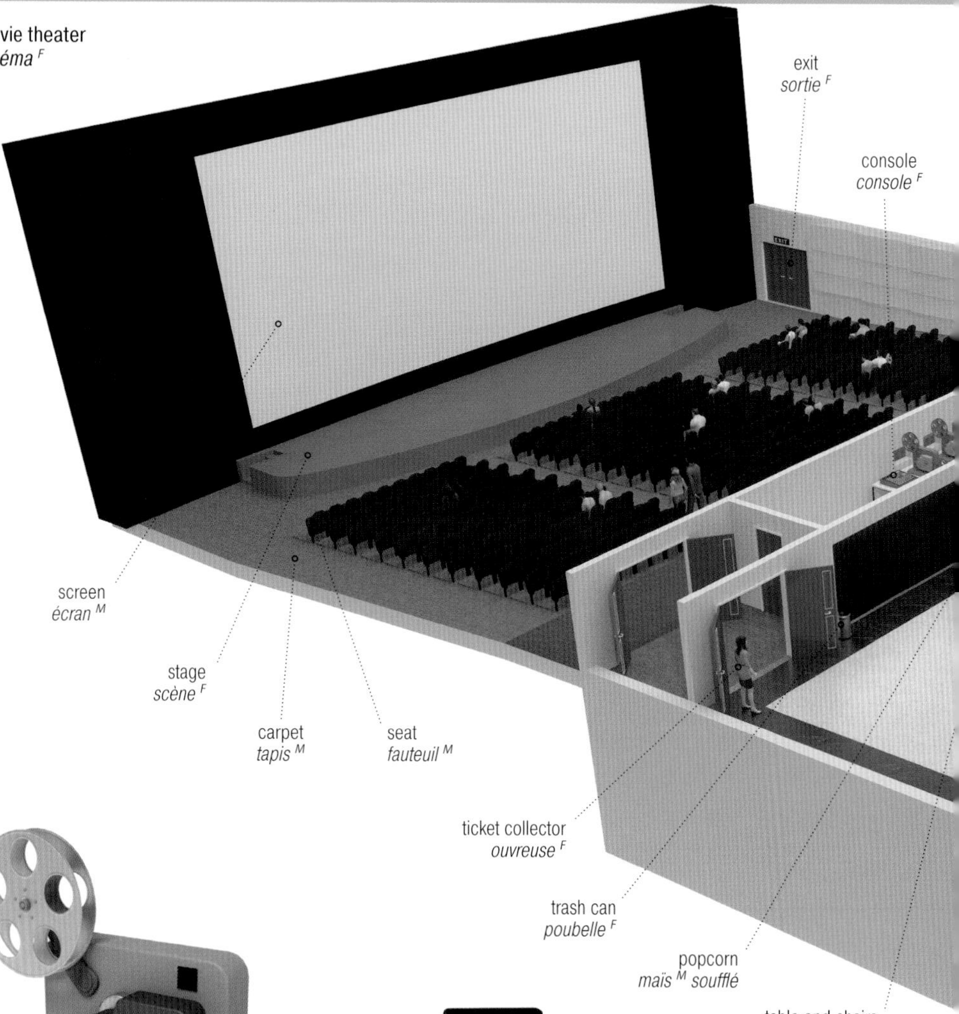

exit
sortie [F]

console
console [F]

screen
écran [M]

stage
scène [F]

carpet
tapis [M]

seat
fauteuil [M]

ticket collector
ouvreuse [F]

trash can
poubelle [F]

popcorn
maïs [M] *soufflé*

table and chairs
table [F] *et chaises* [F]

counter
comptoir [M]

film projector
projecteur [M] *de films* [M]

digital projector
projecteur [M] *numérique*

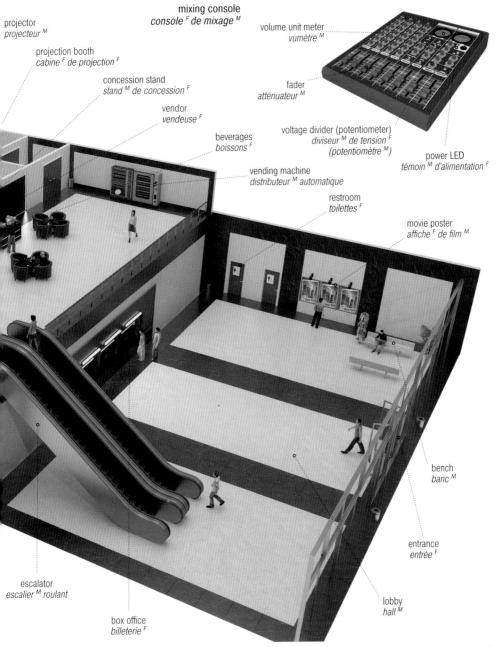

mixing console
console ᶠ de mixage ᴹ

projector
projecteur ᴹ

volume unit meter
vumètre ᴹ

projection booth
cabine ᶠ de projection ᶠ

concession stand
stand ᴹ de concession ᶠ

fader
atténuateur ᴹ

vendor
vendeuse ᶠ

voltage divider (potentiometer)
diviseur ᴹ de tension ᶠ
(potentiomètre ᴹ)

beverages
boissons ᶠ

power LED
témoin ᴹ d'alimentation ᶠ

vending machine
distributeur ᴹ automatique

restroom
toilettes ᶠ

movie poster
affiche ᶠ de film ᴹ

bench
banc ᴹ

entrance
entrée ᶠ

escalator
escalier ᴹ roulant

lobby
hall ᴹ

box office
billeterie ᶠ

television show
émission ᶠ *de télévision* ᶠ

stage
scène ᶠ

desk
bureau ᴹ

scenery
décor ᴹ

host
animateur ᴹ

monitor
moniteur ᴹ

guest
invitée ^F

chair
chaise ^F

electric guitar
guitare ^F

drum kit
batterie ^F

microphone
microphone ^M

television studio
studio [M] *de télévision* [F]

scenery
décor [M]

light
éclairage [M]

monitor
moniteur [M]

truss
grille [F] *d'éclairage* [M]

host
animateur [M]

cable
câble [M]

microphone
microphone [M]

cameraman
caméraman [M]

script
script [M]

stage
scène [F]

guest
invitée ᶠ

singer
chanteuse ᶠ

musician
musicien ᴹ

director
réalisatrice ᴹ

camera
caméra ᶠ

audience member
membre ᴹ de l'auditoire ᴹ

stage
scène ^F

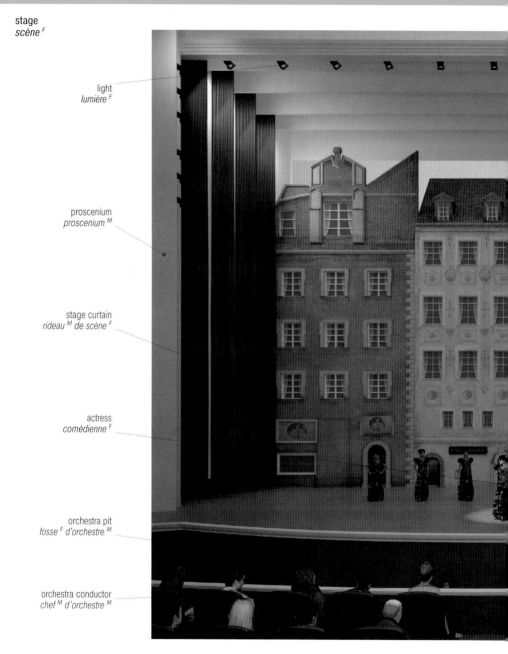

light
lumière ^F

proscenium
proscenium ^M

stage curtain
rideau ^M *de scène* ^F

actress
comédienne ^F

orchestra pit
fosse ^F *d'orchestre* ^M

orchestra conductor
chef ^M *d'orchestre* ^M

beam
frise ꜰ

backdrop
toile ꜰ *de fond* ᴹ

actor
comédien ᴹ

stage
scène ꜰ

audience
public ᴹ

theater
auditorium ^M

mezzanine
mezzanine ^F

balcony
balcon ^M

seat
siège ^M

orchestra
orchestre ^M

opera glasses
jumelles ᶠ de théâtre ᴹ

lens
lentille ᶠ

focusing wheel
molette ᶠ de focalisation ᶠ

body
corps ᴹ

handle
poignée ᶠ

flamenco dancer
danseuse ᶠ de flamenco ᴹ

ruffled sleeve
manches ᶠ à volants ᴹ

ruffled skirt
jupe ᶠ à volants ᴹ

Indian dancer
danseuse ᶠ indienne

maang tikka
maang tikka ᴹ

bindi
bindi ᴹ

nose ring
anneau ᴹ de nez ᴹ

actor
comédien ᴹ

costume
costume ᴹ

panja bracelet
bracelet ᴹ panja

choli
choli ᴹ

bangle
bracelet ᴹ

dupatta
dupatta ᶠ

lehenga
lehenga ᴹ

first position of the arms
première position ^F *des bras* ^M

leotard
léotard ^M

tights
collants ^M

ballet shoes
chaussons ^M *de ballet* ^M

arabesque on pointe
arabesque ^F *sur pointe* ^F

jeté
jeté ^M

front attitude on pointe
attitude ^F *devant en pointe* ^F

grand jeté
grand jeté ^M

second position of the arms
deuxième position ^F *des bras* ^M

third position of the arms
troisième position ^F *des bras* ^M

fourth position of the arms
quatrième position ^F des bras ^M

fifth position of the arms
cinquième position ^F des bras ^M

backward attitude on pointe
attitude ^F derrière en pointe ^F

retiré on pointe
retiré ^M sur pointe ^F

pas de bourrée
pas ^M de bourrée ^F

ballet moves
scènes ^F de ballet ^F

arabesque
arabesque ^F

back bend
inclinaison ^F arrière

entrechat
entrechat ^M

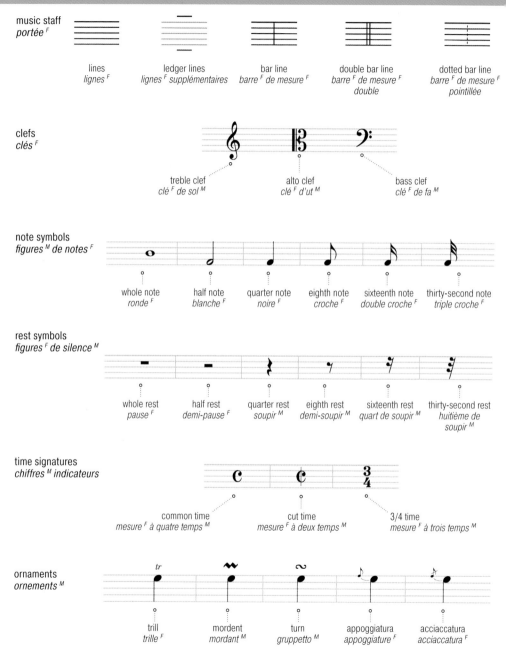

music staff
portée F

lines
lignes F

ledger lines
lignes F supplémentaires

bar line
barre F de mesure F

double bar line
barre F de mesure F
double

dotted bar line
barre F de mesure F
pointillée

clefs
clés F

treble clef
clé F de sol M

alto clef
clé F d'ut M

bass clef
clé F de fa M

note symbols
figures M de notes F

whole note
ronde F

half note
blanche F

quarter note
noire F

eighth note
croche F

sixteenth note
double croche F

thirty-second note
triple croche F

rest symbols
figures F de silence M

whole rest
pause F

half rest
demi-pause F

quarter rest
soupir M

eighth rest
demi-soupir M

sixteenth rest
quart de soupir M

thirty-second rest
huitième de
soupir M

time signatures
chiffres M indicateurs

common time
mesure F à quatre temps M

cut time
mesure F à deux temps M

3/4 time
mesure F à trois temps M

ornaments
ornements M

trill
trille F

mordent
mordant M

turn
gruppetto M

appoggiatura
appoggiature F

acciaccatura
acciaccatura F

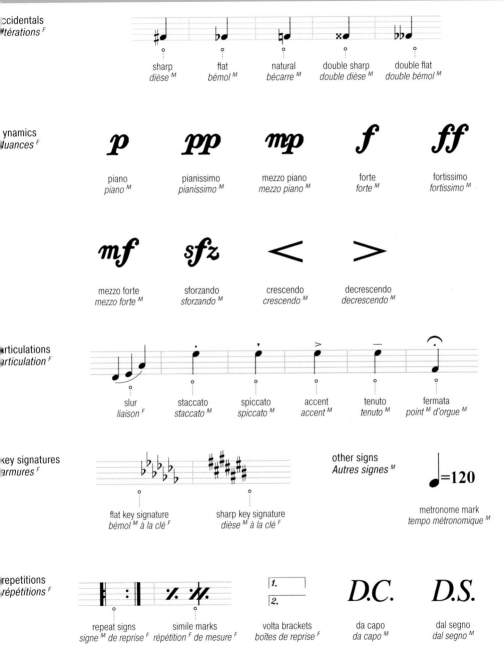

ccidentals
ltérations [F]

sharp	flat	natural	double sharp	double flat
dièse [M]	bémol [M]	bécarre [M]	double dièse [M]	double bémol [M]

ynamics
luances [F]

piano	pianissimo	mezzo piano	forte	fortissimo
piano [M]	pianissimo [M]	mezzo piano [M]	forte [M]	fortissimo [M]

mezzo forte	sforzando	crescendo	decrescendo
mezzo forte [M]	sforzando [M]	crescendo [M]	decrescendo [M]

rticulations
rticulation [F]

slur	staccato	spiccato	accent	tenuto	fermata
liaison [F]	staccato [M]	spiccato [M]	accent [M]	tenuto [M]	point [M] d'orgue [M]

‹ey signatures
armures [F]

other signs
Autres signes [M]

flat key signature	sharp key signature
bémol [M] à la clé [F]	dièse [M] à la clé [F]

metronome mark
tempo métronomique [M]

repetitions
répétitions [F]

repeat signs	simile marks	volta brackets	da capo	dal segno
signe [M] de reprise [F]	répétition [F] de mesure [F]	boîtes de reprise [F]	da capo [M]	dal segno [M]

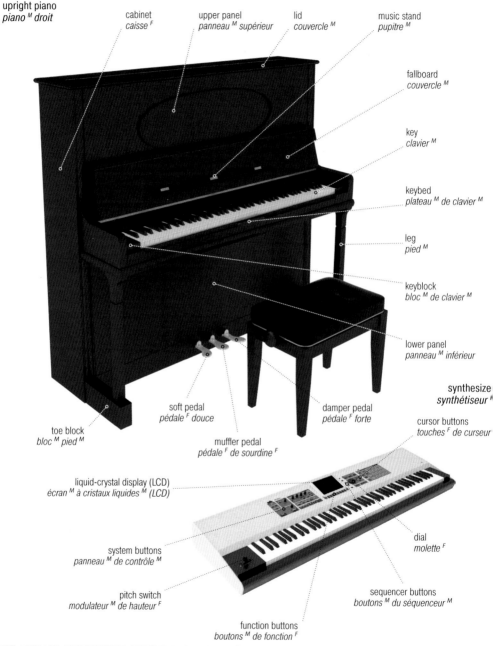

upright piano
piano M *droit*

cabinet
caisse F

upper panel
panneau M *supérieur*

lid
couvercle M

music stand
pupitre M

fallboard
couvercle M

key
clavier M

keybed
plateau M *de clavier* M

leg
pied M

keyblock
bloc M *de clavier* M

lower panel
panneau M *inférieur*

toe block
bloc M *pied* M

soft pedal
pédale F *douce*

muffler pedal
pédale F *de sourdine* F

damper pedal
pédale F *forte*

synthesize
synthétiseur M

cursor buttons
touches F *de curseur*

liquid-crystal display (LCD)
écran M *à cristaux liquides* M *(LCD)*

dial
molette F

system buttons
panneau M *de contrôle* M

pitch switch
modulateur M *de hauteur* F

sequencer buttons
boutons M *du séquenceur* M

function buttons
boutons M *de fonction* F

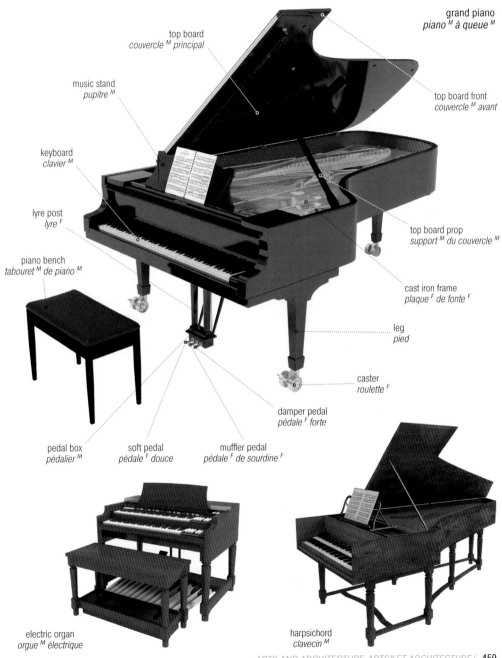

grand piano
piano M *à queue* M

top board
couvercle M *principal*

top board front
couvercle M *avant*

music stand
pupitre M

keyboard
clavier M

top board prop
support M *du couvercle* M

lyre post
lyre F

piano bench
tabouret M *de piano* M

cast iron frame
plaque F *de fonte* F

leg
pied

caster
roulette F

damper pedal
pédale F *forte*

pedal box
pédalier M

soft pedal
pédale F *douce*

muffler pedal
pédale F *de sourdine* F

electric organ
orgue M *électrique*

harpsichord
clavecin M

drum kit
batterie F

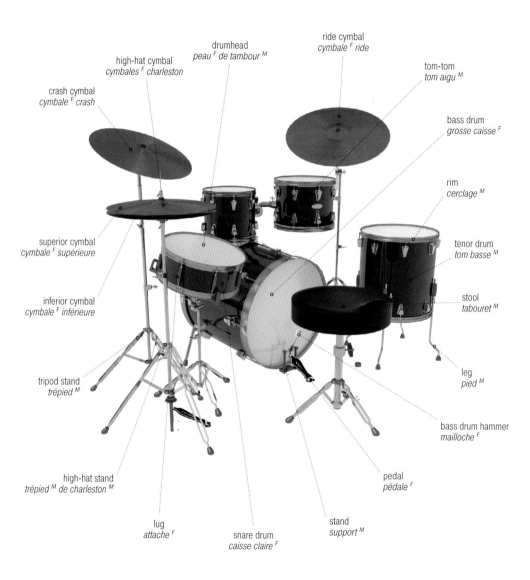

high-hat cymbal
cymbales F *charleston*

drumhead
peau F *de tambour* M

ride cymbal
cymbale F *ride*

tom-tom
tom aigu M

crash cymbal
cymbale F *crash*

bass drum
grosse caisse F

rim
cerclage M

superior cymbal
cymbale F *supérieure*

tenor drum
tom basse M

inferior cymbal
cymbale F *inférieure*

stool
tabouret M

tripod stand
trépied M

leg
pied M

high-hat stand
trépied M *de charleston* M

bass drum hammer
mailloche F

pedal
pédale F

lug
attache F

snare drum
caisse claire F

stand
support M

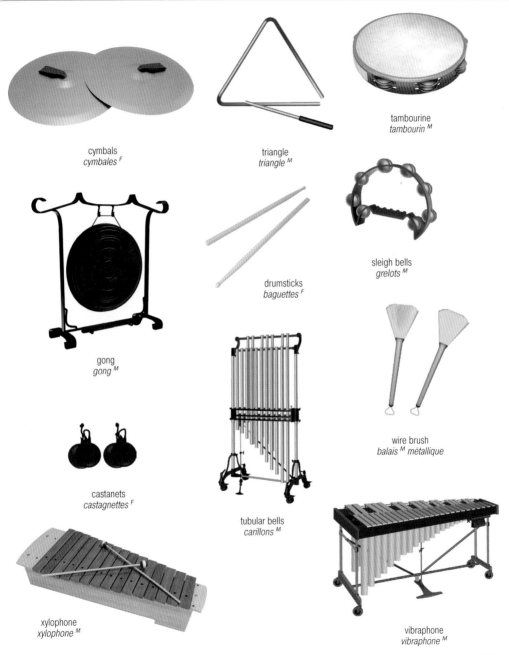

cymbals
cymbales F

triangle
triangle M

tambourine
tambourin M

gong
gong M

drumsticks
baguettes F

sleigh bells
grelots M

castanets
castagnettes F

tubular bells
carillons M

wire brush
balais M métallique

xylophone
xylophone M

vibraphone
vibraphone M

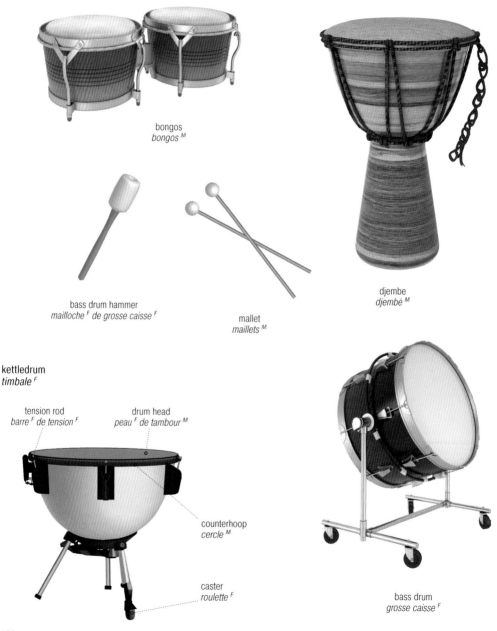

bongos
bongos [M]

bass drum hammer
mailloche [F] *de grosse caisse* [F]

mallet
maillets [M]

djembe
djembé [M]

kettledrum
timbale [F]

tension rod
barre [F] *de tension* [F]

drum head
peau [F] *de tambour* [M]

counterhoop
cercle [M]

caster
roulette [F]

bass drum
grosse caisse [F]

Brass instruments
Cuivres [M]

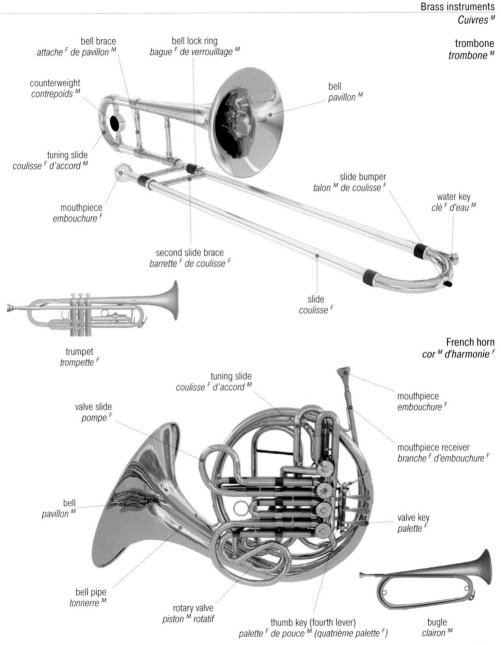

bell brace
attache [F] *de pavillon* [M]

bell lock ring
bague [F] *de verrouillage* [M]

trombone
trombone [M]

counterweight
contrepoids [M]

bell
pavillon [M]

tuning slide
coulisse [F] *d'accord* [M]

slide bumper
talon [M] *de coulisse* [F]

water key
clé [F] *d'eau* [M]

mouthpiece
embouchure [F]

second slide brace
barrette [F] *de coulisse* [F]

slide
coulisse [F]

trumpet
trompette [F]

French horn
cor [M] *d'harmonie* [F]

tuning slide
coulisse [F] *d'accord* [M]

mouthpiece
embouchure [F]

valve slide
pompe [F]

mouthpiece receiver
branche [F] *d'embouchure* [F]

bell
pavillon [M]

valve key
palette [F]

bell pipe
tonnerre [M]

rotary valve
piston [M] *rotatif*

thumb key (fourth lever)
palette [F] *de pouce* [M] (*quatrième palette* [F])

bugle
clairon [M]

tuba
tuba ^M

saxhorn
saxhorn ^M

euphonium
euphonium ^M

cornet
cornet ^M

Woodwind instruments
Instruments ^M *à vent* ^M *en bois* ^M

saxophone
saxophone ^M

octave key
clé ^F *d'octave* ^F

mouthpiece
bec ^F

neck
bocal ^M

reed
anche ^F

neck cork
liège ^M

ligature
bague ^F *de serrage* ^M

recorder
flute ^F *à bec* ^M

bell
pavillon ^M

panpipe
flûte de Pan ^F

shoe
ligature ^F

key
clé ^F

key/finger button
bouton ^M *de clé* ^F

key guard
garde-clés ^M

thumb rest
repose-pouce ^M

bow
culasse ^F

tube
tuyau ^M

English horn
cor M anglais

bassoon
basson M

contrabassoon
contrebasson M

concert flute
flûte F traversière

clarinet
clarinette F

bass clarinet
clarinette F basse

treble flute
flûte F soprano

oboe
hautbois M

piccolo
piccolo M

cello
violoncelle^M

violin and bow
violon^M *et archet*

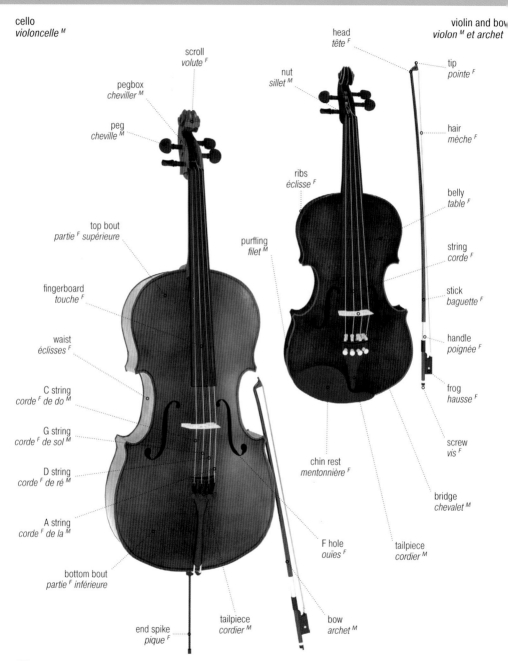

head
tête^F

scroll
volute^F

nut
sillet^M

tip
pointe^F

pegbox
cheviller^M

peg
cheville^M

hair
mèche^F

ribs
éclisse^F

belly
table^F

top bout
partie^F *supérieure*

purfling
filet^M

string
corde^F

fingerboard
touche^F

stick
baguette^F

waist
éclisses^F

handle
poignée^F

C string
corde^F *de do*^M

frog
hausse^F

G string
corde^F *de sol*^M

D string
corde^F *de ré*^M

screw
vis^F

chin rest
mentonnière^F

A string
corde^F *de la*^M

bridge
chevalet^M

bottom bout
partie^F *inférieure*

F hole
ouïes^F

tailpiece
cordier^M

end spike
pique^F

tailpiece
cordier^M

bow
archet^M

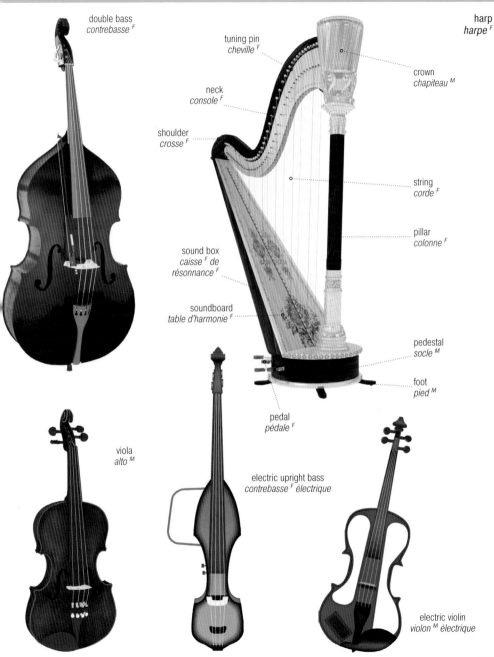

double bass
contrebasse [F]

harp
harpe [F]

tuning pin
cheville [F]

crown
chapiteau [M]

neck
console [F]

shoulder
crosse [F]

string
corde [F]

pillar
colonne [F]

sound box
caisse [F] *de résonnance* [F]

soundboard
table d'harmonie [F]

pedestal
socle [M]

foot
pied [M]

pedal
pédale [F]

viola
alto [M]

electric upright bass
contrebasse [F] *électrique*

electric violin
violon [M] *électrique*

bass guitar
basse F

electric guitar
guitare F électrique

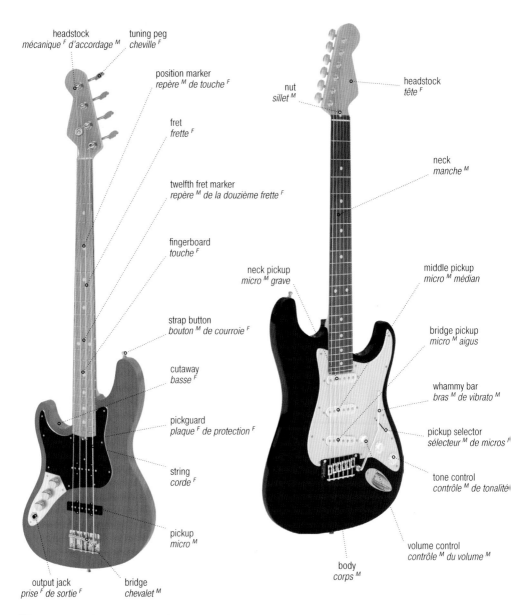

headstock
mécanique F d'accordage M

tuning peg
cheville F

position marker
repère M de touche F

nut
sillet M

headstock
tête F

fret
frette F

neck
manche M

twelfth fret marker
repère M de la douzième frette F

fingerboard
touche F

neck pickup
micro M grave

middle pickup
micro M médian

strap button
bouton M de courroie F

bridge pickup
micro M aigus

cutaway
basse F

whammy bar
bras M de vibrato M

pickguard
plaque F de protection F

pickup selector
sélecteur M de micros F

string
corde F

tone control
contrôle M de tonalité

pickup
micro M

volume control
contrôle M du volume M

output jack
prise F de sortie F

bridge
chevalet M

body
corps M

acoustic guitar
guitare [F] *acoustique*

headstock
tête [F]

peg
cheville [F]

nut
sillet [M]

fret
frette [F]

neck
manche [M]

distortion pedal
pédale [F] *de distorsion* [F]

heel
talon [M]

ribs
éclisse [F]

rosette
rosace [F]

sound hole
rosace [F]

semi-acoustic guitar
guitare [F] *semi-acoustique*

purfling
filet [M]

string
corde [F]

bridge
sillet [M] *de chevalet* [M]

soundboard
table [F] *d'harmonie* [F]

amplifier
amplificateur [M]

guitar case
étui [M] *à guitare* [F]

concertina
concertina ^M

harmonium
harmonium ^M

melodica
mélodica ^M

harmonica
harmonica ^M

accordion
accordéon ^M

bayan
bayan ^M

Australian instruments
Instruments [M] d'Australie [F]

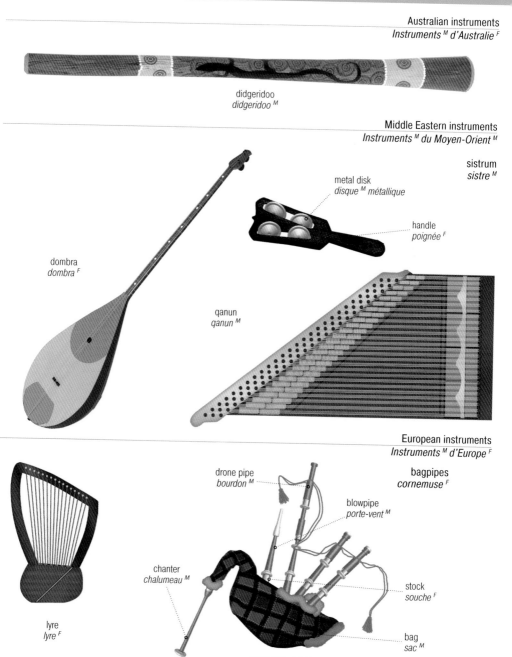

didgeridoo
didgeridoo [M]

Middle Eastern instruments
Instruments [M] du Moyen-Orient [M]

sistrum
sistre [M]

metal disk
disque [M] métallique

handle
poignée [F]

dombra
dombra [F]

qanun
qanun [M]

European instruments
Instruments [M] d'Europe [F]

drone pipe
bourdon [M]

bagpipes
cornemuse [F]

blowpipe
porte-vent [M]

chanter
chalumeau [M]

stock
souche [F]

lyre
lyre [F]

bag
sac [M]

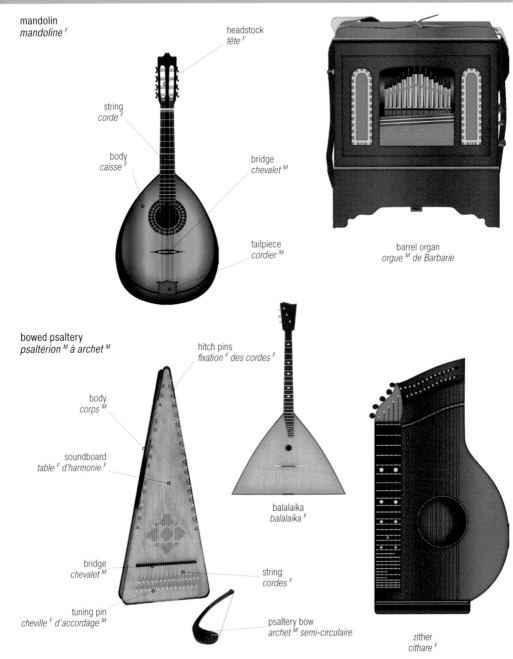

mandolin
mandoline F

headstock
tête F

string
corde F

body
caisse F

bridge
chevalet M

tailpiece
cordier M

barrel organ
orgue M *de Barbarie*

bowed psaltery
psaltérion M *à archet* M

hitch pins
fixation F *des cordes* F

body
corps M

soundboard
table F *d'harmonie* F

balalaika
balalaïka F

bridge
chevalet M

string
cordes F

tuning pin
cheville F *d'accordage* M

psaltery bow
archet M *semi-circulaire*

zither
cithare F

African instruments
Instruments ^M *d'Afrique* ^F

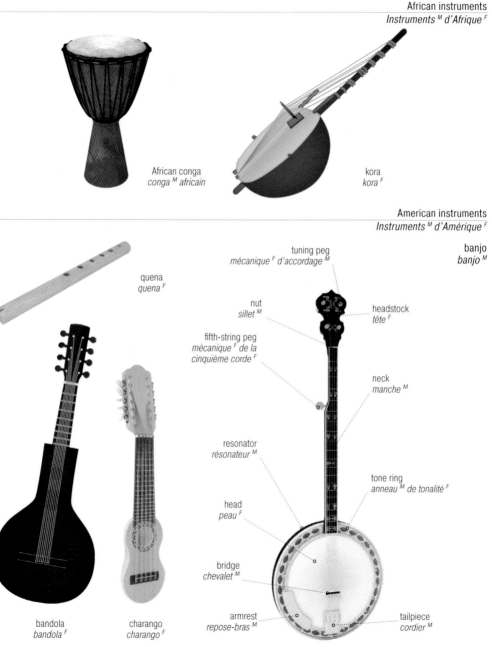

African conga
conga ^M *africain*

kora
kora ^F

American instruments
Instruments ^M *d'Amérique* ^F

tuning peg
mécanique ^F *d'accordage* ^M

banjo
banjo ^M

quena
quena ^F

nut
sillet ^M

headstock
tête ^F

fifth-string peg
mécanique ^F *de la
cinquième corde* ^F

neck
manche ^M

resonator
résonateur ^M

tone ring
anneau ^M *de tonalité* ^F

head
peau ^F

bridge
chevalet ^M

bandola
bandola ^F

charango
charango ^F

armrest
repose-bras ^M

tailpiece
cordier ^M

Asian instruments
Instruments [M] *d'Asie* [F]

guzheng
guzheng [M]

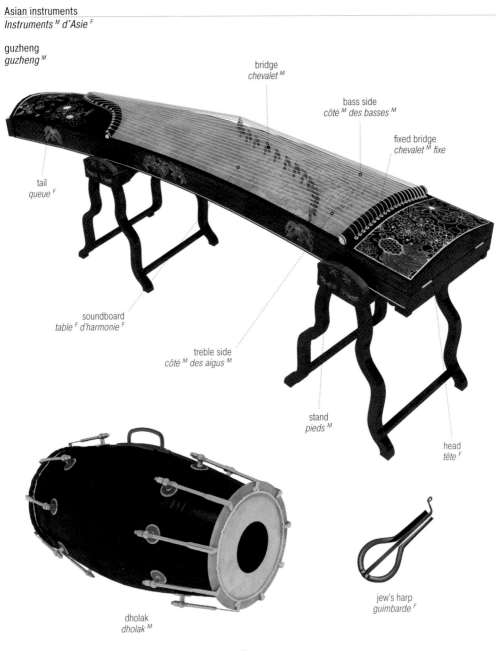

bridge
chevalet [M]

bass side
côté [M] *des basses* [M]

fixed bridge
chevalet [M] *fixe*

tail
queue [F]

soundboard
table [F] *d'harmonie* [F]

treble side
côté [M] *des aigus* [M]

stand
pieds [M]

head
tête [F]

dholak
dholak [M]

jew's harp
guimbarde [F]

guqin
qugin M

shehnai
shehnai F

double reed
anche F *double*

staple
tube M

ivory needle
aiguille F *d'ivoire* M

finger hole
trou M *de doigt* M

bell
pavillon M

huqin
huqin M

pipa
pipa M

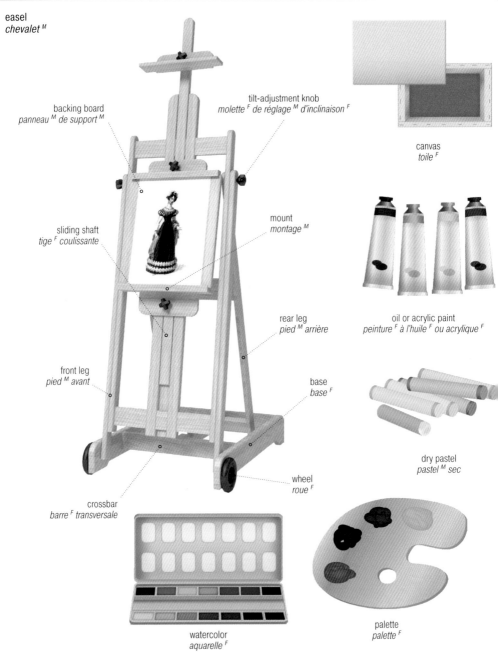

easel
chevalet ᴹ

backing board
panneau ᴹ *de support* ᴹ

tilt-adjustment knob
molette ᶠ *de réglage* ᴹ *d'inclinaison* ᶠ

canvas
toile ᶠ

sliding shaft
tige ᶠ *coulissante*

mount
montage ᴹ

oil or acrylic paint
peinture ᶠ *à l'huile* ᶠ *ou acrylique* ᶠ

rear leg
pied ᴹ *arrière*

front leg
pied ᴹ *avant*

base
base ᶠ

dry pastel
pastel ᴹ *sec*

wheel
roue ᶠ

crossbar
barre ᶠ *transversale*

watercolor
aquarelle ᶠ

palette
palette ᶠ

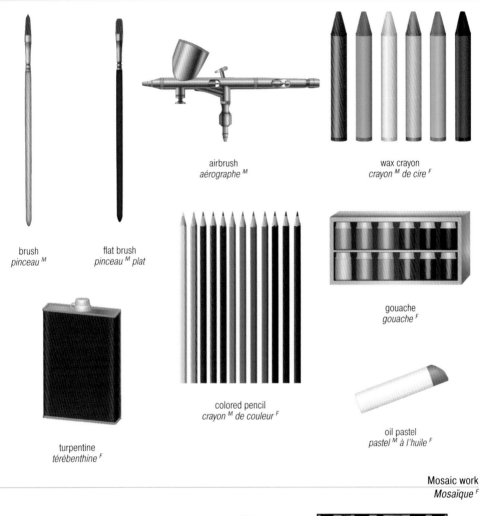

airbrush
aérographe ᴹ

wax crayon
crayon ᴹ de cire ᶠ

brush
pinceau ᴹ

flat brush
pinceau ᴹ plat

gouache
gouache ᶠ

colored pencil
crayon ᴹ de couleur ᶠ

oil pastel
pastel ᴹ à l'huile ᶠ

turpentine
térébenthine ᶠ

Mosaic work
Mosaïque ᶠ

glue
colle ᶠ

tessera
tesselles ᶠ

mosaic
mosaïque ᶠ

Embroidery
Broderie F

satin stitch
point M de satin M

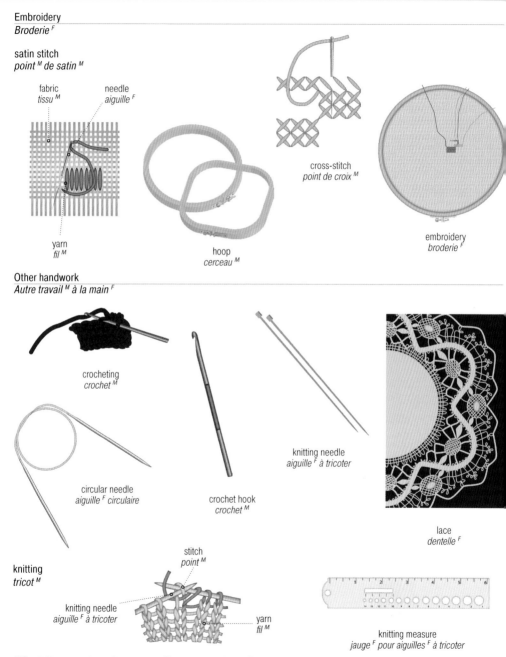

fabric
tissu M

needle
aiguille F

cross-stitch
point de croix M

yarn
fil M

hoop
cerceau M

embroidery
broderie F

Other handwork
Autre travail M à la main F

crocheting
crochet M

circular needle
aiguille F *circulaire*

crochet hook
crochet M

knitting needle
aiguille F *à tricoter*

lace
dentelle F

knitting
tricot M

stitch
point M

knitting needle
aiguille F *à tricoter*

yarn
fil M

knitting measure
jauge F *pour aiguilles* F *à tricoter*

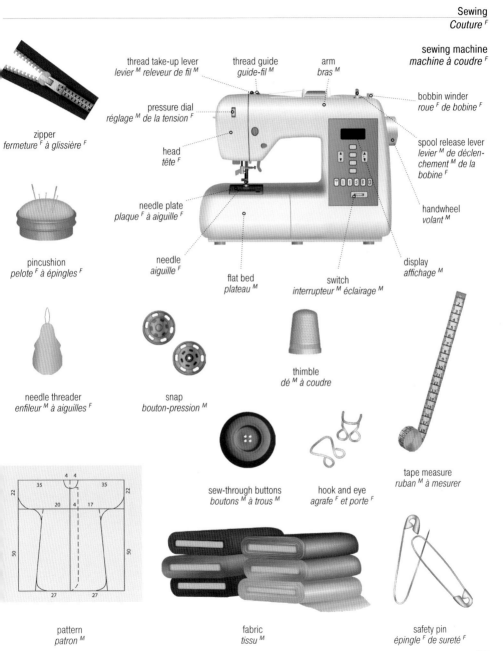

sewing machine
machine à coudre [F]

thread take-up lever
levier [M] *releveur de fil* [M]

thread guide
guide-fil [M]

arm
bras [M]

bobbin winder
roue [F] *de bobine* [F]

pressure dial
réglage [M] *de la tension* [F]

zipper
fermeture [F] *à glissière* [F]

head
tête [F]

spool release lever
levier [M] *de déclen-chement* [M] *de la bobine* [F]

needle plate
plaque [F] *à aiguille* [F]

handwheel
volant [M]

pincushion
pelote [F] *à épingles* [F]

needle
aiguille [F]

flat bed
plateau [M]

switch
interrupteur [M] *éclairage* [M]

display
affichage [M]

needle threader
enfileur [M] *à aiguilles* [F]

snap
bouton-pression [M]

thimble
dé [M] *à coudre*

tape measure
ruban [M] *à mesurer*

sew-through buttons
boutons [M] *à trous* [M]

hook and eye
agrafe [F] *et porte* [F]

pattern
patron [M]

fabric
tissu [M]

safety pin
épingle [F] *de sureté* [F]

cathedral
cathédrale ^F

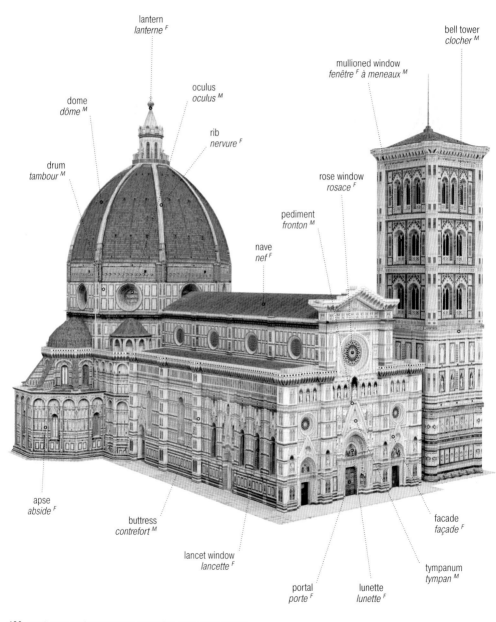

lantern
lanterne ^F

bell tower
clocher ^M

mullioned window
fenêtre ^F *à meneaux* ^M

oculus
oculus ^M

dome
dôme ^M

rib
nervure ^F

drum
tambour ^M

rose window
rosace ^F

pediment
fronton ^M

nave
nef ^F

apse
abside ^F

buttress
contrefort ^M

facade
façade ^F

lancet window
lancette ^F

tympanum
tympan ^M

portal
porte ^F

lunette
lunette ^F

mosque
mosquée F

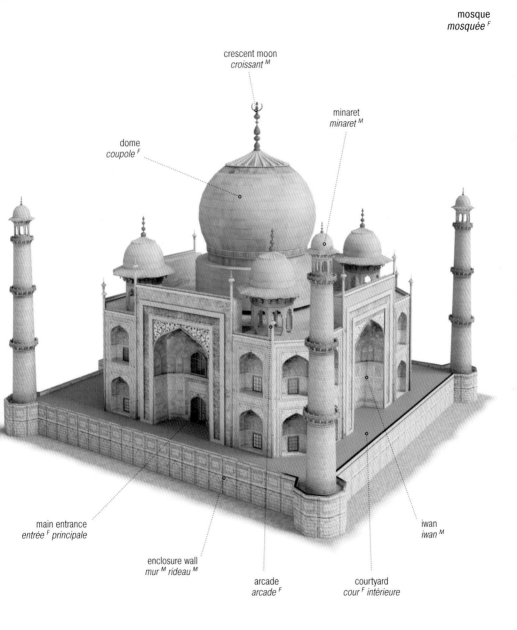

crescent moon
croissant M

minaret
minaret M

dome
coupole F

main entrance
entrée F *principale*

iwan
iwan M

enclosure wall
mur M *rideau* M

arcade
arcade F

courtyard
cour F *intérieure*

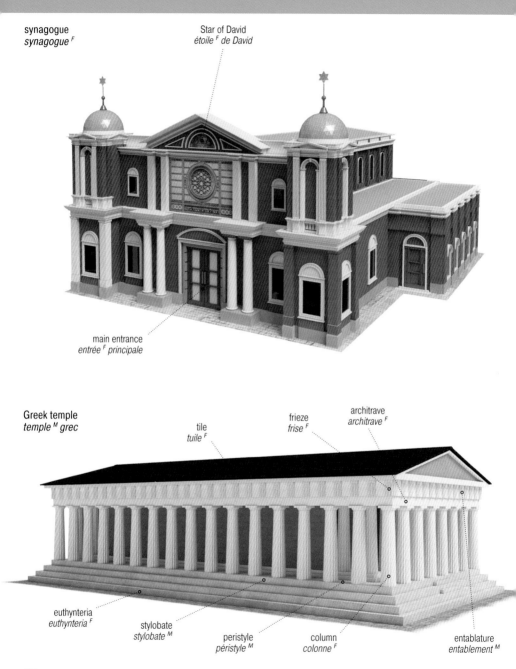

synagogue
synagogue ^F

Star of David
étoile ^F *de David*

main entrance
entrée ^F *principale*

Greek temple
temple ^M *grec*

tile
tuile ^F

frieze
frise ^F

architrave
architrave ^F

euthynteria
euthynteria ^F

stylobate
stylobate ^M

peristyle
péristyle ^M

column
colonne ^F

entablature
entablement ^M

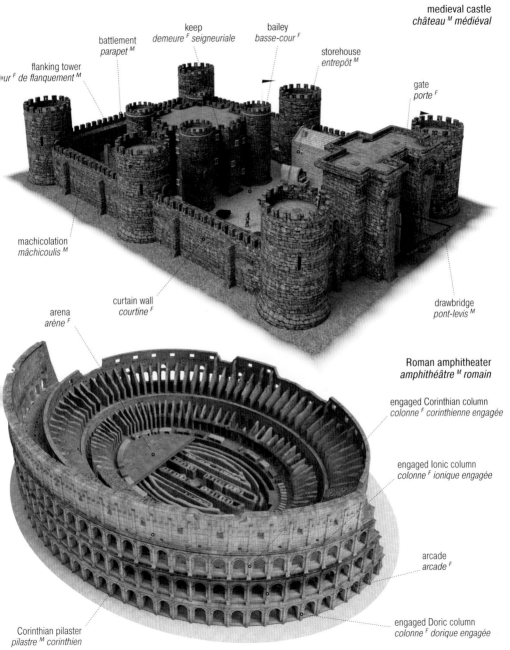

medieval castle
château ^M médiéval

keep
demeure ^F seigneuriale

bailey
basse-cour ^F

battlement
parapet ^M

storehouse
entrepôt ^M

flanking tower
ur ^F de flanquement ^M

gate
porte ^F

machicolation
mâchicoulis ^M

arena
arène ^F

curtain wall
courtine ^F

drawbridge
pont-levis ^M

Roman amphitheater
amphithéâtre ^M romain

engaged Corinthian column
colonne ^F corinthienne engagée

engaged Ionic column
colonne ^F ionique engagée

arcade
arcade ^F

engaged Doric column
colonne ^F dorique engagée

Corinthian pilaster
pilastre ^M corinthien

SPORTS

SPORTS

soccer field
terrain ^M de soccer ^M

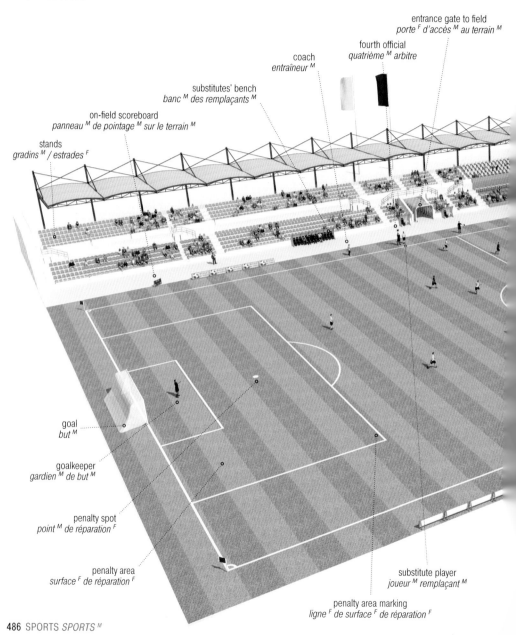

entrance gate to field
porte ^F d'accès ^M au terrain ^M

fourth official
quatrième ^M arbitre

coach
entraîneur ^M

substitutes' bench
banc ^M des remplaçants ^M

on-field scoreboard
panneau ^M de pointage ^M sur le terrain ^M

stands
gradins ^M / estrades ^F

goal
but ^M

goalkeeper
gardien ^M de but ^M

penalty spot
point ^M de réparation ^F

penalty area
surface ^F de réparation ^F

substitute player
joueur ^M remplaçant ^M

penalty area marking
ligne ^F de surface ^F de réparation ^F

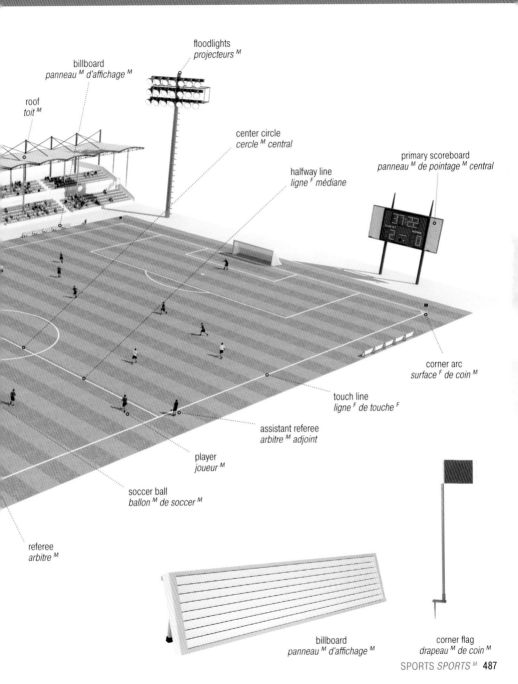

floodlights
projecteurs ^M

billboard
panneau ^M *d'affichage* ^M

roof
toit ^M

center circle
cercle ^M *central*

halfway line
ligne ^F *médiane*

primary scoreboard
panneau ^M *de pointage* ^M *central*

corner arc
surface ^F *de coin* ^M

touch line
ligne ^F *de touche* ^F

assistant referee
arbitre ^M *adjoint*

player
joueur ^M

soccer ball
ballon ^M *de soccer* ^M

referee
arbitre ^M

billboard
panneau ^M *d'affichage* ^M

corner flag
drapeau ^M *de coin* ^M

soccer ball
ballon M *de soccer* M

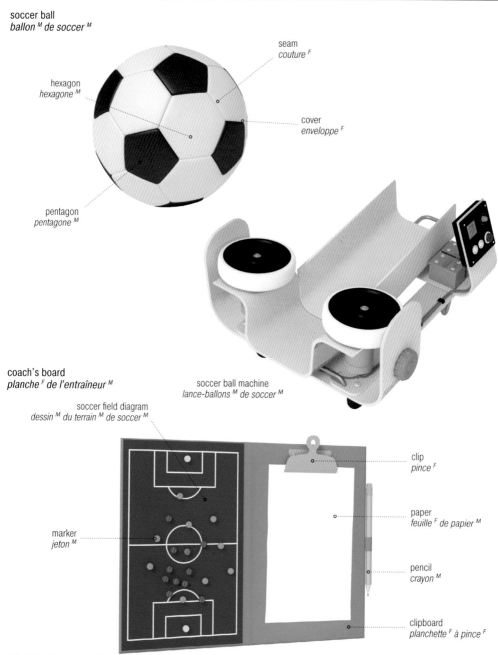

seam
couture F

hexagon
hexagone M

cover
enveloppe F

pentagon
pentagone M

soccer ball machine
lance-ballons M *de soccer* M

coach's board
planche F *de l'entraîneur* M

soccer field diagram
dessin M *du terrain* M *de soccer* M

clip
pince F

paper
feuille F *de papier* M

marker
jeton M

pencil
crayon M

clipboard
planchette F *à pince* F

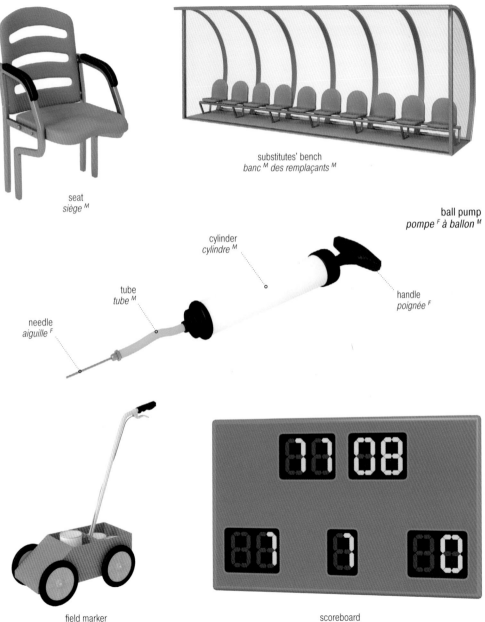

substitutes' bench
banc ^M *des remplaçants* ^M

seat
siège ^M

ball pump
pompe ^F *à ballon* ^M

cylinder
cylindre ^M

handle
poignée ^F

tube
tube ^M

needle
aiguille ^F

field marker
traceur ^M *de terrain* ^M

scoreboard
panneau ^M *de pointage* ^M

Referee's equipment
Équipement ^M *d'arbitre* ^M

referee's shelter
abri ^M *d'arbitre* ^M

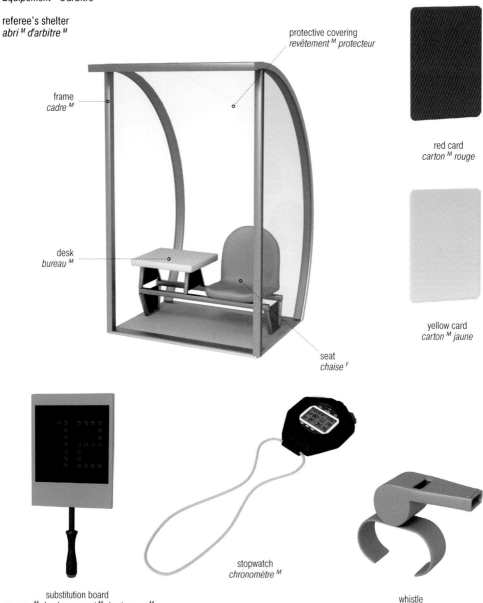

protective covering
revêtement ^M *protecteur*

frame
cadre ^M

red card
carton ^M *rouge*

desk
bureau ^M

yellow card
carton ^M *jaune*

seat
chaise ^F

stopwatch
chronomètre ^M

substitution board
panneau ^M *de changement* ^M *des joueurs* ^M

whistle
sifflet ^M

Soccer player and equipment
Joueur ^M *et équipement* ^M *de soccer* ^M

shin guard
protège-tibia ^M

soccer player
joueur ^M *de soccer* ^M

jersey
maillot ^M

shorts
short ^M

goalkeeper's glove
gant ^M *de gardien* ^M *de but* ^M

tongue
languette ^F

lace
lacet ^M

stud
pointe ^F

soccer cleats
crampons ^M

heel
talon ^M

toe
orteil ^M

American football field
terrain M *de football* M *américain*

referee
arbitre M *en chef* M

team area
zone F *de l'équipe* F

line judge
juge M *de mêlée*

end zone
zone F *des buts* M

billboard
panneau M *d'affichage* M

concession stand
casse-croûte M

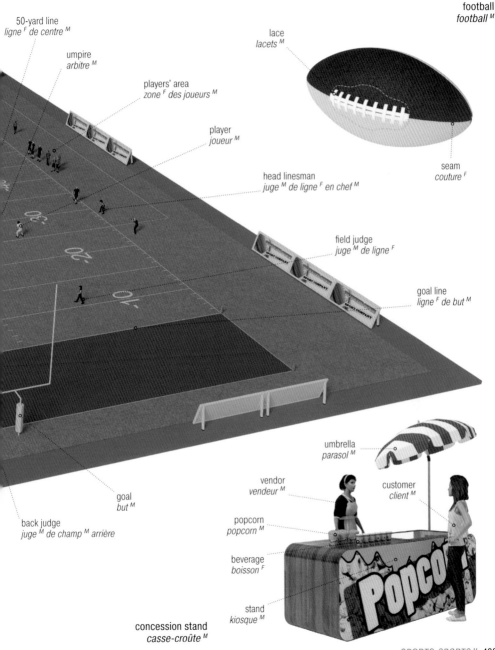

50-yard line
ligne F de centre M

umpire
arbitre M

players' area
zone F des joueurs M

player
joueur M

head linesman
juge M de ligne F en chef M

field judge
juge M de ligne F

goal line
ligne F de but M

goal
but M

back judge
juge M de champ M arrière

football
football M

lace
lacets M

seam
couture F

umbrella
parasol M

vendor
vendeur M

customer
client M

popcorn
popcorn M

beverage
boisson F

stand
kiosque M

concession stand
casse-croûte M

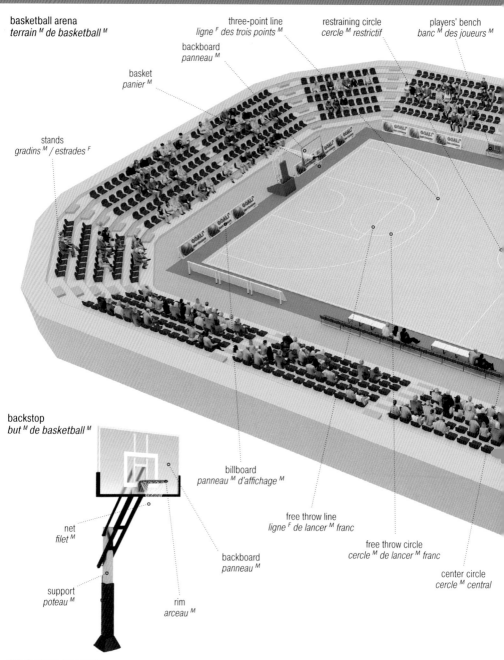

basketball arena
terrain ^M de basketball ^M

three-point line
ligne ^F des trois points ^M

restraining circle
cercle ^M restrictif

players' bench
banc ^M des joueurs ^M

backboard
panneau ^M

basket
panier ^M

stands
gradins ^M / estrades ^F

backstop
but ^M de basketball ^M

billboard
panneau ^M d'affichage ^M

free throw line
ligne ^F de lancer ^M franc

free throw circle
cercle ^M de lancer ^M franc

center circle
cercle ^M central

net
filet ^M

backboard
panneau ^M

support
poteau ^M

rim
arceau ^M

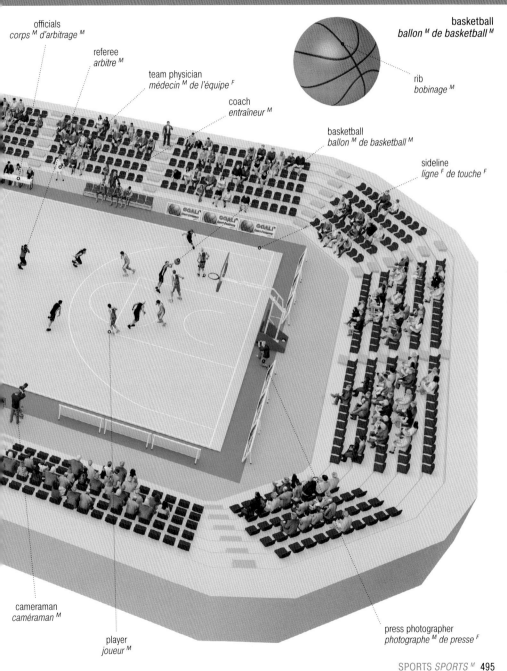

officials
corps ᴹ d'arbitrage ᴹ

referee
arbitre ᴹ

team physician
médecin ᴹ de l'équipe ᶠ

coach
entraîneur ᴹ

basketball
ballon ᴹ de basketball ᴹ

rib
bobinage ᴹ

basketball
ballon ᴹ de basketball ᴹ

sideline
ligne ᶠ de touche ᶠ

cameraman
caméraman ᴹ

player
joueur ᴹ

press photographer
photographe ᴹ de presse ᶠ

Basketball moves
Mouvements M *du basketball* M

layup
tir M *déposé*

hook shot
tir M *à bras* M *roulé*

holding
tenir le ballon M

dribbling
dribbler

pump fake
feinte F *de passe* F

baseball glove: bottom view
gant M de baseball M : vue F du dessous M

thumb
pouce M

strap
patte F

palm
paume F

lace
lacets M

finger
doigt M

cross section of a baseball
coupe F de la balle F

yarn ball
balle F de fil M retors

cork center
centre M de liège M

baseball glove: top view
gant M de baseball M : vue F du dessus M

stitches
couture F

cover
enveloppe F

bat
bâton M

baseball field (baseball diamond)
terrain ^M _de baseball_ ^M

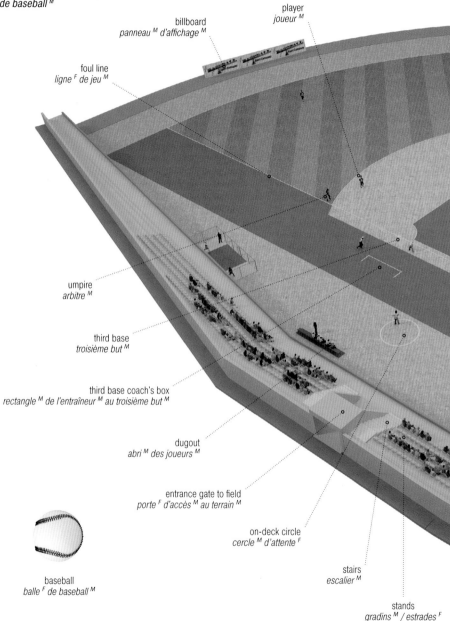

player
joueur ^M

billboard
panneau ^M _d'affichage_ ^M

foul line
ligne ^F _de jeu_ ^M

umpire
arbitre ^M

third base
troisième but ^M

third base coach's box
rectangle ^M _de l'entraîneur_ ^M _au troisième but_ ^M

dugout
abri ^M _des joueurs_ ^M

entrance gate to field
porte ^F _d'accès_ ^M _au terrain_ ^M

on-deck circle
cercle ^M _d'attente_ ^F

stairs
escalier ^M

stands
gradins ^M / _estrades_ ^F

baseball
balle ^F _de baseball_ ^M

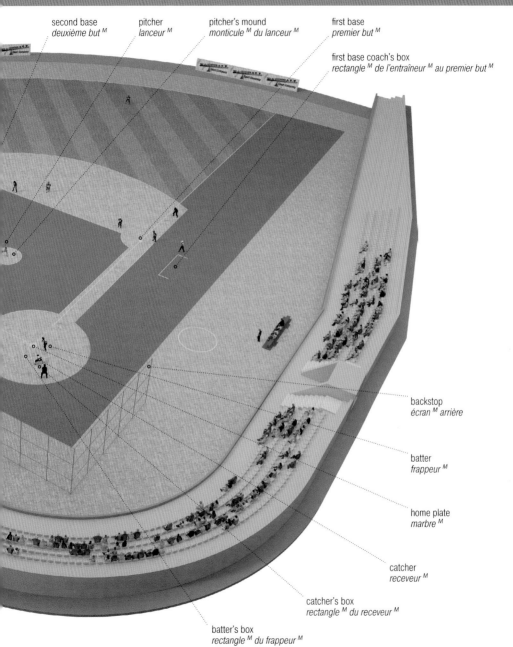

second base
deuxième but ^M

pitcher
lanceur ^M

pitcher's mound
monticule ^M _du lanceur_ ^M

first base
premier but ^M

first base coach's box
rectangle ^M _de l'entraîneur_ ^M _au premier but_ ^M

backstop
écran ^M _arrière_

batter
frappeur ^M

home plate
marbre ^M

catcher
receveur ^M

catcher's box
rectangle ^M _du receveur_ ^M

batter's box
rectangle ^M _du frappeur_ ^M

volleyball court
terrain ^M *de volleyball* ^M

center attacker
attaquant ^M *central*

left attacker
attaquant ^M *gauche*

right attacker
attaquant ^M *droit*

vertical side band
bande ^F *verticale de côté* ^M

right back
arrière ^M *droit*

umpire
deuxième arbitre ^M

scorekeeper
marqueur ^M

net
filet ^M

post
poteau ^M

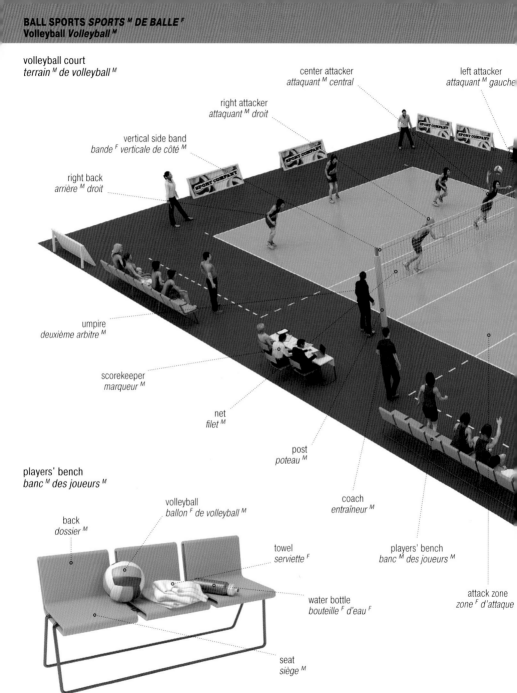

players' bench
banc ^M *des joueurs* ^M

back
dossier ^M

volleyball
ballon ^F *de volleyball* ^M

towel
serviette ^F

coach
entraîneur ^M

players' bench
banc ^M *des joueurs* ^M

water bottle
bouteille ^F *d'eau* ^F

attack zone
zone ^F *d'attaque*

seat
siège ^M

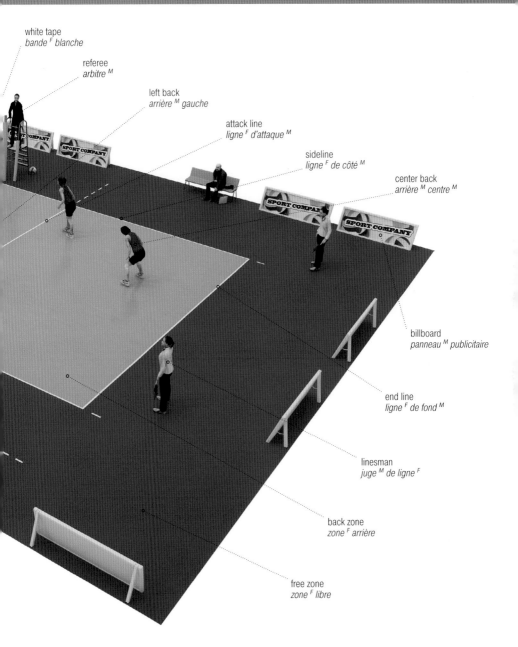

white tape
bande F *blanche*

referee
arbitre M

left back
arrière M *gauche*

attack line
ligne F *d'attaque* M

sideline
ligne F *de côté* M

center back
arrière M *centre* M

billboard
panneau M *publicitaire*

end line
ligne F *de fond* M

linesman
juge M *de ligne* F

back zone
zone F *arrière*

free zone
zone F *libre*

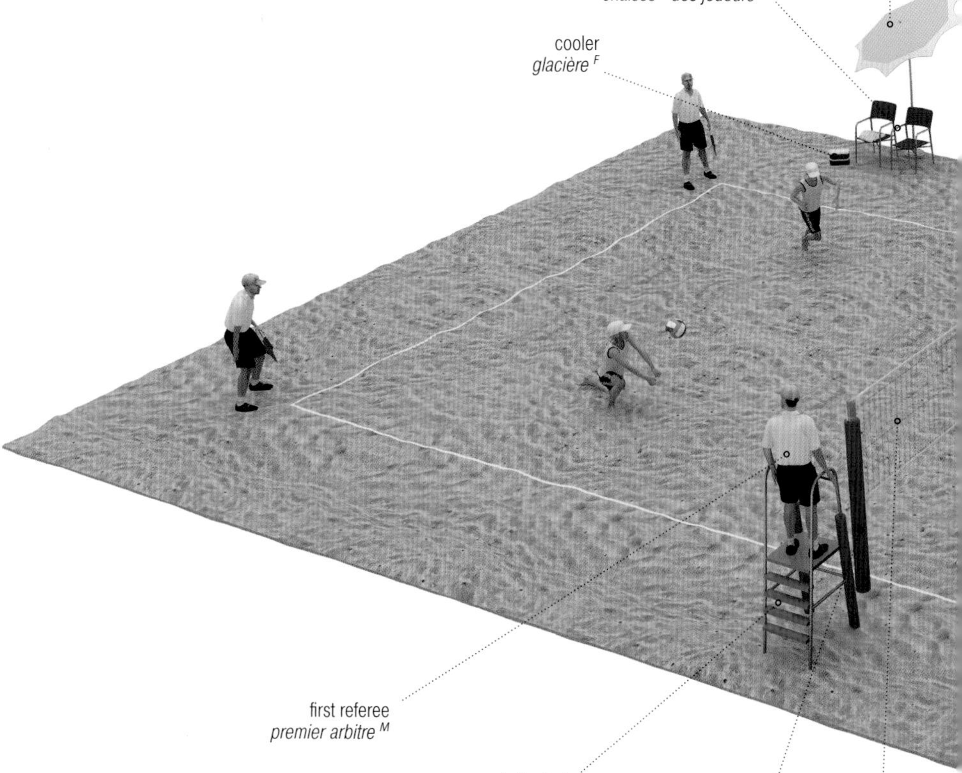

beach volleyball court
terrain M *de volleyball* M *de plage* F

umbrella
parasol M

players' chairs
chaises F *des joueurs* M

cooler
glacière F

first referee
premier arbitre M

umpire's chair
chaise F *d'arbitre* M

stand
poteau M

net
filet M

beach volleyball
ballon M *de volleyball* M *de plage* F

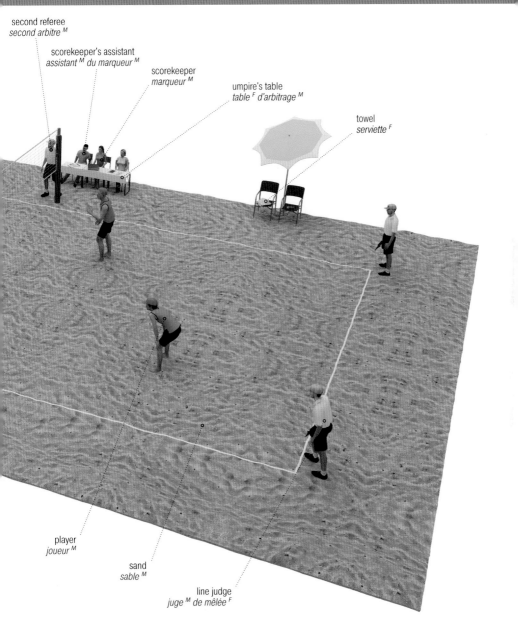

second referee
second arbitre M

scorekeeper's assistant
assistant M du marqueur M

scorekeeper
marqueur M

umpire's table
table F d'arbitrage M

towel
serviette F

player
joueur M

sand
sable M

line judge
juge M de mêlée F

badminton court
court M *de badminton* M

umpire
arbitre M *de chaise* F

towel
serviette F

water bottle
bouteille F *d'eau* F

long service line
ligne F *de fond* M

racket bag
étui M *à raquette* F

billboard
panneau M *d'affichage* M

center line
ligne F *médiane*

doubles sideline
ligne F *de double* M

short service line
ligne F *de service* M *court*

back boundary line
ligne F *de fond* M

singles sideline
ligne F *de simple* M

linesman
juge M *de ligne* F

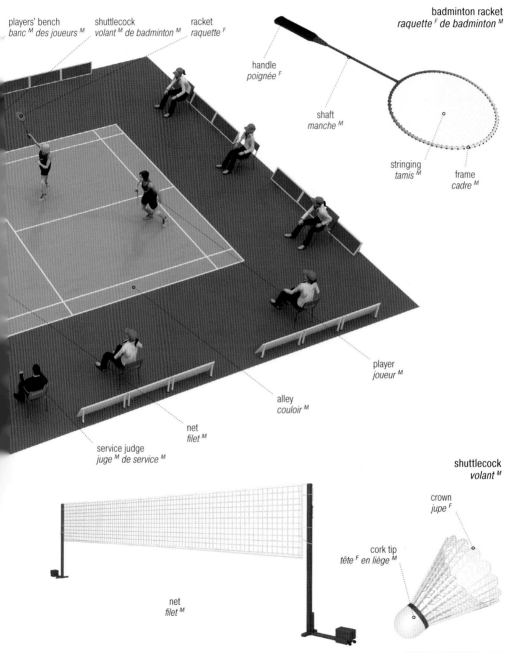

badminton racket
raquette F *de badminton* M

players' bench
banc M *des joueurs* M

shuttlecock
volant M *de badminton* M

racket
raquette F

handle
poignée F

shaft
manche M

stringing
tamis M

frame
cadre M

player
joueur M

alley
couloir M

net
filet M

service judge
juge M *de service* M

net
filet M

shuttlecock
volant M

crown
jupe F

cork tip
tête F *en liège* M

tennis court
court ^M *de tennis* ^M

cameraman
caméraman ^M

player's bench
banc ^M *des joueurs* ^M

chair umpire
arbitre ^M *de chaise* ^F

service line
ligne ^F *de service* ^M

alley
couloir ^M

tennis racket
raquette ^F *de tennis* ^M

ball boy
ramasseur ^M *de balles* ^F

billboard
panneau ^M *d'affichage* ^M

stairs
escalier ^M

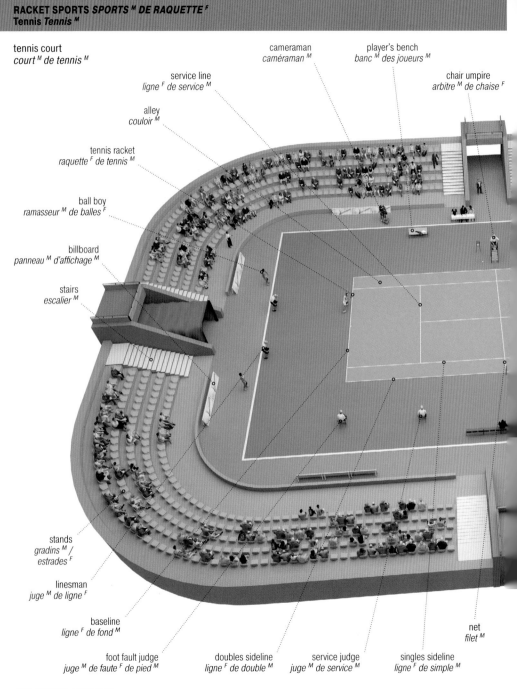

stands
gradins ^M /
estrades ^F

linesman
juge ^M *de ligne* ^F

baseline
ligne ^F *de fond* ^M

net
filet ^M

foot fault judge
juge ^M *de faute* ^F *de pied* ^M

doubles sideline
ligne ^F *de double* ^M

service judge
juge ^M *de service* ^M

singles sideline
ligne ^F *de simple* ^M

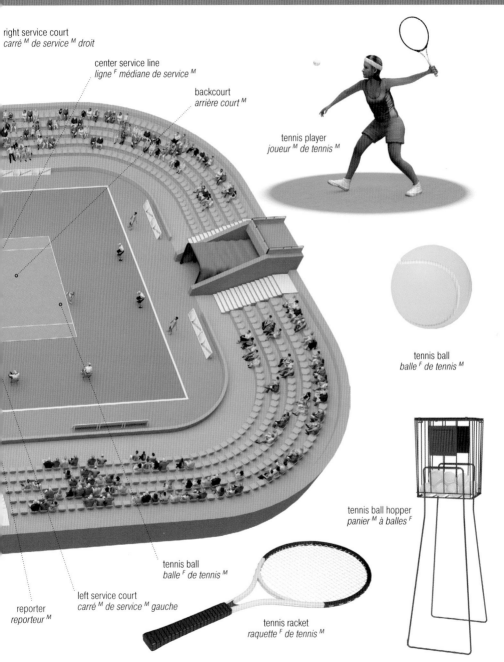

right service court
carré ^M de service ^M droit

center service line
ligne ^F médiane de service ^M

backcourt
arrière court ^M

tennis player
joueur ^M de tennis ^M

tennis ball
balle ^F de tennis ^M

tennis ball hopper
panier ^M à balles ^F

tennis ball
balle ^F de tennis ^M

left service court
carré ^M de service ^M gauche

reporter
reporteur ^M

tennis racket
raquette ^F de tennis ^M

table tennis court
court ᴹ *de tennis* ᴹ *de table* ᶠ

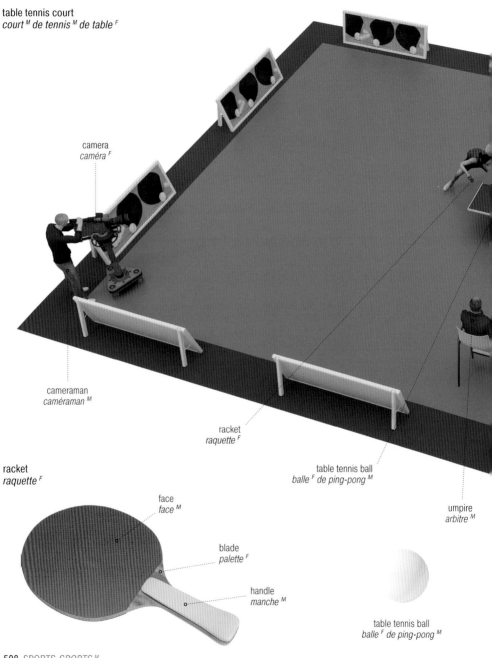

camera
caméra ᶠ

cameraman
caméraman ᴹ

racket
raquette ᶠ

racket
raquette ᶠ

face
face ᴹ

blade
palette ᶠ

handle
manche ᴹ

table tennis ball
balle ᶠ *de ping-pong* ᴹ

umpire
arbitre ᴹ

table tennis ball
balle ᶠ *de ping-pong* ᴹ

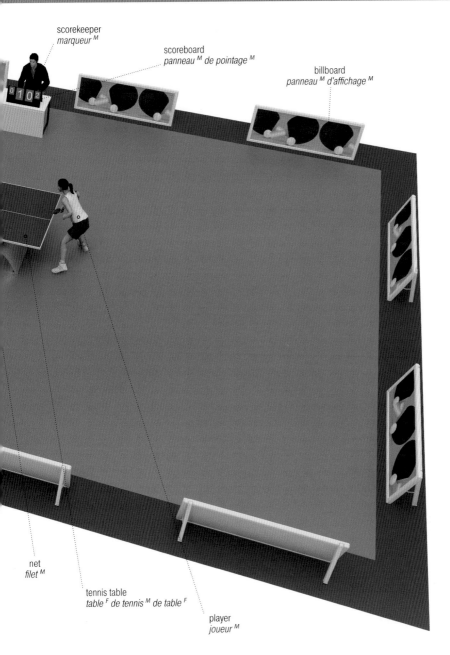

scorekeeper
marqueur ^M

scoreboard
panneau ^M *de pointage* ^M

billboard
panneau ^M *d'affichage* ^M

net
filet ^M

tennis table
table ^F *de tennis* ^M *de table* ^F

player
joueur ^M

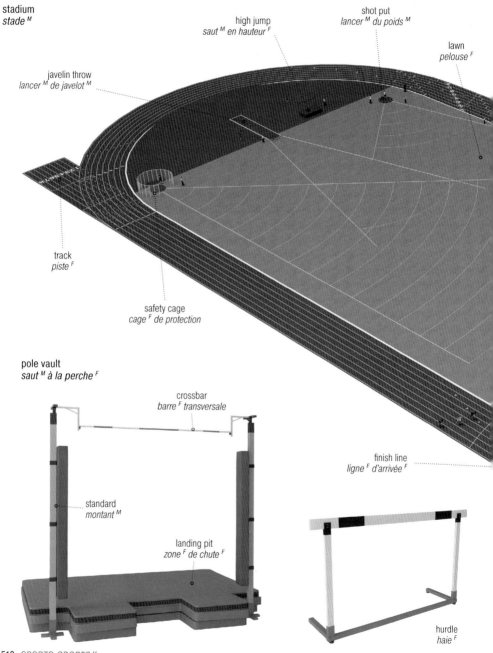

stadium
stade ^M

high jump
saut ^M *en hauteur* ^F

shot put
lancer ^M *du poids* ^M

lawn
pelouse ^F

javelin throw
lancer ^M *de javelot* ^M

track
piste ^F

safety cage
cage ^F *de protection*

pole vault
saut ^M *à la perche* ^F

crossbar
barre ^F *transversale*

finish line
ligne ^F *d'arrivée* ^F

standard
montant ^M

landing pit
zone ^F *de chute* ^F

hurdle
haie ^F

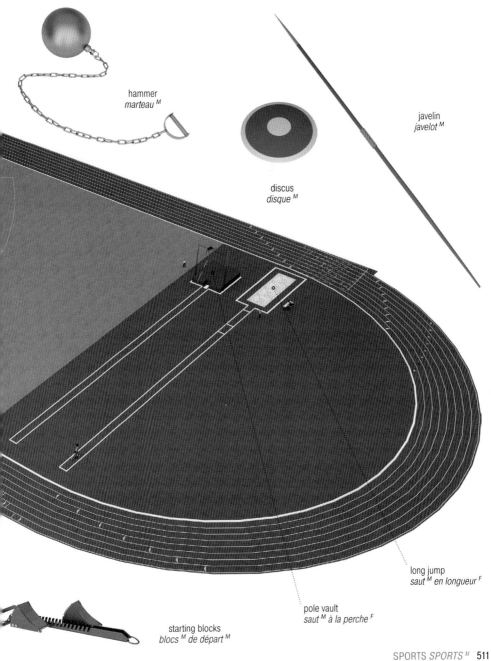

hammer
marteau [M]

javelin
javelot [M]

discus
disque [M]

long jump
saut [M] *en longueur* [F]

pole vault
saut [M] *à la perche* [F]

starting blocks
blocs [M] *de départ* [M]

artistic gymnastics
gymnastique ^F *artistique*

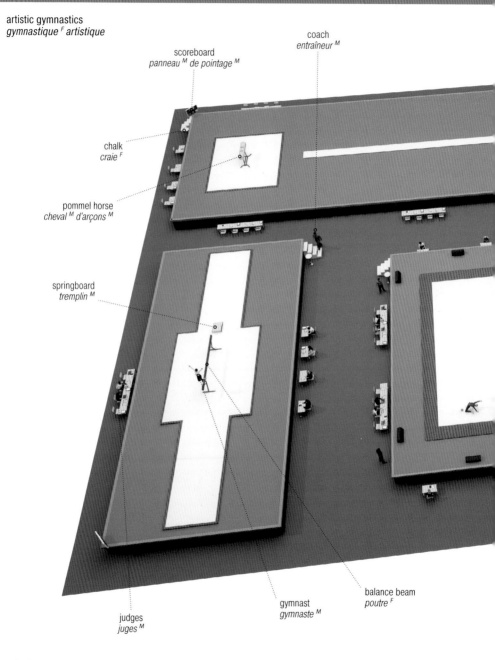

coach
entraîneur ^M

scoreboard
panneau ^M *de pointage* ^M

chalk
craie ^F

pommel horse
cheval ^M *d'arçons* ^M

springboard
tremplin ^M

balance beam
poutre ^F

gymnast
gymnaste ^M

judges
juges ^M

vault
cheval M

parallel bars
barres F *parallèles*

uneven parallel bars
barres F *asymétriques*

rings
anneaux M

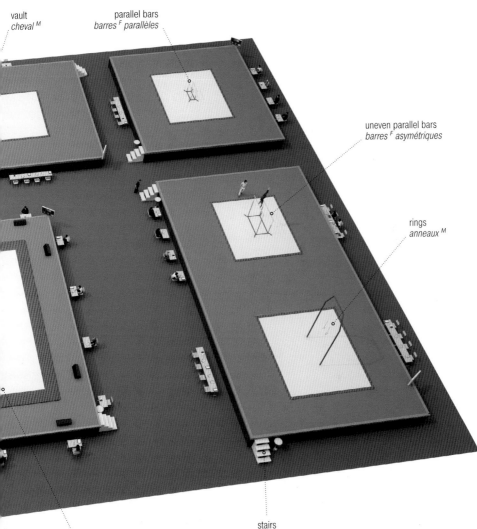

stairs
escalier M

spring floor
tapis M

Artistic gymnastics equipment
Équipement [M] *pour gymnastique* [F] *artistique*

uneven bars
barres [F] *asymétriques*

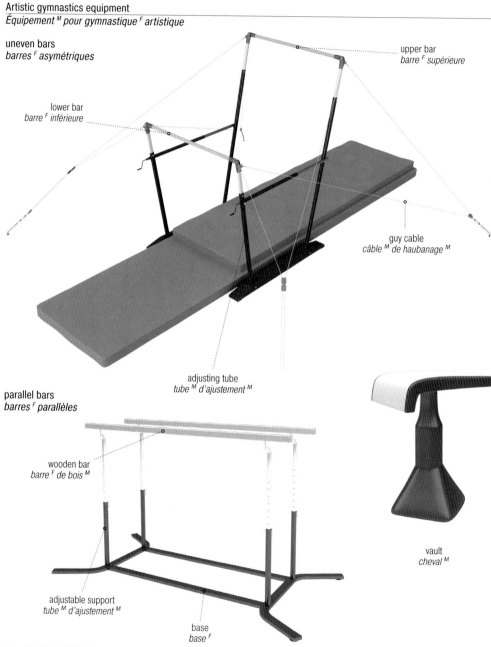

upper bar
barre [F] *supérieure*

lower bar
barre [F] *inférieure*

guy cable
câble [M] *de haubanage* [M]

adjusting tube
tube [M] *d'ajustement* [M]

parallel bars
barres [F] *parallèles*

wooden bar
barre [F] *de bois* [M]

adjustable support
tube [M] *d'ajustement* [M]

base
base [F]

vault
cheval [M]

pommel horse
cheval ^M *d'arçons* ^M

saddle
selle ^F

pommel
arçon ^M

neck
cou ^M

horse
cheval ^M

croup
croupe ^F

base
piètement ^M

height adjustment
réglage ^M *de la hauteur* ^F

chalk bowl
recipient ^M *à talc* ^M

anti-slip shoe
patin ^M *antidérapant*

springboard
tremplin ^M

balance beam
poutre ^F

vaulting horse
cheval ^M

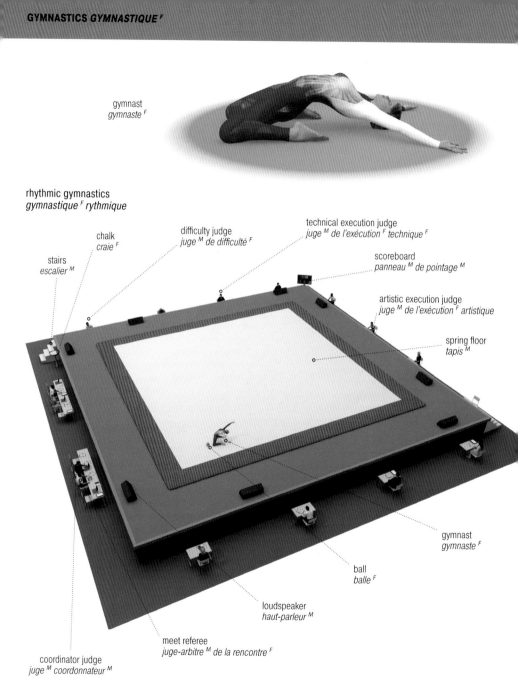

gymnast
gymnaste F

rhythmic gymnastics
gymnastique F *rythmique*

chalk
craie F

difficulty judge
juge M *de difficulté* F

technical execution judge
juge M *de l'exécution* F *technique* F

scoreboard
panneau M *de pointage* M

stairs
escalier M

artistic execution judge
juge M *de l'exécution* F *artistique*

spring floor
tapis M

gymnast
gymnaste F

ball
balle F

loudspeaker
haut-parleur M

meet referee
juge-arbitre M *de la rencontre* F

coordinator judge
juge M *coordonnateur* M

golf cart: front view
voiturette ^F *de golf* ^M : *vue* ^F *de face* ^F

roof
toit ^M

back
dossier ^M

seat
siège ^M

tire
pneu ^M

golf cart: back view
voiturette ^F *de golf* ^M : *vue* ^F *arrière*

club
bâton ^M *de golf* ^M

steering wheel
volant ^M

strap
courroie ^F

cup holder
porte-gobelet ^M

golf bag
sac ^M *de golf* ^M

storage compartment
compartiment ^M
de rangement ^M

armrest
accoudoir ^M

basket
panier ^M

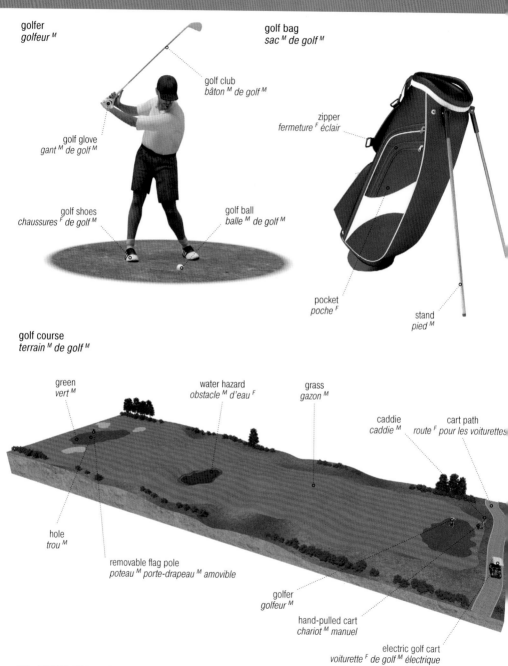

golfer
golfeur ^M

golf bag
sac ^M *de golf* ^M

golf club
bâton ^M *de golf* ^M

zipper
fermeture ^F *éclair*

golf glove
gant ^M *de golf* ^M

golf shoes
chaussures ^F *de golf* ^M

golf ball
balle ^M *de golf* ^M

pocket
poche ^F

stand
pied ^M

golf course
terrain ^M *de golf* ^M

green
vert ^M

water hazard
obstacle ^M *d'eau* ^F

grass
gazon ^M

caddie
caddie ^M

cart path
route ^F *pour les voiturettes*

hole
trou ^M

removable flag pole
poteau ^M *porte-drapeau* ^M *amovible*

golfer
golfeur ^M

hand-pulled cart
chariot ^M *manuel*

electric golf cart
voiturette ^F *de golf* ^M *électrique*

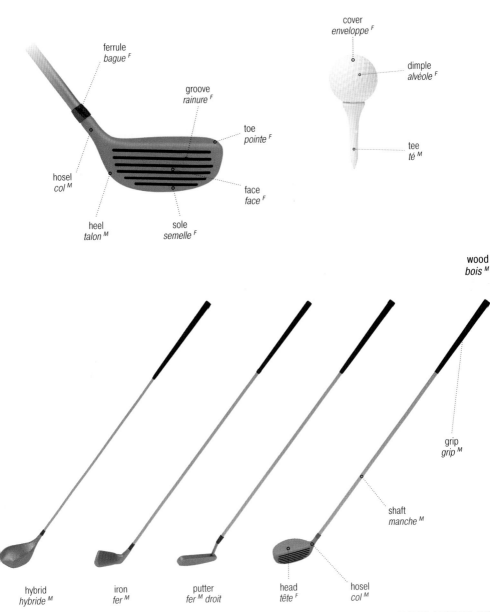

clubhead
tête [F] *d'un club* [M] *de golf* [M]

golf ball
balle [M] *de golf* [M]

cover
enveloppe [F]

dimple
alvéole [F]

tee
té [M]

ferrule
bague [F]

groove
rainure [F]

toe
pointe [F]

hosel
col [M]

face
face [F]

heel
talon [M]

sole
semelle [F]

wood
bois [M]

grip
grip [M]

shaft
manche [M]

hybrid
hybride [M]

iron
fer [M]

putter
fer [M] *droit*

head
tête [F]

hosel
col [M]

boxing ring
ring M de boxe F

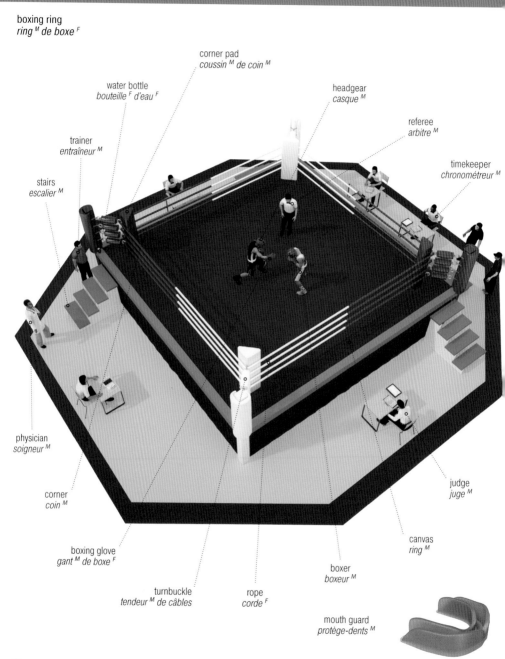

corner pad
coussin M de coin M

water bottle
bouteille F d'eau F

headgear
casque M

referee
arbitre M

trainer
entraîneur M

timekeeper
chronométreur M

stairs
escalier M

physician
soigneur M

judge
juge M

corner
coin M

canvas
ring M

boxing glove
gant M de boxe F

boxer
boxeur M

turnbuckle
tendeur M de câbles

rope
corde F

mouth guard
protège-dents M

heavy bag
punching-bag ^M / *sac* ^M *d'entraînement* ^M

shock-absorbing spring
ressort ^M *absorbeur* ^M *de chocs* ^M

stand
support ^M

eestanding heavy bag
nching-bag ^M autoportant /
ic ^M d'entraînement ^M autoportant

chain
chaîne ^F

punching bag
punching-bag ^M

stitching
couture ^F

base
socle ^M

rubber foot
pied ^M *en caoutchouc* ^M

oxing gloves
ants ^M de boxe ^F

strap
patte ^F

laces
lacets ^M

speed bag
ballon ^M *rapide*

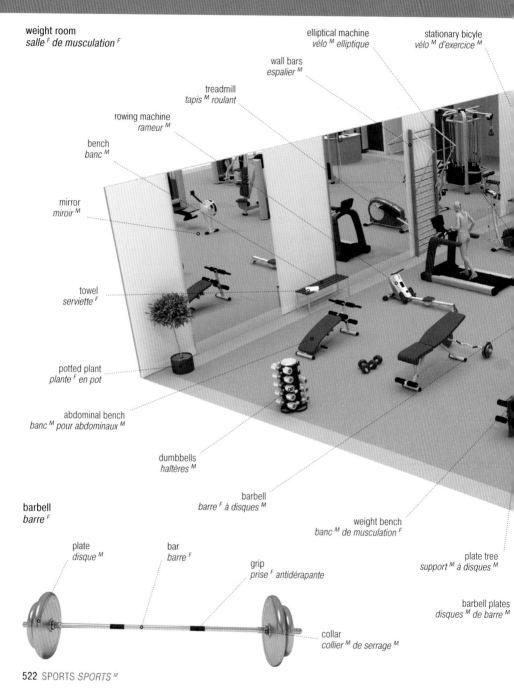

weight room
salle ᶠ de musculation ᶠ

elliptical machine
vélo ᴹ elliptique

stationary bicycle
vélo ᴹ d'exercice ᴹ

wall bars
espalier ᴹ

treadmill
tapis ᴹ roulant

rowing machine
rameur ᴹ

bench
banc ᴹ

mirror
miroir ᴹ

towel
serviette ᶠ

potted plant
plante ᶠ en pot

abdominal bench
banc ᴹ pour abdominaux ᴹ

dumbbells
haltères ᴹ

barbell
barre ᶠ à disques ᴹ

weight bench
banc ᴹ de musculation ᶠ

plate tree
support ᴹ à disques ᴹ

barbell
barre ᶠ

plate
disque ᴹ

bar
barre ᶠ

grip
prise ᶠ antidérapante

barbell plates
disques ᴹ de barre ᴹ

collar
collier ᴹ de serrage ᴹ

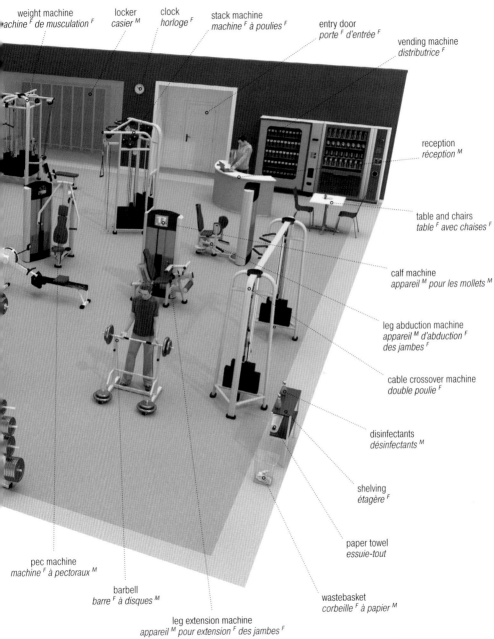

weight machine
machine [F] *de musculation* [F]

locker
casier [M]

clock
horloge [F]

stack machine
machine [F] *à poulies* [F]

entry door
porte [F] *d'entrée* [F]

vending machine
distributrice [F]

reception
réception [M]

table and chairs
table [F] *avec chaises* [F]

calf machine
appareil [M] *pour les mollets* [M]

leg abduction machine
appareil [M] *d'abduction* [F]
des jambes [F]

cable crossover machine
double poulie [F]

disinfectants
désinfectants [M]

shelving
étagère [F]

paper towel
essuie-tout

wastebasket
corbeille [F] *à papier* [M]

pec machine
machine [F] *à pectoraux* [M]

barbell
barre [F] *à disques* [M]

leg extension machine
appareil [M] *pour extension* [F] *des jambes* [F]

reception area
comptoir M *d'accueil* M

locker
casier M

bottled water
bouteille F *d'eau* F

flower vase
vase M *à fleurs* F

door
porte F

laptop computer
ordinateur M *portatif*

lock
verrou M

desk
comptoir M

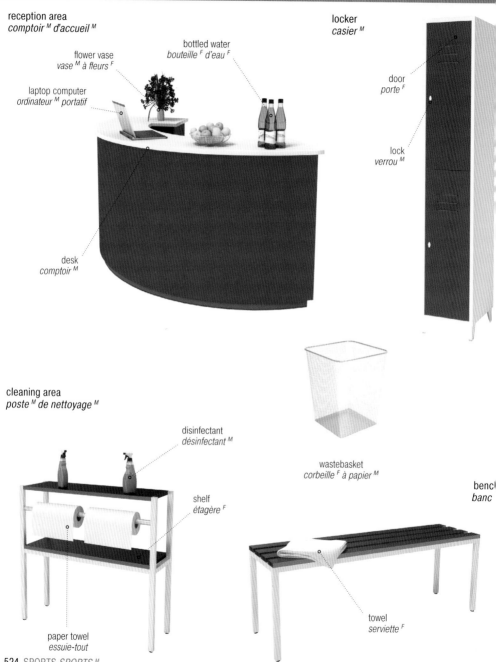

cleaning area
poste M *de nettoyage* M

disinfectant
désinfectant M

wastebasket
corbeille F *à papier* M

shelf
étagère F

bench
banc

paper towel
essuie-tout

towel
serviette F

fixed dumbbells
haltères ^M *préchargés*

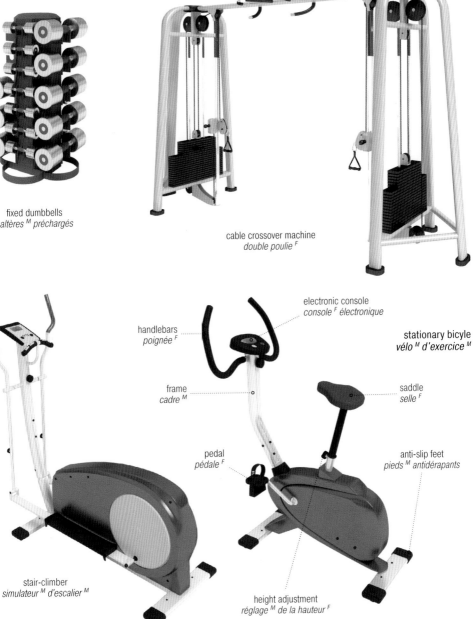

cable crossover machine
double poulie ^F

electronic console
console ^F *électronique*

handlebars
poignée ^F

stationary bicycle
vélo ^M *d'exercice* ^M

frame
cadre ^M

saddle
selle ^F

pedal
pédale ^F

anti-slip feet
pieds ^M *antidérapants*

stair-climber
simulateur ^M *d'escalier* ^M

height adjustment
réglage ^M *de la hauteur* ^F

treadmill
tapis ^{M} *roulant*

display
écran ^{M}

electronic console
console ^{F} *électronique*

grip
poignée ^{F}

running surface
surface ^{F} *de course* ^{F}

base
base ^{F}

barbell plates and tree
disques ^{M} *pour barres* ^{F} *et support* ^{M}

rowing machine
rameur ^{M}

handle
poignée ^{F}

footrest
repose-pieds ^{M}

display
écran ^{M}

anti-slip foot
pied ^{M} *antidérapant*

adjustable dumbbell
haltère ^{M} *ajustable*

frame
cadre ^{M}

strap
sangle ^{F}

resistance adjustment
réglage ^{M} *de la résistance* ^{F}

sliding seat
siège ^{M} *coulissant*

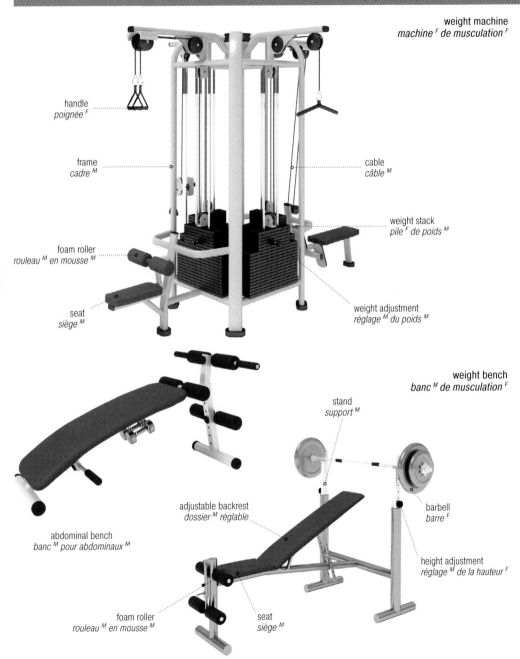

weight machine
machine ^F *de musculation* ^F

handle
poignée ^F

frame
cadre ^M

cable
câble ^M

weight stack
pile ^F *de poids* ^M

foam roller
rouleau ^M *en mousse* ^M

seat
siège ^M

weight adjustment
réglage ^M *du poids* ^M

weight bench
banc ^M *de musculation* ^F

stand
support ^M

adjustable backrest
dossier ^M *réglable*

barbell
barre ^F

abdominal bench
banc ^M *pour abdominaux* ^M

height adjustment
réglage ^M *de la hauteur* ^F

foam roller
rouleau ^M *en mousse* ^M

seat
siège ^M

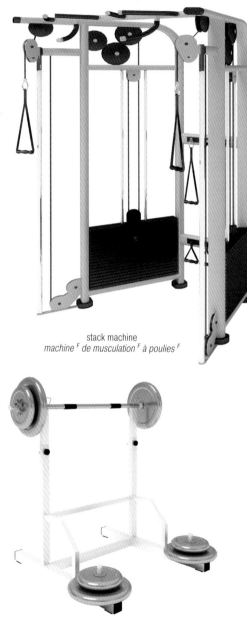

stack machine
machine ^F *de musculation* ^F *à poulies* ^F

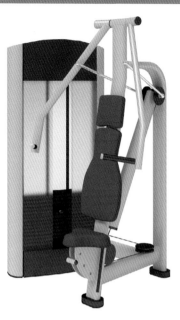

pec machine
machine ^F *à épaules* ^F

barbell stand
porte-haltère ^M

leg extension machine
appareil ^M *pour extension* ^F *des jambes* ^F

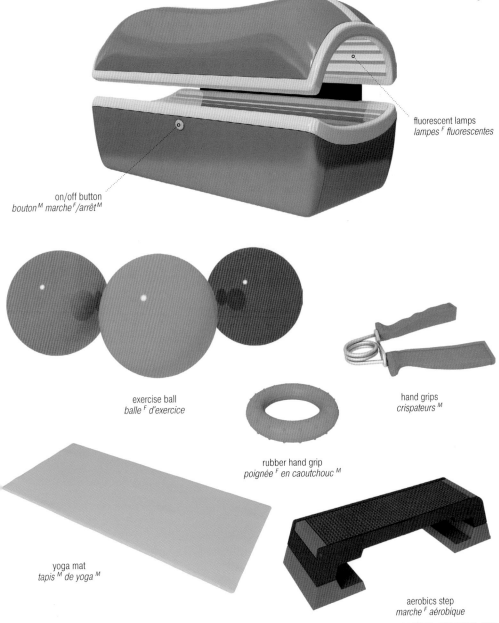

tanning bed
lit ^M *de bronzage* ^M

fluorescent lamps
lampes ^F *fluorescentes*

on/off button
bouton ^M *marche* ^F*/arrêt* ^M

exercise ball
balle ^F *d'exercice*

hand grips
crispateurs ^M

rubber hand grip
poignée ^F *en caoutchouc* ^M

yoga mat
tapis ^M *de yoga* ^M

aerobics step
marche ^F *aérobique*

shoulder stand
chandelle ^F *sur épaules* ^F

standing leg lift
élévation latérale de la jambe - debout

push-up
pompes ^F

scissors
ciseaux ^M

forward bend
flexion ^F *avant*

side lunge
étirements ^M *latéraux*

bra top
haut ^M *de sport* ^M

sweatpants
pantalon ^M *d'exercice* ^M

sneakers
espadrilles ^F

seated forward bend
fente ^F *avant - assis*

shoulder stand scissors
ciseaux ^M *avec chandelle* ^F *sur épaules* ^F

forward lunge
fente ^F *avant*

Skateboarding
Planches ᶠ *à roulettes* ᶠ

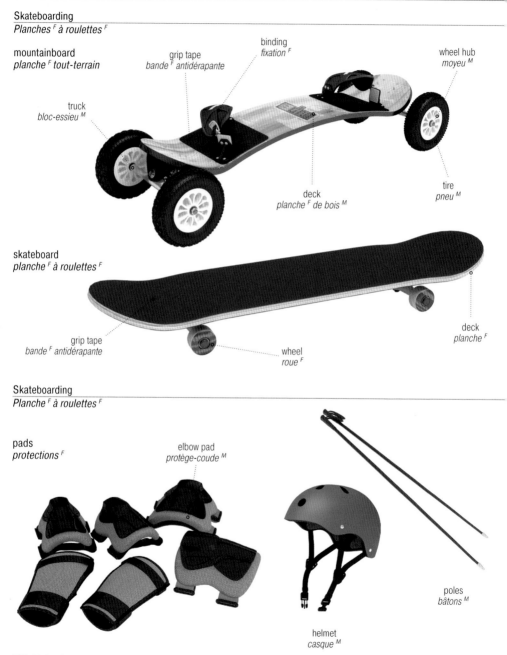

mountainboard
planche ᶠ *tout-terrain*

grip tape
bande ᶠ *antidérapante*

binding
fixation ᶠ

wheel hub
moyeu ᴹ

truck
bloc-essieu ᴹ

deck
planche ᶠ *de bois* ᴹ

tire
pneu ᴹ

skateboard
planche ᶠ *à roulettes* ᶠ

grip tape
bande ᶠ *antidérapante*

wheel
roue ᶠ

deck
planche ᶠ

Skateboarding
Planche ᶠ *à roulettes* ᶠ

pads
protections ᶠ

elbow pad
protège-coude ᴹ

poles
bâtons ᴹ

helmet
casque ᴹ

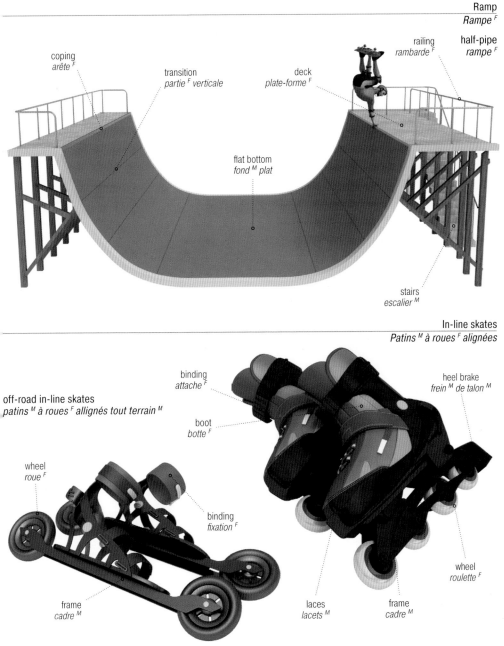

Ramp
Rampe F

railing
rambarde F

half-pipe
rampe F

coping
arête F

transition
partie F *verticale*

deck
plate-forme F

flat bottom
fond M *plat*

stairs
escalier M

In-line skates
Patins M *à roues* F *alignées*

binding
attache F

heel brake
frein M *de talon* M

off-road in-line skates
patins M *à roues* F *allignés tout terrain* M

boot
botte F

wheel
roue F

binding
fixation F

wheel
roulette F

frame
cadre M

laces
lacets M

frame
cadre M

mountain bicycle
vélo ^M de montagne ^F

handlebars
guidon ^M

front brake lever
poignée ^F de frein ^M avant

shifter
manette ^F de dérailleur ^M

rear brake lever
poignée ^F de frein ^M arrière

front fork
fourche ^F avant

front brake
frein ^M avant

hub
moyeu ^M

tire
pneu ^M

rim
jante ^F

spoke
rayon ^M

seat
selle ᶠ

frame
cadre ᴹ

road-racing bicycle
vélo ᴹ *de course* ᶠ

rear brake
frein ᴹ *arrière*

rear derailleur
dérailleur ᴹ *arrière*

chain
chaîne ᶠ

front derailleur
dérailleur ᴹ *avant*

pedal
pédale ᶠ

stand
pied ᴹ

crankset
pédalier ᴹ

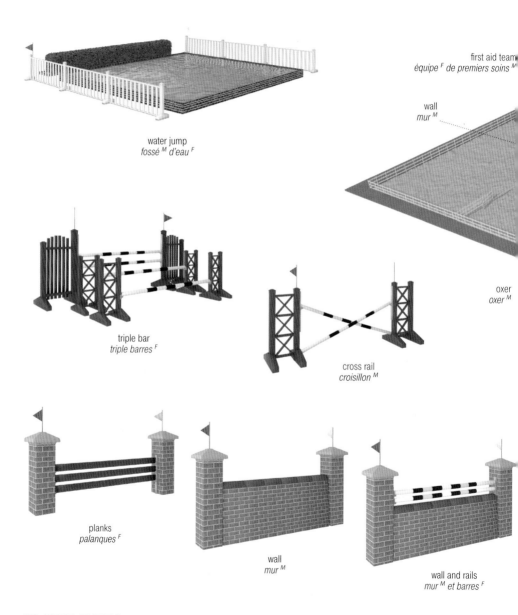

first aid team
équipe ^F de premiers soins ^M

wall
mur ^M

water jump
fossé ^M d'eau ^F

oxer
oxer ^M

triple bar
triple barres ^F

cross rail
croisillon ^M

planks
palanques ^F

wall
mur ^M

wall and rails
mur ^M et barres ^F

powerboat
bateau ^M *à moteur* ^M

engine compartment
compartiment ^M *moteur* ^M

seat
siège ^M

windshield
pare-brise ^M

hull
coque ^F

power racing catamaran
hydroglisseur ^M *de course* ^F

Rowing *Aviron* ^M

whitewater raft
radeau ^M *pneumatique pour rafting* ^M

seat back
dossier ^M *de siège* ^M

ring
anneau ^M

handle
poignée ^F

seat
siège ^M

paddle
rame ^F

double-blade paddle
pagaie ^F *double*

grip
poignée ^F

blade
pale ^F

shaft
manche ^M

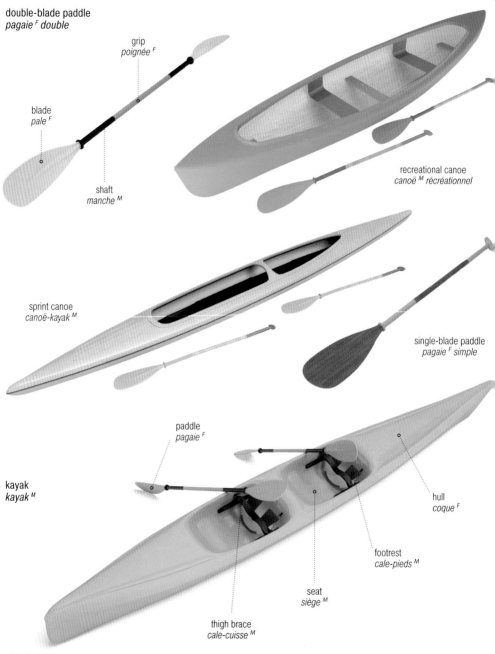

recreational canoe
canoë ^M *récréationnel*

sprint canoe
canoë-kayak ^M

single-blade paddle
pagaie ^F *simple*

paddle
pagaie ^F

kayak
kayak ^M

hull
coque ^F

footrest
cale-pieds ^M

seat
siège ^M

thigh brace
cale-cuisse ^M

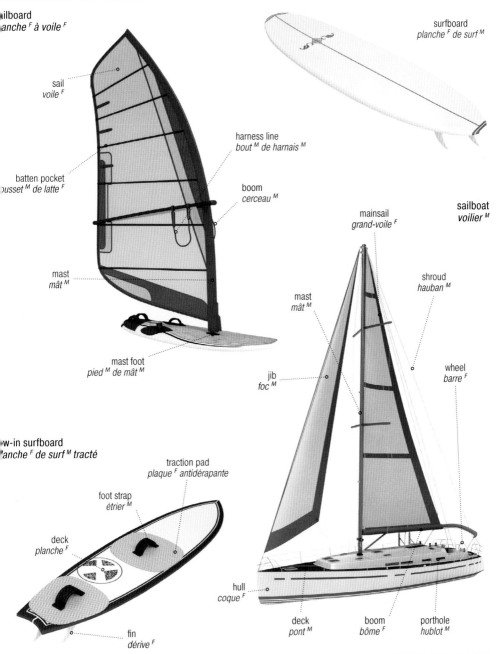

sailboard
planche ^F à voile ^F

surfboard
planche ^F de surf ^M

sail
voile ^F

harness line
bout ^M de harnais ^M

batten pocket
gousset ^M de latte ^F

boom
cerceau ^M

mainsail
grand-voile ^F

sailboat
voilier ^M

mast
mât ^M

shroud
hauban ^M

mast
mât ^M

mast foot
pied ^M de mât ^M

jib
foc ^M

wheel
barre ^F

tow-in surfboard
planche ^F de surf ^M tracté

traction pad
plaque ^F antidérapante

foot strap
étrier ^M

deck
planche ^F

hull
coque ^F

fin
dérive ^F

deck
pont ^M

boom
bôme ^F

porthole
hublot ^M

water polo pool
piscine ᶠ pour water-polo ᴹ

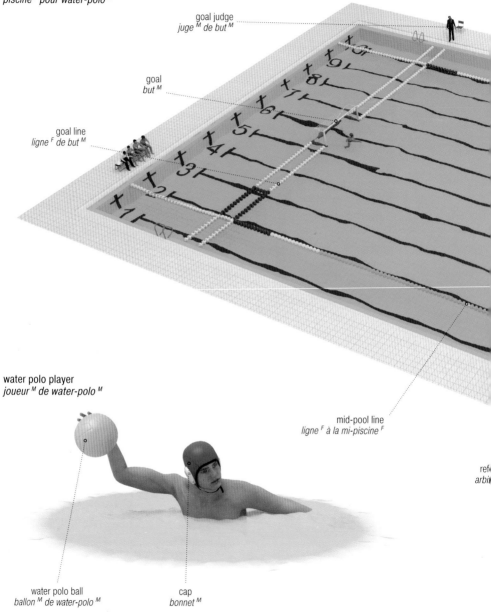

goal judge
juge ᴹ de but ᴹ

goal
but ᴹ

goal line
ligne ᶠ de but ᴹ

water polo player
joueur ᴹ de water-polo ᴹ

mid-pool line
ligne ᶠ à la mi-piscine ᶠ

ref●
arbi●

water polo ball
ballon ᴹ de water-polo ᴹ

cap
bonnet ᴹ

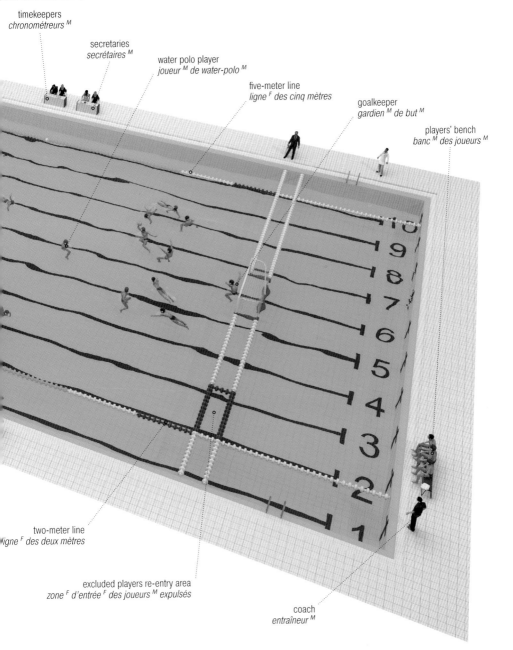

timekeepers
chronométreurs *M*

secretaries
secrétaires *M*

water polo player
joueur *M* *de water-polo* *M*

five-meter line
ligne *F* *des cinq mètres*

goalkeeper
gardien *M* *de but* *M*

players' bench
banc *M* *des joueurs* *M*

two-meter line
ligne *F* *des deux mètres*

excluded players re-entry area
zone *F* *d'entrée* *F* *des joueurs* *M* *expulsés*

coach
entraîneur *M*

Olympic-sized pool
piscine ꟳ olympique

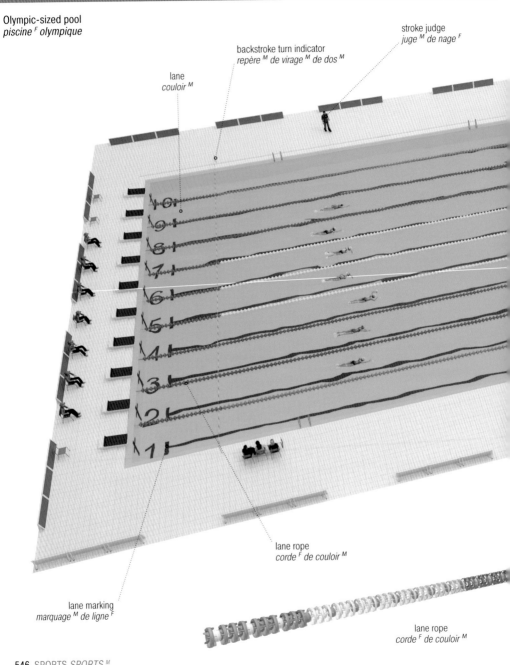

stroke judge
juge ᴹ de nage ꟳ

backstroke turn indicator
repère ᴹ de virage ᴹ de dos ᴹ

lane
couloir ᴹ

lane rope
corde ꟳ de couloir ᴹ

lane marking
marquage ᴹ de ligne ꟳ

lane rope
corde ꟳ de couloir ᴹ

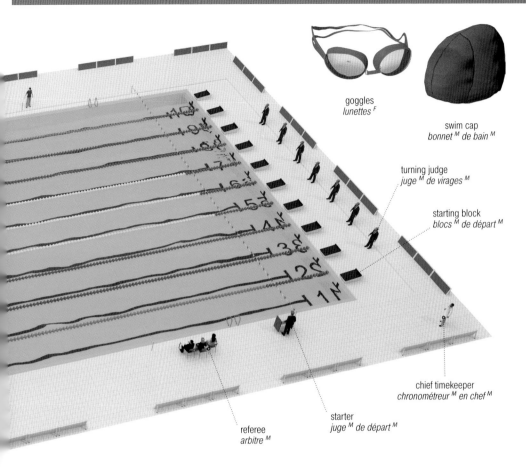

goggles
lunettes ^F

swim cap
bonnet ^M *de bain* ^M

turning judge
juge ^M *de virages* ^M

starting block
blocs ^M *de départ* ^M

chief timekeeper
chronométreur ^M *en chef* ^M

starter
juge ^M *de départ* ^M

referee
arbitre ^M

starting block
bloc ^M *de départ* ^M

lane rope storage reel
dévidoir ^M *à corde* ^F *de couloir* ^M

handrails
rampe ^F

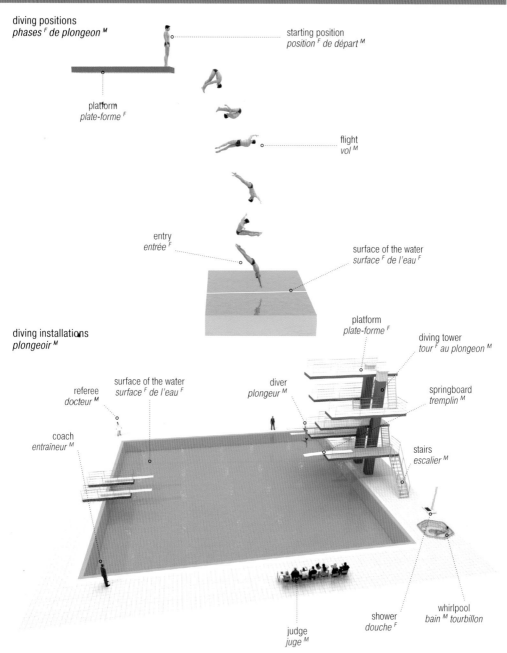

diving positions
phases ꜰ de plongeon ᴹ

starting position
position ꜰ de départ ᴹ

platform
plate-forme ꜰ

flight
vol ᴹ

entry
entrée ꜰ

surface of the water
surface ꜰ de l'eau ꜰ

diving installations
plongeoir ᴹ

platform
plate-forme ꜰ

diving tower
tour ꜰ au plongeon ᴹ

referee
docteur ᴹ

surface of the water
surface ꜰ de l'eau ꜰ

diver
plongeur ᴹ

springboard
tremplin ᴹ

coach
entraîneur ᴹ

stairs
escalier ᴹ

whirlpool
bain ᴹ tourbillon

shower
douche ꜰ

judge
juge ᴹ

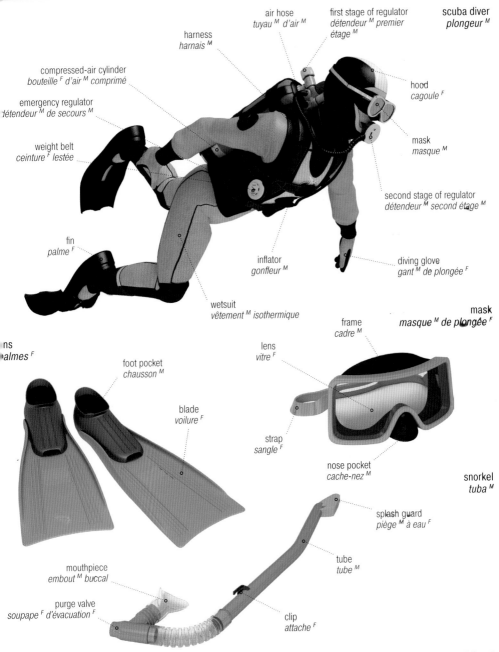

air hose
tuyau M *d'air* M

first stage of regulator
détendeur M *premier étage* M

scuba diver
plongeur M

harness
harnais M

compressed-air cylinder
bouteille F *d'air* M *comprimé*

hood
cagoule F

emergency regulator
détendeur M *de secours* M

mask
masque M

weight belt
ceinture F *lestée*

second stage of regulator
détendeur M *second étage* M

fin
palme F

inflator
gonfleur M

diving glove
gant M *de plongée* F

wetsuit
vêtement M *isothermique*

mask
masque M *de plongée* F

frame
cadre M

ns
almes F

lens
vitre F

foot pocket
chausson M

blade
voilure F

strap
sangle F

nose pocket
cache-nez M

snorkel
tuba M

splash guard
piège M *à eau* F

tube
tube M

mouthpiece
embout M *buccal*

purge valve
soupape F *d'évacuation* F

clip
attache F

rink
patinoire F

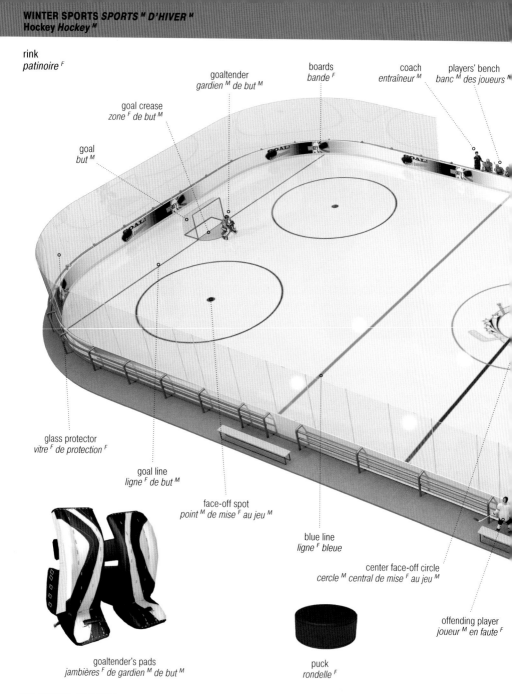

goal crease
zone F *de but* M

goaltender
gardien M *de but* M

boards
bande F

coach
entraîneur M

players' bench
banc M *des joueurs* M

goal
but M

glass protector
vitre F *de protection* F

goal line
ligne F *de but* M

face-off spot
point M *de mise* F *au jeu* M

blue line
ligne F *bleue*

center face-off circle
cercle M *central de mise* F *au jeu* M

offending player
joueur M *en faute* F

goaltender's pads
jambières F *de gardien* M *de but* M

puck
rondelle F

center line
gne ^F centrale

officials' bench
banc ^M des officiels ^M

linesman
juge ^M de ligne ^F

player
joueur ^M

ice
glace ^F

camera
caméra ^F

penalty box
banc ^M des pénalités ^F

referee
arbitre ^M

cameraman
caméraman ^M

helmet
casque ^M

vent
aération ^F

chin strap
jugulaire ^F

hockey player
joueur ^M *de hockey* ^M

glove
gant ^M

player's stick
bâton ^M *de hockey* ^M

hockey skates
patins ^M

tongue
languette ^F

blade
lame ^F

lace
lacet ^M

shaft
manche ^M

toe
orteil ^M

edge
carre ^F

blade
palette ^F / *lame* ^F

figure skates
patins ᴹ *artistiques*

figure skater
patineuse ꟳ *artistique*

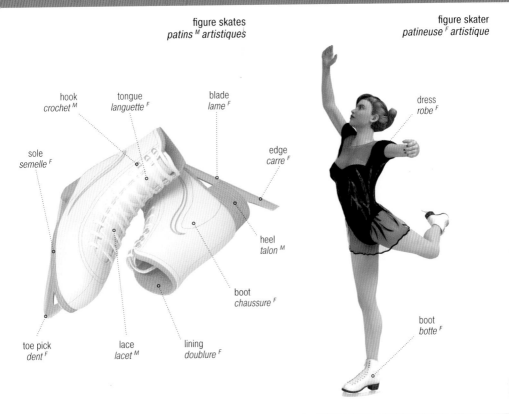

hook
crochet ᴹ

tongue
languette ꟳ

blade
lame ꟳ

dress
robe ꟳ

edge
carre ꟳ

sole
semelle ꟳ

heel
talon ᴹ

boot
chaussure ꟳ

toe pick
dent ꟳ

lace
lacet ᴹ

lining
doublure ꟳ

boot
botte ꟳ

sled
bobsleigh ᴹ

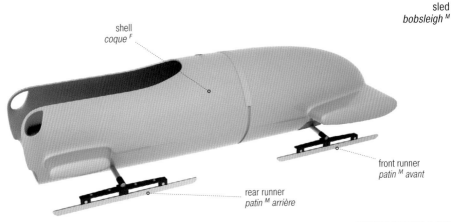

shell
coque ꟳ

front runner
patin ᴹ *avant*

rear runner
patin ᴹ *arrière*

curling stone
pierre ꟳ de curling ᴹ

handle
poignée ꟳ

hog line
ligne ꟳ de jeu ᴹ

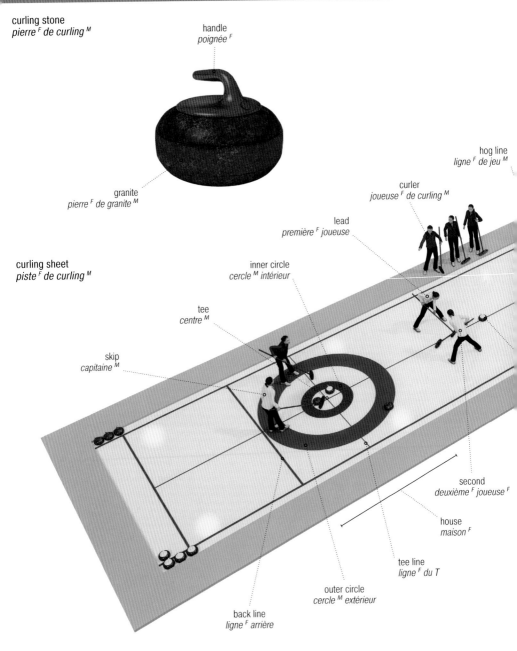

granite
pierre ꟳ de granite ᴹ

curler
joueuse ꟳ de curling ᴹ

lead
première ꟳ joueuse

curling sheet
piste ꟳ de curling ᴹ

inner circle
cercle ᴹ intérieur

tee
centre ᴹ

skip
capitaine ᴹ

second
deuxième ꟳ joueuse ꟳ

house
maison ꟳ

tee line
ligne ꟳ du T

outer circle
cercle ᴹ extérieur

back line
ligne ꟳ arrière

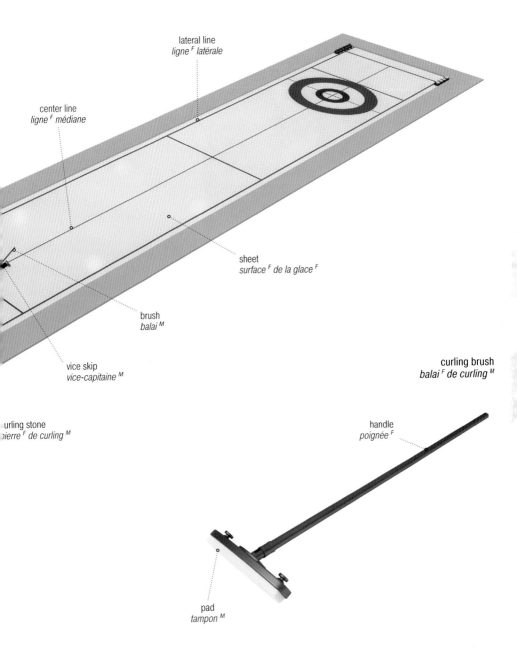

lateral line
ligne F *latérale*

center line
ligne F *médiane*

sheet
surface F *de la glace* F

brush
balai M

vice skip
vice-capitaine M

curling stone
pierre F *de curling* M

curling brush
balai F *de curling* M

handle
poignée F

pad
tampon M

alpine skier
skieur ^M *alpin*

ski boots
bottes ^F *de ski* ^M

ski goggles
lunettes ^F *de ski* ^M

strap
dragonne ^F

strap
attache ^F

upper shell
coque ^F *supérieure*

buckle
boucle ^F

adjustable catch
cran ^M *de réglage* ^M

lower shell
coque ^F *inférieure*

lens
verre ^M

frame
cadre ^M

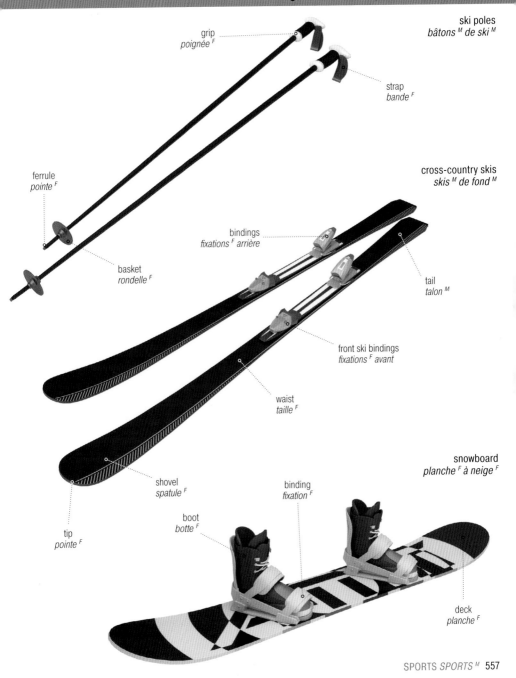

ski poles
bâtons ^M *de ski* ^M

grip
poignée ^F

strap
bande ^F

cross-country skis
skis ^M *de fond* ^M

ferrule
pointe ^F

bindings
fixations ^F *arrière*

tail
talon ^M

basket
rondelle ^F

front ski bindings
fixations ^F *avant*

waist
taille ^F

snowboard
planche ^F *à neige* ^F

shovel
spatule ^F

binding
fixation ^F

boot
botte ^F

tip
pointe ^F

deck
planche ^F

LEISURE AND ENTERTAINMENT

LOISIRS ET DIVERTISSEMENT

plush block
cube M *en peluche* F

interactive toy
jouet M *interactif*

blocks
cubes M

activity gym
portique M *d'éveil* M

mobile
mobile M

stuffed animal
animal M *en peluche* F

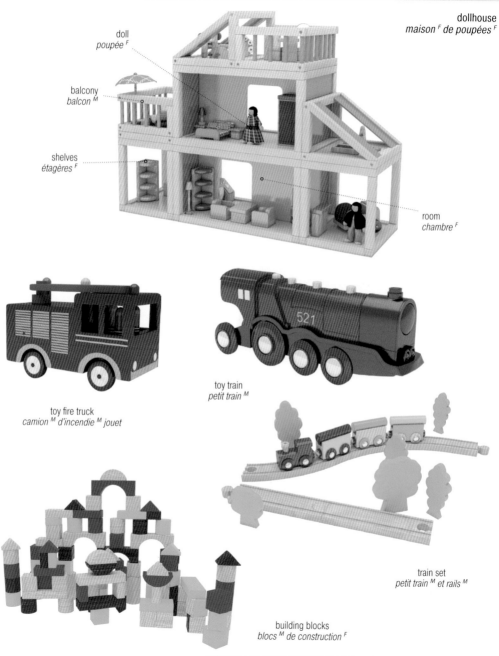

dollhouse
maison ^F *de poupées* ^F

doll
poupée ^F

balcony
balcon ^M

shelves
étagères ^F

room
chambre ^F

toy train
petit train ^M

toy fire truck
camion ^M *d'incendie* ^M *jouet*

train set
petit train ^M *et rails* ^M

building blocks
blocs ^M *de construction* ^F

tricycle
tricycle ᴹ

handlebars
guidon ᴹ

basket
panier ᴹ

seat
siège ᴹ

pedal
pédale ꟳ

rocking toy
jouet ᴹ *à bascule* ꟳ

handle
poignée ꟳ

seat
siège ᴹ

rocker
balancier ᴹ

child's bicycle
vélo ᴹ *pour enfant* ᴹ

handlebars
guidon ᴹ

seat
siège ᴹ

hopper ball
ballon ꟳ *sauteur*

frame
cadre ᴹ

wheel
roue ꟳ

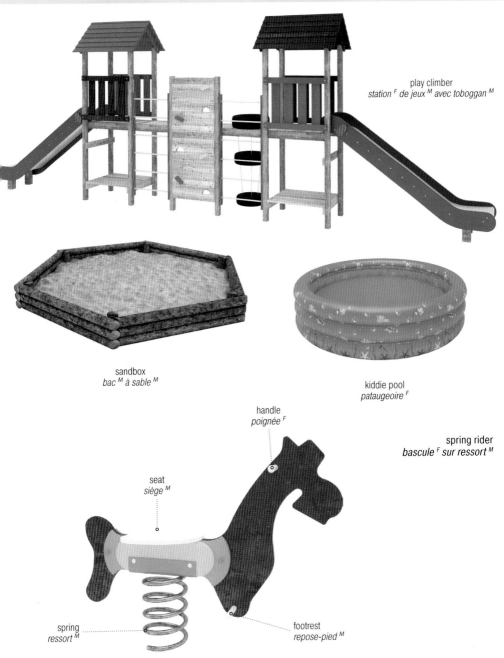

play climber
station ^F de jeux ^M avec toboggan ^M

sandbox
bac ^M à sable ^M

kiddie pool
pataugeoire ^F

handle
poignée ^F

spring rider
bascule ^F sur ressort ^M

seat
siège ^M

spring
ressort ^M

footrest
repose-pied ^M

swing set
portique ᴹ

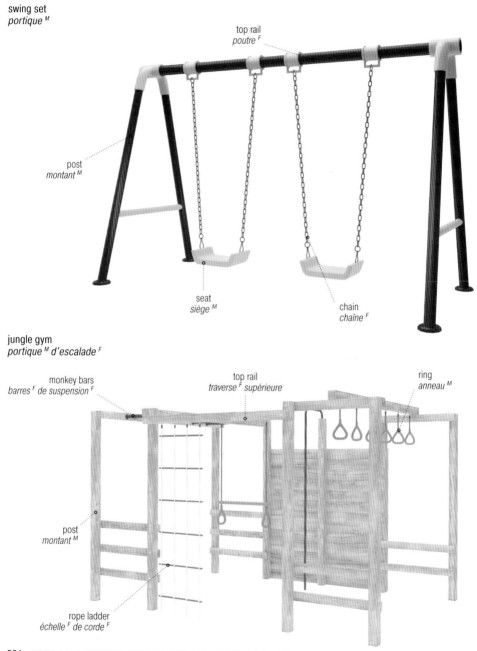

top rail
poutre ꟻ

post
montant ᴹ

seat
siège ᴹ

chain
chaîne ꟻ

jungle gym
portique ᴹ d'escalade ꟻ

monkey bars
barres ꟻ de suspension ꟻ

top rail
traverse ꟻ supérieure

ring
anneau ᴹ

post
montant ᴹ

rope ladder
échelle ꟻ de corde ꟻ

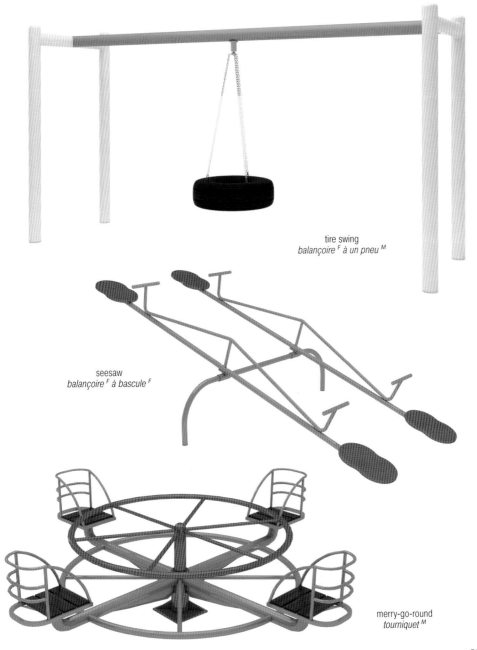

tire swing
balançoire ᶠ à un pneu ᴹ

seesaw
balançoire ᶠ à bascule ᶠ

merry-go-round
tourniquet ᴹ

amusement park rides
manèges ^M de parc ^M d'attractions ^F

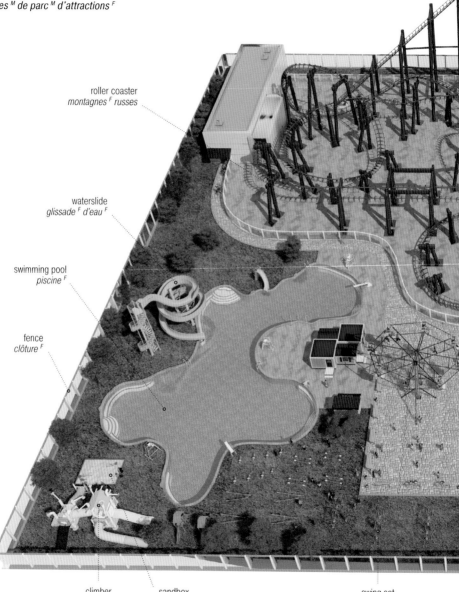

roller coaster
montagnes ^F russes

waterslide
glissade ^F d'eau ^F

swimming pool
piscine ^F

fence
clôture ^F

climber
jeu ^M à grimper

sandbox
bac ^M à sable ^M

swing set
balançoires ^F

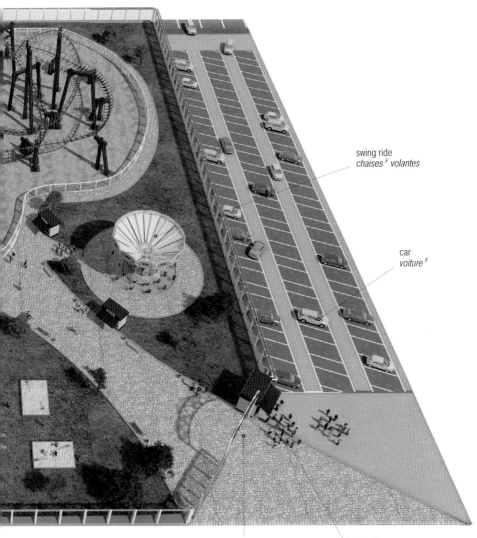

swing ride
chaises ^F *volantes*

car
voiture ^F

entrance
entrée ^F

ticket office
billetterie ^F

Chess
Échecs *M*

black square
case *F* *noire*

chessboard
échiquier *M*

white square
case *F* *blanche*

chess piece
pièce *F* *de jeu* *M* *d'échecs* *M*

pawn
pion *M*

knight
cavalier *M*

rook
tour *F*

bishop
fou *M*

king
roi *M*

queen
reine *F*

Checkers
Jeu ^M *de dames* ^F

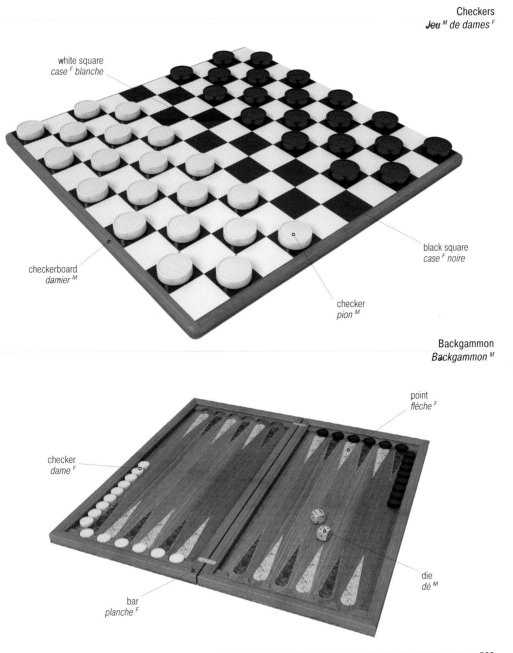

white square
case ^F *blanche*

black square
case ^F *noire*

checkerboard
damier ^M

checker
pion ^M

Backgammon
Backgammon ^M

point
flèche ^F

checker
dame ^F

die
dé ^M

bar
planche ^F

bowling
jeu ᴹ de quilles ᴹ

score screen
écran ᴹ de pointage ᴹ

ball return
renvoi ᴹ de la boule ᶠ

chair
chaise ᶠ

shoe rack
étagère ᶠ à chaussures ᶠ

shoe rental counter
comptoir ᴹ de location ᶠ

table
table ᶠ

score console
écran ᴹ de saisie ᶠ

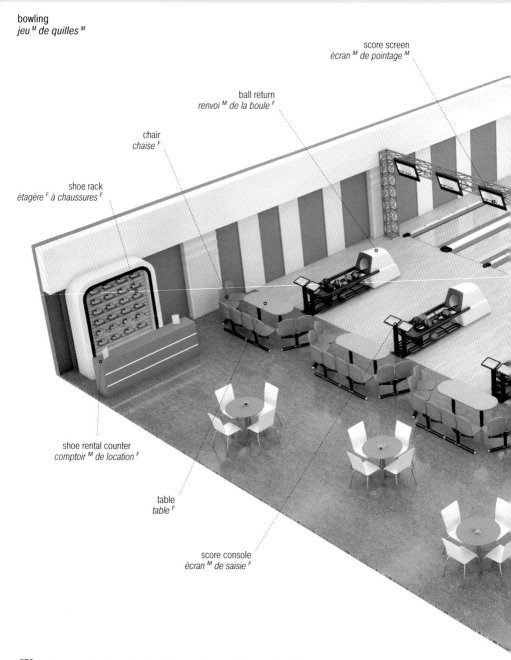

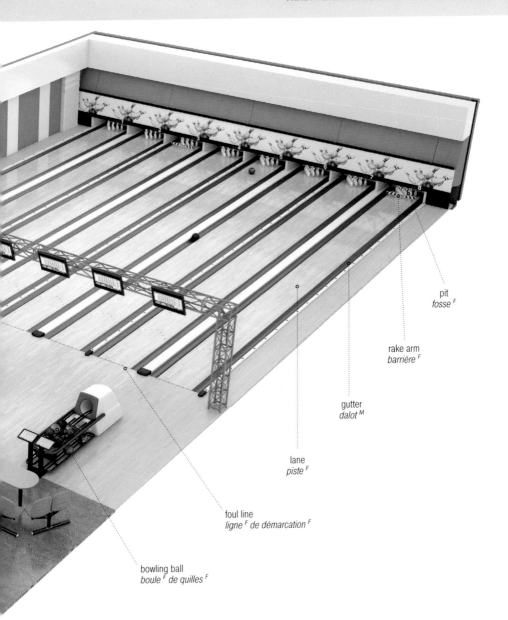

pit
fosse ᶠ

rake arm
barrière ᶠ

gutter
dalot ᴹ

lane
piste ᶠ

foul line
ligne ᶠ *de démarcation* ᶠ

bowling ball
boule ᶠ *de quilles* ᶠ

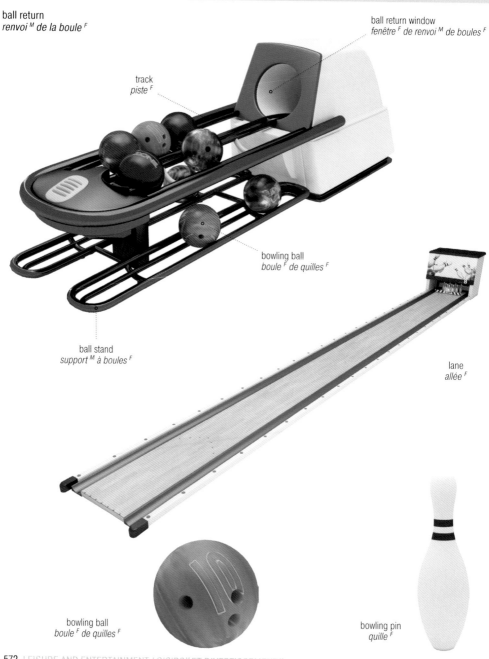

ball return
renvoi [M] *de la boule* [F]

ball return window
fenêtre [F] *de renvoi* [M] *de boules* [F]

track
piste [F]

bowling ball
boule [F] *de quilles* [F]

ball stand
support [M] *à boules* [F]

lane
allée [F]

bowling ball
boule [F] *de quilles* [F]

bowling pin
quille [F]

billiard table
table **F** *de billard* **M**

pocket
poche **F**

pool cue
baguette **F** *de billard* **M**

table leg
patte **F** *de table* **F**

ball
boule **F** *de billard* **M**

rail
bande **F**

felt
feutre **M**

billiards rack
support **M** *de baguettes* **F** *de billard* **M**

billiards chalk
craie **F** *de billard* **M**

snooker table
table **F** *de snooker* **M**

electronic dartboard
jeu ᴹ de fléchettes ꟳ électronique

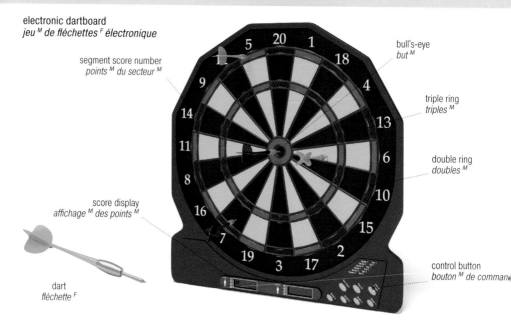

segment score number
points ᴹ du secteur ᴹ

bull's-eye
but ᴹ

triple ring
triples ᴹ

double ring
doubles ᴹ

score display
affichage ᴹ des points ᴹ

control button
bouton ᴹ de comman◖

dart
fléchette ꟳ

bowling game
jeu ᴹ vidéo ꟳ de quilles ꟳ

claw crane machine
machine ꟳ attrape-peluches ꟳ

maze game
jeu ᴹ de labyrinthe ᴹ

score display
tableau [M] *de pointage* [M]

air hockey table
table [F] *de hockey* [M] *pneumatique*

goal
but [M]

face-off spot
_ne_ [F] *de mise* [F] *au jeu* [M]

goalie mallet
poussoir [M]

playing surface
surface [F] *de jeu* [M]

center face-off circle
cercle [M] *central de mise* [F] *au jeu* [M]

puck return
renvoi [M] *de la rondelle* [F]

soccer table
table [M] *de soccer* [M]

fighting game
jeu [M] *de combat* [M]

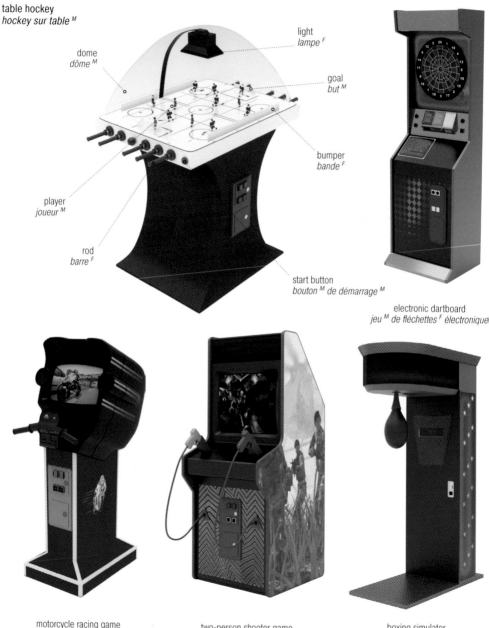

table hockey
hockey sur table ^M

dome
dôme ^M

light
lampe ^F

goal
but ^M

bumper
bande ^F

player
joueur ^M

rod
barre ^F

start button
bouton ^M *de démarrage* ^M

electronic dartboard
jeu ^M *de fléchettes* ^F *électronique*

motorcycle racing game
jeu ^M *de course* ^F *de moto* ^F

two-person shooter game
jeu ^M *de tir* ^M *à deux joueurs* ^M

boxing simulator
simulateur ^M *de boxe* ^F

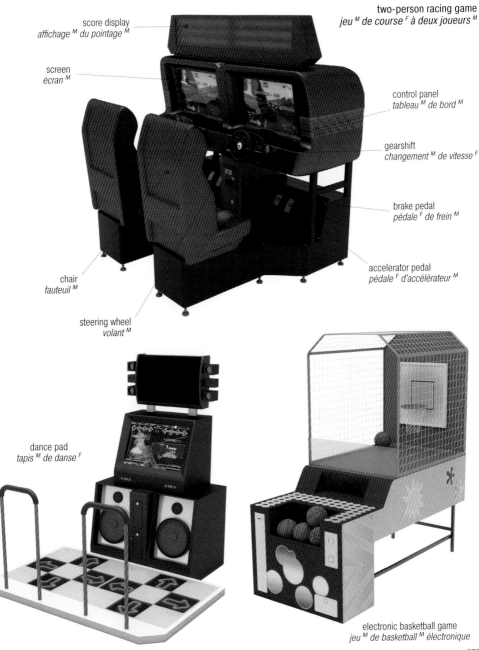

two-person racing game
jeu ^M *de course* ^F *à deux joueurs* ^M

score display
affichage ^M *du pointage* ^M

screen
écran ^M

control panel
tableau ^M *de bord* ^M

gearshift
changement ^M *de vitesse* ^F

brake pedal
pédale ^F *de frein* ^M

accelerator pedal
pédale ^F *d'accélérateur* ^M

chair
fauteuil ^M

steering wheel
volant ^M

dance pad
tapis ^M *de danse* ^F

electronic basketball game
jeu ^M *de basketball* ^M *électronique*

roulette table
table F *de roulette* F

chip
jeton M

croupier's area
place F *du croupier* M

layout
grille F

chip holder
porte-jetons M

roulette wheel
roulette F

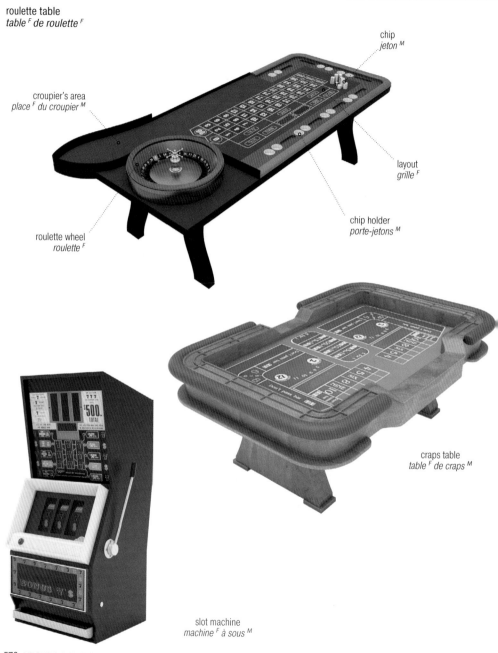

craps table
table F *de craps* M

slot machine
machine F *à sous* M

casino poker table
table [F] *de poker* [M] *de casino* [M]

poker table
table [F] *de poker* [M]

card table
table [F] *à jeu* [M] *de cartes* [F]

Suits
Couleurs ᶠ

hearts
cœur ᴹ

diamonds
carreau ᴹ

clubs
trèfle ᴹ

spades
pique ᶠ

Face cards and special cards
Figures ᶠ et cartes ᶠ spéciales

jack
valet ᴹ

queen
reine ᶠ

king
roi ᴹ

ace
as ᴹ

joker
joker ᴹ

Standard poker hands
Mains ᶠ de poker ᴹ standards

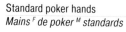

one pair
paire ᶠ

two pairs
double paire ᶠ

three of a kind
brelan ᴹ

straight
suite ᶠ

flush
couleur ᶠ

full house
main ᶠ pleine

four of a kind
carré ᴹ

straight flush
quinte ᶠ couleur ᶠ

royal flush
quinte ᶠ royale

tent
tente ᶠ

patio umbrella
parasol ᴹ

pole
arceau ᴹ

cooler
glacière ᶠ

guy line
hauban ᴹ

wall
habitacle ᴹ

floor
plancher ᴹ

ntern
nterne ᶠ

handle
poignée ᶠ

hook
crochet ᴹ

lamp
lampe ᶠ

globe
globe ᴹ

on/off button
bouton ᴹ *d'alimentation* ᶠ

housing
boîtier ᴹ

folding camp stool
tabouret ᴹ *de camping* ᴹ *pliant*

seat
siège ᴹ

leg
patte ᴹ

skid-proof foot
patin ᶠᴹ *antidérapant*

backpack
sac à dos ᴹ

pocket knife
couteau ᴹ *de poche* ᶠ

flashlight
lampe ᶠ *de poche* ᶠ

sleeping bag
sac ᴹ *de couchage* ᴹ

thermal jug
pot ᴹ *isolant*

lounge chair
chaise ᶠ *longue*

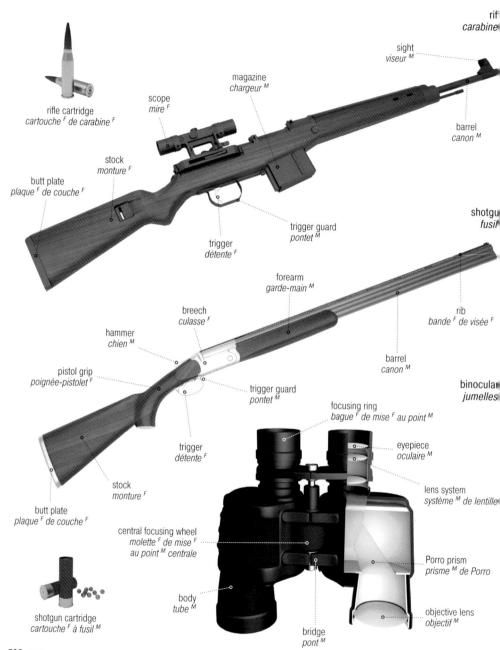

rif
carabine

sight
viseur M

magazine
chargeur M

scope
mire F

rifle cartridge
cartouche F *de carabine* F

barrel
canon M

stock
monture F

butt plate
plaque F *de couche* F

trigger guard
pontet M

shotgu
fusil

trigger
détente F

forearm
garde-main M

breech
culasse F

rib
bande F *de visée* F

hammer
chien M

barrel
canon M

pistol grip
poignée-pistolet F

binocula
jumelles

trigger guard
pontet M

focusing ring
bague F *de mise* F *au point* M

eyepiece
oculaire M

trigger
détente F

lens system
système M *de lentille*

central focusing wheel
molette F *de mise* F
au point M *centrale*

stock
monture F

Porro prism
prisme M *de Porro*

butt plate
plaque F *de couche* F

body
tube M

objective lens
objectif M

shotgun cartridge
cartouche F *à fusil* M

bridge
pont M

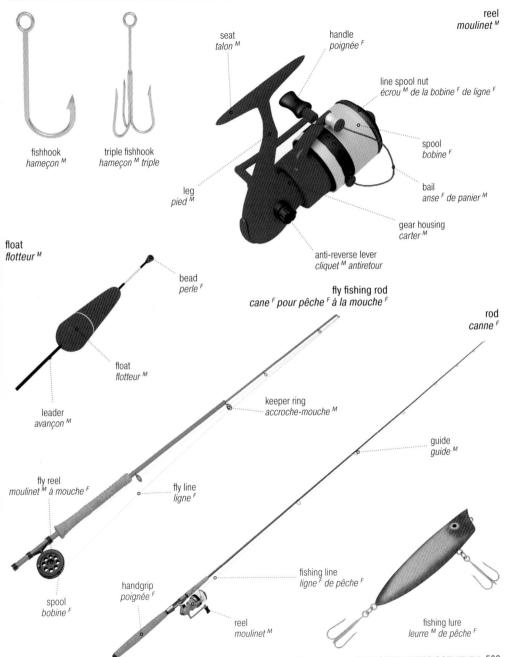

reel
moulinet [M]

seat
talon [M]

handle
poignée [F]

line spool nut
écrou [M] *de la bobine* [F] *de ligne* [F]

spool
bobine [F]

bail
anse [F] *de panier* [M]

gear housing
carter [M]

leg
pied [M]

anti-reverse lever
cliquet [M] *antiretour*

fishhook
hameçon [M]

triple fishhook
hameçon [M] *triple*

float
flotteur [M]

bead
perle [F]

float
flotteur [M]

leader
avançon [M]

fly fishing rod
cane [F] *pour pêche* [F] *à la mouche* [F]

rod
canne [F]

keeper ring
accroche-mouche [M]

guide
guide [M]

fly reel
moulinet [M] *à mouche* [F]

fly line
ligne [F]

spool
bobine [F]

handgrip
poignée [F]

fishing line
ligne [F] *de pêche* [F]

reel
moulinet [M]

fishing lure
leurre [M] *de pêche* [F]

OFFICE

BUREAU

cubicles
postes ^M de travail ^M modulaires

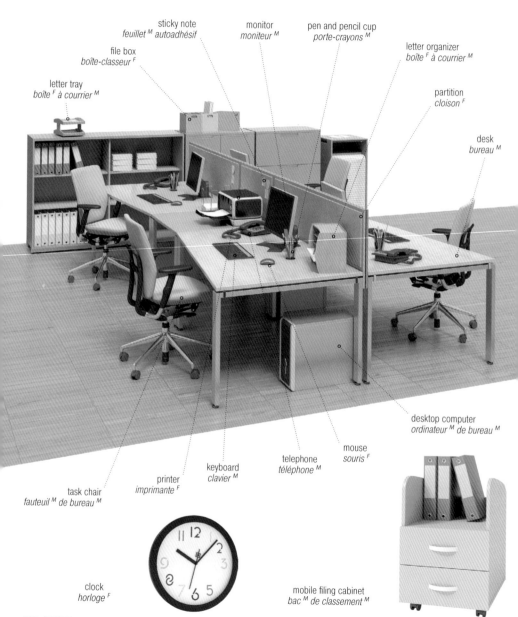

sticky note
feuillet ^M autoadhésif

monitor
moniteur ^M

pen and pencil cup
porte-crayons ^M

file box
boîte-classeur ^F

letter organizer
boîte ^F à courrier ^M

letter tray
boîte ^F à courrier ^M

partition
cloison ^F

desk
bureau ^M

desktop computer
ordinateur ^M de bureau ^M

mouse
souris ^F

telephone
téléphone ^M

keyboard
clavier ^M

printer
imprimante ^F

task chair
fauteuil ^M de bureau ^M

clock
horloge ^F

mobile filing cabinet
bac ^M de classement ^M

call center
centre M *d'appels* M

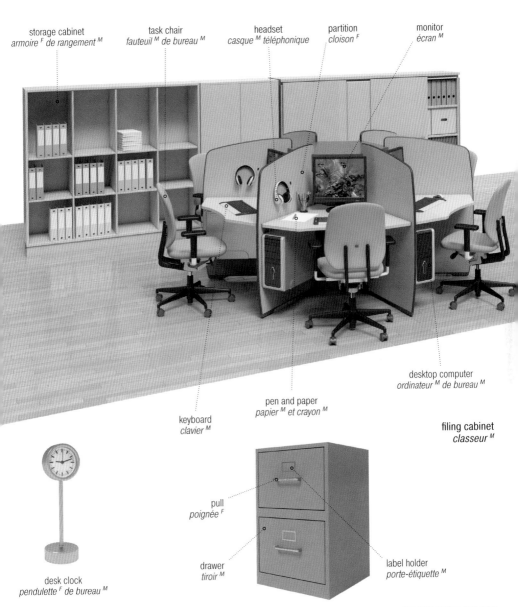

storage cabinet
armoire F *de rangement* M

task chair
fauteuil M *de bureau* M

headset
casque M *téléphonique*

partition
cloison F

monitor
écran M

desktop computer
ordinateur M *de bureau* M

pen and paper
papier M *et crayon* M

keyboard
clavier M

filing cabinet
classeur M

pull
poignée F

drawer
tiroir M

label holder
porte-étiquette M

desk clock
pendulette F *de bureau* M

reception
réception ^M

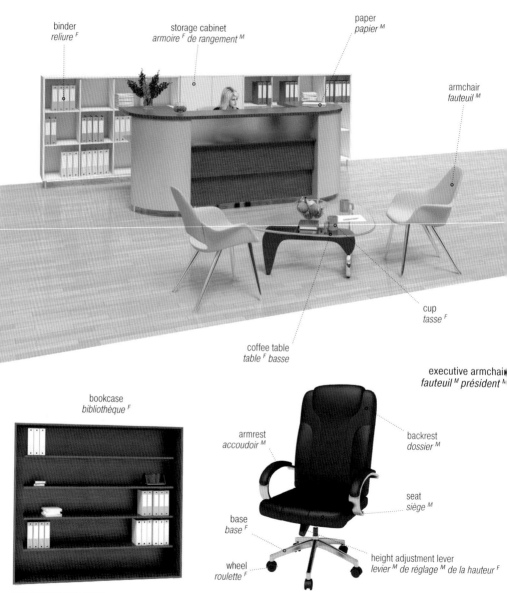

binder
reliure ^F

storage cabinet
armoire ^F de rangement ^M

paper
papier ^M

armchair
fauteuil ^M

cup
tasse ^F

coffee table
table ^F basse

executive armchair
fauteuil ^M président ^M

bookcase
bibliothèque ^F

armrest
accoudoir ^M

backrest
dossier ^M

base
base ^F

seat
siège ^M

wheel
roulette ^F

height adjustment lever
levier ^M de réglage ^M de la hauteur ^F

conference room
salle ꟳ de conférence ꟳ

binder
reliure ꟳ

flip chart
tableau ᴹ de papier ᴹ

watercooler
fontaine ꟳ réfrigérée

file box
boîte-classeur ꟳ

telephone
téléphone ᴹ

executive armchair
fauteuil ᴹ de direction ᴹ

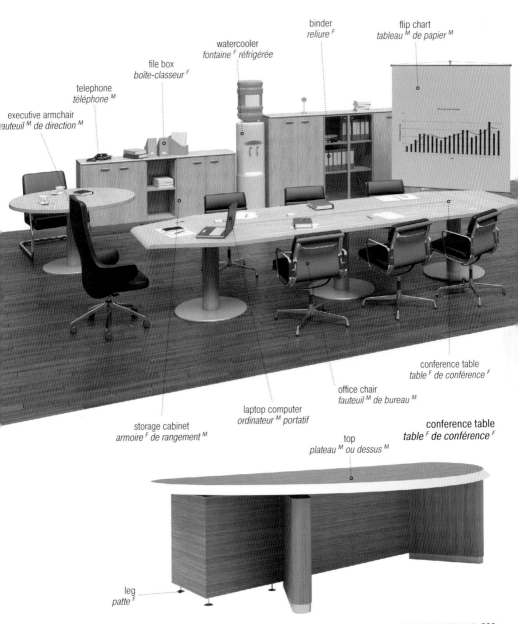

storage cabinet
armoire ꟳ de rangement ᴹ

laptop computer
ordinateur ᴹ portatif

office chair
fauteuil ᴹ de bureau ᴹ

conference table
table ꟳ de conférence ꟳ

top
plateau ᴹ ou dessus ᴹ

conference table
table ꟳ de conférence ꟳ

leg
patte ꟳ

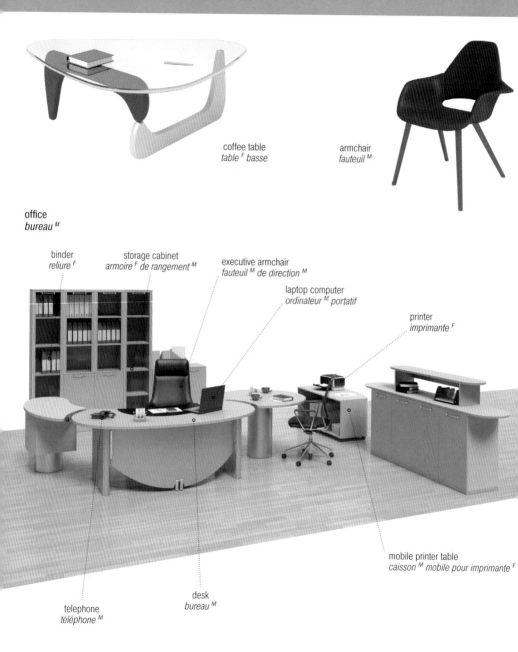

coffee table
table ^F *basse*

armchair
fauteuil ^M

office
bureau ^M

binder
reliure ^F

storage cabinet
armoire ^F *de rangement* ^M

executive armchair
fauteuil ^M *de direction* ^M

laptop computer
ordinateur ^M *portatif*

printer
imprimante ^F

mobile printer table
caisson ^M *mobile pour imprimante* ^F

desk
bureau ^M

telephone
téléphone ^M

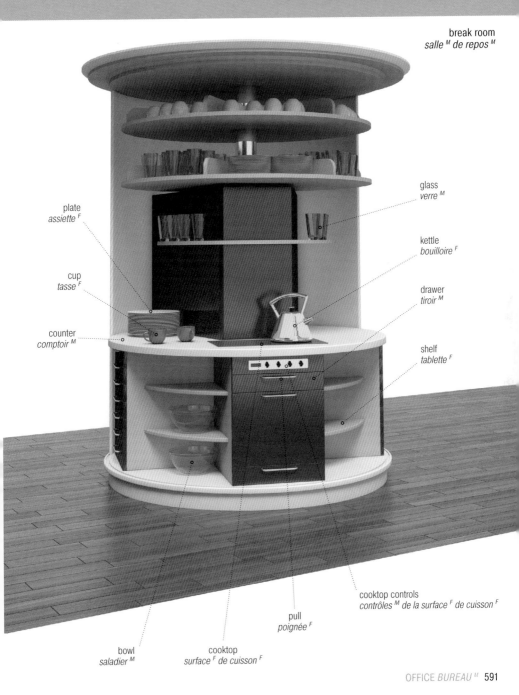

break room
salle ^M de repos ^M

glass
verre ^M

kettle
bouilloire ^F

drawer
tiroir ^M

shelf
tablette ^F

plate
assiette ^F

cup
tasse ^F

counter
comptoir ^M

cooktop controls
contrôles ^M de la surface ^F de cuisson ^F

pull
poignée ^F

bowl
saladier ^M

cooktop
surface ^F de cuisson ^F

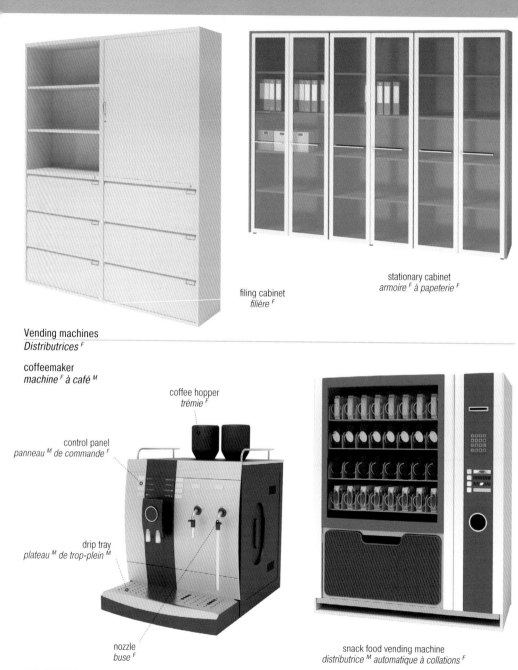

filing cabinet
filière ᶠ

stationary cabinet
armoire ᶠ *à papeterie* ᶠ

Vending machines
Distributrices ᶠ

coffeemaker
machine ᶠ *à café* ᴹ

coffee hopper
trémie ᶠ

control panel
panneau ᴹ *de commande* ᶠ

drip tray
plateau ᴹ *de trop-plein* ᴹ

nozzle
buse ᶠ

snack food vending machine
distributrice ᴹ *automatique à collations* ᶠ

coffee machine
machine ^F *à café* ^M

hot and cold beverage vending machine
distributrice ^F *de boissons* ^F *chaudes et froides*

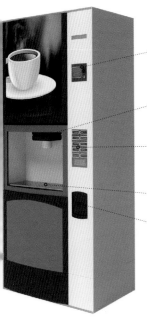

bill acceptor
distributrice ^F *acceptant*
les billets ^F

nozzle
buse ^F

drink selection keypad
clavier ^M *de sélection* ^F
de la boisson ^F

drip tray
plateau ^M *de trop-plein* ^M

change return slot
fenêtre ^F *de retour* ^M
de la monnaie ^F

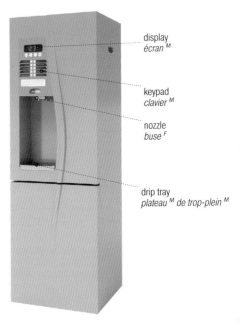

display
écran ^M

keypad
clavier ^M

nozzle
buse ^F

drip tray
plateau ^M *de trop-plein* ^M

beverage vending machine
distributrice ^F *de boissons* ^F

display
présentoir ^M

beverage bottle
bouteille ^F

bill acceptor
distributrice ^F *acceptant les billets* ^F

keypad
clavier ^M

laptop computer
ordinateur M *portatif* M

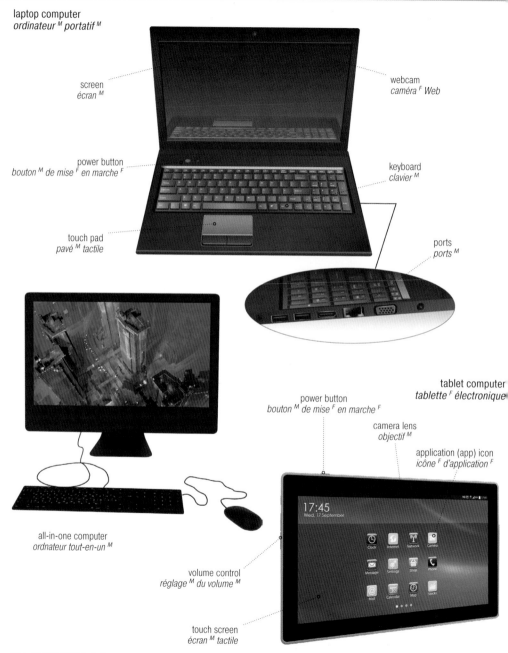

screen
écran M

webcam
caméra F *Web*

power button
bouton M *de mise* F *en marche* F

keyboard
clavier M

touch pad
pavé M *tactile*

ports
ports M

tablet computer
tablette F *électronique*

power button
bouton M *de mise* F *en marche* F

camera lens
objectif M

application (app) icon
icône F *d'application* F

all-in-one computer
ordnateur tout-en-un M

volume control
réglage M *du volume* M

touch screen
écran M *tactile*

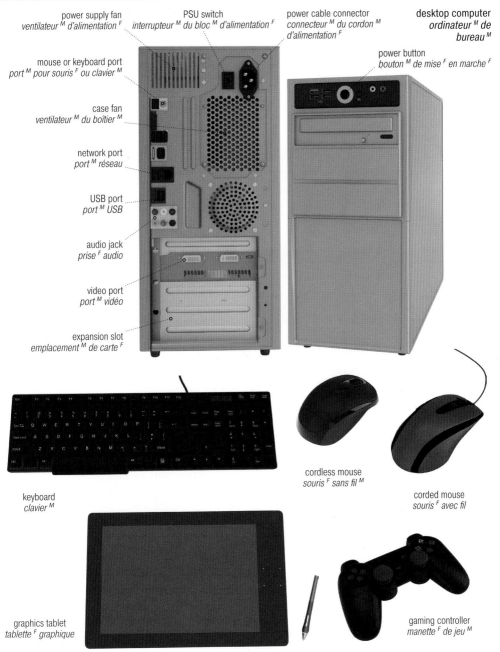

power supply fan
ventilateur ^M *d'alimentation* ^F

PSU switch
interrupteur ^M *du bloc* ^M *d'alimentation* ^F

power cable connector
connecteur ^M *du cordon* ^M
d'alimentation ^F

desktop computer
ordinateur ^M *de*
bureau ^M

mouse or keyboard port
port ^M *pour souris* ^F *ou clavier* ^M

power button
bouton ^M *de mise* ^F *en marche* ^F

case fan
ventilateur ^M *du boîtier* ^M

network port
port ^M *réseau*

USB port
port ^M *USB*

audio jack
prise ^F *audio*

video port
port ^M *vidéo*

expansion slot
emplacement ^M *de carte* ^F

keyboard
clavier ^M

cordless mouse
souris ^F *sans fil* ^M

corded mouse
souris ^F *avec fil*

graphics tablet
tablette ^F *graphique*

gaming controller
manette ^F *de jeu* ^M

Printers, copiers and scanners
Imprimantes, F *photocopieuses* F *et scanners* M

laser printer
imprimante F *laser*

plotter
traceur M

ink cartridge
cartouche F *d'encre* F

toner cartridge
cartouche F *de toner* M

flatbed scanner
scanneur M

paper tray
plateau M *d'alimentation* F *en papier* M

sheetfed scanner
scanneur M *à chargeur* M

cover
couvercle M

belt
courroie F

scan head
tête F *de lecture* F

platen glass
glace F *d'exposition*

control panel
panneau M *de commande* F

power button
bouton M *de mise* F *en marche* F

output tray
plateau M *de sortie* F

ink-jet printer
imprimante [M] *à jet* [M] *d'encre* [F]

control panel
panneau [M] *de commande* [F]

display
écran [M]

copier
photocopieur [M]

power button
bouton [M] *de mise* [F] *en marche* [F]

memory card
carte [F] *mémoire* [F]

Other electronic devices *Autres appareils* [M] *électriques*

headset
casque [M] *d'écoute* [F]

headband
serre-tête [M]

smartphone
téléphone [M] *intelligent*

power button
bouton [M] *de mise* [F] *en marche* [F]

receiver
récepteur [M]

camera lens
objectif [M]

earpiece
écouteur [M]

volume control
bouton [M] *de volume* [M]

touch screen
écran [M] *tactile*

application (app) icon
icône [F] *d'application* [F]

back button
bouton [M] *précédent* [M]

microphone
micro [M]

cable
câble [M]

menu button
bouton [M] *de la barre* [F] *de menus* [M]

home button
bouton [M] *démarrage* [M]

microphone
micro M

handset cord
cordon M *de combiné* M

display
écran M

keypad
clavier M

telephone
téléphone M

handset
combiné M

push button
bouton-poussoir M

speed dial button
bouton M *de composition* F *abrégée*

speed dial directory
répertoire M *de numéros* M *abrégé*

webcam
caméra F *Web*

automatic document feeder
dispositif M *d'alimentation* F *automatique*

fax
télécopieur M

power button
bouton M *de mise* F *en marche* F

handset
combiné M

start button
bouton M *démarrer*

wireless router
routeur M *sans fil* M

display
écran M

indicator light
voyant M

handset cord
cordon M *de combiné* M

Internet stick
clé F *Internet* M

antenna
antenne F

power button
bouton M *de mise* F *en marche* F

printing calculator
calculatrice ^F *à imprimante* ^F

calculator
calculatrice ^F

paper roll
rouleau ^M *de papier* ^M

key
touche ^F

screen
écran ^M

shredder
déchiqueteuse ^F

control button
bouton ^M *de commande* ^F

cutting head
tête ^F *de coupe* ^M

lid
couvercle ^M

pocket calculator
calculatrice ^F *de poche* ^F

waste basket
corbeille ^F *à papier* ^M

monitor
écran ^M

label maker
étiqueteuse F

external hard drive
lecteur M *de disque* M *dur externe*

display
écran M

navigation buttons
boutons M *de navigation* F

keypad
clavier M

USB flash drive
clé F *USB* M

connector
connecteur M

case
boîtier M

control button
bouton M *de commande* F

cap
bouchon M

digital voice recorder
enregistreur M *numérique*

display
écran M

02/02

01.28:05

control button
bouton M *de commande* F

loudspeaker
haut-parleur M

e-reader
liseuse f

digital clock
horloge ^F *numérique*

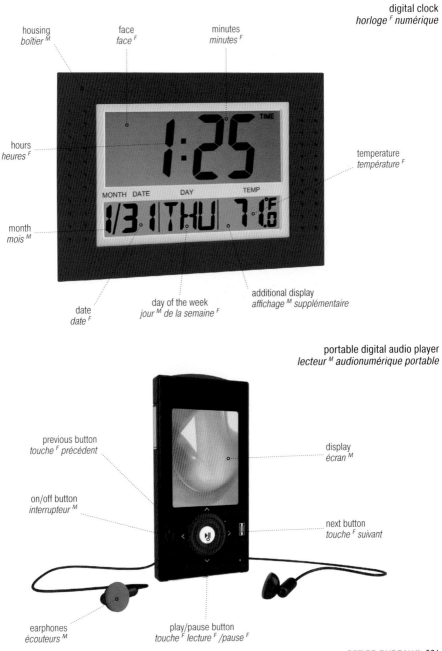

housing
boîtier ^M

face
face ^F

minutes
minutes ^F

hours
heures ^F

temperature
température ^F

month
mois ^M

date
date ^F

day of the week
jour ^M *de la semaine* ^F

additional display
affichage ^M *supplémentaire*

portable digital audio player
lecteur ^M *audionumérique portable*

previous button
touche ^F *précédent*

display
écran ^M

on/off button
interrupteur ^M

next button
touche ^F *suivant*

earphones
écouteurs ^M

play/pause button
touche ^F *lecture* ^F */pause* ^F

single-lens reflex (SLR) digital camera: front view
appareil M *photo* F *numérique reflex mono-objectif : vue* F *de face* F

accessory shoe
griffe F *porte-accessoire*

data display
écran M *de données* F

hot-shoe contact
contact M *électrique*

shutter release button
déclencheur M

mode dial
molette F *de sélection* M

focus setting ring
bague F *de mise* F *au point* M

neckstrap eyelet
oeillet M *d'attache* F

lens
objectif M

camery body
boîtier M *de l'appareil* M *photo*

single-lens reflex (SLR) digital camera: back view
appareil M *photo* F *numérique reflex mono-objectif :*
vue F *arrière* F

lens aperture scale
échelle F *d'ouverture* F *de l'objectif* M

viewfinder
viseur M

menu button
touche F *de sélection* F *des menus* M

AF-ON

settings display button
bouton M *d'affichage* M *des*
paramètres M

image review button
touche F *de visualisation* F *des images* F

erase button
touche F *d'effacement* M

display
écran M

enlarge button
bouton M *d'agrandissement* M

laptop power supply
bloc ^M *d'alimentation pour ordinateur* ^M *portatif*

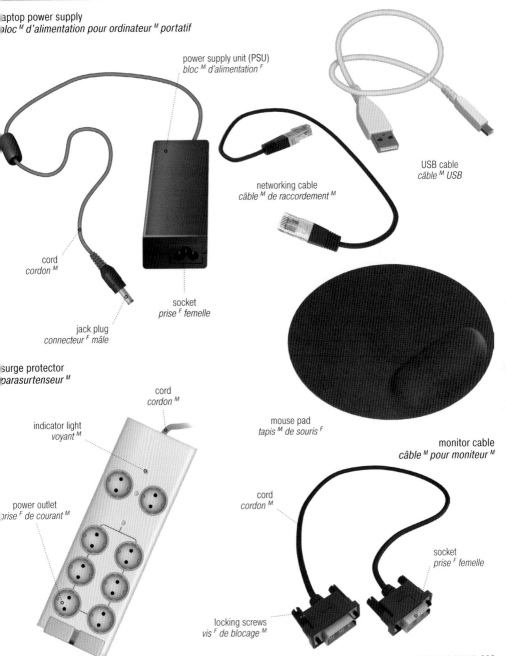

power supply unit (PSU)
bloc ^M *d'alimentation* ^F

USB cable
câble ^M *USB*

networking cable
câble ^M *de raccordement* ^M

cord
cordon ^M

socket
prise ^F *femelle*

jack plug
connecteur ^F *mâle*

surge protector
parasurtenseur ^M

cord
cordon ^M

indicator light
voyant ^M

mouse pad
tapis ^M *de souris* ^F

monitor cable
câble ^M *pour moniteur* ^M

power outlet
prise ^F *de courant* ^M

cord
cordon ^M

socket
prise ^F *femelle*

locking screws
vis ^F *de blocage* ^M

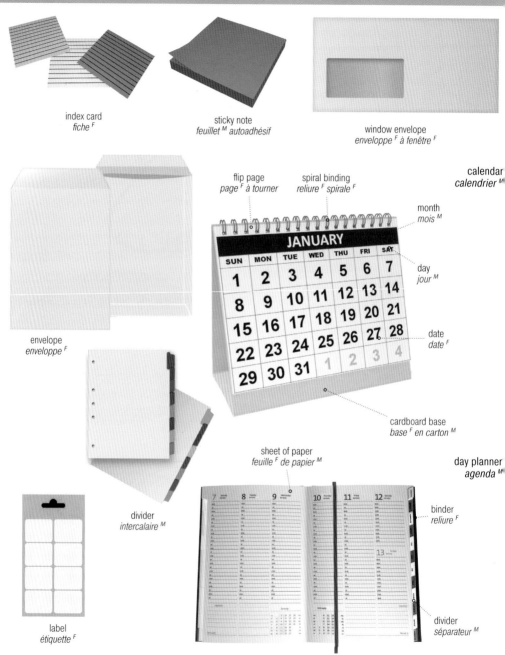

index card
fiche F

sticky note
feuillet M *autoadhésif*

window envelope
enveloppe F *à fenêtre* F

calendar
calendrier M

flip page
page F *à tourner*

spiral binding
reliure F *spirale* F

month
mois M

JANUARY

SUN	MON	TUE	WED	THU	FRI	SAT
1	2	3	4	5	6	7
8	9	10	11	12	13	14
15	16	17	18	19	20	21
22	23	24	25	26	27	28
29	30	31	1	2	3	4

day
jour M

date
date F

envelope
enveloppe F

cardboard base
base F *en carton* M

sheet of paper
feuille F *de papier* M

day planner
agenda M

divider
intercalaire M

binder
reliure F

divider
séparateur M

label
étiquette F

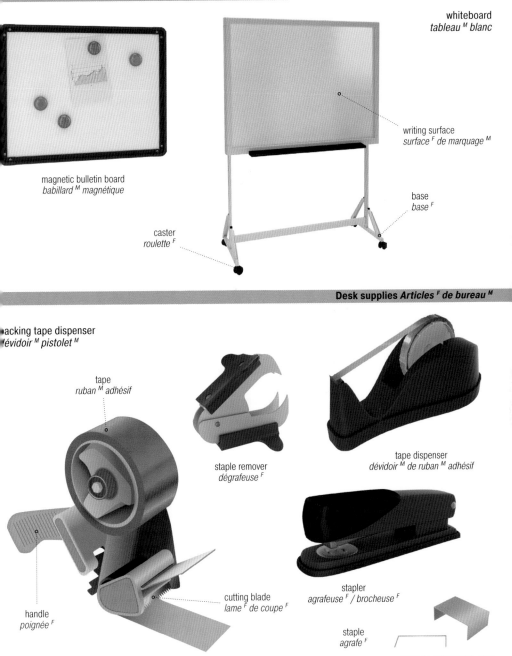

whiteboard
tableau ^M *blanc*

writing surface
surface ^F *de marquage* ^M

magnetic bulletin board
babillard ^M *magnétique*

base
base ^F

caster
roulette ^F

Desk supplies *Articles* ^F *de bureau* ^M

packing tape dispenser
dévidoir ^M *pistolet* ^M

tape
ruban ^M *adhésif*

staple remover
dégrafeuse ^F

tape dispenser
dévidoir ^M *de ruban* ^M *adhésif*

cutting blade
lame ^F *de coupe* ^F

stapler
agrafeuse ^F / *brocheuse* ^F

handle
poignée ^F

staple
agrafe ^F

set square
équerre F

pencil sharpene
taille-crayon M

blade
lame F

paper punch
perforatrice F

glue stick
bâton M *de colle* F

box cutte
couteau M *à lame* F *rétractable*

slide lock
verrou M

blade
lame F

handle
poignée F

correction tape
ruban M *correcteur*

paper clip
trombone M

eraser
gomme F *à effacer*

pushpin
punaise F

ruler
règle F

handle
poignée F

paper cutte
cisaille F / *massicot* M

clamp lock
vis F *de serrage* M

paper guide
guide-feuille M

base
base F

wastebasket
corbeille F *à papier* M

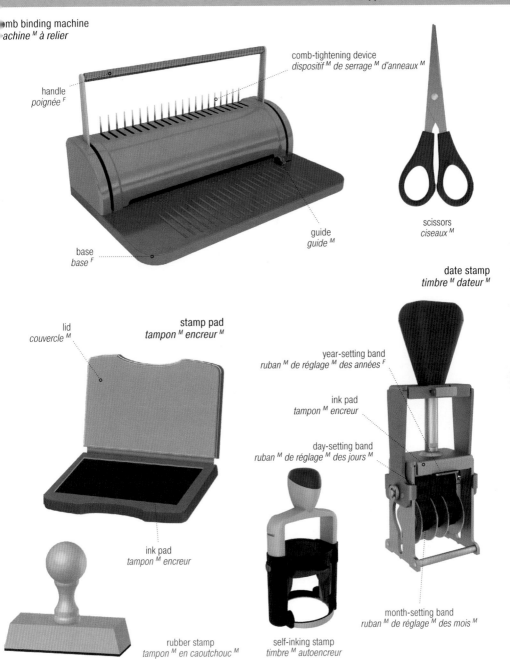

mb binding machine
achine M *à relier*

comb-tightening device
dispositif M *de serrage* M *d'anneaux* M

handle
poignée F

scissors
ciseaux M

guide
guide M

base
base F

date stamp
timbre M *dateur* M

lid
couvercle M

stamp pad
tampon M *encreur* M

year-setting band
ruban M *de réglage* M *des années* F

ink pad
tampon M *encreur*

day-setting band
ruban M *de réglage* M *des jours* M

ink pad
tampon M *encreur*

rubber stamp
tampon M *en caoutchouc* M

self-inking stamp
timbre M *autoencreur*

month-setting band
ruban M *de réglage* M *des mois* M

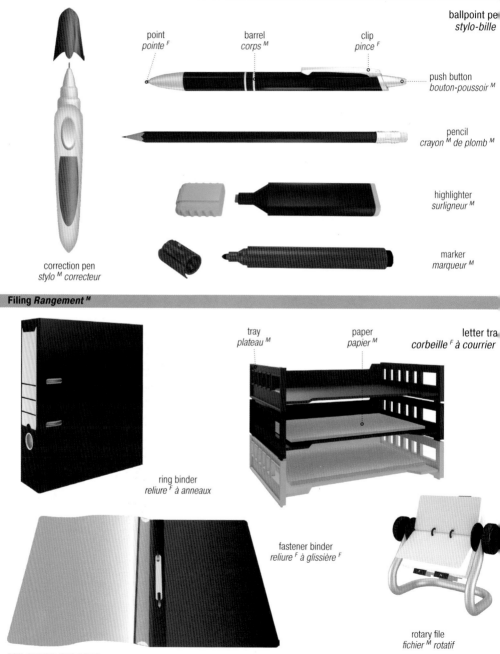

ballpoint pen
stylo-bille

point
pointe F

barrel
corps M

clip
pince F

push button
bouton-poussoir M

pencil
crayon M de plomb M

highlighter
surligneur M

marker
marqueur M

correction pen
stylo M correcteur

Filing *Rangement M*

tray
plateau M

paper
papier M

letter tray
corbeille F à courrier

ring binder
reliure F à anneaux

fastener binder
reliure F à glissière F

rotary file
fichier M rotatif

TRANSPORTS

interchange
échangeur ᴹ

car
voiture ᴹ

arch bridge
pont ᴹ *à arches* ᶠ

road marking
signalisation ᶠ *routière*

traffic sign
panneau ᴹ *routier*

roadway
chaussée ᶠ

billboard (back view)
panneau ᴹ *d'affichage* ᴹ *(vue* ᶠ *de derrière* ᴹ*)*

safety railing
rampe ᶠ *de sécurité* ᶠ

road worker
travailleur ᴹ *routier*

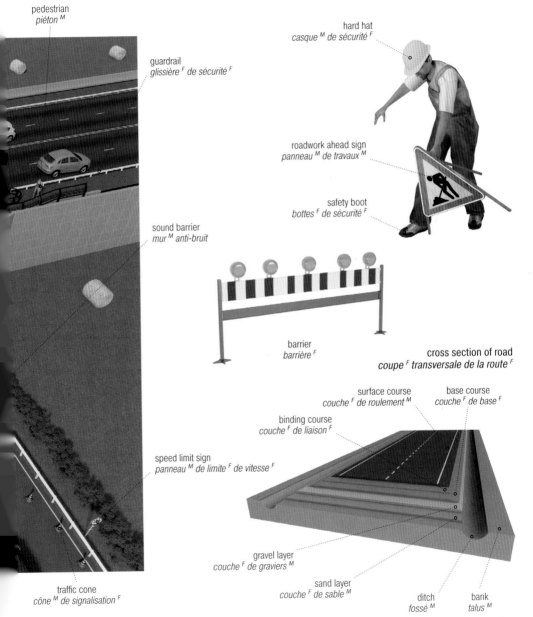

road worker
travailleur M *routier*

pedestrian
piéton M

hard hat
casque M *de sécurité* F

guardrail
glissière F *de sécurité* F

roadwork ahead sign
panneau M *de travaux* M

safety boot
bottes F *de sécurité* F

sound barrier
mur M *anti-bruit*

barrier
barrière F

cross section of road
coupe F *transversale de la route* F

surface course
couche F *de roulement* M

base course
couche F *de base* F

binding course
couche F *de liaison* F

speed limit sign
panneau M *de limite* F *de vitesse* F

gravel layer
couche F *de graviers* M

sand layer
couche F *de sable* M

ditch
fossé M

bank
talus M

traffic cone
cône M *de signalisation* F

arch bridge
pont *M* *en arc* *M*

parapet
parapet *M*

deck
pont *M*

pier
débarcadère *M*

spandrel column
allège *F*

suspension bridge
pont *M* *suspendu*

suspension cable
câble *M* *de suspension* *F*

tower
colonne *F*

suspender
suspente *F*

deck
pont *M*

center span
travée *F* *centrale*

girder
poutre *F*

tower foundation
fondation *F* *de la colonne* *F*

viaduct
viaduc *M*

side span
travée *F* *latérale*

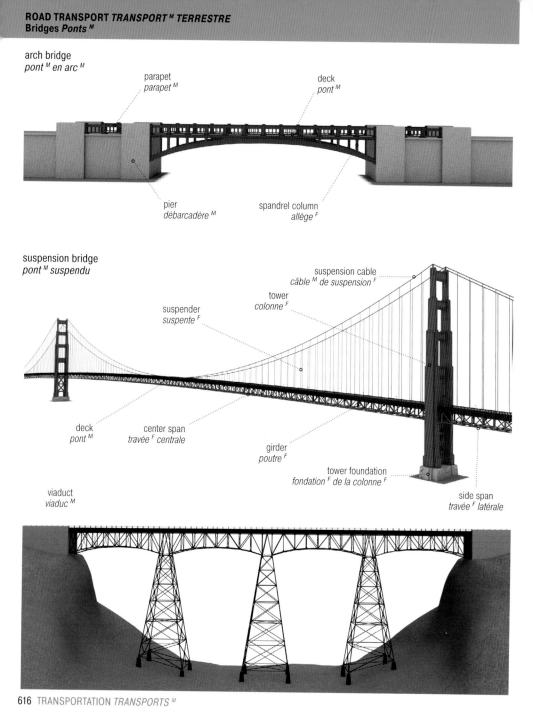

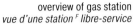

overview of gas station
vue d'une station **F** *libre-service*

car
automobile **F**

gas station attendant
employé **M** *de station-service* **F**

driver
conducteur **M**

service bay
aire **F** *de service* **M**

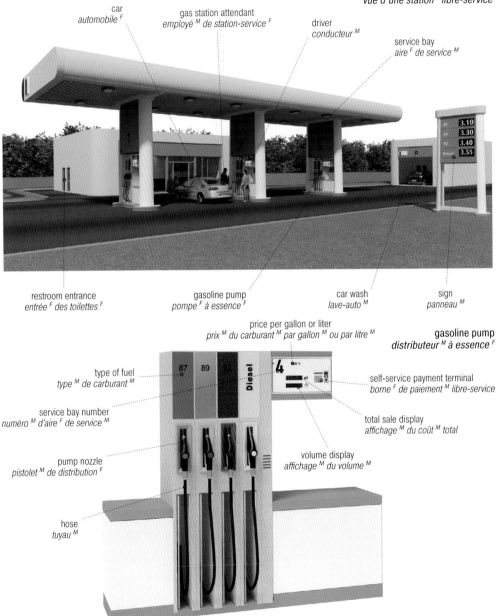

restroom entrance
entrée **F** *des toilettes* **F**

gasoline pump
pompe **F** *à essence* **F**

car wash
lave-auto **M**

sign
panneau **M**

price per gallon or liter
prix **M** *du carburant* **M** *par gallon* **M** *ou par litre* **M**

gasoline pump
distributeur **M** *à essence* **F**

type of fuel
type **M** *de carburant* **M**

self-service payment terminal
borne **F** *de paiement* **M** *libre-service*

service bay number
numéro **M** *d'aire* **F** *de service* **M**

total sale display
affichage **M** *du coût* **M** *total*

pump nozzle
pistolet **M** *de distribution* **F**

volume display
affichage **M** *du volume* **M**

hose
tuyau **M**

Car accessories
Accessoires *M* *automobiles*

jack
cric *M*

jumper cables
câble *M* *de démarrage* *M*

fire extinguisher
extincteur *M*

bicycle rack
porte-vélo *M*

sun visor
pare-soleil *M*

floor mat
tapis *M* *de sol* *M*

snow brush with scraper
balai-neige *M* *à grattoir* *M*

ski rack
porte-ski *M*

trailer hitch
attelage *M* *de remorque* *F*

scraper
grattoir *M*

roller shade
store *M* *à ressort* *M*

infant car seat
siège *M* *de sécurité* *F* *pour bébé* *M*

booster car seat
siège *M* *d'appoint* *M*

child car seat
siège *M* *d'auto* *F* *pour enfant* *M*

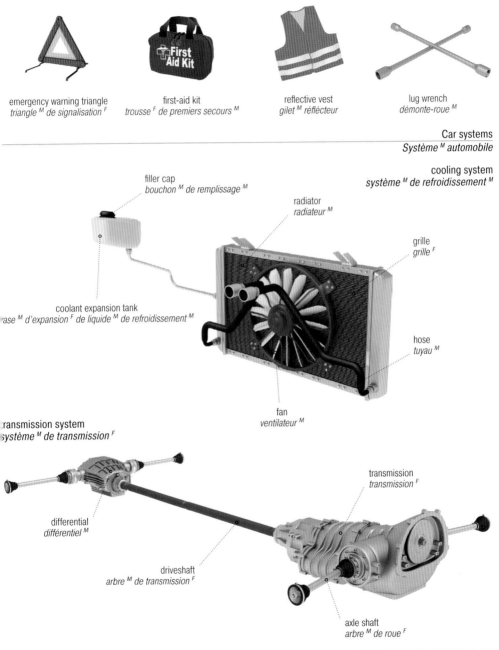

emergency warning triangle
triangle ^M de signalisation ^F

first-aid kit
trousse ^F de premiers secours ^M

reflective vest
gilet ^M réflécteur

lug wrench
démonte-roue ^M

Car systems
Système ^M automobile

cooling system
système ^M de refroidissement ^M

filler cap
bouchon ^M de remplissage ^M

radiator
radiateur ^M

grille
grille ^F

coolant expansion tank
ase ^M d'expansion ^F de liquide ^M de refroidissement ^M

hose
tuyau ^M

fan
ventilateur ^M

transmission system
système ^M de transmission ^F

transmission
transmission ^F

differential
différentiel ^M

driveshaft
arbre ^M de transmission ^F

axle shaft
arbre ^M de roue ^F

braking system
système ^M *de freinage* ^M

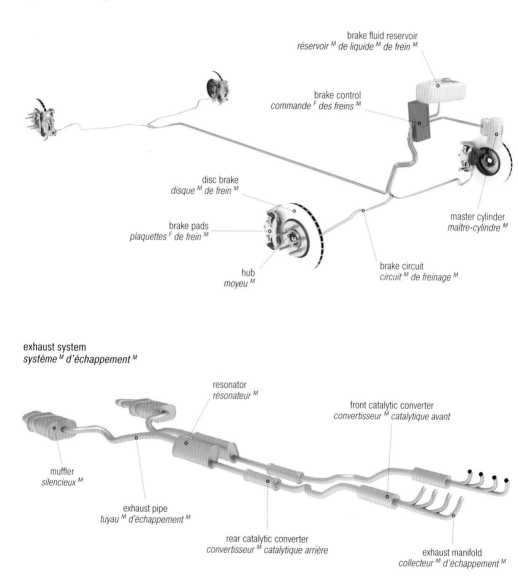

brake fluid reservoir
réservoir ^M *de liquide* ^M *de frein* ^M

brake control
commande ^F *des freins* ^M

disc brake
disque ^M *de frein* ^M

brake pads
plaquettes ^F *de frein* ^M

master cylinder
maître-cylindre ^M

hub
moyeu ^M

brake circuit
circuit ^M *de freinage* ^M

exhaust system
système ^M *d'échappement* ^M

resonator
résonateur ^M

front catalytic converter
convertisseur ^M *catalytique avant*

muffler
silencieux ^M

exhaust pipe
tuyau ^M *d'échappement* ^M

rear catalytic converter
convertisseur ^M *catalytique arrière*

exhaust manifold
collecteur ^M *d'échappement* ^M

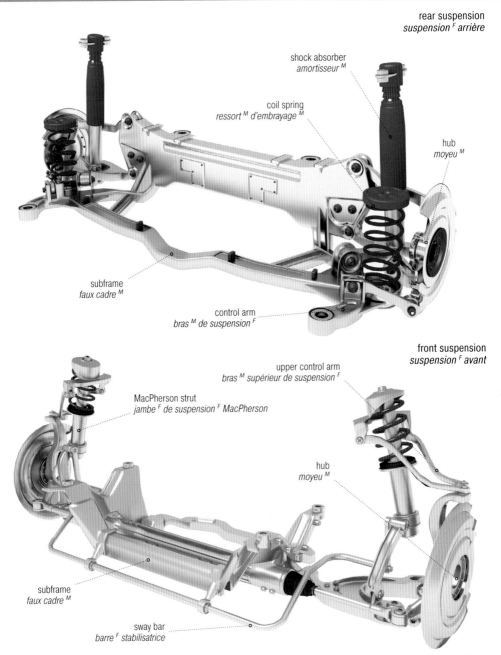

rear suspension
suspension F *arrière*

shock absorber
amortisseur M

coil spring
ressort M *d'embrayage* M

hub
moyeu M

subframe
faux cadre M

control arm
bras M *de suspension* F

front suspension
suspension F *avant*

upper control arm
bras M *supérieur de suspension* F

MacPherson strut
jambe F *de suspension* F *MacPherson*

hub
moyeu M

subframe
faux cadre M

sway bar
barre F *stabilisatrice*

engine
moteur M

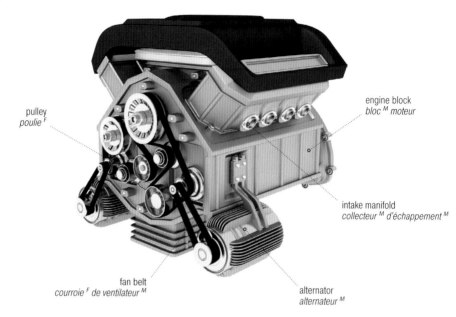

pulley
poulie F

engine block
bloc M *moteur*

intake manifold
collecteur M *d'échappement* M

fan belt
courroie F *de ventilateur* M

alternator
alternateur M

four-stroke engine cycle
cycle M *d'un moteur* M *à quatre temps* M

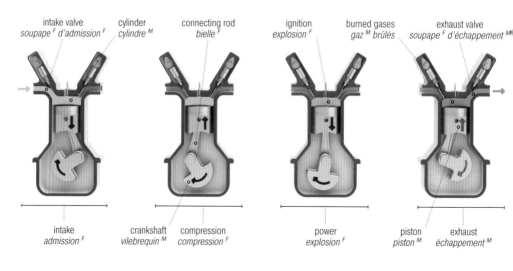

intake valve
soupape F *d'admission* F

cylinder
cylindre M

connecting rod
bielle F

ignition
explosion F

burned gases
gaz M *brûlés*

exhaust valve
soupape F *d'échappement* M

intake
admission F

crankshaft
vilebrequin M

compression
compression F

power
explosion F

piston
piston M

exhaust
échappement M

rear fascia
panneau ᴹ *arrière*

trunk seal
joint ᴹ *de coffre* ᴹ

brake light
feu ᴹ *de freinage* ᴹ

bumper molding
moulure ᴹ *de pare-chocs* ᴹ

front fascia
panneau ᴹ *avant*

grille
grille ᶠ *du radiateur* ᴹ

high beam
feu ᴹ *de route* ᶠ

low beam
feu ᴹ *de croisement* ᴹ

fog light
phare ᴹ *antibrouillard*

bumper molding
moulure ᴹ *de pare-chocs* ᴹ

turn signal
clignotant ᴹ

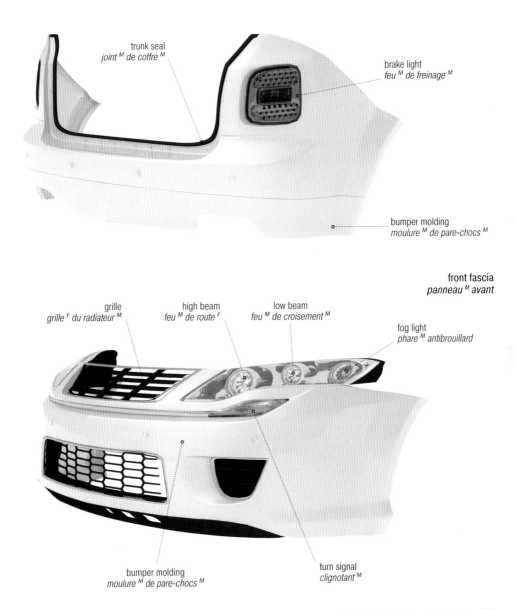

bucket seats
sièges ^M *baquet*

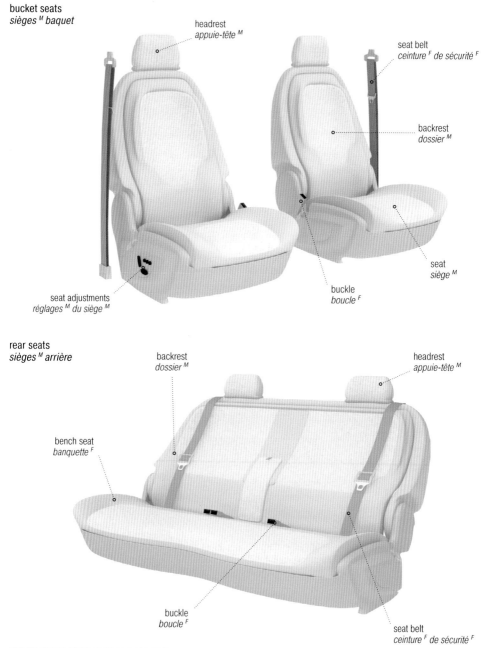

headrest
appuie-tête ^M

seat belt
ceinture ^F *de sécurité* ^F

backrest
dossier ^M

seat
siège ^M

buckle
boucle ^F

seat adjustments
réglages ^M *du siège* ^M

rear seats
sièges ^M *arrière*

backrest
dossier ^M

headrest
appuie-tête ^M

bench seat
banquette ^F

buckle
boucle ^F

seat belt
ceinture ^F *de sécurité* ^F

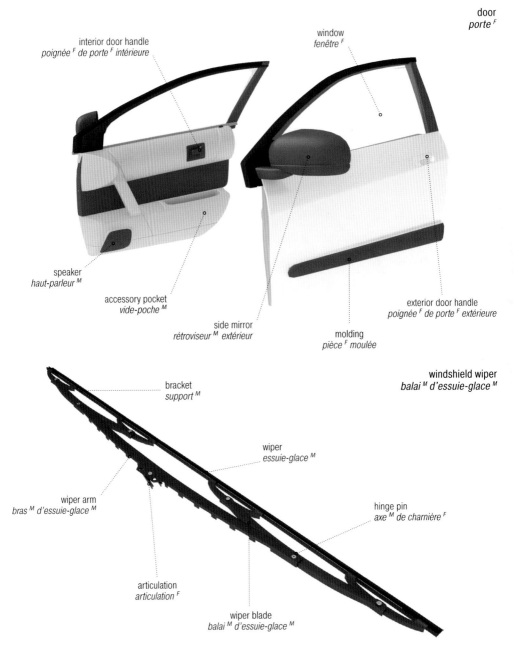

door
porte ^F

interior door handle
poignée ^F *de porte* ^F *intérieure*

window
fenêtre ^F

speaker
haut-parleur ^M

accessory pocket
vide-poche ^M

side mirror
rétroviseur ^M *extérieur*

molding
pièce ^F *moulée*

exterior door handle
poignée ^F *de porte* ^F *extérieure*

windshield wiper
balai ^M *d'essuie-glace* ^M

bracket
support ^M

wiper
essuie-glace ^M

wiper arm
bras ^M *d'essuie-glace* ^M

hinge pin
axe ^M *de charnière* ^F

articulation
articulation ^F

wiper blade
balai ^M *d'essuie-glace* ^M

instrument panel
tableau ᴹ *de bord* ᴹ

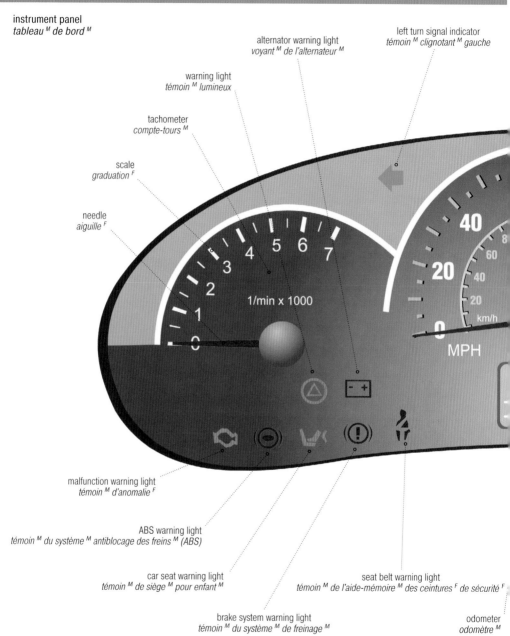

alternator warning light
voyant ᴹ *de l'alternateur* ᴹ

left turn signal indicator
témoin ᴹ *clignotant* ᴹ *gauche*

warning light
témoin ᴹ *lumineux*

tachometer
compte-tours ᴹ

scale
graduation ᶠ

needle
aiguille ᶠ

malfunction warning light
témoin ᴹ *d'anomalie* ᶠ

ABS warning light
témoin ᴹ *du système* ᴹ *antiblocage des freins* ᴹ *(ABS)*

car seat warning light
témoin ᴹ *de siège* ᴹ *pour enfant* ᴹ

seat belt warning light
témoin ᴹ *de l'aide-mémoire* ᴹ *des ceintures* ᶠ *de sécurité* ᶠ

brake system warning light
témoin ᴹ *du système* ᴹ *de freinage* ᴹ

odometer
odomètre ᴹ

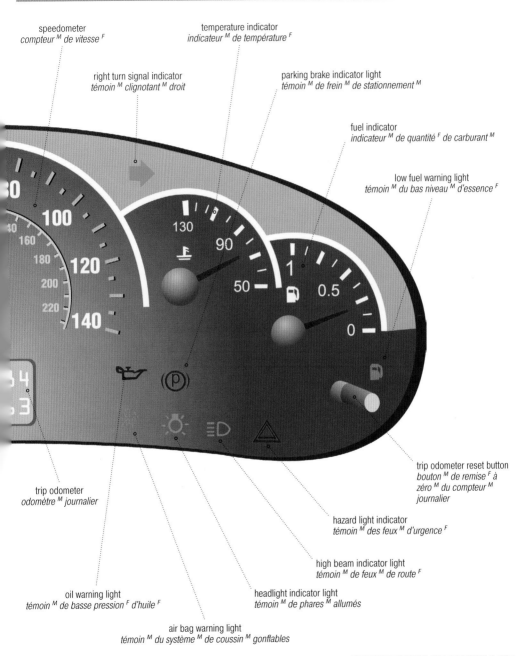

speedometer
compteur M _de vitesse_ F

temperature indicator
indicateur M _de température_ F

right turn signal indicator
témoin M _clignotant_ M _droit_

parking brake indicator light
témoin M _de frein_ M _de stationnement_ M

fuel indicator
indicateur M _de quantité_ F _de carburant_ M

low fuel warning light
témoin M _du bas niveau_ M _d'essence_ F

trip odometer reset button
bouton M _de remise_ F _à zéro_ M _du compteur_ M _journalier_

trip odometer
odomètre M _journalier_

hazard light indicator
témoin M _des feux_ M _d'urgence_ F

high beam indicator light
témoin M _de feux_ M _de route_ F

oil warning light
témoin M _de basse pression_ F _d'huile_ F

headlight indicator light
témoin M _de phares_ M _allumés_

air bag warning light
témoin M _du système_ M _de coussin_ M _gonflables_

tires
roues ^F

tread
bande ^F *de roulement* ^M

hubcap
enjoliveur ^M

bolt
écrou ^M

brake pads
plaquettes ^F *de frein* ^M

shock absorber
amortisseur ^M

suspension coil spring
ressort ^M *hélicoïdal de suspension* ^F

disc brake
disque ^M *de frein* ^M

leaf spring
ressort ^M *à lames* ^F

tire
pneu ^M

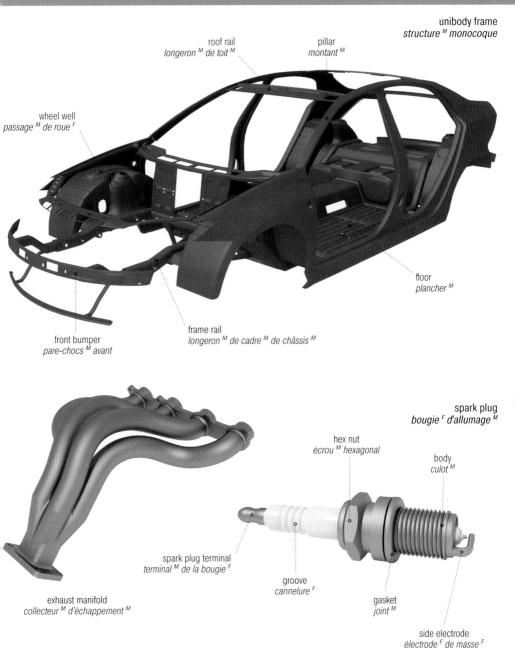

unibody frame
structure ^M *monocoque*

roof rail
longeron ^M *de toit* ^M

pillar
montant ^M

wheel well
passage ^M *de roue* ^F

floor
plancher ^M

front bumper
pare-chocs ^M *avant*

frame rail
longeron ^M *de cadre* ^M *de châssis* ^M

spark plug
bougie ^F *d'allumage* ^M

hex nut
écrou ^M *hexagonal*

body
culot ^M

spark plug terminal
terminal ^M *de la bougie* ^F

groove
cannelure ^F

gasket
joint ^M

side electrode
électrode ^F *de masse* ^F

exhaust manifold
collecteur ^M *d'échappement* ^M

radiator
radiateur[M]

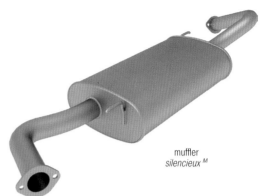

muffler
silencieux[M]

catalytic converter
convertisseur[M] *catalytique*

air filter
filtre[M] *à air*

fuel filter
filtre[M] *à carburant*[M]

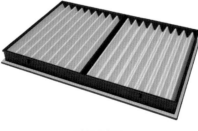

cabin air filter
filtre[M] *à air*[M] *d'habitacle*[M]

oil filter
filtre[M] *à huile*[F]

battery
batterie[F]

dashboard
tableau ^M *de bord* ^M

ignition switch
commutateur ^M *d'allumage* ^M

onboard computer
ordinateur ^M *de bord* ^M

rearview mirror
rétroviseur ^M

vanity mirror
miroir ^M *de pare-soleil* ^M

instrument panel
tableau ^M *de bord* ^M

audio system
système ^M *audio*

sun visor
pare-soleil ^M

steering wheel
volant ^M

clutch pedal
pédale ^F *d'embrayage* ^M

vent
ventilation ^F

panel
panneau ^M

brake pedal
pédale ^F *de frein* ^M

windshield wiper
essuie-glace ^M

glove compartment
boîte ^F *à gants* ^M

gas pedal
pédale ^F *d'accélérateur* ^M

parking brake button
frein ^M *à main* ^F

driving mode selector
sélecteur ^M *de mode* ^M *de conduite* ^F

gearshift lever
levier ^M *de vitesse* ^F

center console
console ^F *centrale*

exterior
extérieur M

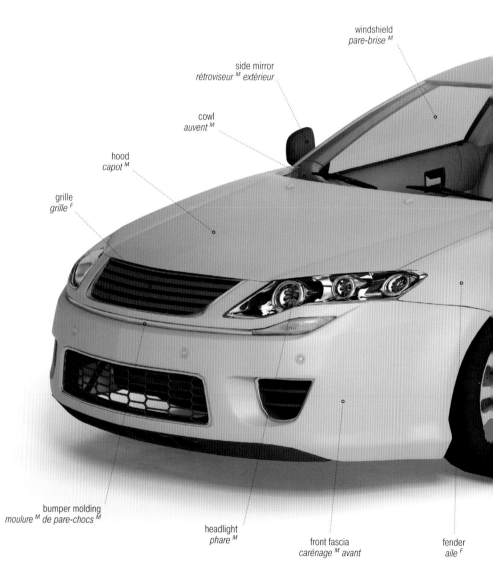

windshield
pare-brise M

side mirror
rétroviseur M *extérieur*

cowl
auvent M

hood
capot M

grille
grille F

bumper molding
moulure M *de pare-chocs* M

headlight
phare M

front fascia
carénage M *avant*

fender
aile F

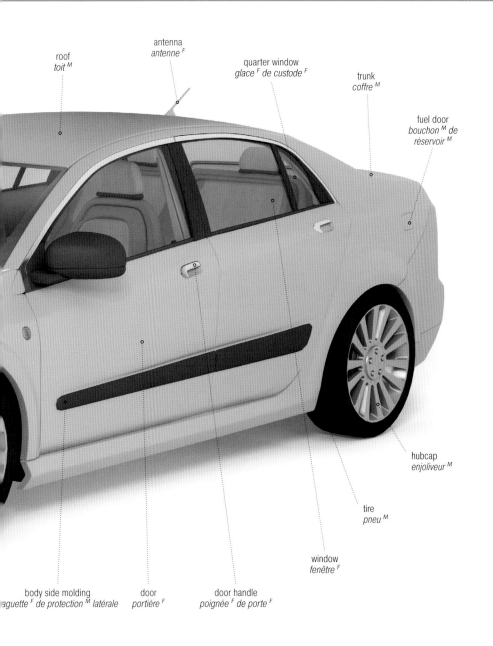

roof
toit ^M

antenna
antenne ^F

quarter window
glace ^F *de custode* ^F

trunk
coffre ^M

fuel door
bouchon ^M *de*
réservoir ^M

hubcap
enjoliveur ^M

tire
pneu ^M

window
fenêtre ^F

body side molding
aguette ^F *de protection* ^M *latérale*

door
portière ^F

door handle
poignée ^F *de porte* ^F

Types of cars
Type ^{M} *de carrosserie* ^{F}

electric car
voiture ^{F} *électrique*

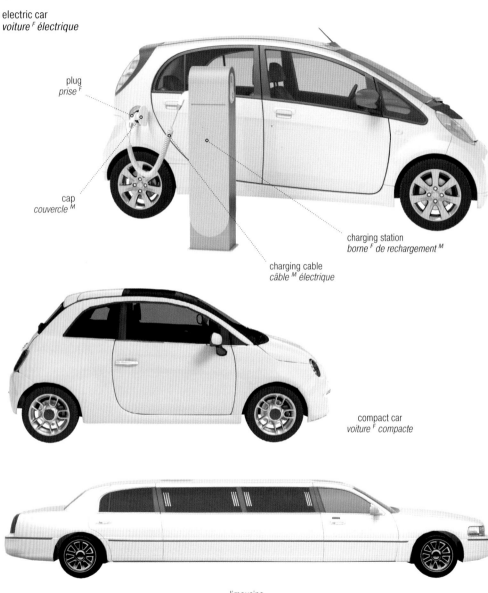

plug
prise ^{F}

cap
couvercle ^{M}

charging station
borne ^{F} *de rechargement* ^{M}

charging cable
câble ^{M} *électrique*

compact car
voiture ^{F} *compacte*

limousine
limousine ^{F}

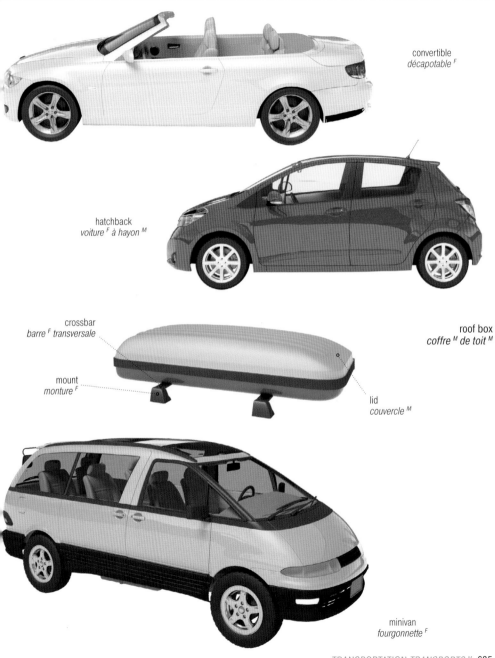

convertible
décapotable ^F

hatchback
voiture ^F *à hayon* ^M

crossbar
barre ^F *transversale*

roof box
coffre ^M *de toit* ^M

mount
monture ^F

lid
couvercle ^M

minivan
fourgonnette ^F

crossover vehicle
vehicule [M] *multisegment*

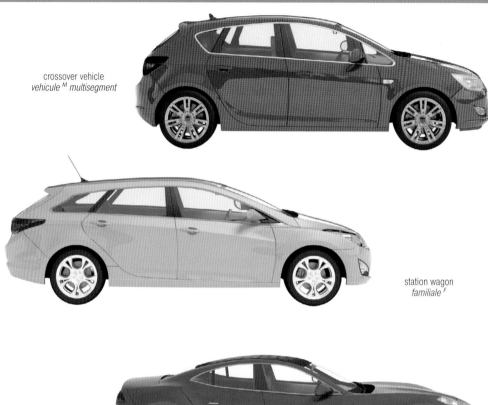

station wagon
familiale [F]

sports car
voiture [F] *de sport* [M]

coupe
coupé [F]

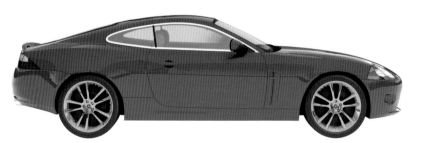

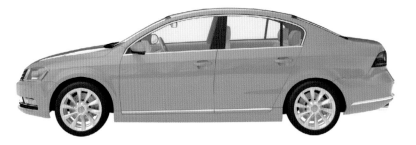

sedan
berline F

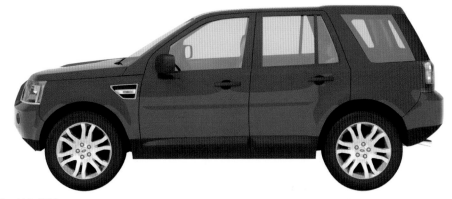

sport utility vehicle (SUV)
véhicule M *utilitaire sport* M

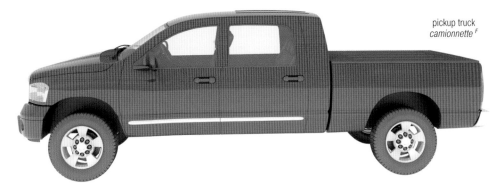

pickup truck
camionnette F

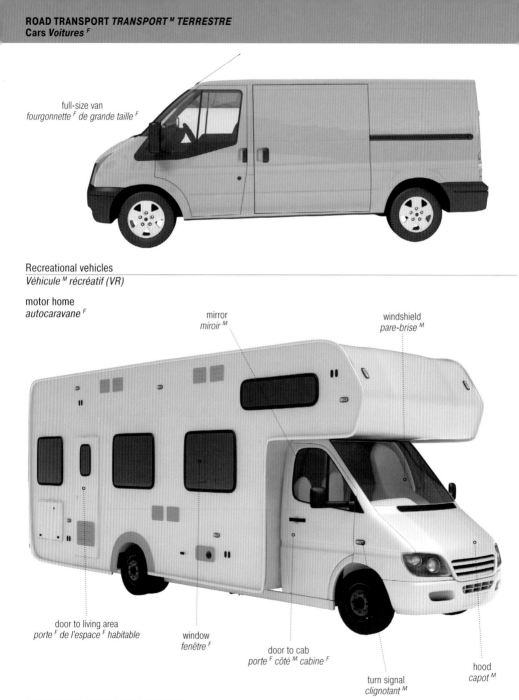

full-size van
fourgonnette ^F *de grande taille* ^F

Recreational vehicles
Véhicule ^M *récréatif (VR)*

motor home
autocaravane ^F

mirror
miroir ^M

windshield
pare-brise ^M

door to living area
porte ^F *de l'espace* ^F *habitable*

window
fenêtre ^F

door to cab
porte ^F *côté* ^M *cabine* ^F

turn signal
clignotant ^M

hood
capot ^M

teardrop trailer
roulotte F

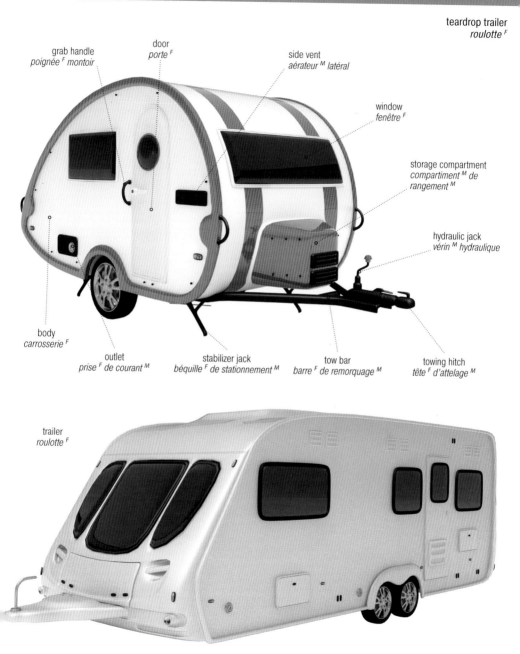

grab handle
poignée F *montoir*

door
porte F

side vent
aérateur M *latéral*

window
fenêtre F

storage compartment
compartiment M *de
rangement* M

hydraulic jack
vérin M *hydraulique*

body
carrosserie F

outlet
prise F *de courant* M

stabilizer jack
béquille F *de stationnement* M

tow bar
barre F *de remorquage* M

towing hitch
tête F *d'attelage* M

trailer
roulotte F

sport bike
moto ^F *de sport* ^M

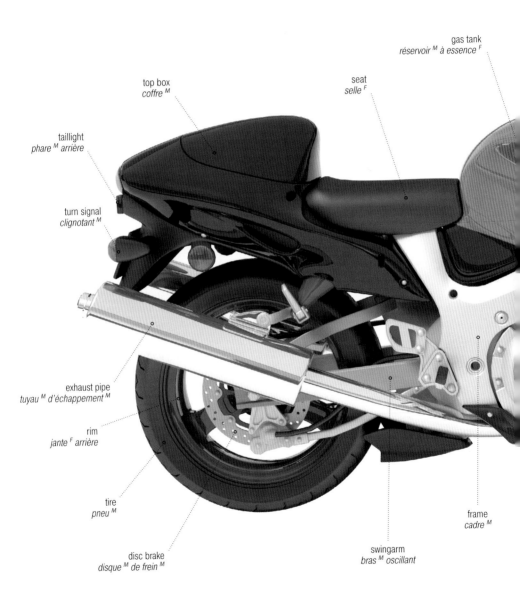

gas tank
réservoir ^M *à essence* ^F

top box
coffre ^M

seat
selle ^F

taillight
phare ^M *arrière*

turn signal
clignotant ^M

exhaust pipe
tuyau ^M *d'échappement* ^M

rim
jante ^F *arrière*

tire
pneu ^M

disc brake
disque ^M *de frein* ^M

swingarm
bras ^M *oscillant*

frame
cadre ^M

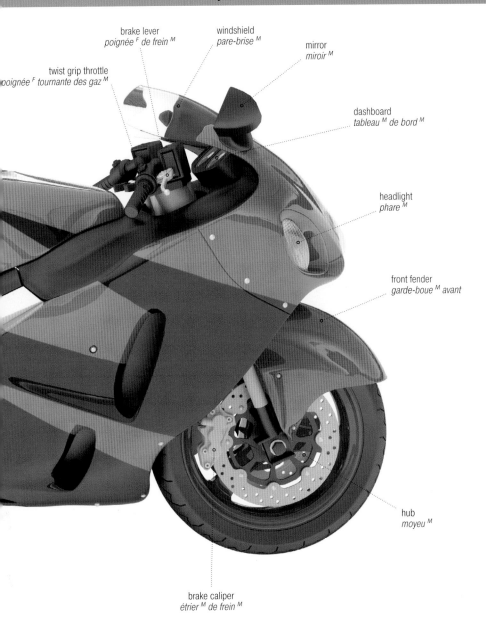

brake lever
poignée F de frein M

windshield
pare-brise M

mirror
miroir M

twist grip throttle
poignée F tournante des gaz M

dashboard
tableau M de bord M

headlight
phare M

front fender
garde-boue M avant

hub
moyeu M

brake caliper
étrier M de frein M

touring motorcycle
moto ^F *de route* ^F

driver's seat
selle ^F *conducteur* ^M

passenger's seat
selle ^F *passager* ^M

windshield
pare-brise ^M

backrest
dossier ^M

top box
coffre ^M

saddlebag
sacoche ^F

passenger's grab handle
poignée ^F *de soutien* ^M
pour le passager ^M

passenger's footrest
repose-pieds ^M *passager* ^M

driver's footrest
repose-pieds ^M

brake pedal
pédale ^F *de frein* ^M

motor scooter
scooter ^M

off-road motorcycle
moto ^F *tout-terrain*

all-terrain vehicle (ATV)
véhicule ^M *tout-terrain* ^M *(VTT)*

headlight
phare ^M

handlebars
guidon ^M

brake lever
poignée ^F *de frein* ^M

handgrip
poignée ^F

gas tank
réservoir ^M *à essence* ^F

seat
siège ^M

rear cargo rack
porte-bagages ^M *arrière*

front cargo rack
porte-bagages ^M *avant*

rear fender
garde-boue ^M *avant*

front bumper
pare-chocs ^M *avant*

footrest
marchepied ^M

tire
pneu ^M

shock absorber
amortisseur ^M

front fender
garde-boue ^M *avant*

motocross motorcycle
moto-cross ^F

standard motorcycle
moto ^F *standard*

mirror
miroir ^M

brake lever
poignée ^F *de frein* ^M

clutch lever
levier ^M *d'embrayage* ^M

handgrip
poignée ^F

seat
siège ^M

fuel tank
réservoir ^M *à essence* ^F

dashboard
tableau ^M *de bord* ^M

turn signal
clignotant ^M

headlight
phare ^M

front fender
garde-boue ^M *avant*

muffler
silencieux ^M

frame
cadre ^M

disc brake
disque ^M *de frein* ^M

exhaust pipe
tuyau ^M *d'échappement* ^M

V-twin engine
bimoteur ^M *en V*

front fork
fourche ^F *avant*

brake caliper
étrier ^M *de frein* ^M

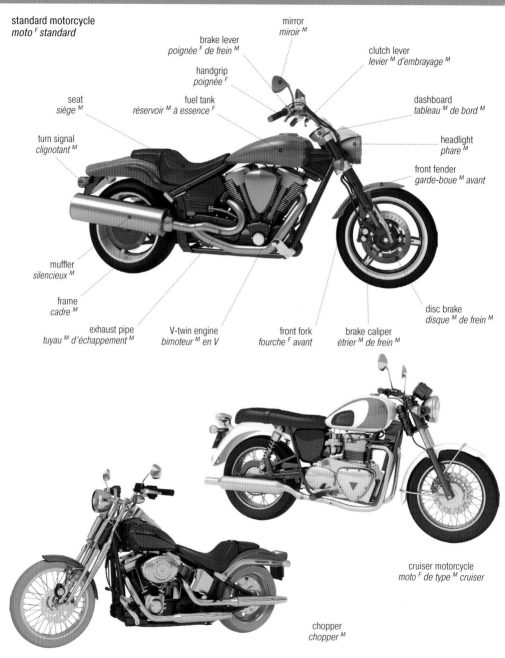

cruiser motorcycle
moto ^F *de type* ^M *cruiser*

chopper
chopper ^M

balance bicycle
vélo ^M *d'apprentissage* ^M

tricycle
tricycle ^M

scooter
trottinette ^F

child carrier
siège ^M *pour enfant* ^M

backpack
sac ^M *à dos* ^M

BMX bicycle
vélocross ^M

mountain bicycle
vélo ^M *de montagne* ^F

touring bicycle
vélo ^M *de cyclotourisme* ^M

tandem bicycle
tandem ^M

child bike trailer
remorque ^F *de vélo* ^M *pour enfant*

cruiser bicycle
vélo M *de plage* F

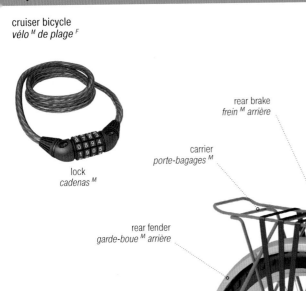

lock
cadenas M

seat
siège M

brake cable
câble M *de frein* M

rear brake
frein M *arrière*

carrier
porte-bagages M

rear fender
garde-boue M *arrière*

mudguard
garde-boue M

spoke
rayon M *de roue* F

rim
chaînes F *à neige* F *obligatoires*

tire
avion M *volant à basse altitude* F

chain
chaîne F

chain wheel
plateau M

pedal
pédale F

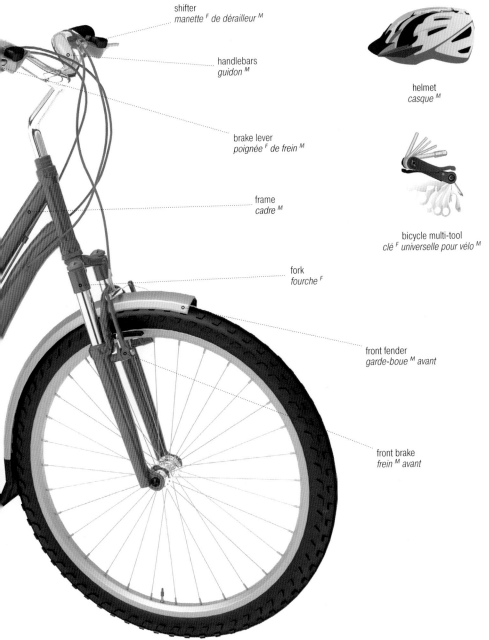

shifter
manette ^F *de dérailleur* ^M

handlebars
guidon ^M

brake lever
poignée ^F *de frein* ^M

frame
cadre ^M

fork
fourche ^F

front fender
garde-boue ^M *avant*

front brake
frein ^M *avant*

helmet
casque ^M

bicycle multi-tool
clé ^F *universelle pour vélo* ^M

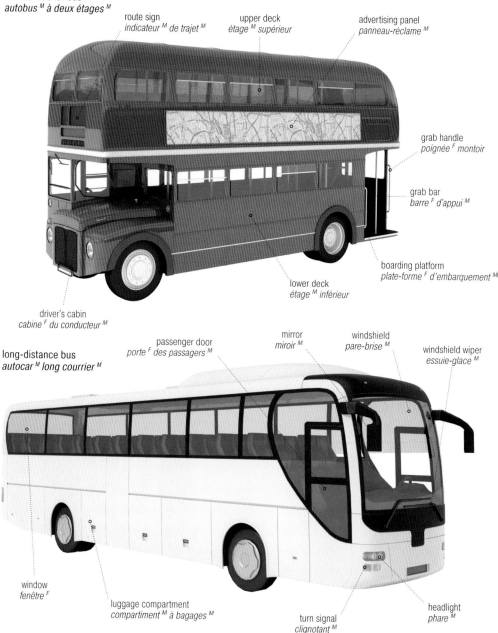

double-decker bus
autobus *M* *à deux étages* *M*

route sign
indicateur *M* *de trajet* *M*

upper deck
étage *M* *supérieur*

advertising panel
panneau-réclame *M*

grab handle
poignée *F* *montoir*

grab bar
barre *F* *d'appui* *M*

boarding platform
plate-forme *F* *d'embarquement* *M*

lower deck
étage *M* *inférieur*

driver's cabin
cabine *F* *du conducteur* *M*

long-distance bus
autocar *M* *long courrier* *M*

passenger door
porte *F* *des passagers* *M*

mirror
miroir *M*

windshield
pare-brise *M*

windshield wiper
essuie-glace *M*

window
fenêtre *F*

luggage compartment
compartiment *M* *à bagages* *M*

turn signal
clignotant *M*

headlight
phare *M*

city bus
autobus ^M *de ville* ^F

minibus
minibus ^M

double-decker long-distance bus
autobus ^M *longue distance* ^F *à deux étages* ^M

articulated bus
autobus M *articulé*

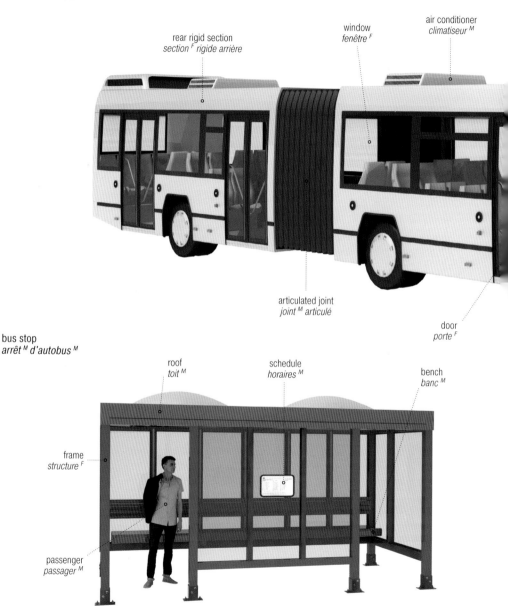

rear rigid section
section F *rigide arrière*

window
fenêtre F

air conditioner
climatiseur M

articulated joint
joint M *articulé*

door
porte F

bus stop
arrêt M *d'autobus* M

roof
toit M

schedule
horaires M

bench
banc M

frame
structure F

passenger
passager M

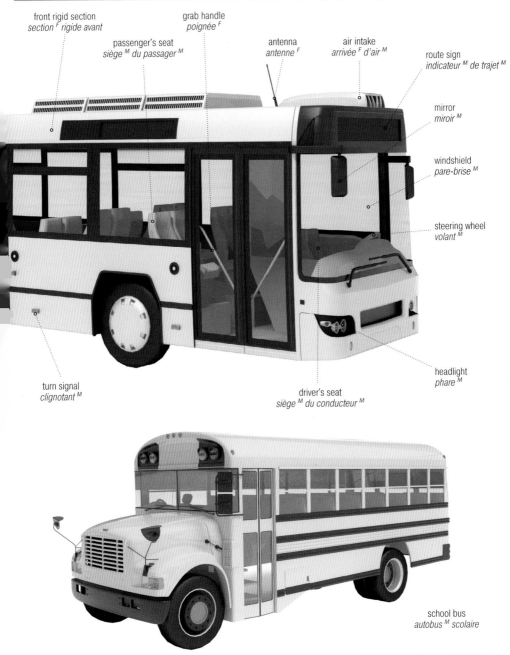

front rigid section
section ^F *rigide avant*

grab handle
poignée ^F

passenger's seat
siège ^M *du passager* ^M

antenna
antenne ^F

air intake
arrivée ^F *d'air* ^M

route sign
indicateur ^M *de trajet* ^M

mirror
miroir ^M

windshield
pare-brise ^M

steering wheel
volant ^M

turn signal
clignotant ^M

driver's seat
siège ^M *du conducteur* ^M

headlight
phare ^M

school bus
autobus ^M *scolaire*

semitrailer
semi-remorque M

cab
cabine F

air horn
avertisseur M *pneumatique*

windshield
pare-brise M

West Coast mirror
rétroviseur M *West Coast*

door
porte F

headlight
phare M

turn signal
clignotant M

gas tank cap
bouchon M *du réservoir* M *d'essence* F

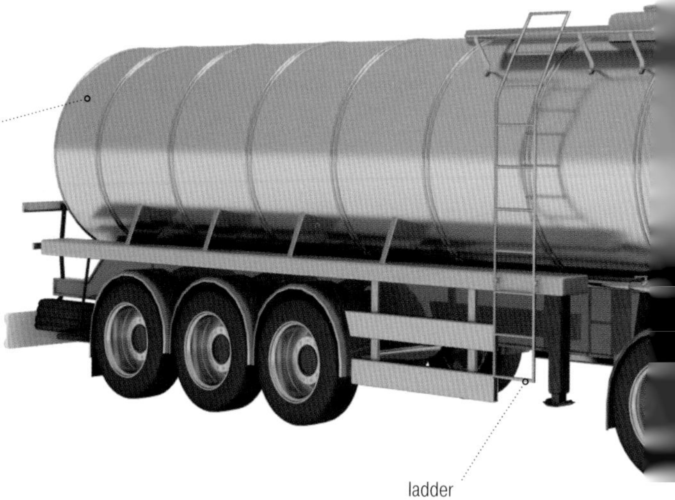

tank body
citerne F

ladder
échelle F

semitrailer
semi-remorque [M]

tank trailer
remorque-citerne [F]

step
marchepied [M]

cab
cabine [F]

West Coast mirror
rétroviseur [M] *West Coast*

radiator grille
grille [F] *du radiateur* [M]

headlight
phare [M]

fuel tank
réservoir [M] *d'essence* [F]

turn signal
clignotant [M]

semitrailer cab
cabine F *de semi-remorque* M

steering wheel
volant M

speaker
haut-parleur M

gearshift lever
levier M *de vitesse* F

armrest
accoudoir M

sleeper cab
cabine F *couchette* F

clutch pedal
pédale F *d'embrayage* M

brake pedal
pédale F *de frein* M

gas pedal
pédale F *d'accélérateur* M

instrument panel
tableau M *de bord* M

seat
siège M

dump truck
camion-benne ^M

cement truck
camion-malaxeur ^M

truck and tandem trailer
camion ^M *et remorque* ^F *tandem*

semitrailer with sleeper cab
semi-remorque ^M *avec cabine* ^F *couchette* ^F

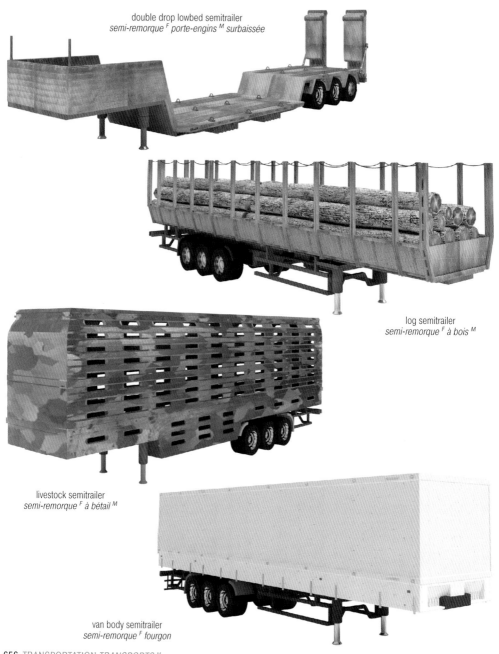

double drop lowbed semitrailer
semi-remorque ^F *porte-engins* ^M *surbaissée*

log semitrailer
semi-remorque ^F *à bois* ^M

livestock semitrailer
semi-remorque ^F *à bétail* ^M

van body semitrailer
semi-remorque ^F *fourgon*

tank trailer
remorque-citerne^F

automobile transport semitrailer
semi-remorque^F *porte-voitures*

truck tractor
porteur-remorqueur^M

box van
fourgonnette^F *à caisse*^F

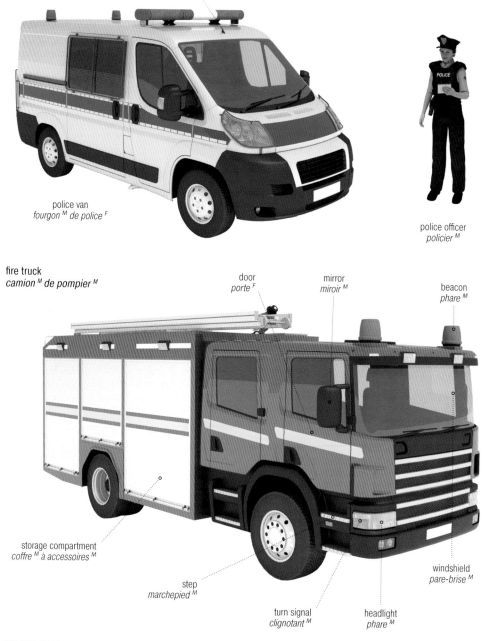

police van
fourgon ᴹ *de police* ᶠ

police officer
policier ᴹ

fire truck
camion ᴹ *de pompier* ᴹ

door
porte ᶠ

mirror
miroir ᴹ

beacon
phare ᴹ

storage compartment
coffre ᴹ *à accessoires* ᴹ

step
marchepied ᴹ

turn signal
clignotant ᴹ

headlight
phare ᴹ

windshield
pare-brise ᴹ

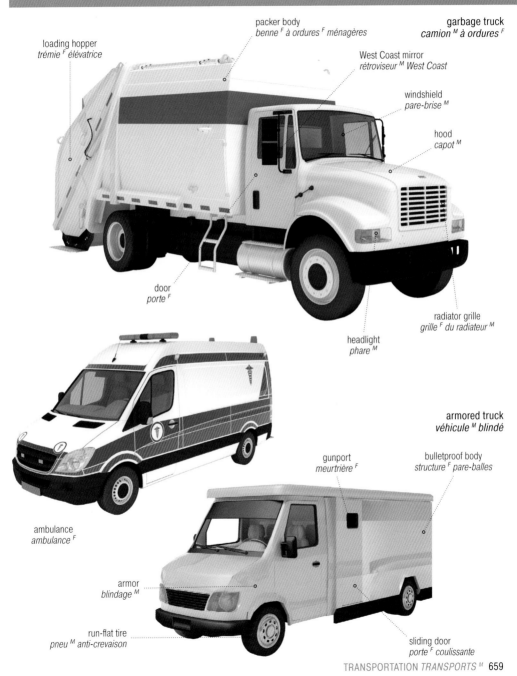

packer body
benne F *à ordures* F *ménagères*

garbage truck
camion M *à ordures* F

loading hopper
trémie F *élévatrice*

West Coast mirror
rétroviseur M *West Coast*

windshield
pare-brise M

hood
capot M

door
porte F

radiator grille
grille F *du radiateur* M

headlight
phare M

armored truck
véhicule M *blindé*

gunport
meurtrière F

bulletproof body
structure F *pare-balles*

ambulance
ambulance F

armor
blindage M

run-flat tire
pneu M *anti-crevaison*

sliding door
porte F *coulissante*

street cleaner
camion ᴹ *balayeur*

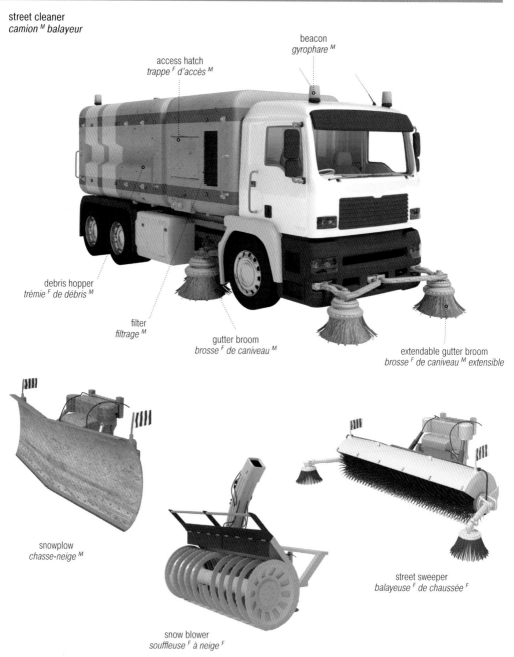

beacon
gyrophare ᴹ

access hatch
trappe ᶠ *d'accès* ᴹ

debris hopper
trémie ᶠ *de débris* ᴹ

filter
filtrage ᴹ

gutter broom
brosse ᶠ *de caniveau* ᴹ

extendable gutter broom
brosse ᶠ *de caniveau* ᴹ *extensible*

snowplow
chasse-neige ᴹ

snow blower
souffleuse ᶠ *à neige* ᶠ

street sweeper
balayeuse ᶠ *de chaussée* ᶠ

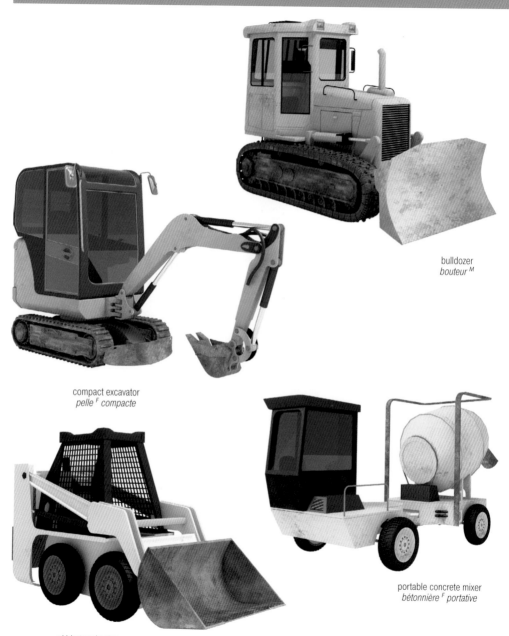

bulldozer
bouteur ᴹ

compact excavator
pelle ᶠ compacte

portable concrete mixer
bétonnière ᶠ portative

skid-steer loader
chargeur ᴹ à direction ᶠ à glissement ᴹ

mini road roller
mini rouleau M compresseur

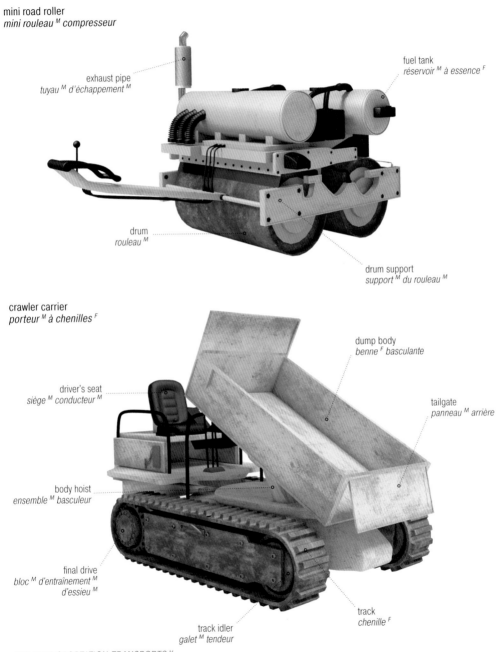

exhaust pipe
tuyau M d'échappement M

fuel tank
réservoir M à essence F

drum
rouleau M

drum support
support M du rouleau M

crawler carrier
porteur M à chenilles F

dump body
benne F basculante

driver's seat
siège M conducteur M

tailgate
panneau M arrière

body hoist
ensemble M basculeur

final drive
*bloc M d'entraînement M
d'essieu M*

track
chenille F

track idler
galet M tendeur

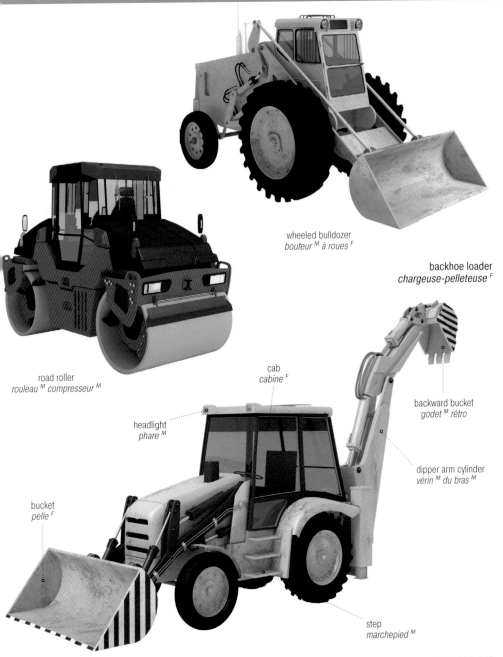

wheeled bulldozer
bouteur ^M *à roues* ^F

backhoe loader
chargeuse-pelleteuse ^F

cab
cabine ^F

backward bucket
godet ^M *rétro*

road roller
rouleau ^M *compresseur* ^M

headlight
phare ^M

dipper arm cylinder
vérin ^M *du bras* ^M

bucket
pelle ^F

step
marchepied ^M

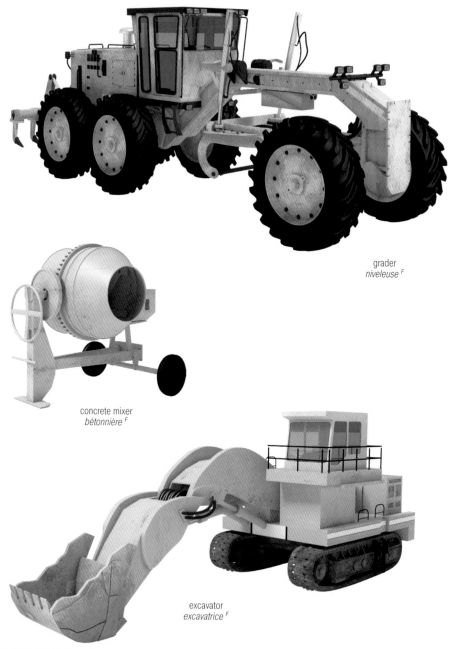

grader
niveleuse ᶠ

concrete mixer
bétonnière ᶠ

excavator
excavatrice ᶠ

haul truck
camion M *de transport* M

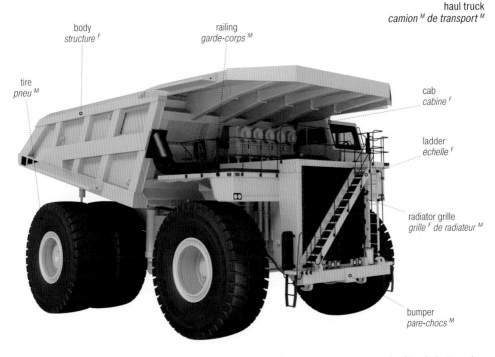

body
structure F

railing
garde-corps M

tire
pneu M

cab
cabine F

ladder
échelle F

radiator grille
grille F *de radiateur* M

bumper
pare-chocs M

haul truck: bottom view
camion M *de transport* M : *vue* F *du dessous* M

tire
roue F

transmission
transmission F

axle shaft
axe M *de roue* F *motrice*

driveshaft
arbre M *de transmission* F

bumper
pare-chocs M

crankcase
carter M *de moteur* M

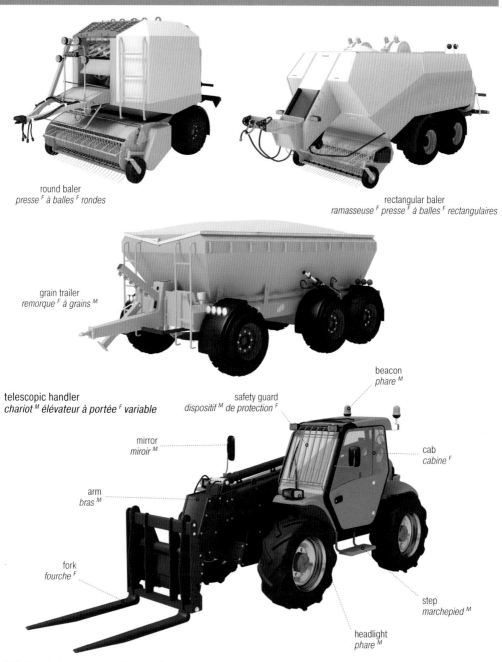

round baler
presse[F] *à balles*[F] *rondes*

rectangular baler
ramasseuse[F] *presse*[F] *à balles*[F] *rectangulaires*

grain trailer
remorque[F] *à grains*[M]

telescopic handler
chariot[M] *élévateur à portée*[F] *variable*

beacon
phare[M]

safety guard
dispositif[M] *de protection*[F]

mirror
miroir[M]

cab
cabine[F]

arm
bras[M]

fork
fourche[F]

step
marchepied[M]

headlight
phare[M]

harvester
moissonneuse F

tractor
tracteur M

horse trailer
remorque F à chevaux M

combine harvester
moissonneuse-batteuse *F*

beacon
gyrophare *M*

cab
cabine *F*

unloading tube
tube *M* *de décharge* *F*

feeding tube
tube *M* *d'alimentation* *F*

rotating auger
vis *F* *d'alimentation* *F*

grain tank
benne *F* *à grains* *M*

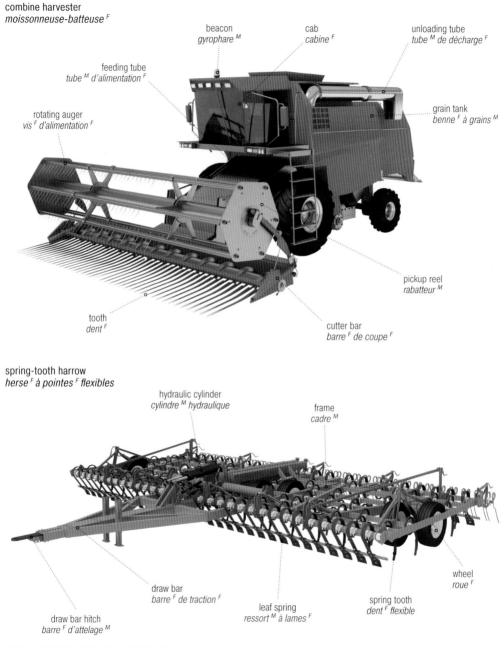

pickup reel
rabatteur *M*

tooth
dent *F*

cutter bar
barre *F* *de coupe* *F*

spring-tooth harrow
herse *F* *à pointes* *F* *flexibles*

hydraulic cylinder
cylindre *M* *hydraulique*

frame
cadre *M*

wheel
roue *F*

draw bar
barre *F* *de traction* *F*

leaf spring
ressort *M* *à lames* *F*

spring tooth
dent *F* *flexible*

draw bar hitch
barre *F* *d'attelage* *M*

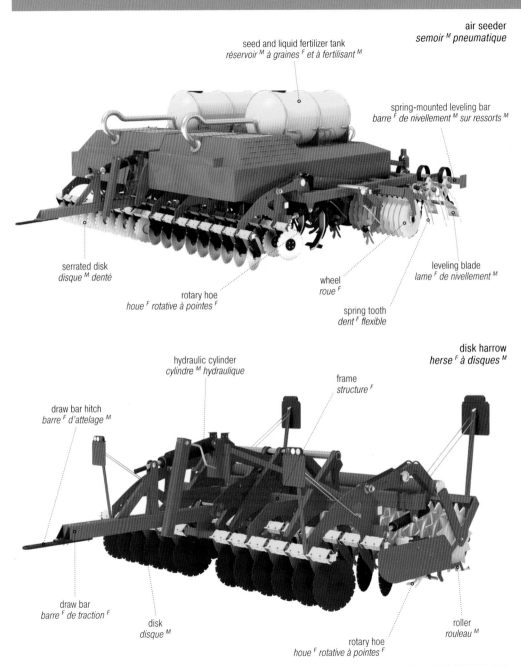

air seeder
semoir [M] *pneumatique*

seed and liquid fertilizer tank
réservoir [M] *à graines* [F] *et à fertilisant* [M]

spring-mounted leveling bar
barre [F] *de nivellement* [M] *sur ressorts* [M]

serrated disk
disque [M] *denté*

leveling blade
lame [F] *de nivellement* [M]

wheel
roue [F]

rotary hoe
houe [F] *rotative à pointes* [F]

spring tooth
dent [F] *flexible*

disk harrow
herse [F] *à disques* [M]

hydraulic cylinder
cylindre [M] *hydraulique*

frame
structure [F]

draw bar hitch
barre [F] *d'attelage* [M]

draw bar
barre [F] *de traction* [F]

disk
disque [M]

rotary hoe
houe [F] *rotative à pointes* [F]

roller
rouleau [M]

fallen rocks
éboulement M *de rochers* M

pavement ends
fin F *de la voie* F *pavée*

loose gravel
gravillons M

no passing zone
zone F *de non-dépassement* M

signal ahead
feux M *de circulation* F

road narrows
rétrécissement M *de chaussée* F

truck crossing
passage M *pour camions* M

two-way traffic
circulation F *dans les deux sens* M

advisory speed
vitesse F *conseiller*

metric speed limit
limite F *de vitesse* F *métrique*

speed limit
limite F *de vitesse* F

night speed limit
limite F *de vitesse* F
de nuit F

divided highway crossing
passage M *d'autoroute* F
à chaussées F *séparées*

left or through
tourner à gauche ou
avancer tout-droit

bicycle and pedestrian detour
détour M *pour piétons* M
et cyclistes M

exit closed
sortie F *barrée*

school zone or area
zone F *d'écoliers* M

bicycle crossing with share
the road warning
piste F *cyclable, partagez la route* F

handicapped crossing
passage M *pour*
personnes F *handicappées*

pedestrian crossing
passage M
pour piétons M

obstruction to be passed on left
obstruction,F passage M
sur la gauche F

obstruction to be passed on right or left
obstruction,F passage M
sur la gauche F ou la droite F

obstruction to be passed on right
obstruction,F passage M
sur la droite F

right turn only
virage M à droite F
uniquement

intersection lane control
signalisation F
d'intersection F

two-way left turn only
tourner à gauche dans les
deux sens M uniquement

straight ahead only
aller tout-droit
uniquement

truck weight limit
poids M limite pour
camions M

railroad crossing
passage M à niveau M

reserved for handicapped parking
stationnement M réservé pour les
personnes F handicapées

HOV lane ahead
voie F réservée
au covoiturage M

road ending at T intersection
route F finissant en
intersection F en T

sharp curve to left (arrow)
virage M serré à gauche
(flèche F)

sharp curve to left (chevron)
virage M serré à gauce
(chevron M)

detour
détour M

do not enter
ne pas entrer

wrong way
mauvais sens M

yield
cédez le passage M

stop
arrêt M

270-degree loop
boucle F à 270 degrés M

curve
virage M

hairpin curve
courbe F serrée

curve with speed advisory
*courbe F avec vitesse F
recommandée*

circular intersection ahead
rond-point M

side road (right)
*route F secondaire
(à droite)*

winding road
virages M

reverse turns
série F de virages M

right curve and minor road
*virage M à droite F et route F
secondaire*

cross road ahead
intersection F

limited vehicle storage space
*entrepôt M pour véhicules M
limités*

T intersection ahead
intersection F en T

merging traffic
trafic M entrant

added lane
nouvelle voie F

merge
engage dans la circulation F

added lane
voie F supplémentaire

divided highway ahead
*autoroute F à chaussées F
séparées*

road narrows
*rétrécissement M
par la droite F*

flagger ahead
signaleur M

road works
travaux M routiers

cattle crossing
passage ^{M} de bétail ^{M}

trucks rollover warning with speed advisory
risque ^{M} de renversement ^{M} et vitesse ^{F} recommandée

low clearance ahead
hauteur ^{F} limitée

no bicycles
interdit aux vélos ^{M}

no pedestrian crossing
traversée ^{F} de piétons ^{M} interdite

no large trucks
gros ^{M} camions ^{M} interdits

no parking
stationnement ^{M} interdit

no left turn
terdiction ^{F} de tourner à gauche ^{F}

no right turn
interdiction ^{F} de tourner à droite ^{F}

no left or u turns
virages ^{M} à gauche et demi-tour ^{M} interdits

no straight through
interdit d'aller tout droit

no U turn
demi-tour ^{M} interdit

slippery when wet
risque ^{M} de chaussée ^{F} glissante

railroad crossing
passage ^{M} à niveau ^{M}

deer crossing
passage ^{M} de cerfs ^{M}

tow away zone
risque ^{M} de remorquage ^{M}

keep left
serrez à gauche ^{F}

one way traffic
sens ^{M} unique

Airport exterior
Vue ᶠ *extérieure de l'aéroport* ᴹ

maintenance hangar
hangar ᴹ *de maintenance* ᶠ

runway
piste ᶠ *d'envol* ᴹ

road
route ᶠ

parking lot
stationnement ᴹ

passenger terminal
aérogare ᶠ *passagers* ᴹ

taxiway
piste ^F *de circulation* ^F *et d'attente* ^F

control tower
tour ^F *de contrôle* ^M

control tower cab
cabine ^F *de tour* ^F *de contrôle* ^M

maneuvering area
aire ^F *de manoeuvre* ^F

service road
route ^F *de service* ^M

taxiway line
ligne ^F *de voie* ^F *de circulation* ^F

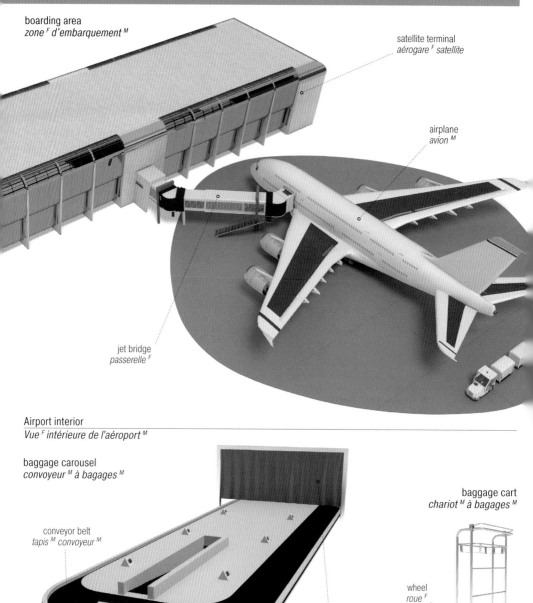

boarding area
zone^F *d'embarquement*^M

satellite terminal
aérogare^F *satellite*

airplane
avion^M

jet bridge
passerelle^F

Airport interior
Vue^F *intérieure de l'aéroport*^M

baggage carousel
convoyeur^M *à bagages*^M

baggage cart
chariot^M *à bagages*^M

conveyor belt
tapis^M *convoyeur*^M

wheel
roue^F

curtain
rideau^M

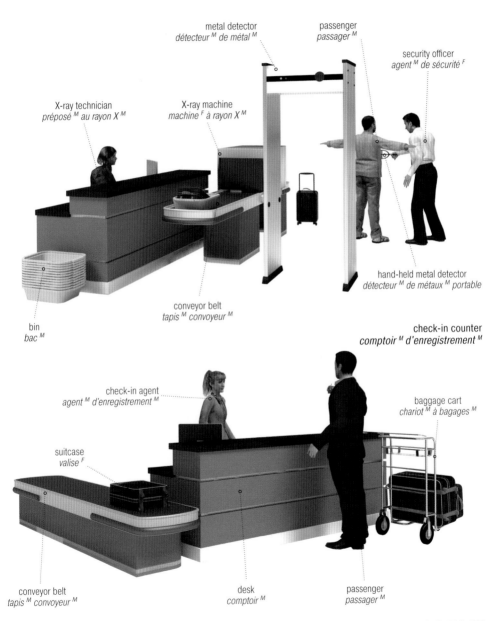

security checkpoint
contrôle^M *de sécurité*^F

metal detector
détecteur^M *de métal*^M

passenger
passager^M

security officer
agent^M *de sécurité*^F

X-ray technician
préposé^M *au rayon X*^M

X-ray machine
machine^F *à rayon X*^M

hand-held metal detector
détecteur^M *de métaux*^M *portable*

conveyor belt
tapis^M *convoyeur*^M

bin
bac^M

check-in counter
comptoir^M *d'enregistrement*^M

check-in agent
agent^M *d'enregistrement*^M

baggage cart
chariot^M *à bagages*^M

suitcase
valise^F

conveyor belt
tapis^M *convoyeur*^M

desk
comptoir^M

passenger
passager^M

departure area
aire ᶠ de départ ᴹ

coffee shop
café ᴹ

restroom
toilettes ᶠ

baggage check-in counter
comptoir ᴹ d'enregistrement ᴹ des bagages ᴹ

flight information board
tableau ᴹ d'affichage ᴹ des vols ᴹ

escalator
escalier ᴹ mécanique

self-service check-in kiosk
borne ᶠ d'enregistrement ᴹ libre-service

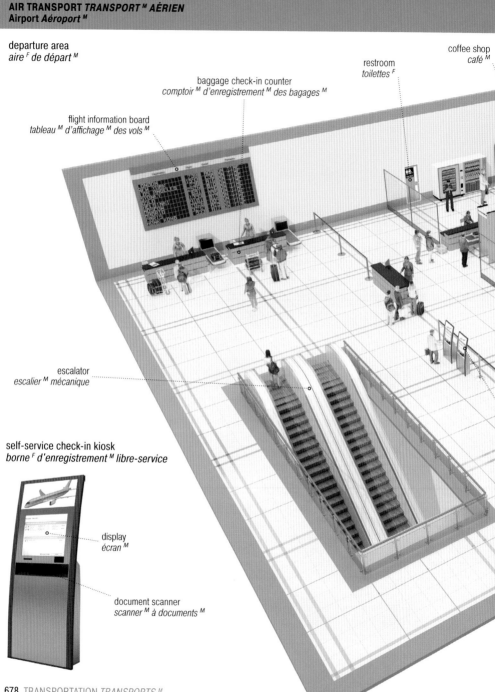

display
écran ᴹ

document scanner
scanner ᴹ à documents ᴹ

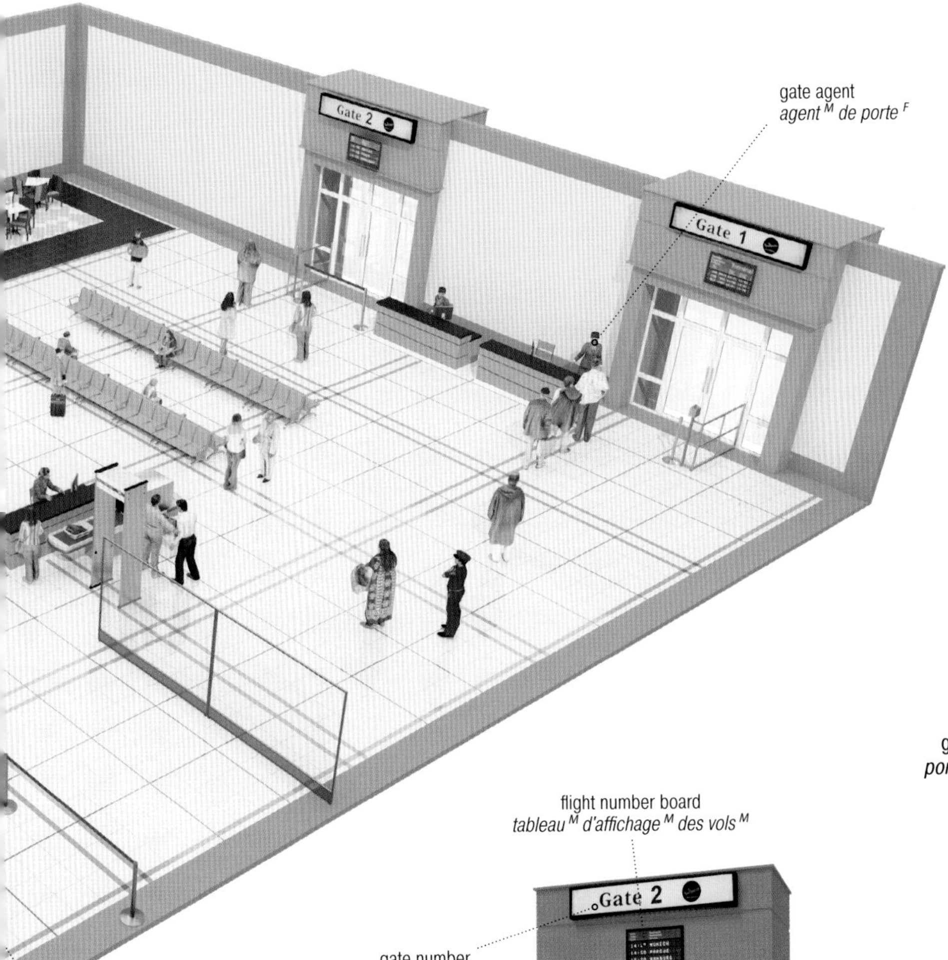

gate agent
agent [M] *de porte* [F]

gate
porte [F]

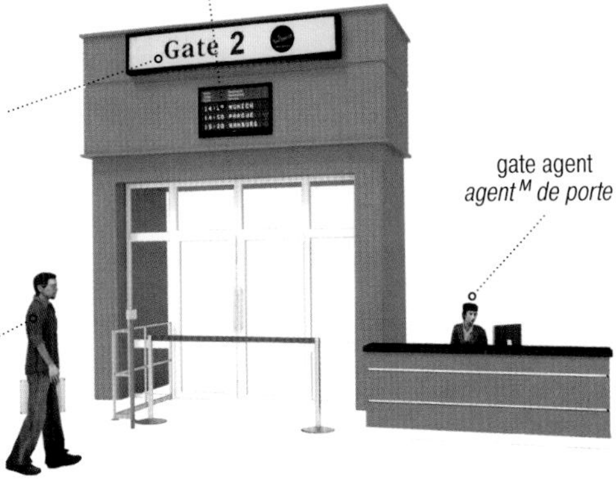

flight number board
tableau [M] *d'affichage* [M] *des vols* [M]

gate number
numéro [M] *de porte* [F] *d'embarquement* [M]

gate agent
agent [M] *de porte* [F]

self-service check-in kiosk
borne [F] *d'enregistrement* [M] *libre-service*

passenger
passager [M]

arrival area
aire ^F *d'arrivée* ^F

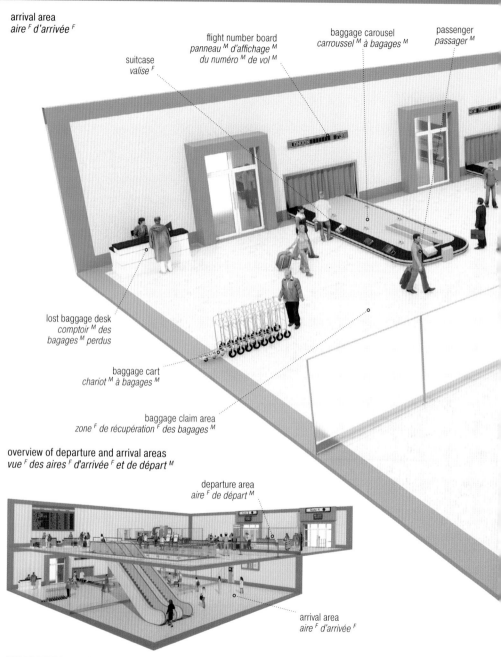

suitcase
valise ^F

flight number board
panneau ^M *d'affichage* ^M
du numéro ^M *de vol* ^M

baggage carousel
carroussel ^M *à bagages* ^M

passenger
passager ^M

lost baggage desk
comptoir ^M *des*
bagages ^M *perdus*

baggage cart
chariot ^M *à bagages* ^M

baggage claim area
zone ^F *de récupération* ^F *des bagages* ^M

overview of departure and arrival areas
vue ^F *des aires* ^F *d'arrivée* ^F *et de départ* ^M

departure area
aire ^F *de départ* ^M

arrival area
aire ^F *d'arrivée* ^F

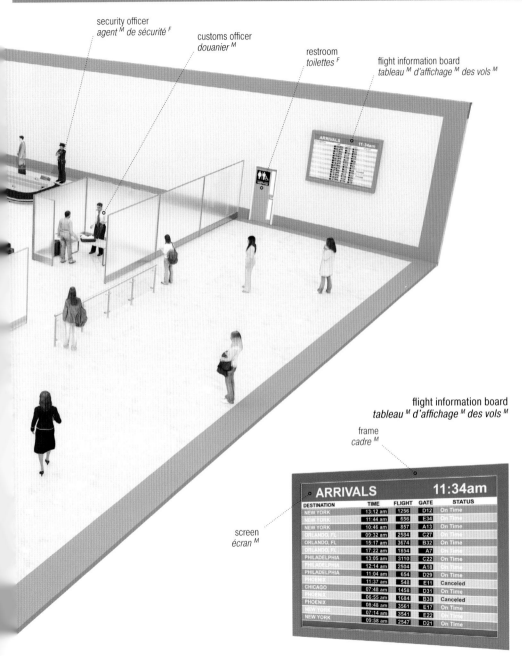

security officer
agent M *de sécurité* F

customs officer
douanier M

restroom
toilettes F

flight information board
tableau M *d'affichage* M *des vols* M

flight information board
tableau M *d'affichage* M *des vols* M

frame
cadre M

screen
écran M

ARRIVALS				11:34am
DESTINATION	TIME	FLIGHT	GATE	STATUS
NEW YORK	13:12 am	1256	D12	On Time
NEW YORK	11:44 am	656	E34	On Time
NEW YORK	10:46 am	857	A13	On Time
ORLANDO, FL	09:32 am	2584	C27	On Time
ORLANDO, FL	15:17 am	3674	B32	On Time
ORLANDO, FL	17:22 am	1854	A7	On Time
PHILADELPHIA	13:05 am	3110	C22	On Time
PHILADELPHIA	12:14 am	2504	A18	On Time
PHILADELPHIA	11:04 am	654	D29	On Time
PHOENIX	11:37 am	548	E11	Canceled
CHICAGO	07:48 am	1458	D31	On Time
PHOENIX	06:55 am	1684	B38	Canceled
PHOENIX	08:48 am	3561	E17	On Time
NEW YORK	07:14 am	3541	E22	On Time
NEW YORK	09:58 am	2547	D21	On Time

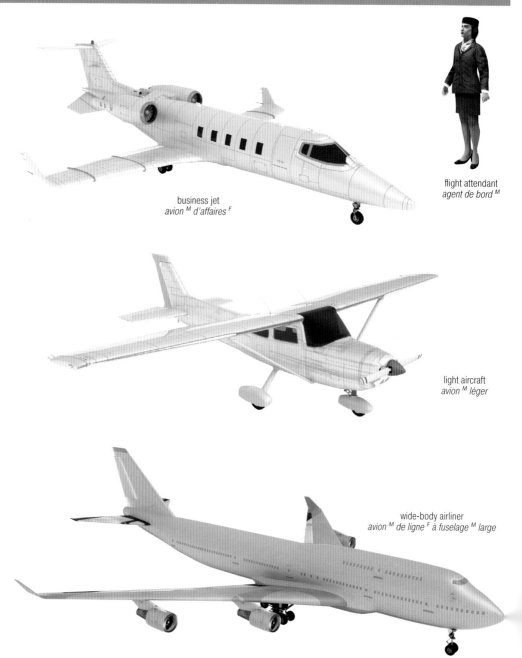

business jet
avion **M** *d'affaires* **F**

flight attendant
agent de bord **M**

light aircraft
avion **M** *léger*

wide-body airliner
avion **M** *de ligne* **F** *à fuselage* **M** *large*

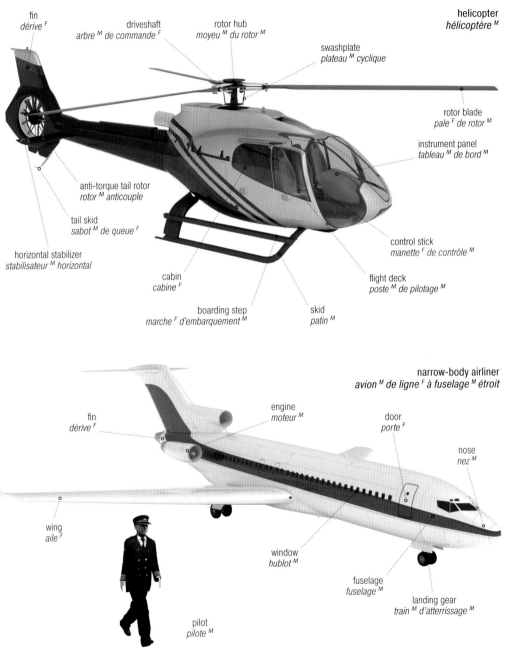

helicopter
hélicoptère M

fin
dérive F

driveshaft
arbre M *de commande* F

rotor hub
moyeu M *du rotor* M

swashplate
plateau M *cyclique*

rotor blade
pale F *de rotor* M

instrument panel
tableau M *de bord* M

anti-torque tail rotor
rotor M *anticouple*

tail skid
sabot M *de queue* F

horizontal stabilizer
stabilisateur M *horizontal*

control stick
manette F *de contrôle* M

cabin
cabine F

flight deck
poste M *de pilotage* M

boarding step
marche F *d'embarquement* M

skid
patin M

narrow-body airliner
avion M *de ligne* F *à fuselage* M *étroit*

fin
dérive F

engine
moteur M

door
porte F

nose
nez M

wing
aile F

window
hublot M

fuselage
fuselage M

landing gear
train M *d'atterrissage* M

pilot
pilote M

catering vehicle
camion ^M *commissariat* ^M

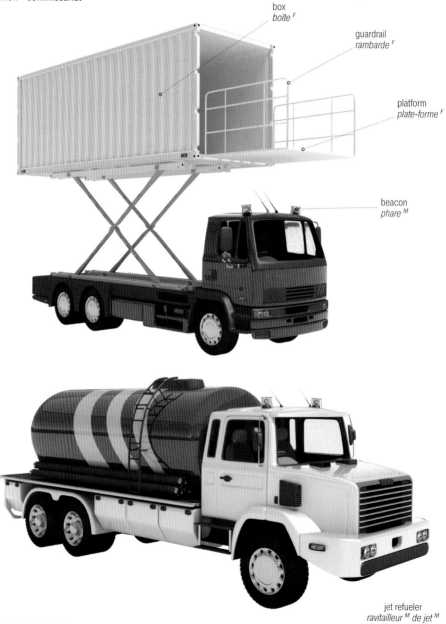

box
boîte ^F

guardrail
rambarde ^F

platform
plate-forme ^F

beacon
phare ^M

jet refueler
ravitailleur ^M *de jet* ^M

baggage conveyor
descente [F] *de bagages* [M]

mobile closed passenger stairs
passerelle [F] *amovible fermée*

mobile passenger stairs
passerelle F *amovible*

retractable boarding platform
plate-forme F *d'embarquement* M *rétractable*

stairs
escalier M

guardrail
garde-corps M

platform light
phare M *de plate-forme* F

flashing beacon
phare M *à éclats* M

cab
cabine F

electrical power unit
groupe M *de gérération* M *électrique*

light-duty truck
camion M *léger*

escort vehicle
véhicule [M] *d'escorte* [F]

service vehicle
véhicule [M] *de service* [M]

mobile loading platform
plate-forme [F] *de chargement* [M]

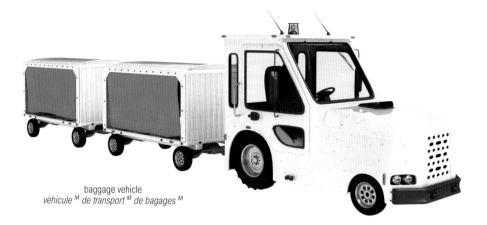

baggage vehicle
véhicule M *de transport* M *de bagages* M

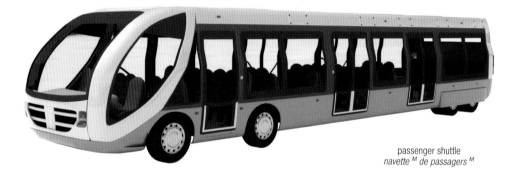

passenger shuttle
navette M *de passagers* M

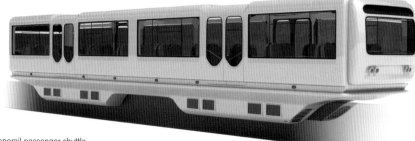

monorail passenger shuttle
monorail M *pour le transfert* M *des passagers* M

snowplow
chasse-neige ^M

fire truck
camion ^M *de pompier* ^M

pushback tug
camion ^M *de remorquage* ^M

passenger station
gare F *de voyageurs* M

clock
horloge F

exit
sortie F

store
boutique F

ticket office
billeterie F

schedules information board
tableau M *d'affichage* M *des horaires* M

platform
quai M

bench
siège M

stairs
escalier M

escalator
escalier M *mécanique*

ticket vending machine
distributrice F *de billets* M

train
train ^M

coffee shop
café ^M

train information board
tableau ^M *d'affichage* ^M *des trains* ^M

commuter train
train ^M *de banlieue* ^F

newsstand
kiosque ^M *à journaux* ^M

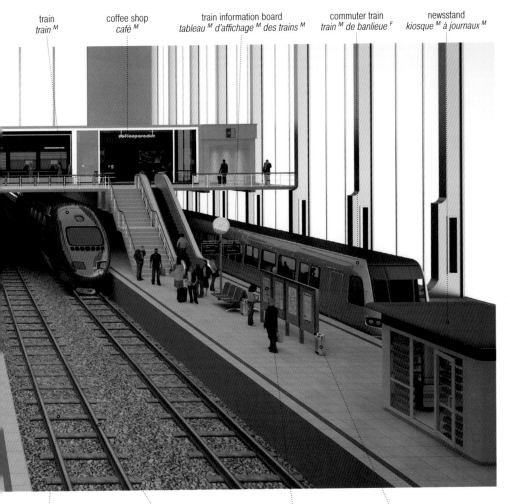

tie
traverse ^F

track
voie ^F *ferrée*

schedules board
horaires ^M

trash can
poubelle ^F

junction
correspondace ᶠ

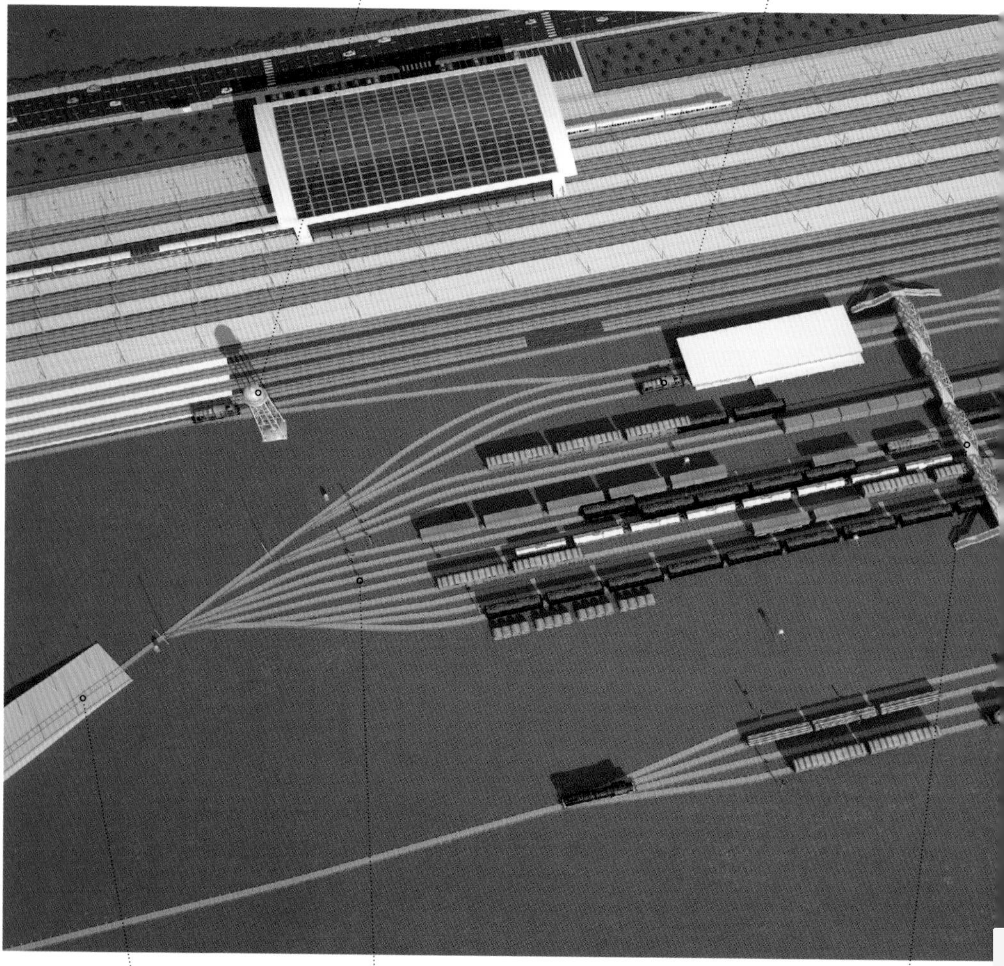

water tower
chateau ᴹ *d'eau* ᶠ

locomotive
locomotive ᶠ

hump
butte ᶠ

signal
signal ᴹ

footbridge
passerelle ᶠ

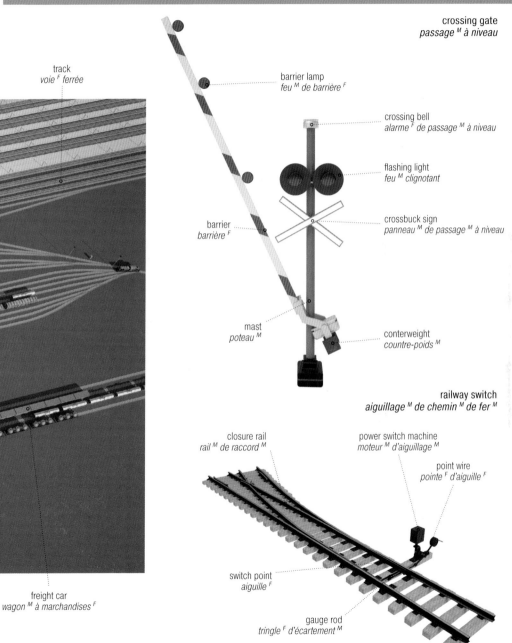

crossing gate
passage M *à niveau*

track
voie F *ferrée*

barrier lamp
feu M *de barrière* F

crossing bell
alarme F *de passage* M *à niveau*

flashing light
feu M *clignotant*

crossbuck sign
panneau M *de passage* M *à niveau*

barrier
barrière F

mast
poteau M

conterweight
countre-poids M

railway switch
aiguillage M *de chemin* M *de fer* M

closure rail
rail M *de raccord* M

power switch machine
moteur M *d'aiguillage* M

point wire
pointe F *d'aiguille* F

switch point
aiguille F

freight car
wagon M *à marchandises* F

gauge rod
tringle F *d'écartement* M

Urban rail transit

Transport M *ferroviaire urbain*

articulated streetcar
tramway M

route sign
indicateur M *de trajet* M

driver's seat
siège M *conducteur* M

passenger's seat
siège M *passager* M

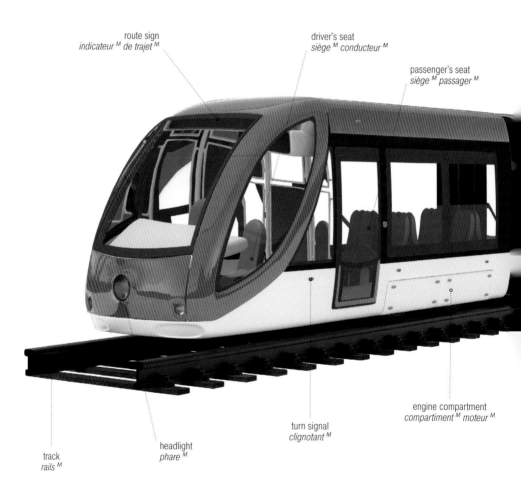

engine compartment
compartiment M *moteur* M

turn signal
clignotant M

track
rails M

headlight
phare M

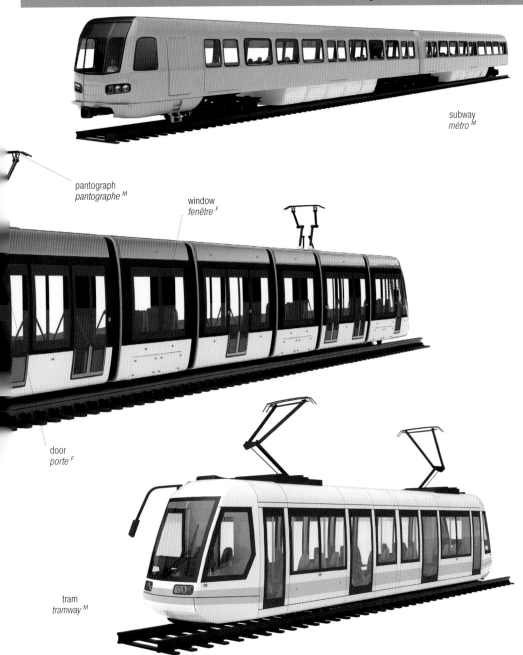

subway
métro M

pantograph
pantographe M

window
fenêtre F

door
porte F

tram
tramway M

Intercity transport
Transport ᴹ *interurbain*

steam locomotive
locomotive ᶠ *à vapeur* ᶠ

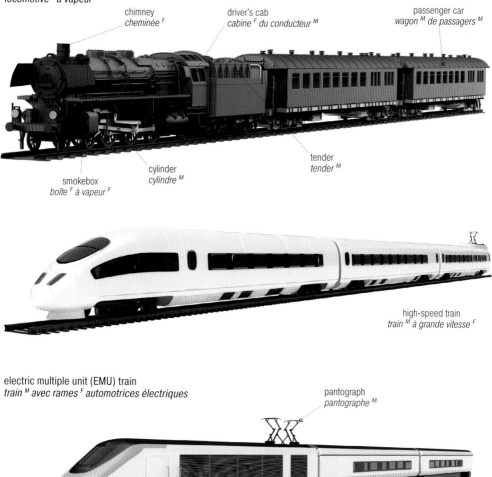

chimney
cheminée ᶠ

driver's cab
cabine ᶠ *du conducteur* ᴹ

passenger car
wagon ᴹ *de passagers* ᴹ

tender
tender ᴹ

cylinder
cylindre ᴹ

smokebox
boîte ᶠ *à vapeur* ᶠ

high-speed train
train ᴹ *à grande vitesse* ᶠ

electric multiple unit (EMU) train
train ᴹ *avec rames* ᶠ *automotrices électriques*

pantograph
pantographe ᴹ

engine compartment
compartiment ᴹ *moteur* ᴹ

headlight
phare ᴹ

Locomotives
Locomotives ^F

diesel locomotive
locomotive ^F *diesel*

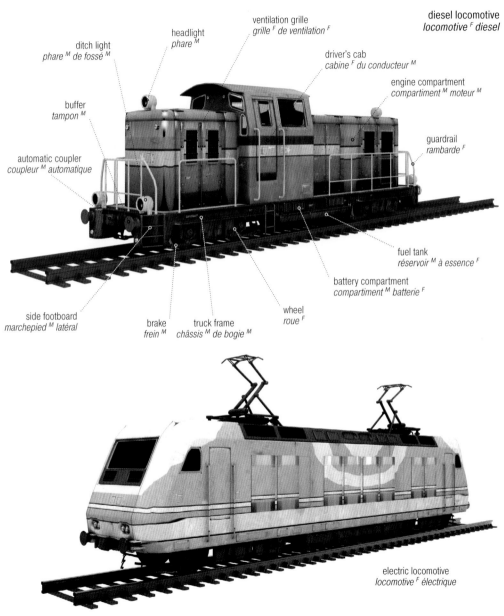

ventilation grille
grille ^F *de ventilation* ^F

headlight
phare ^M

ditch light
phare ^M *de fossé* ^M

driver's cab
cabine ^F *du conducteur* ^M

engine compartment
compartiment ^M *moteur* ^M

buffer
tampon ^M

guardrail
rambarde ^F

automatic coupler
coupleur ^M *automatique*

fuel tank
réservoir ^M *à essence* ^F

battery compartment
compartiment ^M *batterie* ^F

side footboard
marchepied ^M *latéral*

brake
frein ^M

truck frame
châssis ^M *de bogie* ^M

wheel
roue ^F

electric locomotive
locomotive ^F *électrique*

double-ended locomotive
locomotive ^F *double*

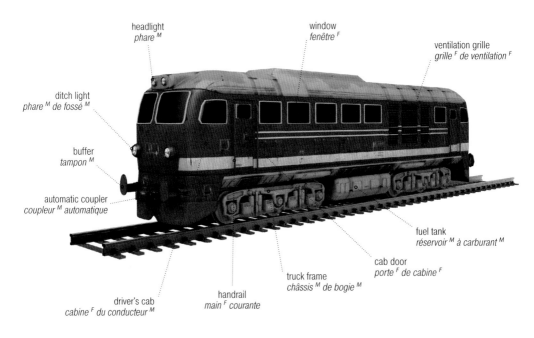

headlight
phare ^M

window
fenêtre ^F

ventilation grille
grille ^F *de ventilation* ^F

ditch light
phare ^M *de fossé* ^M

buffer
tampon ^M

automatic coupler
coupleur ^M *automatique*

fuel tank
réservoir ^M *à carburant* ^M

cab door
porte ^F *de cabine* ^F

truck frame
châssis ^M *de bogie* ^M

driver's cab
cabine ^F *du conducteur* ^M

handrail
main ^F *courante*

Freight cars *Trains* ^M *de marchandises* ^F

double-door boxcar
wagon ^M *couvert à double porte* ^F

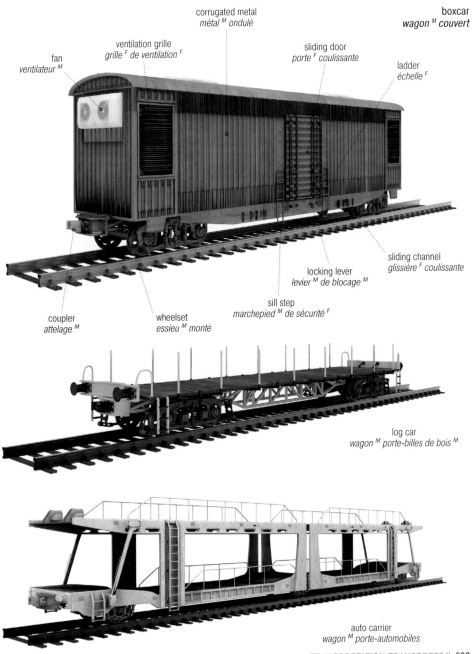

corrugated metal
métal ᴹ *ondulé*

boxcar
wagon ᴹ *couvert*

ventilation grille
grille ᶠ *de ventilation* ᶠ

sliding door
porte ᶠ *coulissante*

fan
ventilateur ᴹ

ladder
échelle ᶠ

sliding channel
glissière ᶠ *coulissante*

locking lever
levier ᴹ *de blocage* ᴹ

coupler
attelage ᴹ

wheelset
essieu ᴹ *monté*

sill step
marchepied ᴹ *de sécurité* ᶠ

log car
wagon ᴹ *porte-billes de bois* ᴹ

auto carrier
wagon ᴹ *porte-automobiles*

tank car
wagon-citerne *M*

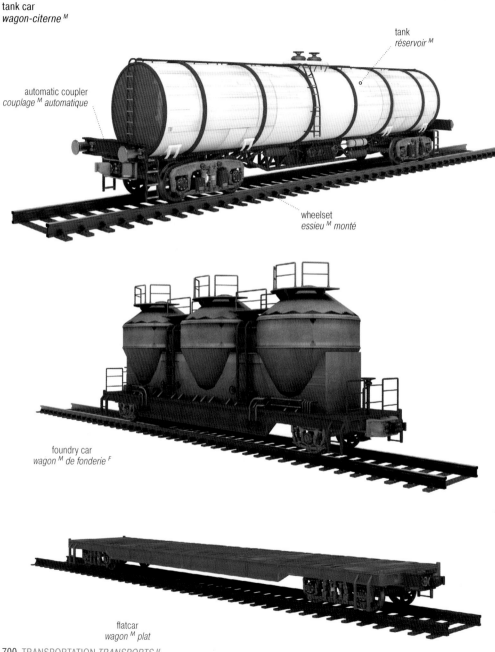

tank
réservoir *M*

automatic coupler
couplage *M* *automatique*

wheelset
essieu *M* *monté*

foundry car
wagon *M* *de fonderie* *F*

flatcar
wagon *M* *plat*

crane car
wagon-grue ^M

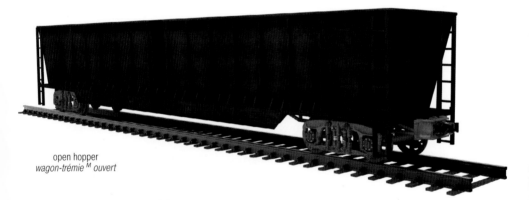

open hopper
wagon-trémie ^M *ouvert*

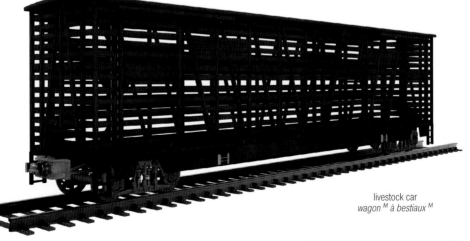

livestock car
wagon ^M *à bestiaux* ^M

subway station
station [F] *de métro* [M]

ticket collector's booth
cabine [F] *du percepteur* [M] *de billets*

city map
plan [M] *de ville* [F]

subway map
plan [M] *du métro* [M]

advertisement
publicité [M]

ticket office
billeterie [F]

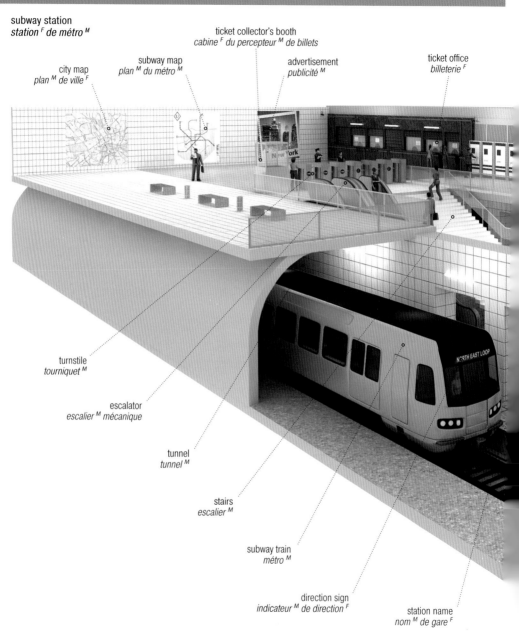

turnstile
tourniquet [M]

escalator
escalier [M] *mécanique*

tunnel
tunnel [M]

stairs
escalier [M]

subway train
métro [M]

direction sign
indicateur [M] *de direction* [F]

station name
nom [M] *de gare* [F]

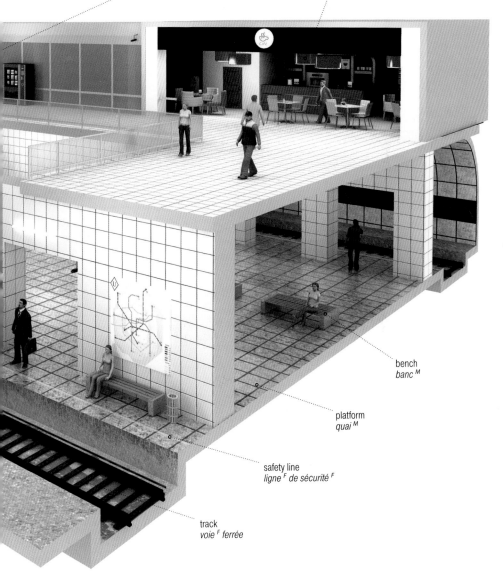

cket vending machine
istributrice F *de billets* M

automatic teller machine (ATM)
guichet M *automatique bancaire (GAB)*

coffee shop
café M

bench
banc M

platform
quai M

safety line
ligne F *de sécurité* F

track
voie F *ferrée*

port
port ᴹ

transit shed
entrepôt ᴹ *de transit* ᴹ
tanker
tanker ᴹ
fuel tank
réservoir ᴹ *à carburant* ᴹ
train
train ᴹ
slipway
cale ᶠ
railroad tracks
voies ᶠ *ferrées*
tugboat
remorqueur ᴹ

gantry crane
grue F à portique M

customs house
bureau M des douanes F

lighthouse
phare M

lantern
lanterne F

gallery
galerie F

container
conteneur M

container ship
navire M porte-conteneurs M

container terminal
terminal M à conteneurs M

tower
tour F

Passenger vessels
Navires ᴹ de croisière ᶠ

cruise ship
paquebot ᴹ de croisière ᶠ

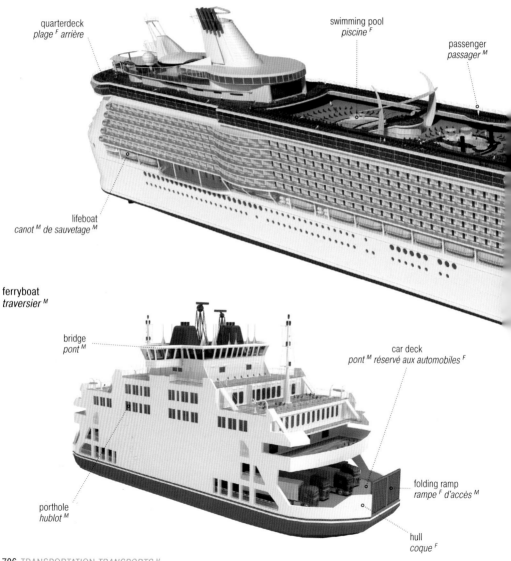

quarterdeck
plage ᶠ arrière

swimming pool
piscine ᶠ

passenger
passager ᴹ

lifeboat
canot ᴹ de sauvetage ᴹ

ferryboat
traversier ᴹ

bridge
pont ᴹ

car deck
pont ᴹ réservé aux automobiles ᶠ

porthole
hublot ᴹ

folding ramp
rampe ᶠ d'accès ᴹ

hull
coque ᶠ

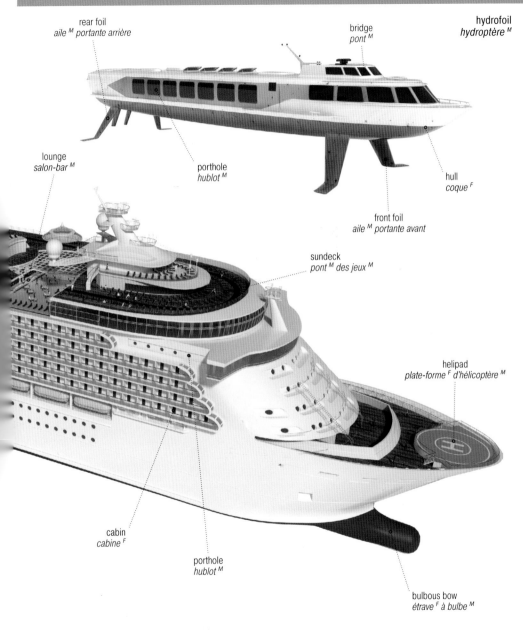

rear foil
aile ^M *portante arrière*

bridge
pont ^M

hydrofoil
hydroptère ^M

lounge
salon-bar ^M

porthole
hublot ^M

hull
coque ^F

front foil
aile ^M *portante avant*

sundeck
pont ^M *des jeux* ^M

helipad
plate-forme ^F *d'hélicoptère* ^M

cabin
cabine ^F

porthole
hublot ^M

bulbous bow
étrave ^F *à bulbe* ^M

Ancillary vessels
Navires M auxiliaires

tugboat
remorqueur M

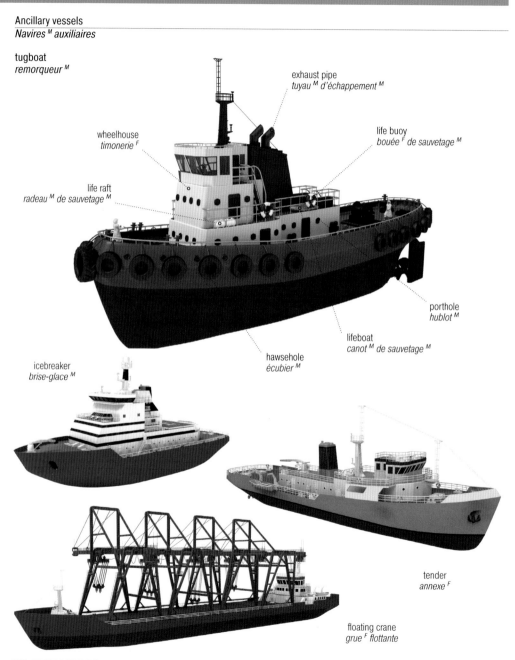

exhaust pipe
tuyau M d'échappement M

wheelhouse
timonerie F

life buoy
bouée F de sauvetage M

life raft
radeau M de sauvetage M

porthole
hublot M

lifeboat
canot M de sauvetage M

hawsehole
écubier M

icebreaker
brise-glace M

tender
annexe F

floating crane
grue F flottante

Cargo and fishing vessels
Navires M cargo et navires M de pêche F

container ship
porte-conteneur M

bridge
passerelle F

container
conteneur M

deck
pont M

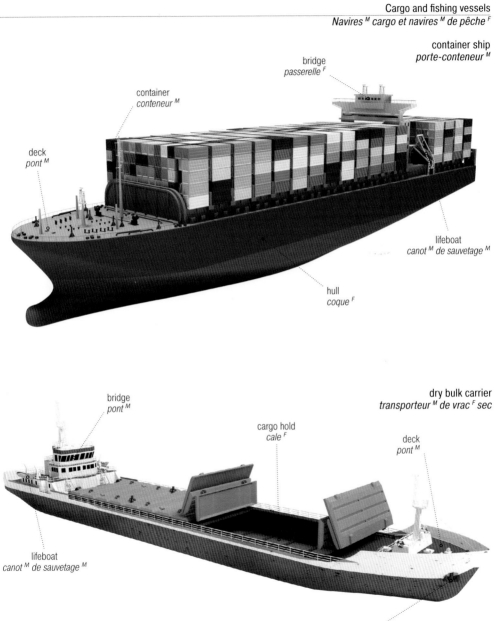

lifeboat
canot M de sauvetage M

hull
coque F

dry bulk carrier
transporteur M de vrac F sec

bridge
pont M

cargo hold
cale F

deck
pont M

lifeboat
canot M de sauvetage M

anchor
ancre F

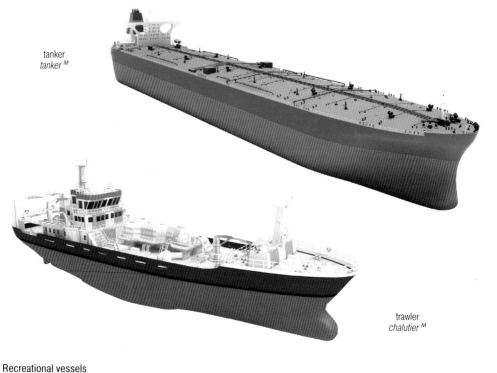

tanker
tanker ᴹ

trawler
chalutier ᴹ

Recreational vessels
Navires ᴹ *de plaisance* ᶠ

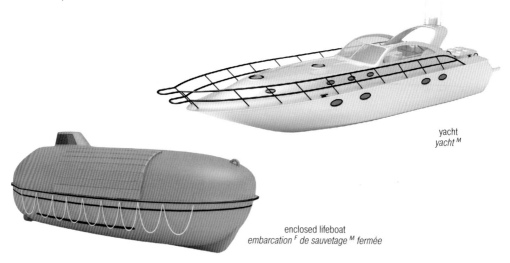

yacht
yacht ᴹ

enclosed lifeboat
embarcation ᶠ *de sauvetage* ᴹ *fermée*

schooner
goélette *ᶠ*

sailboat
voilier *ᴹ*

mainmast
grand mât *ᴹ*

sail
voile *ᶠ*

bowsprit
beaupré *ᴹ*

hull
coque *ᶠ*

foremast
mât *ᴹ* *de misaine* *ᶠ*

mizzenmast
mât *ᴹ* *d'artimon* *ᴹ*

personal watercraft: front view
motomarine ᶠ : vue ᶠ de face ᶠ

personal watercraft: rear view
motomarine ᶠ : vue ᶠ arrière

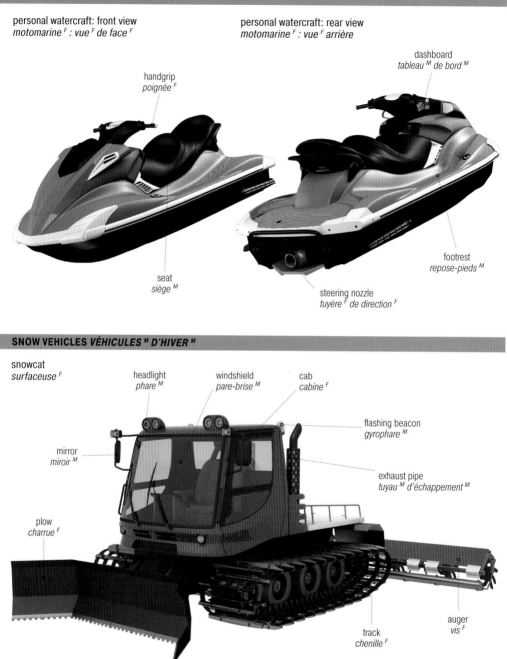

dashboard
tableau ᴹ de bord ᴹ

handgrip
poignée ᶠ

footrest
repose-pieds ᴹ

seat
siège ᴹ

steering nozzle
tuyère ᶠ de direction ᶠ

SNOW VEHICLES *VÉHICULES ᴹ D'HIVER ᴹ*

snowcat
surfaceuse ᶠ

headlight
phare ᴹ

windshield
pare-brise ᴹ

cab
cabine ᶠ

flashing beacon
gyrophare ᴹ

mirror
miroir ᴹ

exhaust pipe
tuyau ᴹ d'échappement ᴹ

plow
charrue ᶠ

auger
vis ᶠ

track
chenille ᶠ

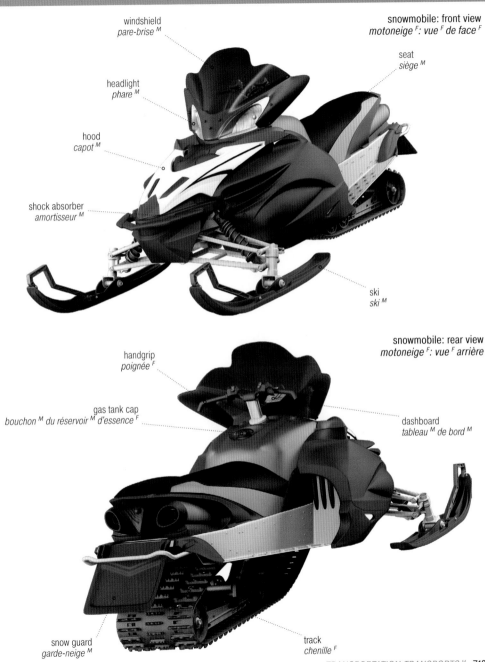

windshield
pare-brise ᴹ

snowmobile: front view
motoneige ᶠ*: vue* ᶠ *de face* ᶠ

seat
siège ᴹ

headlight
phare ᴹ

hood
capot ᴹ

shock absorber
amortisseur ᴹ

ski
ski ᴹ

snowmobile: rear view
motoneige ᶠ*: vue* ᶠ *arrière*

handgrip
poignée ᶠ

gas tank cap
bouchon ᴹ *du réservoir* ᴹ *d'essence* ᶠ

dashboard
tableau ᴹ *de bord* ᴹ

snow guard
garde-neige ᴹ

track
chenille ᶠ

cable car
téléphérique ^M

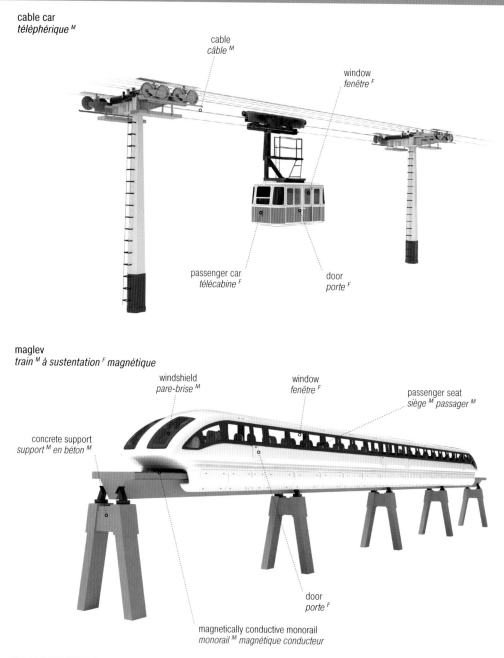

cable
câble ^M

window
fenêtre ^F

passenger car
télécabine ^F

door
porte ^F

maglev
train ^M *à sustentation* ^F *magnétique*

windshield
pare-brise ^M

window
fenêtre ^F

passenger seat
siège ^M *passager* ^M

concrete support
support ^M *en béton* ^M

door
porte ^F

magnetically conductive monorail
monorail ^M *magnétique conducteur*

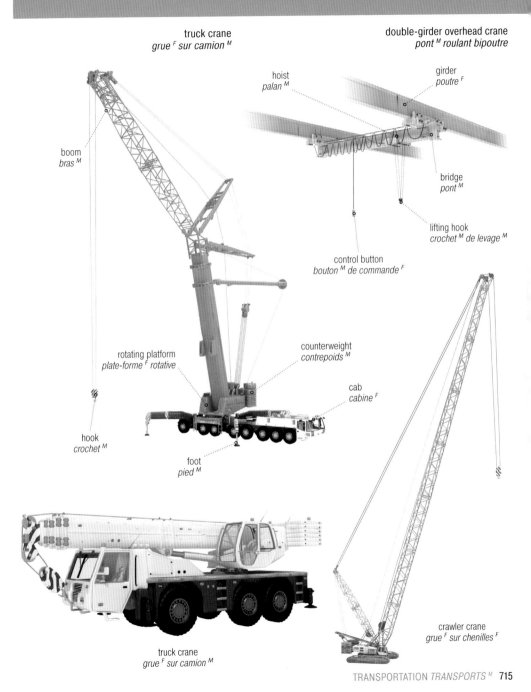

truck crane
grue F *sur camion* M

double-girder overhead crane
pont M *roulant bipoutre*

hoist
palan M

girder
poutre F

boom
bras M

bridge
pont M

lifting hook
crochet M *de levage* M

control button
bouton M *de commande* F

rotating platform
plate-forme F *rotative*

counterweight
contrepoids M

cab
cabine F

hook
crochet M

foot
pied M

truck crane
grue F *sur camion* M

crawler crane
grue F *sur chenilles* F

harbor gantry crane
grue F portuaire à portique F

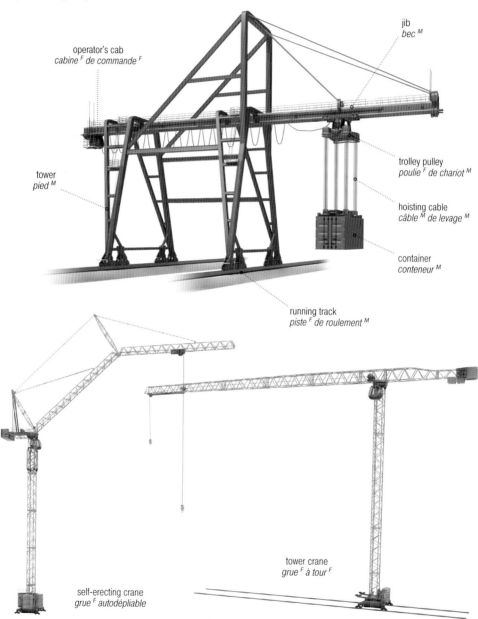

jib
bec M

operator's cab
cabine F de commande F

trolley pulley
poulie F de chariot M

tower
pied M

hoisting cable
câble M de levage M

container
conteneur M

running track
piste F de roulement M

self-erecting crane
grue F autodépliable

tower crane
grue F à tour F

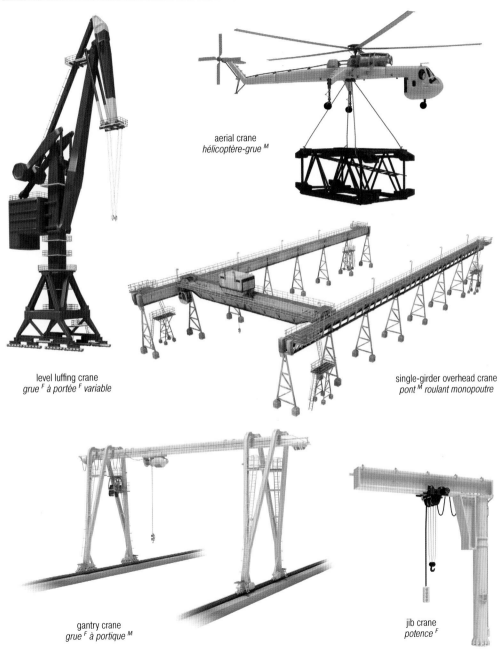

aerial crane
hélicoptère-grue [M]

level luffing crane
grue [F] *à portée* [F] *variable*

single-girder overhead crane
pont [M] *roulant monopoutre*

gantry crane
grue [F] *à portique* [M]

jib crane
potence [F]

SCIENCE

LES SCIENCES

periodic table
tableau^M *périodique*

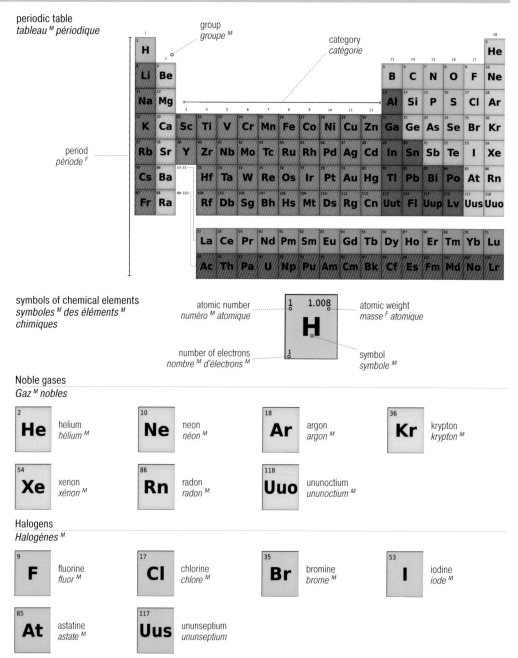

group
groupe^M

category
catégorie

period
période^F

symbols of chemical elements
symboles^M *des éléments*^M
chimiques

atomic number
numéro^M *atomique*

atomic weight
masse^F *atomique*

number of electrons
nombre^M *d'électrons*^M

symbol
symbole^M

Noble gases
Gaz^M *nobles*

He	helium *hélium*^M
Ne	neon *néon*^M
Ar	argon *argon*^M
Kr	krypton *krypton*^M
Xe	xenon *xénon*^M
Rn	radon *radon*^M
Uuo	ununoctium *ununoctium*^M

Halogens
Halogènes^M

F	fluorine *fluor*^M
Cl	chlorine *chlore*^M
Br	bromine *brome*^M
I	iodine *iode*^M
At	astatine *astate*^M
Uus	ununseptium *ununseptium*

Transition metals
Métal [M] *de transition*

 21 **Sc** scandium
scandium [M]

 22 **Ti** titanium
titane [M]

 23 **V** vanadium
vanadium [M]

 24 **Cr** chromium
chrome [M]

 25 **Mn** manganese
manganèse [M]

26 **Fe** iron
fer [M]

27 **Co** cobalt
cobalt [M]

28 **Ni** nickel
nickel [M]

 29 **Cu** copper
cuivre [M]

30 **Zn** zinc
zinc [M]

39 **Y** yttrium
yttrium [M]

40 **Zr** zirconium
zirconium [M]

 41 **Nb** niobium
niobium [M]

42 **Mo** molybdenum
molybdène [M]

43 **Tc** technetium
technétium [M]

44 **Ru** ruthenium
ruthénium [M]

 45 **Rh** rhodium
rhodium [M]

46 **Pd** palladium
palladium [M]

47 **Ag** silver
argent [M]

48 **Cd** cadmium
cadmium [M]

 72 **Hf** hafnium
hafnium [M]

73 **Ta** tantalum
tantale [M]

74 **W** tungsten
tungstène [M]

75 **Re** rhenium
rhénium [M]

 76 **Os** osmium
osmium [M]

77 **Ir** iridium
iridium [M]

78 **Pt** platinum
platine [M]

 79 **Au** gold
or [M]

 80 **Hg** mercury
mercure [M]

 104 **Rf** rutherfordium
rutherfordium [M]

105 **Db** dubnium
dubnium [M]

106 **Sg** seaborgium
seaborgium [M]

 107 **Bh** bohrium
bohrium [M]

 108 **Hs** hassium
hassium [M]

109 **Mt** meitnerium
meitnérium [M]

110 **Ds** darmstadtium
darmstadtium [M]

 111 **Rg** roentgenium
roentgenium [M]

 112 **Cn** copernicium
copernicium [M]

Alkali metals
Métaux [M] *alcalins*

 Li lithium
lithium [M]

 Na sodium
sodium [M]

 K potassium
potassium [M]

 Rb rubidium
rubidium [M]

Cs cesium
césium [M]

Fr francium
francium [M]

Post-transition metals
Métaux [M] *pauvres*

 Al aluminum
aluminium [M]

Ga gallium
gallium [M]

 In indium
indium [M]

 Sn tin
étain [M]

 Tl thallium
thallium [M]

Pb lead
plomb [M]

Bi bismuth
bismuth [M]

Po polonium
polonium [M]

 Uut ununtrium
ununtrium [M]

 Fl flerovium
flérovium [M]

 Uup ununpentium
ununpentium

 Lv livermorium
livermorium [M]

Metalloids
Éléments [M] *non métalliques*

B boron
bore [M]

Si silicon
silicium [M]

Ge germanium
germanium [M]

As arsenic
arsenic [M]

Sb antimony
antimoine [M]

Te tellurium
tellure [M]

Nonmetals
Non-métaux [M]

H hydrogen
hydrogène [M]

C carbon
carbone [M]

N nitrogen
azote [M]

O oxygen
oxygène [M]

P phosphorus
phosphore [M]

S sulfur
soufre [M]

Se selenium
sélénium [M]

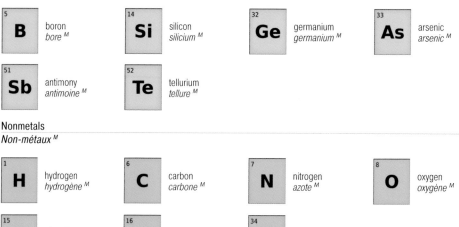

Lanthanides
Lanthanides M

lanthanum
lanthane M

cerium
cérium M

praseodymium
praséodyme M

neodymium
néodyme M

promethium
prométhium M

samarium
samarium M

europium
europium M

gadolinium
gadolinium M

terbium
terbium M

dysprosium
dysprosium M

holmium
holmium M

erbium
erbium M

thulium
thulium M

ytterbium
ytterbium M

lutetium
lutécium M

Actinides
Actinides M

actinium
actinium M

thorium
thorium M

protactinium
protactinium M

uranium
uranium M

neptunium
neptunium M

plutonium
plutonium M

americium
américium M

curium
curium M

berkelium
berkélium M

californium
californium M

einsteinium
einsteinium M

fermium
fermium M

mendelevium
mendélévium M

nobelium
nobélium M

lawrencium
lawrencium M

Alkaline earth metals
Métaux M *alcalino-terreux*

beryllium
béryllium M

magnesium
magnésium M

calcium
calcium M

strontium
strontium M

barium
baryum M

radium
radium M

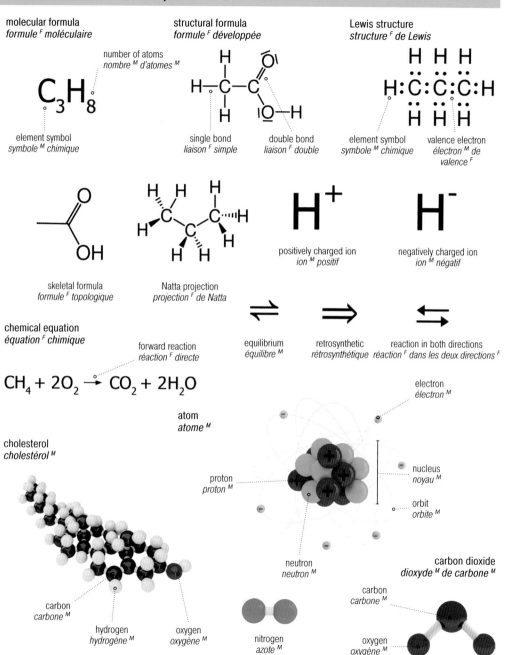

molecular formula
formule F *moléculaire*

number of atoms
nombre M *d'atomes* M

C_3H_8

element symbol
symbole M *chimique*

structural formula
formule F *développée*

single bond
liaison F *simple*

double bond
liaison F *double*

Lewis structure
structure F *de Lewis*

element symbol
symbole M *chimique*

valence electron
électron M *de valence* F

skeletal formula
formule F *topologique*

Natta projection
projection F *de Natta*

H^+

positively charged ion
ion M *positif*

H^-

negatively charged ion
ion M *négatif*

chemical equation
équation F *chimique*

forward reaction
réaction F *directe*

equilibrium
équilibre M

retrosynthetic
rétrosynthétique

reaction in both directions
réaction F *dans les deux directions* F

$CH_4 + 2O_2 \rightarrow CO_2 + 2H_2O$

atom
atome M

electron
électron M

cholesterol
cholestérol M

proton
proton M

nucleus
noyau M

orbit
orbite M

neutron
neutron M

carbon dioxide
dioxyde M *de carbone* M

carbon
carbone M

carbon
carbone M

hydrogen
hydrogène M

oxygen
oxygène M

nitrogen
azote M

oxygen
oxygène M

Kinematics
Cinématique ^F

v

velocity
vitesse ^F

a

acceleration
accélération ^F

g

gravitational acceleration
accélération ^F
gravitationnelle

f

frequency
fréquence ^F

n

rotational frequency
fréquence ^F *de rotation* ^F

λ

wavelength
longueur ^F *d'onde* ^F

ν

kinematic viscosity
viscosité ^F *cinématique*

t

time
temps ^M

T

period duration
durée ^F *de la période* ^F

ω

angular velocity
vitesse ^F *angulaire*

Mechanics
Mécanique ^F

m

mass
masse ^F

F

force
force ^F

J

impulse
impulsion ^F

p

linear momentum
quantité ^F *de mouvement* ^M

I

moment of inertia
moment ^M *d'inertie* ^F

M

moment of force
moment ^M *d'une force* ^F

L

angular momentum
moment ^M *angulaire*

σ

normal tension
tension normale ^F

τ

shear stress
contrainte ^F *de cisaillement* ^M

P

power
puissance ^F

W

work
travail ^M

ρ

density
masse ^F *volumique*

I

intensity
intensité ^F

η

efficiency
rendement ^M

S

entropy
entropie ^F

F_{R}

frictional force
force ^F *de frottement* ^M

γ

specific weight
poids ^M *spécifique*

V

specific volume
volume ^M *spécifique*

Photometry and optics
Photométrie ^F *et optique* ^F

D

diameter
diamètre

I_{V}

luminous intensity
intensité ^F *lumineuse*

Φ_{v}

luminous flux
flux ^M *lumineux*

η

luminous efficacy
efficacité ^F *lumineuse*

L_{v}

luminance
luminance ^F

E_{v}

illuminance
éclairement ^M *lumineux*

M_{v}

luminous exitance
exitance ^F *lumineuse*

H_{v}

luminous exposure
exposition ^F *lumineuse*

f

focal length
distance ^F *focale*

Q_{v}

luminous energy
énergie ^F *lumineuse*

Thermodynamics
Thermodynamique ^F

λ

thermal conductivity
conductivité ^F
thermique

T

absolute temperature
température ^F
absolue

ϑ

Celsius temperature
température ^F *Celsius*

Q

heat
chaleur ^F

U

internal energy
énergie ^F *interne*

E_{th}

thermal energy
énergie ^F *thermique*

μ

chemical potential
potentiel ^M *chimique*

H

enthalpy
enthalpie ^F

Φ_{th}

heat flux
flux ^M *de chaleur* ^F

S

entropy
entropie ^F

C_{th}

thermal capacity
capacité ^F *thermique*

Electricity
Électricité ^F

Y

admittance
admittance ^F

I

electric current
courant ^M *électrique*

J

electric current density
densité ^F *de courant* ^M
électrique

Q

electric charge
charge ^F *électrique*

U

electric tension
tension ^F

φ

phase shift
déphasage ^M

R

resistance
résistance ^F

X

reactance
réactance ^F

Z

impedance
impédance ^F

ρ

specific resistance
résistivité ^F

B

susceptance
susceptance ^F

F_L

Lorentz force
force ^F *de Lorentz*

E

electric field
champ ^M *électrique*

Ψ

water potential
potentiel ^M *hydrique*

D

electric flux density
induction ^F *électrique*

P

polarization
polarisation ^F

α

polarizability
polarisabilité ^F

Magnetism
Magnétisme ^M

P

effective power
puissance ^F *effective*

B

magnetic flux density
densité ^F *de champ* ^M
magnétique

J

magnetic polarization
polarisation ^F
magnétique

ϵ

permittivity
permittivité ^F

M

magnetization
magnétisation ^F

Φ

magnetic flux
flux ^M *magnétique*

C

electric capacity
capacité ^F *électrique*

S

elastance
élastance ^F

L

inductance
inductance ^F

H

magnetic field strength
intensité ^F *du champ* ^M
magnétique

S

apparent power
puissance ^F
apparente

m

magnetic moment
moment ^M *magnétique*

Atomic and molecular quantities
Quantités [F] *d'atomes* [M] *et de molécules* [F]

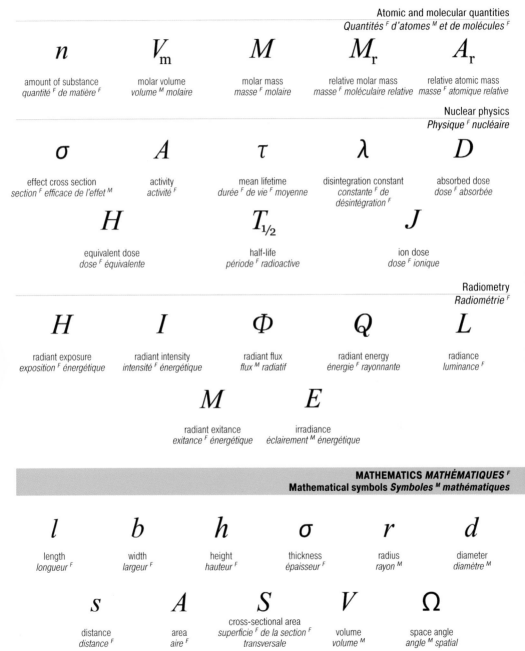

n

amount of substance
quantité [F] *de matière* [F]

V_{m}

molar volume
volume [M] *molaire*

M

molar mass
masse [F] *molaire*

M_{r}

relative molar mass
masse [F] *moléculaire relative*

A_{r}

relative atomic mass
masse [F] *atomique relative*

Nuclear physics
Physique [F] *nucléaire*

σ

effect cross section
section [F] *efficace de l'effet* [M]

A

activity
activité [F]

τ

mean lifetime
durée [F] *de vie* [F] *moyenne*

λ

disintegration constant
constante [F] *de désintégration* [F]

D

absorbed dose
dose [F] *absorbée*

H

equivalent dose
dose [F] *équivalente*

$T_{1/2}$

half-life
période [F] *radioactive*

J

ion dose
dose [F] *ionique*

Radiometry
Radiométrie [F]

H

radiant exposure
exposition [F] *énergétique*

I

radiant intensity
intensité [F] *énergétique*

Φ

radiant flux
flux [M] *radiatif*

Q

radiant energy
énergie [F] *rayonnante*

L

radiance
luminance [F]

M

radiant exitance
exitance [F] *énergétique*

E

irradiance
éclairement [M] *énergétique*

MATHEMATICS *MATHÉMATIQUES* [F]
Mathematical symbols *Symboles* [M] *mathématiques*

l

length
longueur [F]

b

width
largeur [F]

h

height
hauteur [F]

σ

thickness
épaisseur [F]

r

radius
rayon [M]

d

diameter
diamètre [M]

s

distance
distance [F]

A

area
aire [F]

S

cross-sectional area
superficie [F] *de la section* [F] *transversale*

V

volume
volume [M]

Ω

space angle
angle [M] *spatial*

+	−	✕	÷	±
addition/positive *addition F/positif*	subtraction/negative *soustraction F/négatif*	multiplication *multiplication F*	division *division F*	plus or minus *signe M plus M ou moins M*

=	≠	<	>	≤
equals *signe M égal M*	is not equal to *signe M de différence F*	is less than *plus petit que*	is greater than *plus grand que*	is less than or equal to *plus petit ou égal à*

≥	√	%	Σ	∏
is greater than or equal to *plus grand ou égal à*	square root of *racine F carrée*	percent *pourcentage*	sum *somme F*	product *produit M*

Δ	∫	′	°	∞
difference *différence F*	integral *intégrale F*	derivative *dérivée F*	degree *degré M*	infinity *à l'infini M*

∠	⌐	⊥	‖	∅
acute angle *angle M aigu*	right angle *angle M droit*	is perpendicular to *perpendiculaire à*	is parallel to *parallèle à*	diameter *diamètre M*

∪	∩	∅	∈	⊂
union of two sets *union F de deux ensembles M*	intersection of two sets *intersection F de deux ensembles M*	empty set *ensemble M vide*	is an element of *appartient à*	is included in/is a subset of *est compris dans*

∀	∃	ℕ	ℤ	ℚ
universal quantification *quantification F universelle*	existential quantification *quantification F existentielle*	natural numbers *nombres M entiers naturels*	integers *nombres M entiers relatifs*	rational numbers *nombres M rationnels*

$\mathbb{A}$

algebraic numbers
nombres M *algébriques*

$\mathbb{R}$

real numbers
nombres M *réels*

$\mathbb{C}$

complex numbers
nombres M *complexes*

$\mathbb{H}$

quaternions
quaternions M

π

pi
Pi

simple fraction
fraction F *ordinaire*

numerator
numérateur M

$$\frac{3}{4}$$

fraction bar
barre F *de fraction* F

denominator
dénominateur M

e

Euler's number
nombre M *d'Euler*

φ

golden ratio
nombre M *d'or* M

i

imaginary number
nombre M *imaginaire*

I

one
un M

II

two
deux M

III

three
trois M

IV

four
quatre M

V

five
cinq M

VI

six
six M

VII

seven
sept M

VIII

eight
huit M

IX

nine
neuf M

X

ten
dix M

XX

twenty
vingt M

XXX

thirty
trente M

XL

forty
quarante M

L

fifty
cinquante M

LX

sixty
soixante M

XC

ninety
quatre-vingt-dix M

C

one hundred
cent M

D

five hundred
cinq cents M

M

one thousand
mille M

Circle
Cercle M

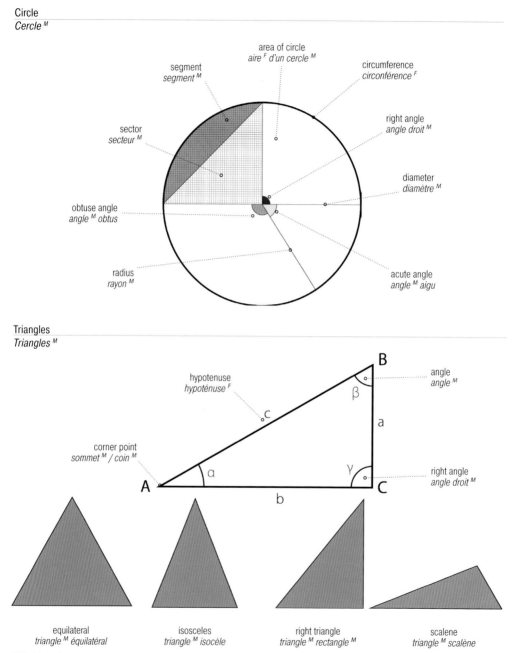

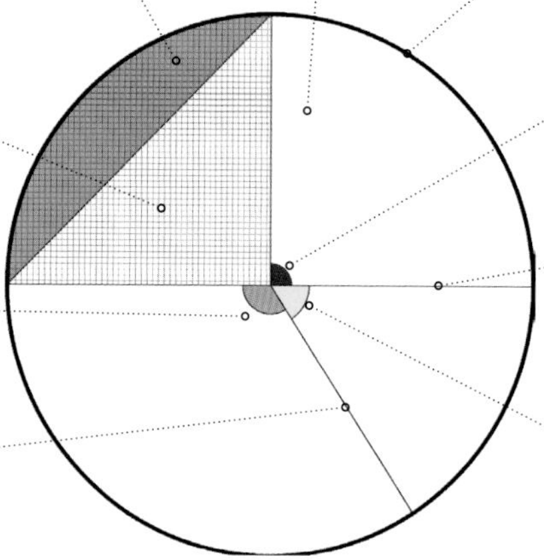
area of circle
aire F *d'un cercle* M
segment
segment M
circumference
circonférence F
sector
secteur M
right angle
angle droit M
diameter
diamètre M
obtuse angle
angle M *obtus*
radius
rayon M
acute angle
angle M *aigu*

Triangles
Triangles M

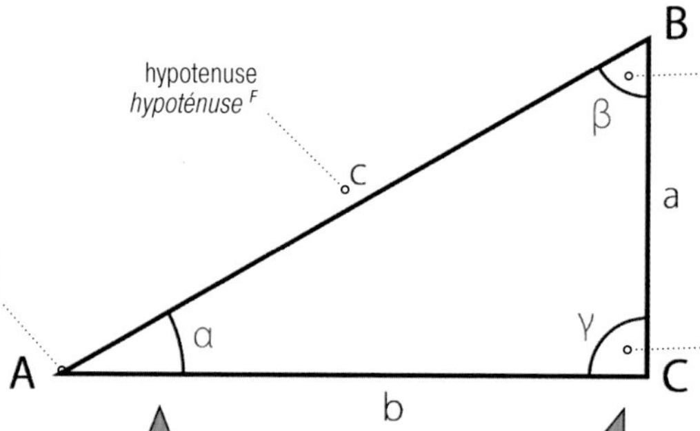
B
angle
angle M
hypotenuse
hypoténuse F
c
β
a
corner point
sommet M / *coin* M
α
γ
A
C
right angle
angle droit M
b

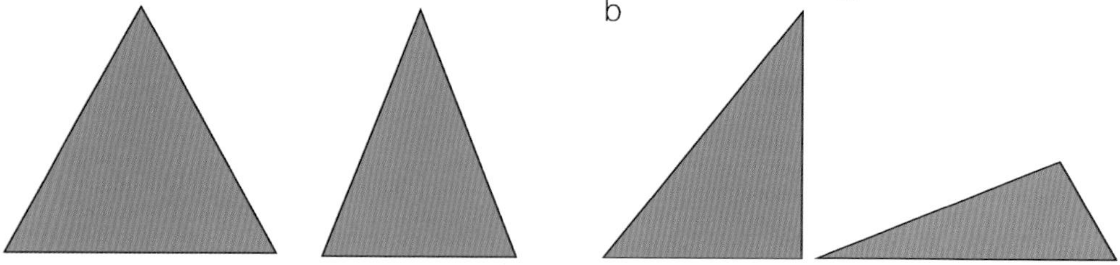
equilateral
triangle M *équilatéral*
isosceles
triangle M *isocèle*
right triangle
triangle M *rectangle* M
scalene
triangle M *scalène*

Polygons
Polygones ^M

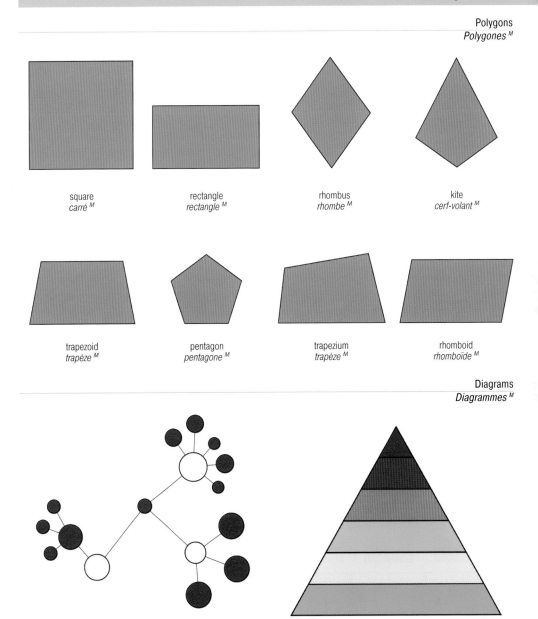

square
carré ^M

rectangle
rectangle ^M

rhombus
rhombe ^M

kite
cerf-volant ^M

trapezoid
trapèze ^M

pentagon
pentagone ^M

trapezium
trapèze ^M

rhomboid
rhomboïde ^M

Diagrams
Diagrammes ^M

cluster diagram
diagramme ^M *à bulles* ^F

pyramid diagram
diagramme ^M *pyramidal*

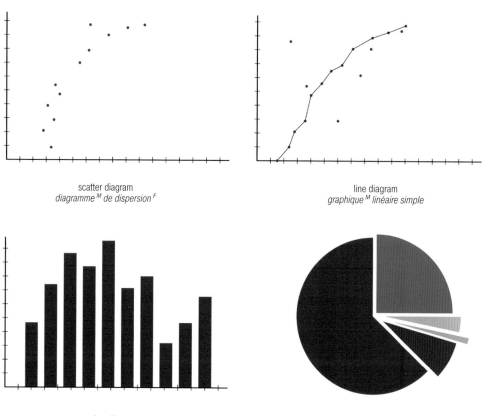

scatter diagram
diagramme ᴹ *de dispersion* ᶠ

line diagram
graphique ᴹ *linéaire simple*

bar diagram
diagramme ᴹ *en barres* ᶠ

pie chart
diagramme ᴹ *circulaire*

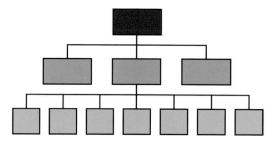

tree diagram
arborescence ᶠ

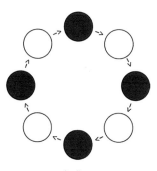

cycle diagram
diagramme ᴹ *cyclique*

Solids
Solides [M]

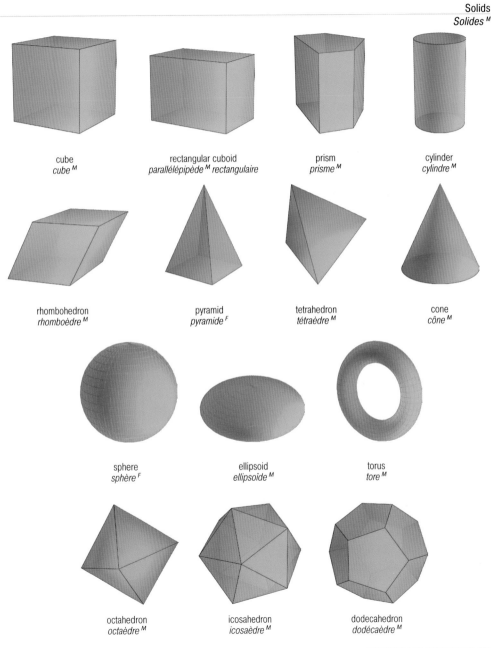

cube
cube [M]

rectangular cuboid
parallélépipède [M] *rectangulaire*

prism
prisme [M]

cylinder
cylindre [M]

rhombohedron
rhomboèdre [M]

pyramid
pyramide [F]

tetrahedron
tétraèdre [M]

cone
cône [M]

sphere
sphère [F]

ellipsoid
ellipsoïde [M]

torus
tore [M]

octahedron
octaèdre [M]

icosahedron
icosaèdre [M]

dodecahedron
dodécaèdre [M]

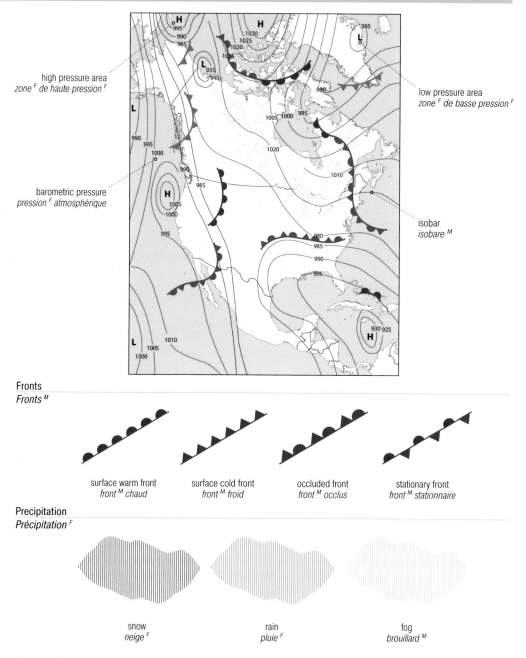

high pressure area
zone [F] *de haute pression* [F]

low pressure area
zone [F] *de basse pression* [F]

barometric pressure
pression [F] *atmosphérique*

isobar
isobare [M]

Fronts
Fronts [M]

surface warm front
front [M] *chaud*

surface cold front
front [M] *froid*

occluded front
front [M] *occlus*

stationary front
front [M] *stationnaire*

Precipitation
Précipitation [F]

snow
neige [F]

rain
pluie [F]

fog
brouillard [M]

station model
modèle [M] *de pointage* [M]

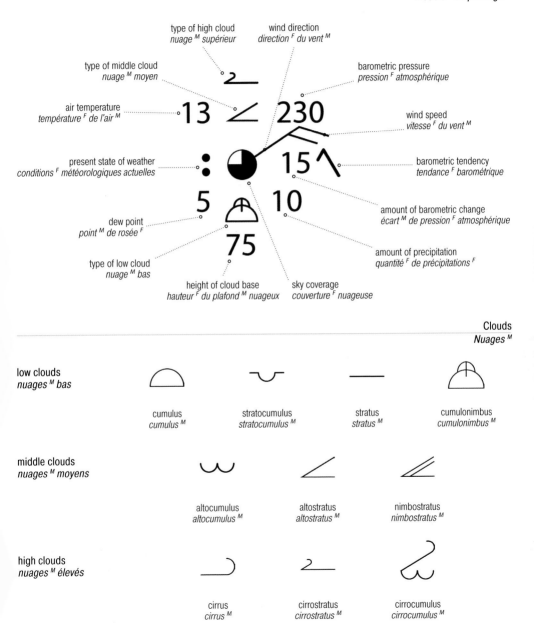

type of high cloud
nuage [M] *supérieur*

wind direction
direction [F] *du vent* [M]

type of middle cloud
nuage [M] *moyen*

barometric pressure
pression [F] *atmosphérique*

air temperature
température [F] *de l'air* [M]

wind speed
vitesse [F] *du vent* [M]

present state of weather
conditions [F] *météorologiques actuelles*

barometric tendency
tendance [F] *barométrique*

amount of barometric change
écart [M] *de pression* [F] *atmosphérique*

dew point
point [M] *de rosée* [F]

amount of precipitation
quantité [F] *de précipitations* [F]

type of low cloud
nuage [M] *bas*

height of cloud base
hauteur [F] *du plafond* [M] *nuageux*

sky coverage
couverture [F] *nuageuse*

Clouds
Nuages [M]

low clouds
nuages [M] *bas*

cumulus
cumulus [M]

stratocumulus
stratocumulus [M]

stratus
stratus [M]

cumulonimbus
cumulonimbus [M]

middle clouds
nuages [M] *moyens*

altocumulus
altocumulus [M]

altostratus
altostratus [M]

nimbostratus
nimbostratus [M]

high clouds
nuages [M] *élevés*

cirrus
cirrus [M]

cirrostratus
cirrostratus [M]

cirrocumulus
cirrocumulus [M]

Precipitation
Précipitations [F]

light intermittent rain
pluie [F] *légère intermittente*

moderate intermittent rain
pluie [F] *modérée intermittente*

heavy intermittent rain
forte pluie [F] *intermittente*

freezing rain
pluie [F] *verglaçante*

light intermittent drizzle
petite bruine [F] *intermittente*

moderate intermittent drizzle
bruine [F] *modérée intermittente*

thick intermittent drizzle
forte bruine [F] *intermittente*

freezing drizzle
bruine [M] *verglaçante*

sleet
giboulée [F]

ice crystals
poudrin [M] *de glace* [F]

intermittent light snow
légère chute [F] *de neige* [F] *intermittente*

continuous moderate snow
chute [F] *de neige* [F] *modérée et continue*

intermittent heavy snow
forte chute [F] *de neige* [F] *intermittente*

graupel (soft hail)
neige [F] *roulée*

haze
brume [F] *sèche*

sandstorm or dust storm
tempête [F] *de poussière* [F] *ou de sable* [M]

well-developed dust or sand whirl
tourbillon [M] *de sable* [M] *ou de poussière* [F] *bien formé*

drifting snow, low
poudrerie, [F] *basse*

drifting snow, high
poudrerie, [F] *élevée*

fog
brouillard [M]

lightning visible, no thunder heard
éclairs [M] *visibles, pas de tonnerre* [M]

thunderstorm
orage [M]

shower of rain and snow, mixed
averse [F] *de pluie* [F] *et de neige,* [F] *mélangées*

snow shower
averse [F] *de neige* [F]

rain shower
averse [F] *de pluie* [F]

funnel clouds or tornadoes
tubas [M] *ou tornades* [F]

hurricane
ouragan [M]

Sky coverage
Partie F du ciel M couverte

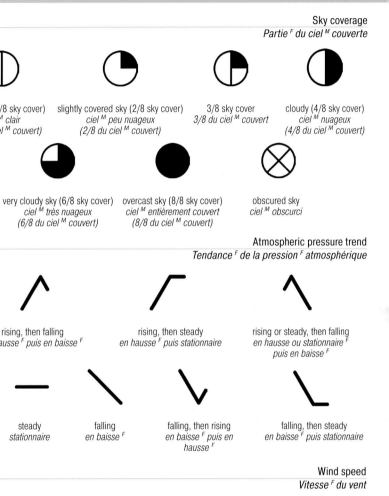

cloudless sky
ciel M sans nuage M

clear sky (1/8 sky cover)
*ciel M clair
(1/8 du ciel M couvert)*

slightly covered sky (2/8 sky cover)
*ciel M peu nuageux
(2/8 du ciel M couvert)*

3/8 sky cover
3/8 du ciel M couvert

cloudy (4/8 sky cover)
*ciel M nuageux
(4/8 du ciel M couvert)*

5/8 sky cover
5/8 du ciel M couvert

very cloudy sky (6/8 sky cover)
*ciel M très nuageux
(6/8 du ciel M couvert)*

overcast sky (8/8 sky cover)
*ciel M entièrement couvert
(8/8 du ciel M couvert)*

obscured sky
ciel M obscurci

Atmospheric pressure trend
Tendance F de la pression F atmosphérique

rising
en hausse F

rising, then falling
en hausse F puis en baisse F

rising, then steady
en hausse F puis stationnaire

rising or steady, then falling
*en hausse ou stationnaire F
puis en baisse F*

falling or steady, then rising
*en baisse F ou stationnaire puis
en hausse F*

steady
stationnaire

falling
en baisse F

falling, then rising
*en baisse F puis en
hausse F*

falling, then steady
en baisse F puis stationnaire

Wind speed
Vitesse F du vent

calm
calme M

gentle breeze
petite brise F

moderate breeze
jolie brise F

fresh breeze
bonne brise F

near gale
grand frais M

gale
coup M de vent M

severe gale
fort coup M de vent M

storm
tempête F

violent storm
violente tempête F

hurricane
ouragan M

subtractive colors
couleurs F *soustractives*

additive colors
couleurs F *primaires additives*

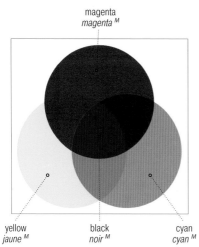

magenta
magenta M

yellow   black   cyan
jaune M   *noir* M   *cyan* M

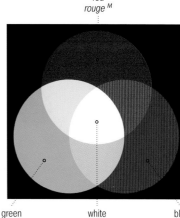

red
rouge M

green   white   blue
vert M   *blanc* M   *bleu* M

Color contrasts *Contrastes* M *de couleurs* F

contrast of hue
contraste M *de teintes* F

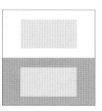

simultaneous contrast
contraste M *simultané*

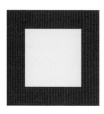

light-dark contrast
contraste M *clair-foncé*

saturation contrast
contraste M *de saturation* F

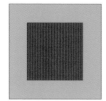

warm-cool contrast
contraste M *de couleurs* F
chaudes et froides

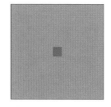

quantity contrast
contraste M *de quantité* F

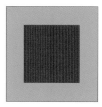

complementary contrast
contraste M *de couleurs* F
complémentaires

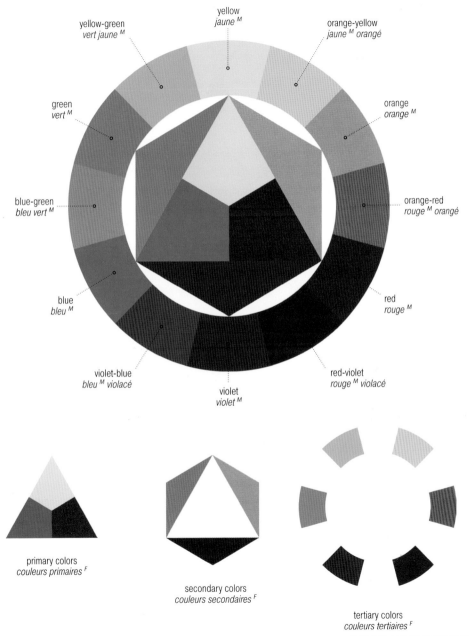

yellow-green
vert jaune [M]

yellow
jaune [M]

orange-yellow
jaune [M] *orangé*

green
vert [M]

orange
orange [M]

blue-green
bleu vert [M]

orange-red
rouge [M] *orangé*

blue
bleu [M]

red
rouge [M]

violet-blue
bleu [M] *violacé*

red-violet
rouge [M] *violacé*

violet
violet [M]

primary colors
couleurs primaires [F]

secondary colors
couleurs secondaires [F]

tertiary colors
couleurs tertiaires [F]

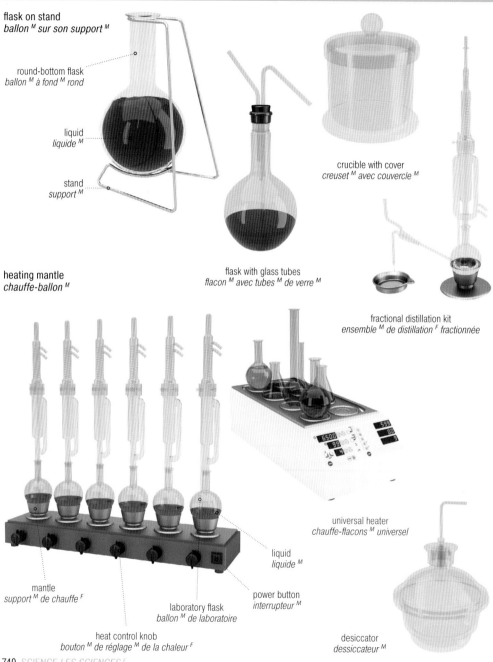

flask on stand
ballon ^M sur son support ^M

round-bottom flask
ballon ^M à fond ^M rond

liquid
liquide ^M

stand
support ^M

crucible with cover
creuset ^M avec couvercle ^M

heating mantle
chauffe-ballon ^M

flask with glass tubes
flacon ^M avec tubes ^M de verre ^M

fractional distillation kit
ensemble ^M de distillation ^F fractionnée

universal heater
chauffe-flacons ^M universel

liquid
liquide ^M

mantle
support ^M de chauffe ^F

power button
interrupteur ^M

laboratory flask
ballon ^M de laboratoire

heat control knob
bouton ^M de réglage ^M de la chaleur ^F

desiccator
dessiccateur ^M

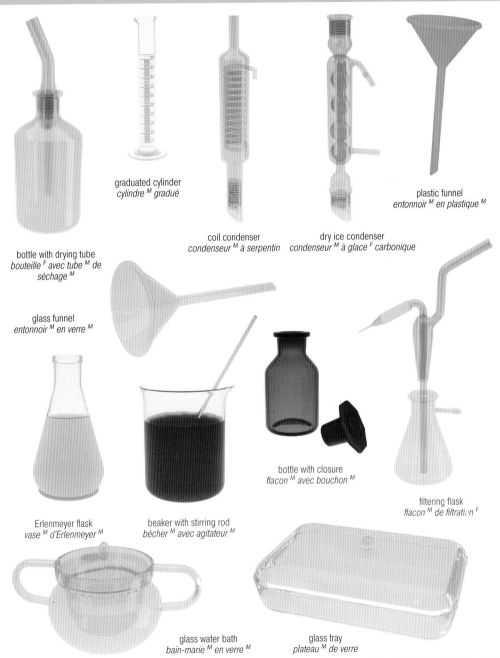

graduated cylinder
cylindre *M* *gradué*

plastic funnel
entonnoir *M* *en plastique* *M*

coil condenser
condenseur *M* *à serpentin*

dry ice condenser
condenseur *M* *à glace* *F* *carbonique*

bottle with drying tube
bouteille *F* *avec tube* *M* *de séchage* *M*

glass funnel
entonnoir *M* *en verre* *M*

bottle with closure
flacon *M* *avec bouchon* *M*

filtering flask
flacon *M* *de filtration* *F*

Erlenmeyer flask
vase *M* *d'Erlenmeyer* *M*

beaker with stirring rod
bécher *M* *avec agitateur* *M*

glass water bath
bain-marie *M* *en verre* *M*

glass tray
plateau *M* *de verre*

ring stand with clamps
support ᴹ annulaire avec pinces ᶠ

separatory funnel
appareil ᴹ à décantation ᶠ

barrel
baril ᴹ / tonneau ᴹ

electronic pipette
pipette ᶠ électronique

filter funnel
entonnoir ᴹ de filtration ᶠ

test tube with stopper
éprouvette ᶠ avec bouchon ᴹ

test tube on stand
*éprouvette ᶠ sur
support ᴹ*

beaker with handle
bécher ᴹ à anse ᶠ

wash bottle
flacon-laveur ᴹ

beaker
bécher ᴹ

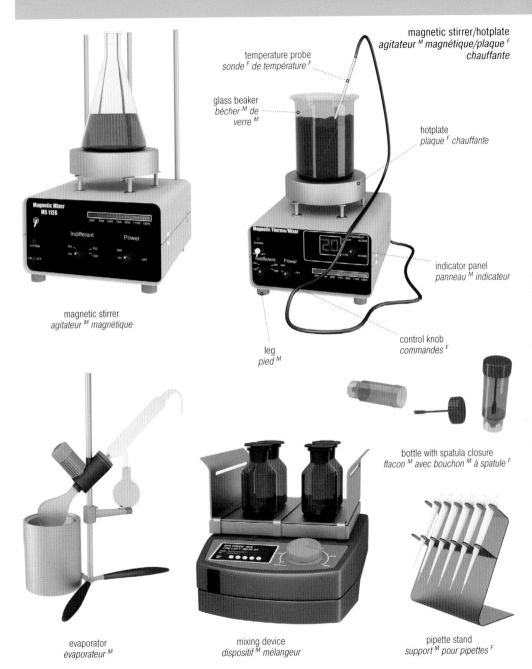

magnetic stirrer/hotplate
agitateur M magnétique/plaque F chauffante

temperature probe
sonde F de température F

glass beaker
bécher M de verre M

hotplate
plaque F chauffante

Magnetic Mixer
MS 112G

20W 30W 50W 70W 90W 110W 130W
Indifferent   Power
SYSTEM
100   300
200   700   MIN
ON   OFF   ON   OFF

Magnetic Thermo/Mixer
temperature
Indifferent Power
OFF
ON 50W 70W 90W 110W 130W

indicator panel
panneau M indicateur

magnetic stirrer
agitateur M magnétique

leg
pied M

control knob
commandes F

bottle with spatula closure
flacon M avec bouchon M à spatule F

evaporator
évaporateur M

mixing device
dispositif M mélangeur

pipette stand
support M pour pipettes F

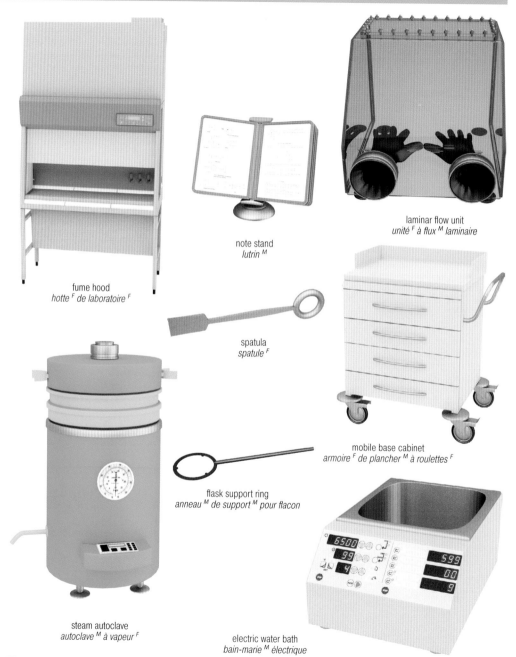

laminar flow unit
unité ᶠ à flux ᴹ laminaire

note stand
lutrin ᴹ

fume hood
hotte ᶠ de laboratoire ᶠ

spatula
spatule ᶠ

mobile base cabinet
armoire ᶠ de plancher ᴹ à roulettes ᶠ

flask support ring
anneau ᴹ de support ᴹ pour flacon

steam autoclave
autoclave ᴹ à vapeur ᶠ

electric water bath
bain-marie ᴹ électrique

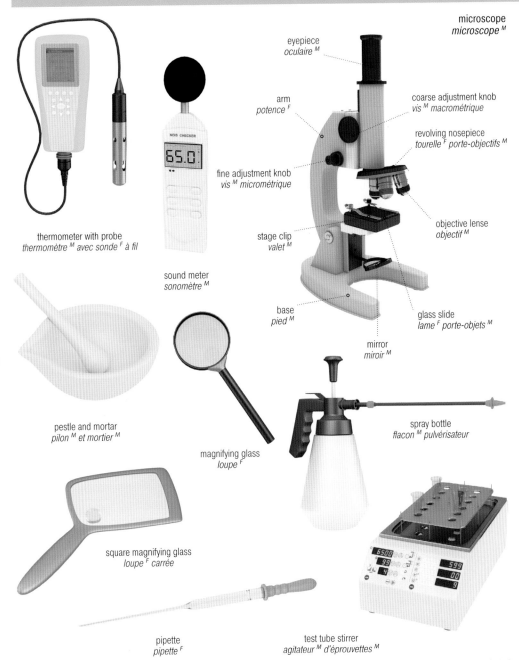

microscope
microscope M

eyepiece
oculaire M

arm
potence F

coarse adjustment knob
vis M *macrométrique*

revolving nosepiece
tourelle F *porte-objectifs* M

fine adjustment knob
vis M *micrométrique*

objective lense
objectif M

thermometer with probe
thermomètre M *avec sonde* F *à fil*

stage clip
valet M

sound meter
sonomètre M

base
pied M

glass slide
lame F *porte-objets* M

mirror
miroir M

pestle and mortar
pilon M *et mortier* M

spray bottle
flacon M *pulvérisateur*

magnifying glass
loupe F

square magnifying glass
loupe F *carrée*

pipette
pipette F

test tube stirrer
agitateur M *d'éprouvettes* M

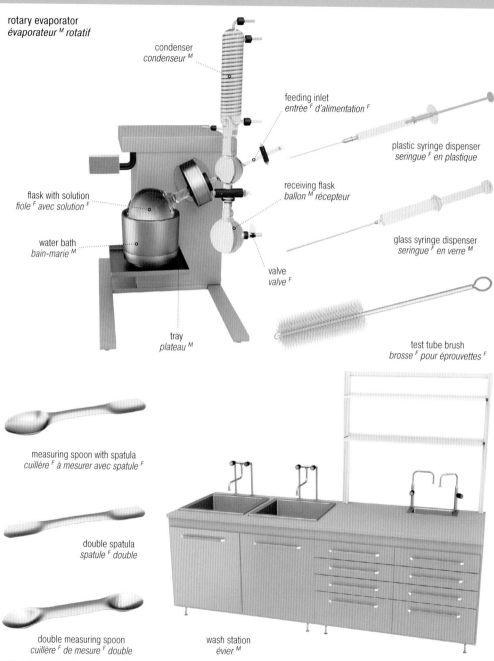

rotary evaporator
évaporateur ᴹ *rotatif*

condenser
condenseur ᴹ

feeding inlet
entrée ᶠ *d'alimentation* ᶠ

plastic syringe dispenser
seringue ᶠ *en plastique*

flask with solution
fiole ᶠ *avec solution* ᶠ

receiving flask
ballon ᴹ *récepteur*

water bath
bain-marie ᴹ

glass syringe dispenser
seringue ᶠ *en verre* ᴹ

valve
valve ᶠ

tray
plateau ᴹ

test tube brush
brosse ᶠ *pour éprouvettes* ᶠ

measuring spoon with spatula
cuillère ᶠ *à mesurer avec spatule* ᶠ

double spatula
spatule ᶠ *double*

double measuring spoon
cuillère ᶠ *de mesure* ᶠ *double*

wash station
évier ᴹ

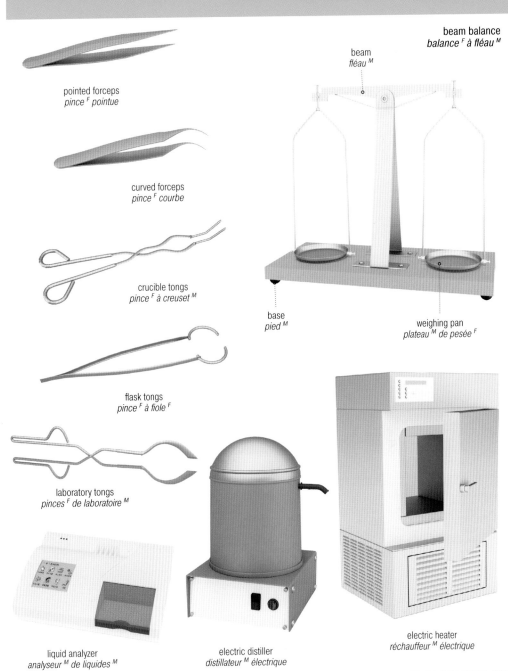

pointed forceps
pince F pointue

curved forceps
pince F courbe

crucible tongs
pince F à creuset M

flask tongs
pince F à fiole F

laboratory tongs
pinces F de laboratoire M

beam balance
balance F à fléau M

beam
fléau M

base
pied M

weighing pan
plateau M de pesée F

liquid analyzer
analyseur M de liquides M

electric distiller
distillateur M électrique

electric heater
réchauffeur M électrique

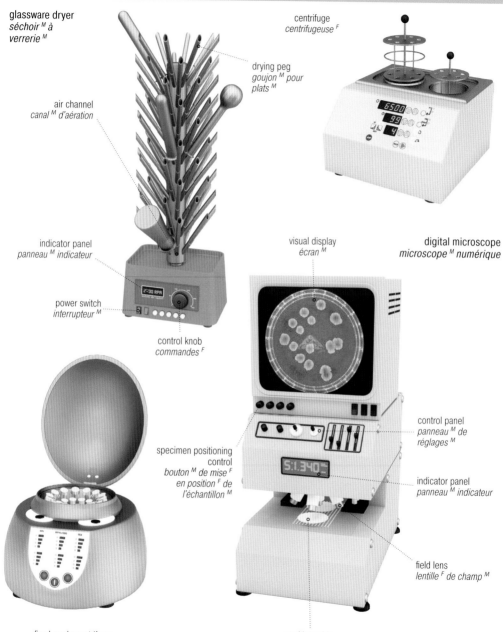

glassware dryer
*séchoir ᴹ à
verrerie ᴹ*

centrifuge
centrifugeuse ᶠ

drying peg
*goujon ᴹ pour
plats ᴹ*

air channel
canal ᴹ d'aération

indicator panel
panneau ᴹ indicateur

power switch
interrupteur ᴹ

control knob
commandes ᶠ

visual display
écran ᴹ

digital microscope
microscope ᴹ numérique

control panel
*panneau ᴹ de
réglages ᴹ*

specimen positioning
control
*bouton ᴹ de mise ᶠ
en position ᶠ de
l'échantillon ᴹ*

indicator panel
panneau ᴹ indicateur

field lens
lentille ᶠ de champ ᴹ

fixed-angle centrifuge
centrifugeuse ᶠ à angle ᴹ fixe

position table
platine ᶠ porte-échantillon ᴹ

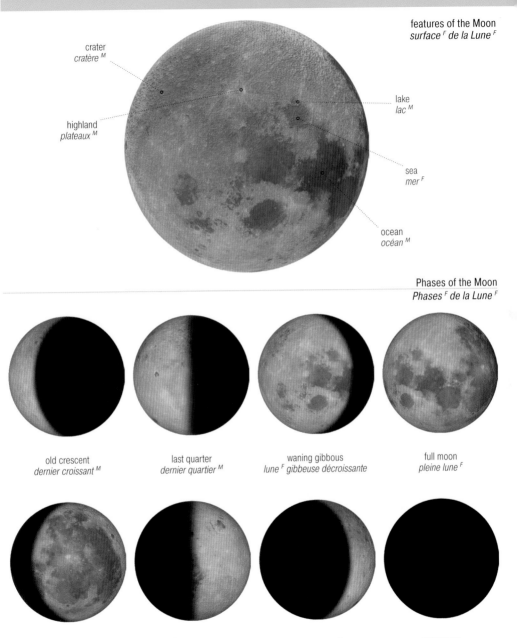

features of the Moon
surface [F] de la Lune [F]

crater
cratère [M]

lake
lac [M]

highland
plateaux [M]

sea
mer [F]

ocean
océan [M]

Phases of the Moon
Phases [F] de la Lune [F]

old crescent
dernier croissant [M]

last quarter
dernier quartier [M]

waning gibbous
lune [F] gibbeuse décroissante

full moon
pleine lune [F]

waxing gibbous
lune [F] gibbeuse croissante

first quarter
premier quartier [M]

new crescent
nouveau croissant [M] de lune [F]

new moon
nouvelle lune [F]

solar system
système M *solaire*

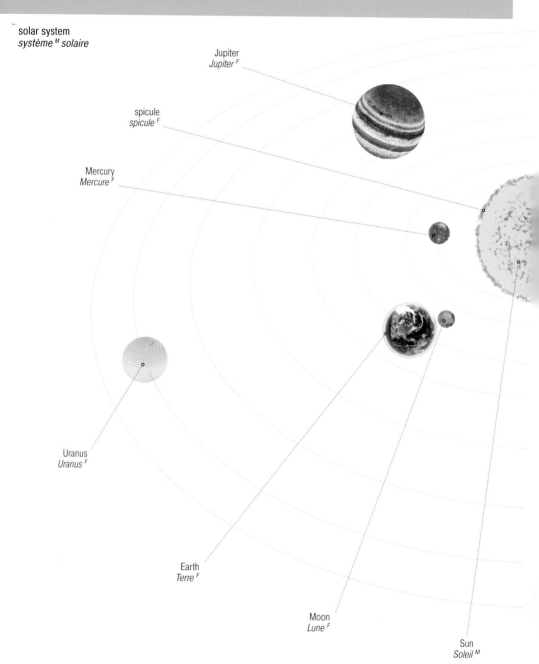

Jupiter
Jupiter F

spicule
spicule F

Mercury
Mercure F

Uranus
Uranus F

Earth
Terre F

Moon
Lune F

Sun
Soleil M

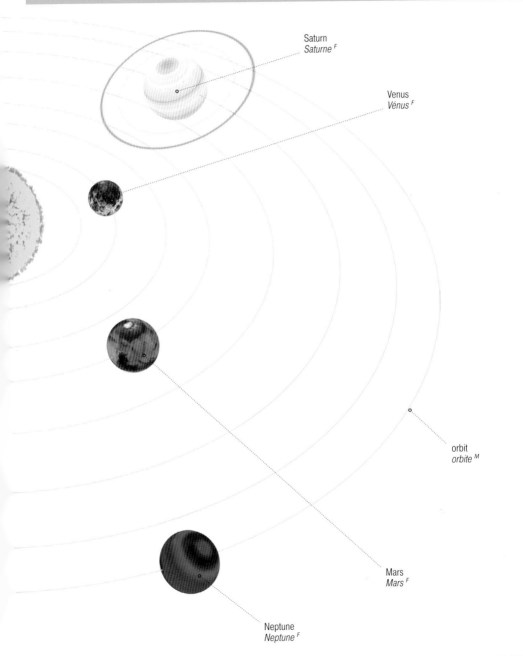

Saturn
Saturne[F]

Venus
Vénus[F]

orbit
orbite[M]

Mars
Mars[F]

Neptune
Neptune[F]

seasons of the year
saisons ^F de l'année ^F

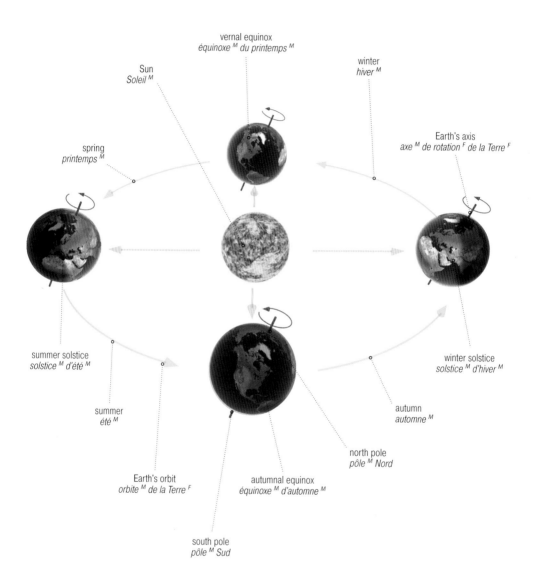

vernal equinox
équinoxe ^M du printemps ^M

winter
hiver ^M

Sun
Soleil ^M

Earth's axis
axe ^M de rotation ^F de la Terre ^F

spring
printemps ^M

summer solstice
solstice ^M d'été ^M

winter solstice
solstice ^M d'hiver ^M

summer
été ^M

autumn
automne ^M

north pole
pôle ^M Nord

Earth's orbit
orbite ^M de la Terre ^F

autumnal equinox
équinoxe ^M d'automne ^M

south pole
pôle ^M Sud

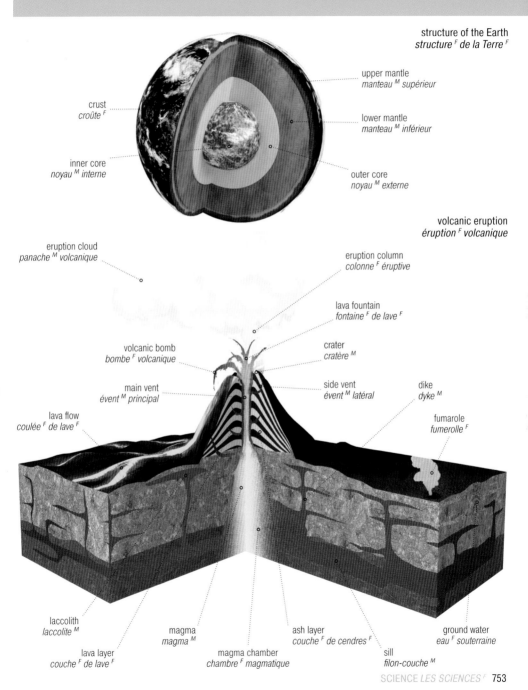

structure of the Earth
structure[F] *de la Terre*[F]

upper mantle
manteau[M] *supérieur*

crust
croûte[F]

lower mantle
manteau[M] *inférieur*

inner core
noyau[M] *interne*

outer core
noyau[M] *externe*

volcanic eruption
éruption[F] *volcanique*

eruption cloud
panache[M] *volcanique*

eruption column
colonne[F] *éruptive*

lava fountain
fontaine[F] *de lave*[F]

volcanic bomb
bombe[F] *volcanique*

crater
cratère[M]

main vent
évent[M] *principal*

side vent
évent[M] *latéral*

dike
dyke[M]

lava flow
coulée[F] *de lave*[F]

fumarole
fumerolle[F]

laccolith
laccolite[M]

magma
magma[M]

ash layer
couche[F] *de cendres*[F]

ground water
eau[F] *souterraine*

lava layer
couche[F] *de lave*[F]

magma chamber
chambre[F] *magmatique*

sill
filon-couche[M]

radio telescope
radiotélescope M

receiver
récepteur M

steerable parabolic reflector
réflecteur M *parabolique orientable*

observatory
observatoire M

parabolic reflector
réflecteur M *parabolique*

rotating dome
dôme F *mobile*

dome shutter
cimier M *mobile*

support structure
structure F *portante*

rotating track
piste F *rotative*

circular track
piste F *circulaire*

laboratory
laboratoire M

door
porte F

telescope
télescope M

finderscope
viseur M

dew shield
pare-buée M

eyepiece
oculaire M

main tube
tube M *principal*

focusing knob
bouton M *de mise au point* F

cradle
berceau M

azimuth fine adjustment
réglage M *précis de l'azimut*

counterweight
contrepoids M

altitude fine adjustment
réglage M *exact de l'altitude*

tripod
trépied M

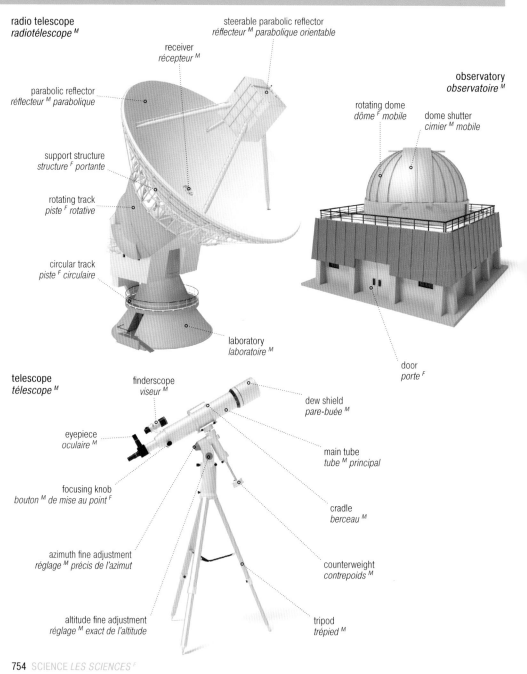

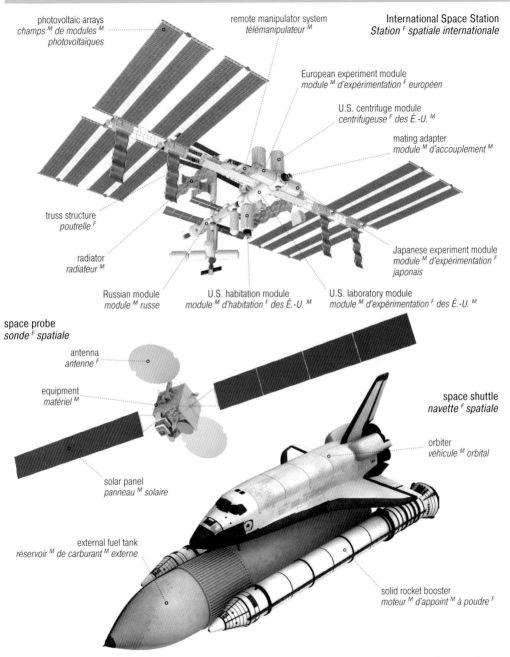

photovoltaic arrays
champs [M] *de modules* [M]
photovoltaïques

remote manipulator system
télémanipulateur [M]

International Space Station
Station [F] *spatiale internationale*

European experiment module
module [M] *d'expérimentation* [F] *européen*

U.S. centrifuge module
centrifugeuse [F] *des É.-U.* [M]

mating adapter
module [M] *d'accouplement* [M]

truss structure
poutrelle [F]

radiator
radiateur [M]

Japanese experiment module
module [M] *d'expérimentation* [F]
japonais

Russian module
module [M] *russe*

U.S. habitation module
module [M] *d'habitation* [F] *des É.-U.* [M]

U.S. laboratory module
module [M] *d'expérimentation* [F] *des É.-U.* [M]

space probe
sonde [F] *spatiale*

antenna
antenne [F]

equipment
matériel [M]

space shuttle
navette [F] *spatiale*

orbiter
véhicule [M] *orbital*

solar panel
panneau [M] *solaire*

external fuel tank
réservoir [M] *de carburant* [M] *externe*

solid rocket booster
moteur [M] *d'appoint* [M] *à poudre* [F]

Moon landing
atterrissage [M] *sur la Lune* [F]

lunar rover
véhicule [M] *lunaire*

landing module
module [M] *lunaire*

Earth
Terre [F]

crater
cratère [M]

surface of the Moon
surface [F] *de la Lune* [F]

astronaut
astronaute [M]

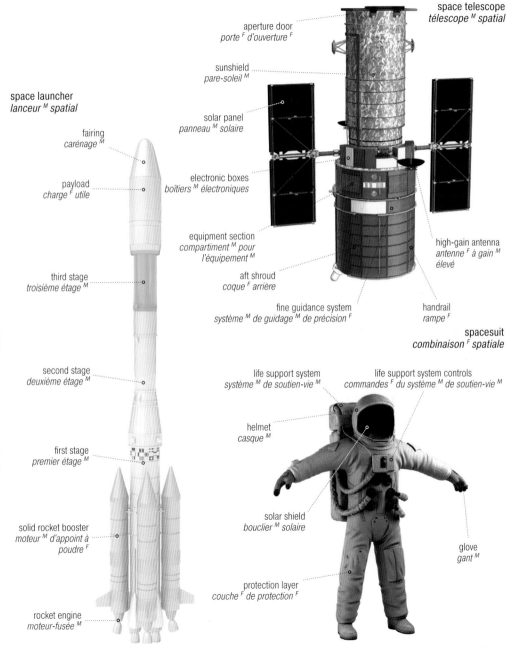

space telescope
télescope [M] *spatial*

aperture door
porte [F] *d'ouverture* [F]

sunshield
pare-soleil [M]

space launcher
lanceur [M] *spatial*

solar panel
panneau [M] *solaire*

fairing
carénage [M]

payload
charge [F] *utile*

electronic boxes
boîtiers [M] *électroniques*

equipment section
compartiment [M] *pour
l'équipement* [M]

third stage
troisième étage [M]

aft shroud
coque [F] *arrière*

high-gain antenna
antenne [F] *à gain* [M]
élevé

fine guidance system
système [M] *de guidage* [M] *de précision* [F]

handrail
rampe [F]

second stage
deuxième étage [M]

spacesuit
combinaison [F] *spatiale*

life support system
système [M] *de soutien-vie* [M]

life support system controls
commandes [F] *du système* [M] *de soutien-vie* [M]

helmet
casque [M]

first stage
premier étage [M]

solid rocket booster
moteur [M] *d'appoint à
poudre* [F]

solar shield
bouclier [M] *solaire*

glove
gant [M]

rocket engine
moteur-fusée [M]

protection layer
couche [F] *de protection* [F]

ENERGY AND INDUSTRY

ÉNERGIE ET INDUSTRIE

solar panel
panneau ᴹ *solaire*

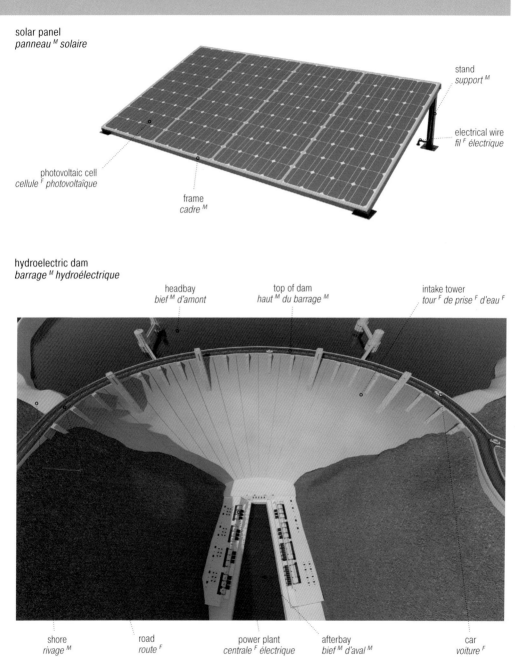

stand
support ᴹ

electrical wire
fil ᶠ *électrique*

photovoltaic cell
cellule ᶠ *photovoltaïque*

frame
cadre ᴹ

hydroelectric dam
barrage ᴹ *hydroélectrique*

headbay
bief ᴹ *d'amont*

top of dam
haut ᴹ *du barrage* ᴹ

intake tower
tour ᶠ *de prise* ᶠ *d'eau* ᶠ

shore
rivage ᴹ

road
route ᶠ

power plant
centrale ᶠ *électrique*

afterbay
bief ᴹ *d'aval* ᴹ

car
voiture ᶠ

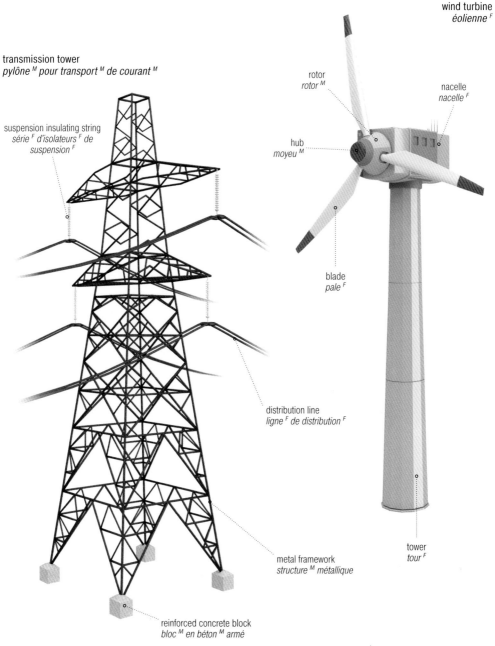

wind turbine
éolienne F

transmission tower
pylône M *pour transport* M *de courant* M

rotor
rotor M

nacelle
nacelle F

suspension insulating string
série F *d'isolateurs* F *de*
suspension F

hub
moyeu M

blade
pale F

distribution line
ligne F *de distribution* F

metal framework
structure M *métallique*

tower
tour F

reinforced concrete block
bloc M *en béton* M *armé*

nuclear power plant
centrale F *nucléaire*

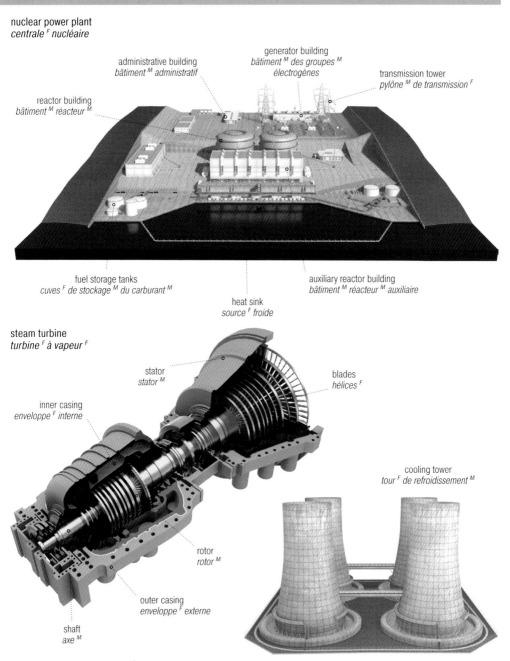

administrative building
bâtiment M *administratif*

generator building
bâtiment M *des groupes* M
électrogènes

transmission tower
pylône M *de transmission* F

reactor building
bâtiment M *réacteur* M

fuel storage tanks
cuves F *de stockage* M *du carburant* M

heat sink
source F *froide*

auxiliary reactor building
bâtiment M *réacteur* M *auxiliaire*

steam turbine
turbine F *à vapeur* F

stator
stator M

blades
hélices F

inner casing
enveloppe F *interne*

cooling tower
tour F *de refroidissement* M

rotor
rotor M

outer casing
enveloppe F *externe*

shaft
axe M

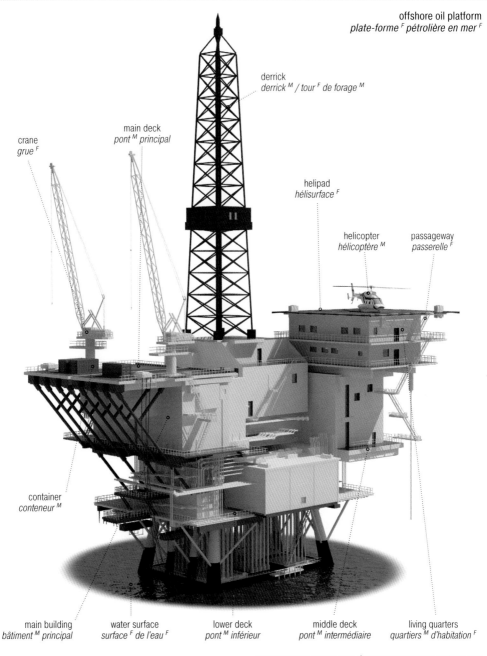

offshore oil platform
plate-forme F *pétrolière en mer* F

derrick
derrick M */ tour* F *de forage* M

main deck
pont M *principal*

crane
grue F

helipad
hélisurface F

helicopter
hélicoptère M

passageway
passerelle F

container
conteneur M

main building
bâtiment M *principal*

water surface
surface F *de l'eau* F

lower deck
pont M *inférieur*

middle deck
pont M *intermédiaire*

living quarters
quartiers M *d'habitation* F

oil tank farm
dépôt ^M *de réservoir* ^M *à essence* ^F

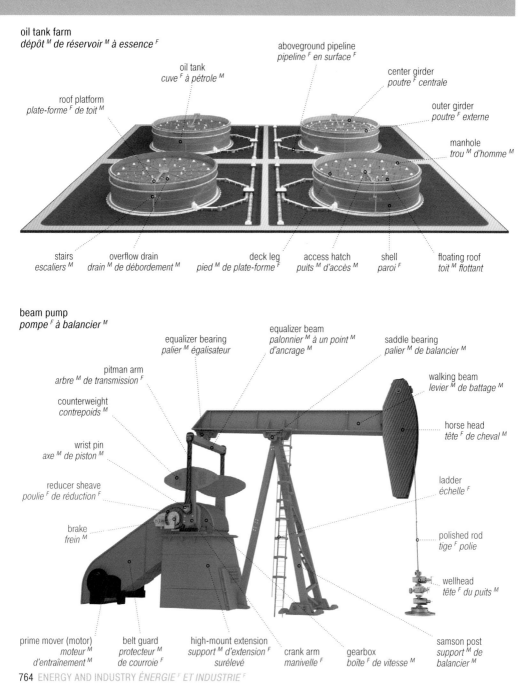

aboveground pipeline
pipeline ^F *en surface* ^F

oil tank
cuve ^F *à pétrole* ^M

center girder
poutre ^F *centrale*

roof platform
plate-forme ^F *de toit* ^M

outer girder
poutre ^F *externe*

manhole
trou ^M *d'homme* ^M

stairs
escaliers ^M

overflow drain
drain ^M *de débordement* ^M

deck leg
pied ^M *de plate-forme* ^F

access hatch
puits ^M *d'accès* ^M

shell
paroi ^F

floating roof
toit ^M *flottant*

beam pump
pompe ^F *à balancier* ^M

equalizer bearing
palier ^M *égalisateur*

equalizer beam
palonnier ^M *à un point* ^M
d'ancrage ^M

saddle bearing
palier ^M *de balancier* ^M

pitman arm
arbre ^M *de transmission* ^F

walking beam
levier ^M *de battage* ^M

counterweight
contrepoids ^M

horse head
tête ^F *de cheval* ^M

wrist pin
axe ^M *de piston* ^M

reducer sheave
poulie ^F *de réduction* ^F

ladder
échelle ^F

brake
frein ^M

polished rod
tige ^F *polie*

wellhead
tête ^F *du puits* ^M

prime mover (motor)
moteur ^M
d'entraînement ^M

belt guard
protecteur ^M
de courroie ^F

high-mount extension
support ^M *d'extension* ^F
surélevé

crank arm
manivelle ^F

gearbox
boîte ^F *de vitesse* ^M

samson post
support ^M *de*
balancier ^M

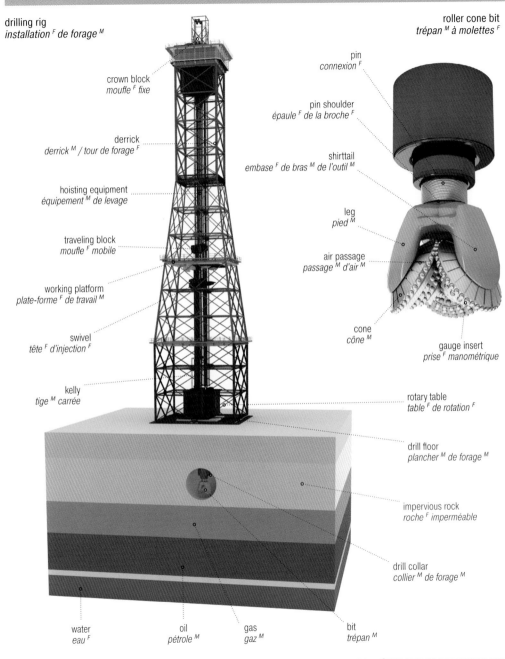

drilling rig
installation ^F *de forage* ^M

roller cone bit
trépan ^M *à molettes* ^F

pin
connexion ^F

crown block
moufle ^F *fixe*

pin shoulder
épaule ^F *de la broche* ^F

derrick
derrick ^M */ tour de forage* ^F

shirttail
embase ^F *de bras* ^M *de l'outil* ^M

hoisting equipment
équipement ^M *de levage*

leg
pied ^M

traveling block
moufle ^F *mobile*

air passage
passage ^M *d'air* ^M

working platform
plate-forme ^F *de travail* ^M

swivel
tête ^F *d'injection* ^F

cone
cône ^M

kelly
tige ^M *carrée*

gauge insert
prise ^F *manométrique*

rotary table
table ^F *de rotation* ^F

drill floor
plancher ^M *de forage* ^M

impervious rock
roche ^F *imperméable*

drill collar
collier ^M *de forage* ^M

water
eau ^F

oil
pétrole ^M

gas
gaz ^M

bit
trépan ^M

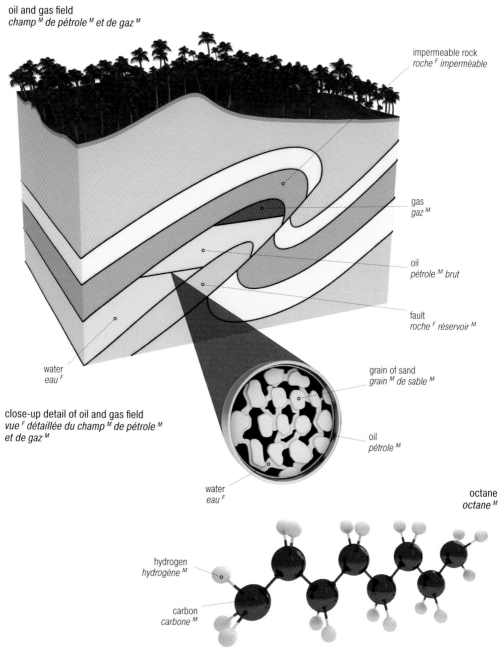

oil and gas field
champ M *de pétrole* M *et de gaz* M

impermeable rock
roche F *imperméable*

gas
gaz M

oil
pétrole M *brut*

fault
roche F *réservoir* M

water
eau F

close-up detail of oil and gas field
vue F *détaillée du champ* M *de pétrole* M
et de gaz M

grain of sand
grain M *de sable* M

oil
pétrole M

water
eau F

octane
octane M

hydrogen
hydrogène M

carbon
carbone M

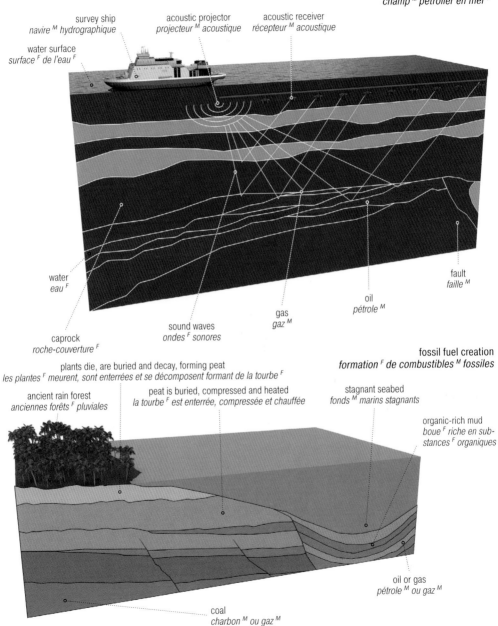

offshore oil field
champ M *pétrolier en mer* F

survey ship
navire M *hydrographique*

acoustic projector
projecteur M *acoustique*

acoustic receiver
récepteur M *acoustique*

water surface
surface F *de l'eau* F

water
eau F

fault
faille M

oil
pétrole M

gas
gaz M

caprock
roche-couverture F

sound waves
ondes F *sonores*

fossil fuel creation
formation F *de combustibles* M *fossiles*

plants die, are buried and decay, forming peat
les plantes F *meurent, sont enterrées et se décomposent formant de la tourbe* F

ancient rain forest
anciennes forêts F *pluviales*

peat is buried, compressed and heated
la tourbe F *est enterrée, compressée et chauffée*

stagnant seabed
fonds M *marins stagnants*

organic-rich mud
boue F *riche en sub-*
stances F *organiques*

oil or gas
pétrole M *ou gaz* M

coal
charbon M *ou gaz* M

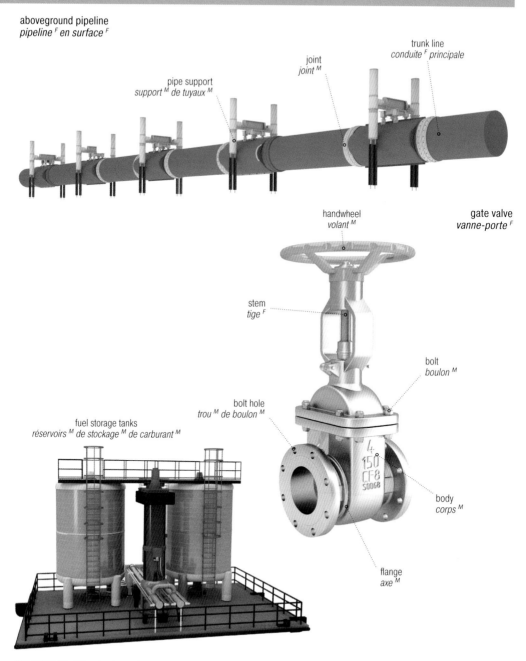

aboveground pipeline
pipeline F *en surface* F

trunk line
conduite F *principale*

joint
joint M

pipe support
support M *de tuyaux* M

handwheel
volant M

gate valve
vanne-porte F

stem
tige F

bolt
boulon M

bolt hole
trou M *de boulon* M

fuel storage tanks
réservoirs M *de stockage* M *de carburant* M

body
corps M

flange
axe M

shrink wrap machine
machine ᶠ d'emballage ᴹ

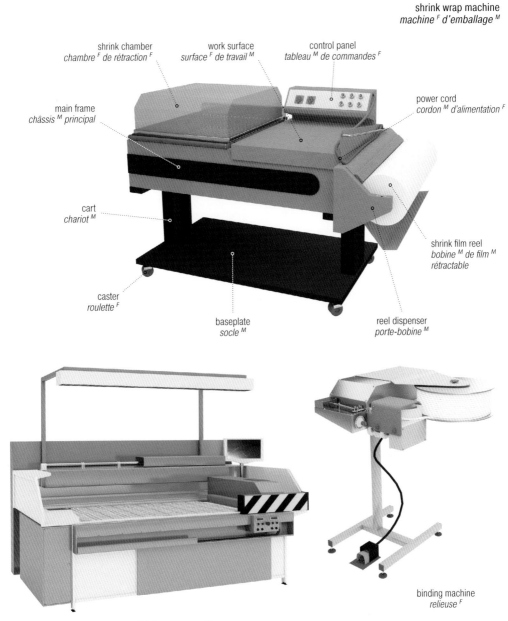

shrink chamber
chambre ᶠ de rétraction ᶠ

work surface
surface ᶠ de travail ᴹ

control panel
tableau ᴹ de commandes ᶠ

power cord
cordon ᴹ d'alimentation ᶠ

main frame
châssis ᴹ principal

cart
chariot ᴹ

shrink film reel
bobine ᴹ de film ᴹ
rétractable

caster
roulette ᶠ

baseplate
socle ᴹ

reel dispenser
porte-bobine ᴹ

binding machine
relieuse ᶠ

fabric-cutting machine
machine ᶠ à découper ᶠ du tissu ᴹ

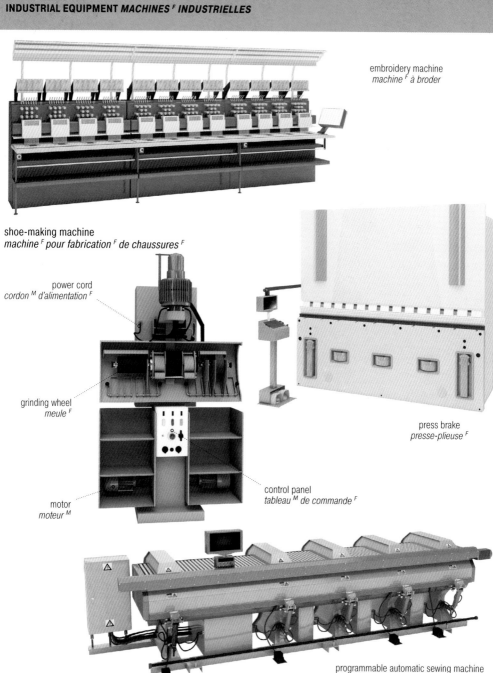

embroidery machine
machine F *à broder*

shoe-making machine
machine F *pour fabrication* F *de chaussures* F

power cord
cordon M *d'alimentation* F

grinding wheel
meule F

motor
moteur M

press brake
presse-plieuse F

control panel
tableau M *de commande* F

programmable automatic sewing machine
machine F *à coudre programmable automatique*

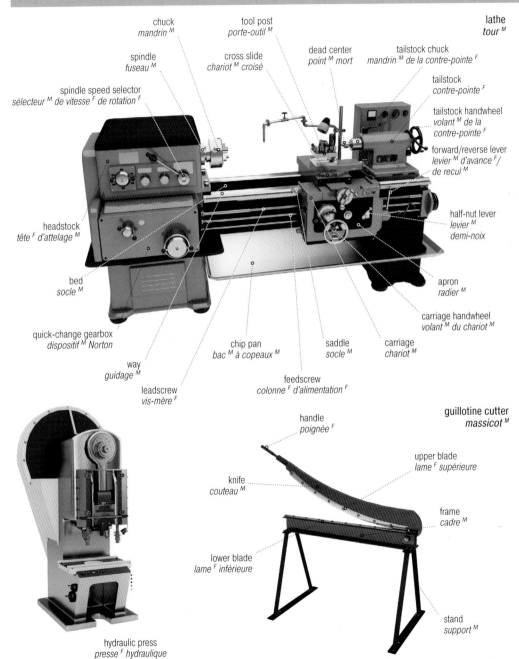

lathe
tour M

chuck
mandrin M

tool post
porte-outil M

dead center
point M *mort*

tailstock chuck
mandrin M *de la contre-pointe* F

spindle
fuseau M

cross slide
chariot M *croisé*

tailstock
contre-pointe F

spindle speed selector
sélecteur M *de vitesse* F *de rotation* F

tailstock handwheel
volant M *de la
contre-pointe* F

forward/reverse lever
levier M *d'avance* F /
de recul M

headstock
tête F *d'attelage* M

half-nut lever
levier M
demi-noix

bed
socle M

apron
radier M

quick-change gearbox
dispositif M *Norton*

carriage handwheel
volant M *du chariot* M

way
guidage M

chip pan
bac M *à copeaux* M

saddle
socle M

carriage
chariot M

leadscrew
vis-mère F

feedscrew
colonne F *d'alimentation* F

guillotine cutter
massicot M

handle
poignée F

upper blade
lame F *supérieure*

knife
couteau M

frame
cadre M

lower blade
lame F *inférieure*

stand
support M

hydraulic press
presse F *hydraulique*

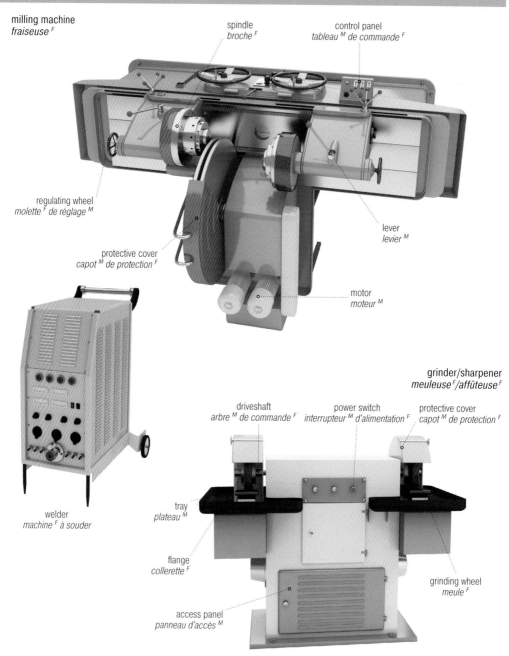

milling machine
fraiseuse F

spindle
broche F

control panel
tableau M *de commande* F

regulating wheel
molette F *de réglage* M

lever
levier M

protective cover
capot M *de protection* F

motor
moteur M

welder
machine F *à souder*

grinder/sharpener
meuleuse F/*affûteuse* F

driveshaft
arbre M *de commande* F

power switch
interrupteur M *d'alimentation* F

protective cover
capot M *de protection* F

tray
plateau M

flange
collerette F

access panel
panneau d'accès M

grinding wheel
meule F

numerical control (NC) machining center
centre M *d'usinage* M *à commande* F *numérique*

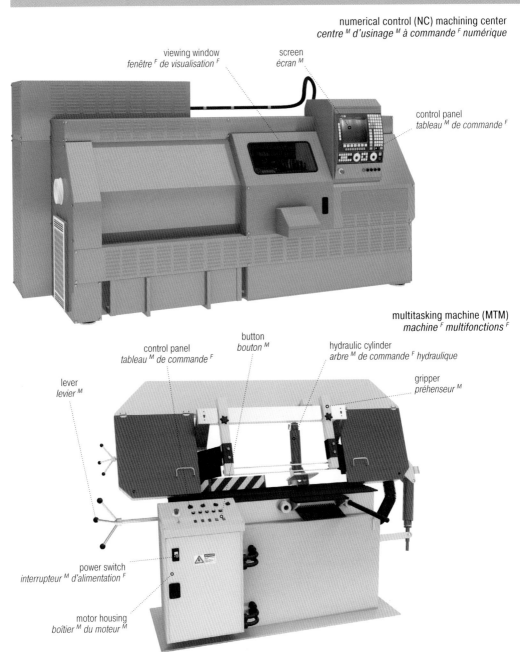

viewing window
fenêtre F *de visualisation* F

screen
écran M

control panel
tableau M *de commande* F

multitasking machine (MTM)
machine F *multifonctions* F

control panel
tableau M *de commande* F

button
bouton M

hydraulic cylinder
arbre M *de commande* F *hydraulique*

lever
levier M

gripper
préhenseur M

power switch
interrupteur M *d'alimentation* F

motor housing
boîtier M *du moteur* M

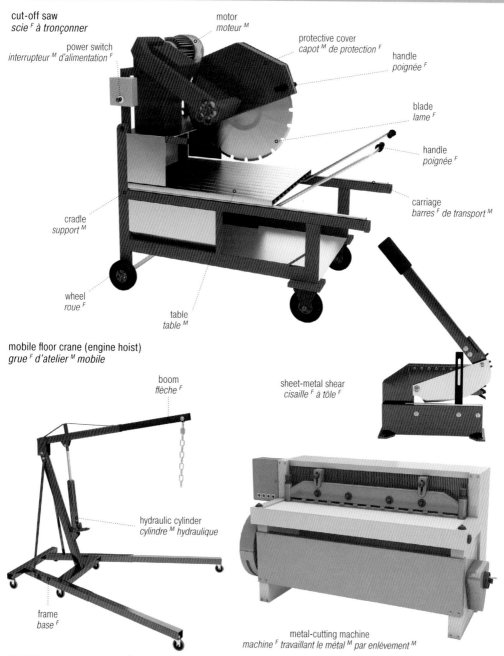

cut-off saw
scie [F] *à tronçonner*

motor
moteur [M]

power switch
interrupteur [M] *d'alimentation* [F]

protective cover
capot [M] *de protection* [F]

handle
poignée [F]

blade
lame [F]

handle
poignée [F]

carriage
barres [F] *de transport* [M]

cradle
support [M]

wheel
roue [F]

table
table [M]

mobile floor crane (engine hoist)
grue [F] *d'atelier* [M] *mobile*

boom
flèche [F]

sheet-metal shear
cisaille [F] *à tôle* [F]

hydraulic cylinder
cylindre [M] *hydraulique*

frame
base [F]

metal-cutting machine
machine [F] *travaillant le métal* [M] *par enlèvement* [M]

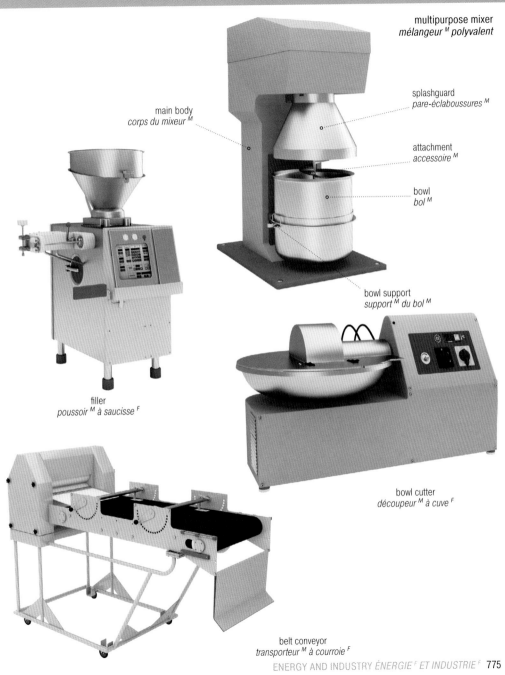

multipurpose mixer
mélangeur M *polyvalent*

splashguard
pare-éclaboussures M

main body
corps du mixeur M

attachment
accessoire M

bowl
bol M

bowl support
support M *du bol* M

filler
poussoir M *à saucisse* F

bowl cutter
découpeur M *à cuve* F

belt conveyor
transporteur M *à courroie* F

part of conveyor system
partie F du système M de convoyeur M

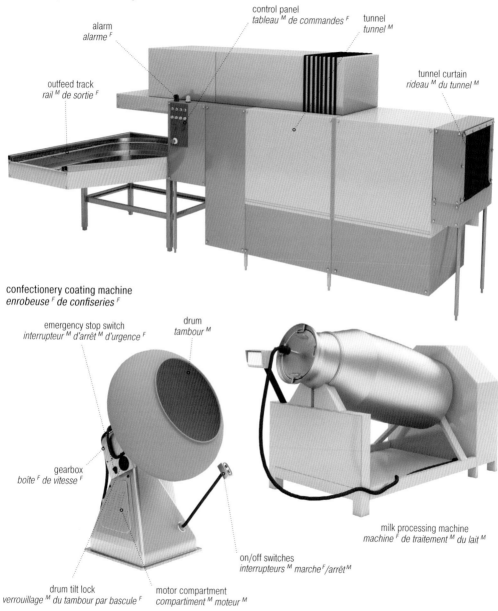

alarm
alarme F

control panel
tableau M de commandes F

tunnel
tunnel M

tunnel curtain
rideau M du tunnel M

outfeed track
rail M de sortie F

confectionery coating machine
enrobeuse F de confiseries F

emergency stop switch
interrupteur M d'arrêt M d'urgence F

drum
tambour M

gearbox
boîte F de vitesse F

milk processing machine
machine F de traitement M du lait M

on/off switches
interrupteurs M marche F/arrêt M

drum tilt lock
verrouillage M du tambour M par bascule F

motor compartment
compartiment M moteur M

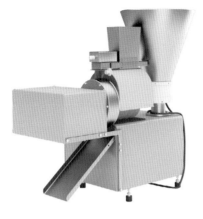

portioning and forming machine
façonneuse F *et portionneuse* F *à pâte*

food slicer
trancheuse F *à aliments* M

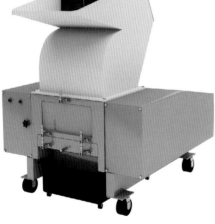

food mill
moulin F

conveyor system feeder
convoyeur M *d'alimentation* F

rib
nervure F

hard hat
casque M *de sécurité* F

peak
visière F

face shield
écran M *facial*

suspension
suspension F

earplugs
bouchons M *d'oreille* F

ear protectors
protège-oreilles M

safety boots
bottes F *de sécurité* F

toe guard
protège-orteils M

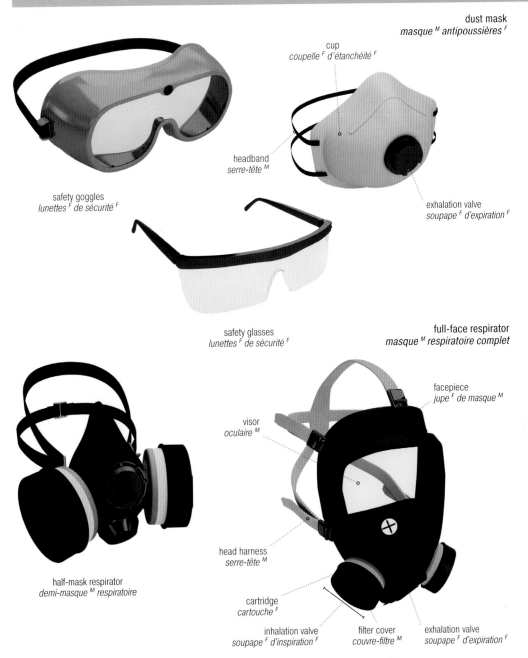

dust mask
masque [M] *antipoussières* [F]

cup
coupelle [F] *d'étanchéité* [F]

headband
serre-tête [M]

safety goggles
lunettes [F] *de sécurité* [F]

exhalation valve
soupape [F] *d'expiration* [F]

safety glasses
lunettes [F] *de sécurité* [F]

full-face respirator
masque [M] *respiratoire complet*

facepiece
jupe [F] *de masque* [M]

visor
oculaire [M]

head harness
serre-tête [M]

half-mask respirator
demi-masque [M] *respiratoire*

cartridge
cartouche [F]

inhalation valve
soupape [F] *d'inspiration* [F]

filter cover
couvre-filtre [M]

exhalation valve
soupape [F] *d'expiration* [F]

ENGLISH INDEX

D

INDEX FRANÇAIS

M